ALLEN GUTWIRTH'S

EXPIRATION

A Brooklyn Story

ISBN Number:

Printed in the United States of America

CREATIVE DIRECTOR, ASHISH LOHRA

DEDICATION

Dedicated to the only remaining living people in my book, Jamie Gutwirth (my son), Jonathan Gutwirth (my grandson), Bella Gutwirth (my granddaughter), and Maggie Gutwirth (my daughter-in-law).

In memories of Elaine Lewis (my soulmate and wife).

Broadway Sam Publishing, New York, New York

Every person in this book is real, unfortunately, they have all expired. Except Jamie, my only son and his family. All locations mentioned in this book are the same, for locations do not expire, and the businesses that were located there are forever changing as well as demographics.

Life is an organism forever mutating. Geography is constant, however people and things expire.

Expiration is a time travel through my life.
Welcome to my world!

FOREWORD

To those who open the cover of this book, curious to learn what it's all about: I recommend you ask your spouse, significant other or physician to see if you have a BAR CODE that has your expiration date.

I believe we all have it, SEEK AND YOU SHALL FIND.

PROLOGUE

This book is dedicated to all who were born in the 1940s and who didn't make it to 2024, unfortunately, I started to read the New York Times from back to front.

My generation was faced with the end of World War II. We were too young for the Korean War and as young adults. Just the right age to be drafted for Vietnam. We tackled Polio, Measles, Mumps and Aids, your generation is faced with COVID-19.

I have to admit that as your grandfather I had much more fun. Having unprotected sex until AIDS and now it's even worse with the COVID-19 pandemic.

All this occurred in a world without iPhones, iPads, music streaming, AI or Google. The Internet of Things (IOT) was nonexistent as was Moore's law. Phone booths were on every corner, and so were answering machines and pagers. Letter writing was typical, and people knew their home addresses without looking at their smartphones. Then Pornography was scarce and there was no need to go to a seedy movie house with guys masturbating. Now, it's all there with a click of a mouse. Meeting a potential mate was face to face on the street, in a bar or at the counter of the cosmetics section in major department stores.

Before internet connectivity, the definition of privacy was a hotel room with a DO NOT DISTURB sign.

PLEASE GUESS THE RIDDLE HIDDEN IN THE BARCODE.

Baby

Adult

WELCOME TO MY LIFE

You Know You Are Old When Your Past Is More Exciting Than Your Future.

TABLE OF CONTENTS

DECADE ONE

My Rebirth

If I remember correctly my parents packed up the car and drove South to Miami, My father was never a nine-five person. Always hustling to make a living. He had developed a relationship with Arthur Klar whose company managed concessions at Music Venues and printed Souvenir Programs that were sold to audiences that went to Broadway Shows. Arthur owned the Concession right at St. John Terrell's Music Circus located on Treasure Island in Miami and hired my dad to run the food concessions and souvenir programs. St. John's concept was to produce Operettas in the round under a Circus Tent at an affordable ticket price.

Exposing Miami audiences to light Operas of the British team Gilbert & Sullivan, Sigmund Romberg Hungarian Born immigrating to the United States was the most prolific. Composer of Operettas such as The Desert Song, The Student Prince, The New Moon, Joining Romberg was Franz Lehar the Merry Widow in its original German Die lustige Witwer which was translated into English by Jeremy Sands.

On route to Miami, our 1948 Chevy blew up in Southern Georgia. The auto repair shop would take a week to repair it, and both my parents decided to buy a new car so that we could continue our journey.

Driving straight through we arrived at Treasure Island as the largest Circus Tent sprang to life. There I was a chubby ten-year-old kid in the middle of the creation of this fantasy world full of actors, prop men, lighting and sound equipment ready to turn the Red, White and Blue Tent to a whole new world. My parents checked into a Motel which was used as a base until the Grand Opening of the First Operetta the Desert Song.

Opening the Concession was a family production, everything arrived at once, A grill powered by Butane to make hot dogs, a freezer for the ice cream, kegs of Beer, Soft drinks, popcorn, Cotton Candy machines and various other items to be sold to the audience. My folks forgot about school for they figured I could learn more about business and life working with them. My father placed me on a wooden box near the entrance to the tent to sell Souvenir programs wearing a red apron for the bargain price of $3.00 when the real price is $2.00. Imagine a chubby kid in a red Apron hawking these special books and learning how to make a change.

I became the Mascot of the entire company, allowed into the inner—sanctum of dressing rooms and props.

How The Past Disappeared

About a month after our arrival after the audience left one of the major Stars of the Desert Song offered me a ride on his 1950 Mg Td Roadster. Rather than sitting inside the car, I decided to stand on the running boards for what was supposed to be a one-minute ride to the exit of the music circus. Thirty seconds into this joy ride I fell off the running board. My father ran to pick me up thinking that all was well. After closing the concession, we returned to the motel and I began to throw up and feel dizzy, at that point, they decided to take me to the emergency room at Jackson Memorial Hospital. After a series of X-rays, the Neurologist assigned to the ER told my parents that if they did not operate immediately, I would die. The surgeon explained that a pebble pierced my skull, and I had a Subdural hematoma which in laymen's terms was a Blood Clot in the Brain. My parents gave their consent for the surgery.

My parents, who at that time were in their early Thirties faced a life-changing occurrence. They just moved to Florida, had little money and were living in a Motel with their only child having emergency surgery. After six hours of waiting in the ER, they were told that the surgery was finished and that I was in the ICU. I was moved to a semi-private room where I was in a Coma for ten days. The surgeon explained that if I survived I would either be unable to walk or see. I was told that all the synagogues in Miami were praying for me. Three weeks later I was discharged from Jackson Memorial and driven to my new home in Indian Creek. My maternal Grandmother came to help my mother. I was paralyzed on my left side and suffered from Double vision. At that time they did not have home Rehab and with the help of my family, I worked on gaining strength on the left side of my body, because I was a true leftie movement slowly returned to my left side. My bout with double vision slowly corrected itself. Having suddenly developed a phobia expecting everything was dirty I washed my hands ten times a day.

In August of 1950, we returned to our one-bedroom apartment which was over a candy store in East New York Brooklyn. My parents gave me the bedroom and they turned what was supposed to be a living room into their bedroom.

Public Schools started in September 1951, my parents were advised that I should not go to a Public School for it was still dangerous. I was assigned a homeschool instructor who came to our apartment three days a week: leaving me an entire afternoon with nothing to do. My life was lonely and I was always under the protective eyes of my mother and Grandparents who lived three blocks away. My daily routine was, going shopping with my mother who purchased fresh Candled eggs, she always brought her egg box along. The candling was to see if there wasn't a chick inside. The food in the 50s was always fresh with few frozen items.

After Shopping, we would visit my grandmother who had a two-bedroom apartment on the second floor of an apartment over a grocery store. Every time I visited, her next-door neighbour Dassa a woman in her late forties would open her door wearing a Flimsy house dress with her breasts exposed, Her blonde hair was always in curlers kissing me on the cheek and handing me a Hershey Bar. My parents were first-generation Americans, my maternal grandparents were from Poland. They immigrated during the early part of the 20th Century. They spoke mainly Yiddish. In those days New York City was the Apparel industry of the USA whose workers were members of the International Garment Workers Union with Ninety percent Jewish skilled labor. My Grandfather was a garment worker presser.

My Grandparents had a tradition of Friday Night Sabbath meals with the entire family which included two uncles and one aunt. My Uncle Charlie who looked like Errol Flynn fought in World War 11 in the Pacific as a chief warrant officer to earn extra money as an infantryman in gliders, my Uncle Mike was based in England flying B-17 bombing raids over Germany as the plane's Navigator. The visits to my grandparents increased to every day of the week for they had a Black and White Television which meant that they were upper-middle class.

By not attending Middle School, I would visit the public basketball court and shoot baskets while all the kids my age were in school. During the Fifties, the radio was the major entertainment device. From Soap Operas, Big Band broadcasting, Crime Shows, and Superheroes, the radio became my only form of entertainment. Seventy years later the Radio is obsolete as a form of entertainment, podcasts are the 21st-century answer to storytelling, when listening to music you have, Spotify, Pandora, Apple Music, Amazon Music, and Sirius.

By the beginning of 1951, it became mandatory to start prepping for my Bar Mitzvah which is mandatory and a rite of passage for a Jewish Boy when he reached thirteen years old. In my neighbourhood, there were at least a dozen synagogues. My Grandfather was active in a small synagogue and enrolled me in a

Hebrew studies group which I tried to avoid until one day the Rabbi told him that I was a no-show. His demands were simple I either study or I am not welcome in his house. I was not going to miss eating Chopped Liver and watching his Black and White TV. In the early 50s, Grandmothers looked like old people when they were in their mid-fifties. She was my Bube and my grandfather was Zeydeh. I never knew their first name.

I was overweight, and my mother would find a way to make me custom pants and make me dress for Sabbath Dinner. I very rarely saw my father who was constantly on the road selling Souvenir programs for Broadway Shows that were traveling across the country. Every week my mother received an envelope with cash. During that period, he travelled with Olivia Havilland when she toured Candida, came home for a few days, and hit the road travelling with Black Entertainers who followed the Green Book Route* Cutting across the South with Bands like Duke Ellington, and Lionel Hampton. Ella Fitzgerald, Sarah Vaugh Touring Southern Texas he decided to stay in Colored Only Boarding Houses. Once he called home and told my mother that he was in Jail in Georgia where he was traveling with a Black Gospel group called the Golden Gate Quartet. They were booked to do Concerts in Black Churches along the Bible Belt. Outside of Atlanta, a State Trooper stopped their Tour Bus to find Liquor and threatened to arrest everyone. Realizing if the group was found guilty of having liquor in a dry county, they would wind up in a Chain Gang. My dad told the Magistrate that the liquor was his and they let the bus go. He spent the night in jail until my mother wired him a Thousand Dollars.

1952 was the year I fell in love with the Most Beautiful Schwinn Bicycle. I spent the entire winter and spring nagging my parents for the Bike. I nagged and they said it was too dangerous, They thought, I would fall and hurt my head or get hit by a car. By June of 1952, we came to a negotiated compromise. I could only ride the bike in Snedekers Park which was two blocks away when either of my parents was there. Agreeing to the negotiation was better than nothing so every day I would walk my Schwinn to the Park accompanied by either my mother or Father. In the building I lived in there weren't any elevators, so I had to bring the bike up one floor and park it in my bedroom along with a stash of Ketchup, Tuna Fish, or other canned goods that my mother purchased when they were on sale. I even had a large Hebrew National Salami which was hung from a nail on my bedroom wall. I thought of it as a Jewish still life.

The New York City Board of Education assigned a Home instructor who would come at about 10 am and work through noon on the Formica Kitchen table while my parents slept in the living room. Being a person who likes to eat I taught myself how to cook. Having nothing to do until my parents woke up, I would spend time doing homework and cleaning my bike. Lovingly I polished the chrome fenders and headlights. If the weather was terrible I would put newspapers on the floor and clean the White Wall tires.

My First Love

In the Summer of 1951, my father had an opportunity to run the Beach Concession on Fire Island which was directly across from Shirley Long Island. The closest Community was Cherry Grove a Summer Gateway for the Gay Community in Manhattan. The only way to get on the Island was by taking a ferry from Shirley to our dock. We moved into a large two-story white house which was about 100 yards from the ocean and the same distance from the bay. On the Main floor were the concession, the men's and women's locker rooms, and Showers. I discovered a peephole by the women's locker room but unfortunately, very few women used this facility. To save money my mother would recycle coffee and dip teabags in brownish tap water. We were surrounded by Sand Dunes and our closest neighbor was the Coast Guard Station.

Weekends were crowded with families who brought their food and made the beach dirty. The seller was ice cream, soft drinks, and an occasional hot dog. One Saturday we had visitors who used the locker rooms and bought food. A member of the group introduced himself as Anthony Benedetto (Tony Bennett). What made him stand out from his crowd was that he gave me a twenty-dollar bill as a tip.

On Labor Day in 1951, we returned to our apartment on Riverdale Avenue. Who said there wasn't a culture in East New York? Some days we were entertained from the courtyard of our building by Opera Singers and Violinists who received applause and dollar donations thrown out the windows. On the Avenues of East New York were walkup tenements barren of trees, on the streets were private homes with fences and gardens all shaded by a canopy of trees

In 1952, my father went on the Road again with the touring Company of South Pacific returning to Brooklyn and preparing us to spend the Summer in Danbury Connecticut where there was a New Summer Stock Theatre. Summer Stock was perfect for young talented musical talent to cut their teeth. Every few weeks there was a new show, and the producers brought in name talents to Headline. Finding lodging that was affordable and within a short distance of the same Red, White, and Blue tent that featured a Theatre in the round, we drove up to Candlewood Lake and rented a Cabin for the Summer.

With the opening of the theatre, my dad bought me a red, white, and blue vest with large pockets to take the money. During intermission, I worked in the Aisles, selling popcorn, candy, and

Good Humor ice cream pops. I was Chubby, about five six with a great hustle. Not only did I sell out, but I made tips.

A few weeks into various productions the producers brought in a famous Actor James Westerfield to star in a Cole Porter Musical "Anything Goes" written by Cole Porter. The Musical took place on an Ocean Liner that made the crossing from New York to London. As the show was going through rehearsals the producer told my father they needed a kid in the show and I was perfect. I went from selling Ice cream to being a cast member. The Summer came to an end I went back to Brooklyn as an actor. In the fall of 1952, my father had it on the road and travelling. Arthur Klar the publisher of the Theatrical Souvenir programs allowed him to sell the programs in Broadway Theatres and Motown reviews that took place in the Large iconic movie theatres that showed films and offered a stage show.

Proudly I would leave my Grandparent's apartment which was on the second floor over a Grocery Store, walk down the stairs in my Boy Scout Uniform and walk three blocks joining my fellow scouts in the Pledge of Allegiance, learning the official Scout handshake. The NRA's representative gave lectures on gun safety and never once discussed the Second Amendment. We discussed Citizenship, Camping, learning how to pitch a tent, and how to survive in the Wilderness. Viewing my surroundings there wasn't any Wilderness except for Canaries which at that time had empty fields and a pier, Central Park, and if you were adventurous Staten Island. My life was perfect at that time for I still had an in-home education, My parents were together and always fighting, which I gathered was the way marriages went. Having figured out how to get my Mother to allow me to ride my bike in the gutter.

My father was always practical, he purchased a basket to carry groceries and a lock to secure my bike when I went into the shop. Every day I journeyed to the A&P Supermarket, always forgetting to buy a few stuff on the list that my Mother gave me so I could return the next day. After my 12th Birthday, which usually came up on Thanksgiving Day or the Wednesday before, the entire family gathered to Celebrate my Birthday. We had a traditional Jewish Thanksgiving with Chopped Liver, Chicken Noodle Soup with real chicken, and brisket meaning we had Friday's Sabbath Dinner on Thursday with a repeat performance the following day.

1953 became the year of planning my Bar Mitzvah which became the domain of my grandfather who arranged for me to have special tutoring from the Rabbi of his School on reading the Haftarah. In other words, I had to read passages from the Torah which was appropriate for the day of my Bar Mitzvah in Hebrew. The Rabbi was smart enough to teach me one Paragraph from the Torah.

In early 1953, my parents started interviewing Banquet Halls to get Quotes which included food, and flowers. Every weekend we would go to various Bar Mitzvahs, sample the food, and listen to the orchestras, In those days they did not have DJ'S. The cost for 25 couples was about $50.00 per couple for a Smorgasbord, a three-course dinner, and $500.00 for a five-piece orchestra.

They finally negotiated on a location which was a Banquet Hall attached to a large Synagogue. That created interiors to Replicate the Hall of Mirrors of Versailles. My Maternal Grandparents agreed to pay half. And my father went to his parents to get the other half. It seems that once a couple gets married the family unit gravitates to the Maternal side of the family. It seemed that my father was somehow distant from his parents who lived about a mile away in the more upscale part of east New York. He had a Brother and a Sister. His parents immigrated from Europe about the same time as my Maternal Grandparents.

I never had a memorable relationship with my paternal grandparents whom we visited about once a month. They lacked the warmth of my Maternal Grandparents. His Brother was married and made a living as a waiter for a Kosher Caterer based in Long Island. My cousins who were twins Beverly and Charlie were a year younger than me. We met about the same time that I visited my Paternal Grandparents. The implosion happened when my father asked his parents for money for my Bar Mitzvah, and they turned him down. Upon reflection a month after my Bar Mitzvah we never visited or saw them again. The dynamics of my mother came into play, she was happy that my father walked away from his family which brought them closer to her parents.

As the months passed, I was on the Bar Mitzvah Path, weekly rehearsal learning a script I didn't understand, I muttered and learned how to Bow to God. I discovered that I was Kohen which meant I was a descendant of priests in ancient Jewry. I would rather be a descendant of Superman. This designation allowed me to be on BIMA and required me to wear sneakers during the high holidays. My goal was to make it to the weekend after my 13th Birthday to make my family proud through this Jewish rite of passage. That evening, I was kissed, pinched, and bestowed with White envelopes containing Cash. It seems every Bar Mitzvah has a relative that looks like they were a Hundred Years old entering with a Cane and wearing a black dress. Everybody in the audience turned and cheered at her entrance. The lady who entered was an

Aunt of my mother's who lived on the Lower Eastside of Manhattan in a four-story walk-up with a bathroom in the hallway. What made her interesting was that she was in her early Seventies and had a bathroom in the hallway. In those days anybody over fifty looked old.

Here I was stuffing my suit pockets with cash or small white envelopes. As expected I had to make a speech. It seems that every Bar Mitzvah speech starts with Today I am a Man. I went through the ritual of thanking my entire family and the neurosurgery team at Jackson Memorial. This reference was understood only by immediate family. Looking back to my Bar Mitzvah the only people my age were my cousins. At the end of the evening, I decided I would love to learn how to set up the smorgasbord table. As my parents said their farewells to their guests I approached Moishe head of catering and asked him if he needed assistance. With a handshake, he told me to report the following Saturday at noon to work with him until 8 pm. And he will pay $3.00 per hour and give me a package of Chopped Liver and other canopies to bring home to the family.

THE BEGINNING OF THE CHOPPED LIVER EXPRESS

My schedule was from 4 pm until 8 pm every Saturday. It started in the kitchen where I worked alongside the waiting staff to bring out the ornate punch bowl which was Sterling Silver, the trays of Chopped Liver, and various other canopies. How lavish the smorgasbord looked, was determined by what package the client purchased. Laying out the various platters of food was an art of mixing the colours of the food interspersed by assorted ferns, and flowers. The goal was to turn the SMORGASBORD TABLE into a piece of art. This reception room of about 5, 000 square feet with Floral Wallpaper of what looked like the French Countryside, had Crystal Sconces and a center Crystal Chandelier with 25 lights with large double White Gold trim doors in the rear that opened into the main dining room Silver. This was the Jewish version of Versailles.

After the set up I went to the coat check room and helped Moishe's Mother check the coats of the guests who started arriving at about 6 pm. Like clockwork, the dinner was being served in the main dining room, which was about 10, 000 Square feet with floor-to-ceiling Mirrors, shiny wood floors with a stage in the rear flanked by entrances and exits to the kitchen. Around the entire Ballroom were Crystal Sconces and, in the Middle, hung a huge Crystal Chandelier with about forty lights.

Between 7 and 8 pm, chimes were rung and the doors to the Banquet Hall opened with great fanfare. I immediately broke down the Smorgasbord and brought the remaining food into the attached Schule where I placed the remaining food in paper containers and started to clean the Punch Bowls. The lights and heat were turned off so they could save money on heating and electricity. The only illumination was a 100-watt bulb near a sink and the table I worked at. The temperature in the SCHULE was below freezing. My job was to clean the punch bowl for the next event the following Saturday.

I arrived home with my food stash which was stretched out until the following week, this employment lasted for five weeks. Moishe told me to come in at 2 pm he had a special assignment for me. Upon entering he walked with me to the Banquet Hall and gave me a sudsy bucket of water, a Brillo pad, a piece of cloth, and rubber gloves. He pointed to the scuff marks on the floor and said he wanted me to remove the black marks on the dance floor.

He left and I was on my knees and I felt that I was in the SAHARA DESERT shoveling sand. Then and there I made a decision that CHOPPED LIVER, PIGS IN A BLANKET, GELFITE FISH, and SMOKED SALMON wasn't for me.

Handing my cleaning equipment to Moshe I told him I resigned and to keep the money he owed me for today.

Arriving home earlier than usual I told my parents that I would rather spend the weekend with them than spend it with BAR MITZAHS and WEDDING leftovers.

I never knew my Grandfather's real name but to me he was Zeydah. As a member of the ILGWU* he was a dapper dresser. Every Saturday afternoon I found him pressing his suit and shining his shoes, at about 6 pm he put on his coat and hat and left my Grandmother. He was an 8X10 Glossy as one of my family discussed where he went.

Every Sunday we would gather to watch ED Sullivan who was a Newspaper Columnist and host of the most-viewed Variety Show on television. During the week we would watch Boxing, Wrestling, Perry Mason, The Lone Ranger, Bonanza, and Gunsmoke. He would get excited and talk to the television in Yiddish. I would say you are right Zeydah.

In the Winter of 1954, my father who still worked for Arthur Klar travelled across the Country selling Souvenir Programs for the country's top Comedy Duo Martin and Lewis. The act was comprised of a handsome Italian Dean Martin and his Comedy Sidekick Jerry Lewis. He was gone for three months. At that point, he gave up travelling across the country. He and Klar decided that he would do local Big Band Concerts and would take me to work with him at the BIG BAND CONCERTS selling Souvenir Programs and bands such as Vaugh Monroe, Duke Ellington, and Lionel Hampton. My Dad and I bonded over the long rides to Connecticut, Long Island, and Maryland. Sometimes rather than heading straight home we would spend the night in a Motel.

In the spring of 1954, I was told that the New York Board of Education determined that I was well enough to start High School. Come September I had to register at THOMAS JEFFERSON HIGH.

SUITS AND HANGERS

My Uncle Charlie asked me to come with him to buy a suit at one of the top Men's Suit stores located on Pitkin Avenue. There were very few men's clothing stores that sold hand-crafted suits.

Charlie who was a spiffy dresser only wanted to own the best. He was working for one of the Top Furriers as a salesman in what was once the Fur Capital of the world located a few blocks from RH Macy's on West 34th Street. As Charlie was being fitted, I roamed around the store which was stocked with Navy Black, and gray suits. Viewing how the salesmen greeted the customers listening to their sales pitch. Approaching the store manager, I asked if he could use a stock boy and someone to box the suits. He asked me who was I with, pointing to my uncle who was spending five Hundred dollars he smiled and asked me if I could work Saturdays and Sundays for $3. 00 an hour, Before I said yes, I asked if he could pay $4. 00 with a big smile we agreed on $3. 50 per hour. My hours were from Noon to 6 pm. Every Saturday I would take my bike and ride it to SAM & MACK and park it in the stock room.

There was a dress code, I had to wear a White shirt with a tie, Gray or Black Trousers, and polished shoes. In the words of Sam, "I represented the image of the store." The first thing I did on my arrival was to make sure all the suits were hanging straight. Sizes 38, 40, 44 regulars, extra-long etc. I noticed that every sale had three steps, the salesmen escorted the buyer who was usually accompanied by a wife or girlfriend. Guiding them to help select the right size, right colour, and perfect fabric. Trying on the jacket, then escorting him to try on the pants, having his partner sit near the fitting mirror, and bringing the tailor to do a proper fitting. After much adulation on how elegant he looked. The customer would look at the price tag and ask if the store can do better on the price. Now the salesman whispers in the customer's ear if he purchases two suits he can give 30% off and he will eat the reduction of his commission.

I discovered to close a large sale that the salesman can give 30% with an added 10%. It was simple math two suites = $800-240=560 -56. 00 =504. Now a good salesman would sell two perfectly coordinated shirts and two Silk Ties.

Sam & Mack has a shoe department with a wonderful pair of shoes that will turn any person into one who would be admired by his clients, customers, and boss. Guaranteeing that he will be a VICE PRESIDENT BY YEARS END. The following weekend the customer will return for his final fitting receiving a confirmation of his Elegance. That's where I came in, I would take the suits handle them with care ready to box them and whisper into the customer's ear that I would include the hangers even though it was against the store rules. Usually, the customer smiles and surreptitiously places bills in my hand. I would make an extra $20. 00 per pay.

Since my father wasn't traveling, I would escort him into Manhattan with the BMT subway which was five blocks away from my house. To make me happy he had a photographer friend put together a composite photo sheet with my stage resume which was ANYTHING GOES in Summer stock. My dream was to be a standup Comedian. He landed a job as a Comedy writer for Milton Berle who had a top variety show on NBC. Upon our arrival in Manhattan, we went to a famous coffee shop where unemployed actors and Comedians hung out. At about four O'clock we would go around the corner to 1650 Broadway where Berle's offices were located. The office had a large leather couch where I would sit immersed in Cigar Smoke. My father disappeared into the writer's room.

Berle would pass me and ask if I had any new Material. He told me to call him Uncle Miltie. I would do some imitations of Jimmy Durante and Red Skelton. Berle would tap me on the head and say to keep working on it. One of the writers passed me and told me to bring my pictures over to the Jackie Gleason office which was in the Park Central Hotel. Walking over to the hotel which was a few blocks away from 1650 Broadway. Gleason had a top Variety Show titled The Cavalcade of Stars. Which was being aired on the Dumont Network which later became the Fox Network owned by Rupert Murdoch News Corp.

Before taking the subway home my father had to stop at Lindy's and buy their famous Cheesecake. Lindy's was right across the street from Berle's office. Entering the restaurant was like entering the New York City culinary temple. All the tables in the front were reserved for Comics and Radio and Television personalities. Heading downtown to 44th Street you had Sadri's whose front tables were reserved for Broadway Producers and entertainers on the Broadway Stage. About a week later I was called by the head of talent for the Cavalcade of Stars to come in for an audition. They were looking for a kid for a sketch they called the Honeymooners where Gleason played a Bus Driver. I got the part. I was the only 13-year-old in my Boy Scout troop who appeared with a major television star.

Lindy's 1956

1954 was a year of achievement, I earned 21 Merit Badges to become an EAGLE SCOUT. I do not know how I earned these badges for they were designed for kids from small towns and rural areas. My survival skills came in handy when I went to Manhattan and visited Central Park. I was able to identify various trees, I knew the difference between a Rat and a squirrel. I could cross against the light and dodge Yellow Cabs.

Spring of 1954 my father accompanied my Boy Scout troop to the wilds of Staten Island where the Scouts had a campground. He planned to make a large turkey for the troop, expecting that the fifty-pound bird would defrost by the time we arrived at the campsite. He planned the entire meal and made stuffing the evening before we left. He bought cans of Cranberry sauce and a giant pan to roast the Turkey. Upon arrival, he discovered that the bird was frozen stiff. We had no other choice but to boil water and give Turkey hot water Enema We finally ate dinner at 8 pm A decade later New York State built the Verrazano Bridge connecting Brooklyn with the Wilderness of the Fifth Borough. With the opening of the bridge, thousands of people who lived in the other Boroughs flocked to buy their piece of Suburbia which was a ferry ride to MANHATTAN.

In September of 1954, I faced the reality of having to go to High School which was a few blocks away from where I lived. This period of adjustment introduced me to the kids that lived in my neighbourhood. Viewing High School as a nine-to-three job that didn't pay me money. This was the first time in my life that I interfaced with girls, it was wonderful for my dick always got hard. They all tried to make themselves older trying to cover up the pimples on their face and sneaking into the bathroom to put on lipstick. My motivation at that time was to find another job. I left SAM & MACK after one of the salesmen told me to Sam that I was selling hangers. When he told me that was against the rules I resigned.

Finally, the Board of Education cleared me to go to High School turning out to be Thomas Jefferson a ten-minute walk from my apartment. I was one of the biggest kids in the class except for the kids who played Basketball or who were on the football team. Usually, I was seated in the back of the room surrounded by these monsters. My goal was to make the teachers love me so at any given moment I would raise my hand to give the correct answer. I was overweight and all the skinny kids would call me names. A couple of months into the Semester they started calling me GUPPY.

By early November my father finally found a profession that was suited for him, and he became a Publicity Man. Creating an alliance with Eddie Jaffe who by 1954 was the go-to man if you wanted to get mentioned in the Gossip Columns of one of New York's daily NEWSPAPERS.

In the Fall of 1954, My father had an idea, his new Associate needed a boy to run errands, do filing, and do other small chores. I jumped at the idea and he set up an interview with Jaffe for the following Sunday afternoon. By that time, I was an Explorer Scout which was created by the BOY SCOUTS OF AMERICA for Boys who were about to be fourteen. This meant shelving my Khaki Uniform and buying a New green outfit. The Explorer Scouts created a rank similar to EAGLE but was called Silver meaning I needed to earn additional Merit Badges. That Sunday I had an Explorer Scout event in mid-town Manhattan. My father arranged a five pm interview at Jaffe's office/apartment which was located on the top floor of a four-story building over an Italian restaurant named ZUCCAS located at 158 West 48th Street. Arriving at 5 pm sharp I rang the buzzer and the street door opened. Someone yelled it was on the top floor. Arriving at an opened door I heard a voice yelling I will be right out. Entering the apartment finding myself in a large living room filled with papers, pants, and shoes scattered around the place. In one corner of the living room was a pond with fish swimming around, flanked by two couches. By the widows that faced 48th Street were two desks with table lamps and phones. Facing the desks were two old swivel chairs.

After fifteen minutes of watching the Gold Fish swim around the pond, the bedroom door opened a Beautiful Tall Blonde Lady exited adjusting her clothes followed by a thin man with glasses about 5'6" and wearing a bathrobe. She kissed him on the head and said she was looking forward to seeing him next week. "You are Sam's Son. Your Father talks about you all the time. He says you want to be a Comic" Jaffe mumbled as he sat down by the desk and started opening a pile of mail.

"Your name is Allen, am I right? You can call me Eddie. Your father told me you are available after school"

I nodded "Yes."

"Your job is to make sure the living room is clean and the refrigerator has food. If you see the bedroom door closed that means I am sleeping. When I get up you can go in and hang my clothes up and file any papers you see around. Pointing to the door of his bedroom There I will leave you a note outlining the chores of the day with Money to buy what I need at the A&P which was on Ninth Avenue between 54th and 55th Street. If I have other instructions, I will call your father with daily instructions for the following day. You will get paid five dollars an hour."

He shook my hand and escorted me to the door. It was a deal. Calculating the amount of money I will earn per week I figured it to be a hundred dollars per week which I will deposit ninety in the savings account that my Mother set up with the three thousand dollars I received from my Bar Mitzvah gifts.

That Monday I wore a shirt and tie to school, with my book bag I met My father at the Subway and we both travelled into the city. The subway fare at that time was fifteen cents. The hour ride into the city allowed me to do my homework assignment.

I was given a key to open the street entrance to the apartments. Reaching the top floor I found Jaffe"s apartment door open with a telephone cord stretched across the floor to the adjoining apartment. As I was about to enter Jaffe's apartment a slightly balding man dressed in a white shirt and tie introduced himself as Joe Russell. For the eight years I worked with Jaffe I never knew what Joe did for a living. I found out that he went to the Greyhound Bus Terminal in search of starry-eyed girls who wanted to be in Show Business. Within an hour he became their mentor offering a place to stay until they started earning money, Cloris Leachman was one of Joe's house guests. My dad told me he was on the payroll of the Copacabana for Joe was the go-between Monte Proser who created the concept and opened the club in 1940 with a faux Décor which he thought that a Brazil Tropical theme should be. The Copa as it was known had a full orchestra a chorus line of Beautiful Copa Girls wearing Carmen Miranda head costumes. Every major Entertainer wanted to Play The Copa.

Proser had money issues by 1950 he was broke. Joe Russell who was a friend of Proser introduced him to Mobster Frank Costello who offered to be his partner. In those days Credit Cards were nonexistent and cash was king. Costello did not trust Proser and needed to ensure that he wasn't skimming money.

Since the Copa was initially Costello's club he bought in a Loyalist Jules Podell who Managed the Kit Kat Club. Within six months Posner was gone and the Canopy over the door was Jules Podell's Copacabana. An entertainer wasn't a star until they played the Copa. Stars like Frank Sinatra, Dean Martin, Jerry Lewis, Sammy Davis Danny Thomas, and The Supremes just to name a few.

This was Joe Russell's monthly meal ticket. I discovered that the third apartment on the floor was used as an office for COMEDY WRITER NAT HIKEN who created two successful series SGT BILKO starring Phil Silvers and CAR 54 WHERE ARE YOU starring Joe E. Ross and Fred Gwynne That was the cast of Neighbors on the top floor. Never once did I see the tenant on the second floor, but I did meet his cats who I found having dinner at Jaffe's Gold Fish pond. I was told he was a Columnist for an Entertainment trade paper the Hollywood Reporter, and a renowned caricaturist.

New York was home to the Daily Mirror, Daily News, The New York Post, The Herald Tribune, and the New York Times not to mention The Wall Street Journal plus two wire services The United Press and Associated Press.

The Mirror, The News, and The Post all had gossip Columns. The Fifties were simpler times and readers who enjoyed reading about the lives of famous and Infamous bought papers.

Most days I arrived and found detailed instructions on the door with instruction to deliver neatly typed envelops by hand to the Columnist of varied Daily Newspaper gossip Columnists the likes of Ed Sullivan, Earl Wilson, Dorothy Kilgallen Liz Smith, Jack Obrian Robert Sylvester, and Walter Winchell - the most powerful Gossip Columnist of the 20th Century who's column was in the Daily Mirror owned by William Randolph Hearst and syndicated to the chain of newspapers owned by the Hearst Corporation. Winchell also had a Network Radio Show which was then called NBC/THE BLUE NETWORK which was the most listened to broadcast from the Depression to the 1957.

Before I left for High School a large white envelope was placed where I ate breakfast with a note DELIVER TO WALTER WINCHELL.

I discovered that Eddie Jaffe was barred forever from placing a client in Winchell's Column due to giving a piece of news that was untrue. Jaffe paid my father to place his clients in Winchell's Column. Three times a week I visited the City Rooms of all the major newspapers in New York. On those days I wore a Sports jacket with Thermals. Walking straight through the lobby saying hello to people at the reception desk, walking straight through the newsroom where people thought I was a copyboy, and dropping off the exclusive tidbits to each Columnist.

Walter Winchell had an apartment at the Saint Moritz on Central Park South. I found out from the doorman what floor was

WINCHELL'S offices on. I waited until the lobby was busy and snook into the Elevator. Arriving on the floor I knocked on a door and was greeted by Winchell's Secretary Rose Bigman. Rose was a nice lady overworked, she asked how I found out where Mr. Winchell's offices my friend at the Mirror gave me the information There who my father was and how he had many clients whom Mr. Winchell's readers would enjoy knowing about: adding that I was an Eagle Scout, working part-time to save money for college. As the Elevator door closed I told her I would be by once or twice a week.

Since I saw myself as a member of EDDIE JAFFE's Public Relations firm I had to look great, that meant finding a great Barber. En route to the subway, I had to walk under elevated Subway tracks which went West cutting across East New York to get to the BMT* which went North to South going directly into Manhattan, passing Fortunoff who sold household items, and giftware at great prices. Whose entrance was on Livonia Avenue, walking towards the Subway I Passed a Barber Shop where there was a group of guys pitching pennies, Big urban areas had sidewalks many of which were boxes creating natural lines. The coin that got close to the line would win the pot, pennies were props for dollars. The other group would be reading the Sports Pages of the New York Post or The Daily News all waiting outside to get in. Asking one of the guys who were standing in front of the door leaning on the Traditional Red and White swirling poles with a white globe a top who were they waiting for, He looked at me as if I was stupid and said MIKE Da barber. It seems that people in the know of his great talents and the camaraderie of the shops' clientele drew customers from all five Boroughs to have DA BARBER STYLE THEIR HAIR.

Suddenly a large RED Cadillac Eldorado pulled up in front of the crowd and the door on the passenger side opened and out stepped a natty dressed guy wearing a signing blue suit with Black Slick Back hair. They all moved aside as if he were Jesus walking through the Gates of Jerusalem to open the door. All the clients came off the street as he took off his suit jacket hung it up and donned his black Barber Apron. I was told by one of his hairy patrons that he was MIKE DA BARBER. I discovered that DA BARBER was a degenerate gambler and went to the race track or Trotters four or five times a week. If he won, it was guaranteed that he would not show up to cut hair. In those days DA BARBER charged $10.00 per haircut. Approaching the Da Barber I asked how long a wait. He looked at me and said come back Saturday Morning I am certain to be in. The hairstyle was a slick back front which ended in a ducktail in the back. All the other guys in school were wearing what was called motorcycle jackets which were all leather having many zippers. My Parents told me that wearing the jacket told the world that I was a bad kid.

That was the beginning of my interest in Da Barber. His store was across the street from Curly's poolroom which guaranteed that a good majority of his clients were all individual contractors involved in illegitimate businesses. Some were bookies who would cover sporting events, some were number runners, and others were the 1954 version of Credit Card Companies that at that time didn't exist, they were called SHYLOCKS which was a modern-day tribute to William Shakespeare's Merchant of Venice. It was a very simple business, you needed say a hundred Dollars to begin,

Mr Silvers a Cigar Chomping who was overweight and owned a Large White Eldorado loaned you the hundred dollars with a 20% interest-rated compound daily. Meaning after seven days you owned $120.00 and so on. Usually, small businesses borrow money in Thousands of dollars to pay the rent, payroll etc. Usually, the money came from a mob-connected guy who enjoyed beating up deadbeats who could not come up with the money in the time agreed to pay off the debt. This form of business as we would say today was an economic safety net with two downsides, you were either killed or you had a new partner, the mob. Now you are not an owner but an employee, if they discovered your hand was in the Cookie Jar you are liquidated. I now found a way to get free haircuts by arriving early at the Barber Shop and selling my turn to the next. Included in this cast of characters was a person called THE HOODLUM RABBI who was Autistic but in the Fifties he was just retarded. One of the wise guys in the Barber Shop used a telephone in a candy store around the corner and called the pay phone inside the Barber Shop. One of the guys inside answered the phone and said there was a call for the HOODLUM RABBI, picking up the phone he became flustered and within seconds hung up and started shaking. Mike asked what was wrong and the Hoodlum Rabbi blurted out that THE HOODLUM PRIEST CALLED HIM THREATENING TO KILL HIM IF HE INSISTED ON USING HOODLUM in his name. About ten minutes later the phone rang again in the shop. Da Barber picked up the phone and told the POPE was calling him from the Vatican to tell him that the HOODLUM PRIEST was sorry. This incident made me aware that the world was filled with ASSHOLES.

Middle-class people were not aware of the Diner's Club which came on the market in 1953. This operated with the concept of a credit card that allows you to make purchases and repay them totally or partially, The Diner's Club became the business model for today's Credit Cards which in reality are legitimate Shylock's charging exorbitant interest on monies owed by the users. Credit Cards became a cash cow for the banking industry which for many years were allowed low interest rates for the use of Capital but charged high interest rates from card users.

I soon learned that the DA BARBER was cutting the hair of up-coming talents who grew up in the Neighborhood, among them was Steve Lawrence who married my first wife's cousin Edith Gormezano a Sephardic Jew whose stage name was Eydie Gorme.

Getting off the BMT on 48th Street in Manhattan was always filled with excitement for I didn't know who or what would be in Jaffe's office. One afternoon I was working in the living room where I found a guy in his twenties sleeping on the couch. Jaffe introduced me to Marlon who was a friend of a friend who needed a place to stay until he got his own apartment. He was in town to shoot a movie called ON THE WATERFRONT, also studying with Lee Strasberg's Actor Studio.

When Jaffe finally woke up I figured it would be nice if I made him Breakfast of Eggs and Toast. Wearing a silk Bathrobe, he went into the Living Room and ate while Joe Russell told him about his new sleepovers which he recruited from the GRAY HOUND BUS TERMINAL.

Entering his bedroom newspapers were scattered with Various opened and unopened mails. He was a good friend of the writer Dick Condon and there were notes from John Wayn scattered across the room were suit jackets without pants, shirts with food stains, ties, and various raincoats. I always wondered where Jaffe's pants were. I later realized he would visit women either Hookers or Strippers and have sex with them, one day after his ordeal, he left his pants, put on his raincoat, grabbed a cab and came home at four in the Morning. In the afternoon a beautiful woman knocked on the door, gave me the pants and told me to tell Eddie she loved him.

One afternoon I was sitting in the office with my father, A man walked into the apartment went straight to the bathroom took a shower, dressed up, walked into the living room and said "Tell Eddie Thanks" and left. I asked my father if he knew him. My Dad just shrugged and went back to work.

Other neighbourhood kids played stickball, basketball, and other sports. My sport was roaming around Midtown Manhattan sneaking into newspaper City Rooms, delivering saucy paragraphs on the accounts of Jaffe's clients written by my father to columnists.

In 1954, an event changed the dynamics of the Friday Night rituals, the death of my Uncle Charlie from testicular Cancer which devasted my Zaydah and Mother. A year later my Aunt Helen who was still living with my Grandparents at the old age of thirty finally married her boss and moved out of the house leaving my Maternal grandparents empty nesters. The death of his son took the zest out of my Zaydah's life. By the end of 1954, he had a sudden heart attack and passed away. His death was taken hardest by my Father and Mother. To my father, I supposed he was the dad he always wanted and to my Mother, there was truly a unique bond which was unravelled to me for 17 years.

After my Zaydah's death, I moved into my Aunt's now empty bedroom and stayed with my Bubbah for almost a year, going straight to school during this period I found a fresh breakfast with warm bread and freshly baked cakes. Unbeknownst to me she would get up at 6 a.m. and go down to buy fresh bread and pastries at the local Bakery which was a block away.

In 1955, I went to the Supreme Theatre movie house and paid fifty Cents to see a movie called BLACK BOARD JUNGLE Starring Glenn Ford who played a teacher Sidney Poitier and introduced movie audiences to teen rebellion. The soundtrack movie score was composed by BILL HALEY AND THE COMETS titled ROCK AROUND THE CLOCK.

It was a depiction of an inner city High School where white teenagers ran havoc over the teaching staff. I was going to a New York City High School. The only havoc I experienced was outside the girls' bathroom where they all lined up to put on makeup and lipstick. In those days parents wanted their daughters to look like young Jewish Virgins when they left their home. I did not have time to be rebellious, I wanted to make money.

Radio stations around the country were all playing ROCK N ROLL. Sam Katzman a producer of B movies and Cheap Horror films hired Eddie Jaffe and my Father to handle publicity for the New York opening ROCK AROUND THE CLOCK, starring Bill Haley And The Comets, The Platters, Tony Martinez and his Band

and Freddie Bell and Bellboys, introducing New York radio DJ Alan Freed. Alan Freed was a natural at casting. Freed who in 1951 was a Cleveland Ohio Radio DJ by the name of Alan Freed known to his listeners as Moondog introduced RHYTHM AND BLUES created by Black Musical Talent to White Midwest Audiences. In 1951, Freed was hired by New York Radio station WINS where he coined the name ROCK N ROLL. This new sound caught on with a teenage audience and WINS became a top Radio Station. Its owners syndicated Freed's broadcast to top Markets across the country, Freed was the Father of Rock N ROLL. He handily packed Large Ornate Movie Theatres across the country with Musical soloists such as Bill Haley and the Comets, Little Richard, Jerry Lee Lewis, Fats Domino, Ray Charles, The Platters, Sam Cooke, Jackie Wilson all backed by big bands.

The plan was to amass a hundred teenagers from schools across the City handing them free tickets and telling them to scream, cry and shout as the stars arrived at the Palace Theatre on Broadway which in the Fifties went from Vaudeville to showing movies. Today the same theatre is used for major Broadway Musicals. The make-believe riot made all the major Newspapers in New York, radio coverage, and WPIX television which was owned by the NEW YORK DAILY NEWS, In the mid-fifties, the advent of television was just happening.

While in High School I became more sociable and realized that my penis was used for more things than urinating. The multi-function of my Penis was discovered when I had a great dream and woke up with a wet bed and a hand full of gooey stuff. The word got out that I was on the Jackie Gleason Show and the kids in my neighborhood all wanted to be my friends. None of us lived in a single-family home that had a finished basement we all lived in Apartments.

On Pennsylvania Avenue across from our high school, there were attached two-family homes that had finished basements. We were in great need of a space for our club meetings and twenty-five of us agreed to pay $2.50 as weekly dues. They all agreed and made me the treasurer aka President. The owner of the house was Mrs. Shapiro a Polish lady who spoke little English but Yiddish. I charmed her by using some of the Yiddish terms that my Bubbe taught me. After joining her for a glass of Tea and home-baked cake she agreed to a rent of $40.00 a month upfront. I gave her the money and she made me swear not to make much noise during our meetings. As she hugged me I noticed she had numbers on her forearm and realized she was a HOLOCAUST SURVIVOR.

This transaction took place on a Friday afternoon and the club members were waiting to hear whether I made the deal. Following me to the Subway, we discussed meeting there the following evening after Sabbath to respect Mrs. Shapiro and view the space. On Saturday afternoon I had to accompany my father to Pitkin Avenue to buy a pair of shoes, the name of the shoe store was REGAL SHOES. While my father was trying on shoes I viewed a large RED SIGN that had chipped paint and said REGAL. When my Dad finished paying for the shoes I asked the manager if I could have the sign. He said sure take it.

A block away from THE REGAL SHOE STORE was a supermarket whose manager knew my mother. I asked to borrow a shopping cart to help transport my large sign.

There I was on Pitkin Avenue on a Saturday afternoon wheeling a large REGAL SIGN accompanied by my father making sure that the sign did not tip over. My crew was hanging out in front of Mrs. Shapiro's house waiting for me to arrive with the key for the side door that led into the basement. Arriving with the Giant Sign in a cart, they all asked what the sign was about. Pointing at the SIGN which had paint peeling off I said "This is the official name of our club REGAL HOUSE."

Entering the dimly lit basement which was loaded with old furniture and various Nick-Nacks. We found a broken-down couch old lamps and a couple of end tables. The sign helped with our colour scheme, so we decided to paint the walls A VIBRANT ORANGE. One of our members' father was an electrician who happened to have a small Crystal Chandelier which replaced the one naked bulb which was hanging in the middle of the room. There was a small bathroom whose walls were peeling and we painted that Interior vibrant blue and changed the toilet seat. All that was missing was a radio a folding table with four folding chairs which cost us under a hundred dollars and the space was completed within 72 hours. The main mission of our members was to invite girls over to what we called our ROCK N ROLL PARTIES which if you were lucky was a make-out party. By eleven pm the girls had to go home escorted by guys who had Semen stained pants. During the week some guys used their allowances to play poker and drink THUNDERBIRD produced by Gallo Wineries and cost under ten dollars.

One night I witnessed my close friend Irving Schwartz lose all of his allowance to stay in the game and bet his Bar Mitzvah watch. Guess what, he lost his watch. The asshole who won it put it on the floor and stepped on it. This incident almost tore the club apart. Luckily we developed a code of conduct. Dues must be paid on time, $2.50 each Friday. If you miss a week you are charged 15% interest, which I learned from hanging out at Da Barber. Miss two weeks you are out of the club. Word got out at Thomas Jefferson High School where we were all going into our Junior year that being a member of REGAL HOUSE was cool and a place to hang out. We created a membership committee where each founding member can recommend a future member who needs a unanimous vote to join. We put a lid on twenty-five members, we needed to set up standards for our members and a code of conduct which we called the RULES OF REGAL.

No Drugs, No forcing yourself on a girl that says n, No loud noise after 11 p.m. No markers when in a card game, when broke you leave the game, and no excessive drinking. One Friday night one of our founding members Ricky got really drunk, we put a towel like a turban on his head, carried him out and placed him in a chair in the middle of Pennsylvania Avenue which was a wide two-way street. After five minutes of watching cars wiz by we poured a bucket of water over him, and stepped back to view his reaction when he realized he was in the middle of the street with cars whizzing by, we escorted him back into the club to dry off. After that incident, he never drank more than one glass of THUNDERBIRD.

For keeping the clubhouse clean we had a rotating roster of members who would eventually hook up with a girl who would come in and clean the club.

Working for Eddie Jaffe after school made the weeks go by. Straightening out of his bedroom, filing, and delivering fresh gossip items to my list, in every City room I entered the receptionist thought I was an employee.

In 2016, My scouting days were over for I reached the highest Ranks in both the Boy Scouts and Explorers. In my Junior year in High School, I tried to bring up my grades. I was an outstanding student in History, Biology, and English excelled at Lunch, and terrible in Physical ED. The instructor wanted me to climb up a rope, and do push-ups, I failed in Algebra, Geometry and Spanish. In New York to graduate you had to take State Regent Exams. I failed the Math Regent twice, and Spanish once.

I finally passed the Math Regent by cheating, I wrote the formulas on my hands. In early 2016, Jaffe and my father landed a deal at THE CONCORD HOTEL. Which was the premiere Summer getaway for wealthy Jewish Families who fled the five Boroughs of Manhattan. Traveling two hours to the CATSKILL Region Middle Class Jewish Families rented Bungalows where the families stayed, and the Husbands came up to visit on Weekends on their vacations. The small town which was the Centerpiece of what was called the Jewish Alps Monticello was surrounded by all the Hotels that offered an abundance of food, entertainment, and other amenities. The Bungalow communities were near Kiamesha Lake. This was the land where Jewish Princesses would find their Jewish Prince Charming.

The Concord was the most elegant of the hotels in the region. Its owners were the Winarick family and its patriarch was Arthur Winarick. Legend has it that Arthur was the founder of Jeris Hair tonics and during Prohibition, he sold excess Alcohol to Bootleggers. He, like many other Jewish Russian Immigrants travelled to the Catskills. He went to Grossinger's Hotel built as the ultimate luxury resort in the Catskill. Arthur was a man who always thought of doing better, driving through the area he found a dilapidated hotel called Ideal Plaza which was heavily in debt. He purchased over 2, 000 acres of Natural beauty, which was dirt cheap. He was farsighted to realize that the Next Generation of New York Jews who became successful would want luxury.

His vision was to create a hotel that would outdo Grossinger's, after renovating the existing Ideal Plaza with an indoor Tropical theme pool, in 1951 he hired architect Morris Lapidus who built iconic Hotels in Miami Beach such as the Fontainebleau and the Eden Roc. Like the Catskills Miami Beach became the winter retreat for middle-class New York Jews. Winarick's vision was a hotel with 1, 500 hundred Guest rooms and a dining room that could seat 3, 000 people, an indoor and outdoor pool, a golf course, a baseball field, and eventually a three thousand-seat theatre with unobstructed views of the stage.

Jaffe didn't like to leave New York, my father was assigned to the account and we drove up to the Concord on the first weekend of April 1956 which happened to be the second night of Passover. The Concord was the only HIGH-RISE building in the Catskills, towering over all the existing resorts in the area. Checking in we were escorted to a top-floor suite. I tagged along with my father who was greeted by the Manager of the Hotel Ray Parker who turned out to be married to Winarick's daughter, and Phil Greenwald director of entertainment.

Roaming through the hotel I came across the daily entertainment schedule. 9 am hiking in the woodland owned by the hotel, 10 am softball, and 11 am volleyball. Lunch was followed by dancing lessons given by Tony and Marie, during the fifties Latin dancing was all the rage. Mambo, Cha Cha, Merengue, Tango. Every hotel had Latin Bands that rotated with big American dance bands and orchestras.

Tony and Maria had a class of fifty guests whose feet were always going in the wrong direction, the class was full of mainly women, 4 pm was Simon Sez with a bottle of Champagne given as a final prize to the person who survives.

Saturday was the big night where guests displayed how rich they were, the couples and families entered the dining room displaying their furs, jewellery, and gowns. It was a procession of Jews who wanted to display their wealth to their peers. The main attraction of what entertainers called the Catskills BORSCHT BELT describes the area of Hotels and Bungalow Colonies in Sullivan County where an abundance of Food was served to the guests. Two different agents booked talents that played the circuit. The agent that secondary acts can depend on Charlie Rapp. If he enjoyed your talent you would get a Summer Contract which included beaches, Clubs and every hotel in Sullivan County. William Morris the top talent agency that represented the most famous entertainers assigned Lee Solomon to spend time with Philly Greenwald. Lee was a fashion plate, he always had a tan and his hair perfectly combed.

That evening after the show in the 1.500-seat theatre everyone went to the Coffee Shop for another round of desserts. The Jewish

American Princesses went to the Night Owl lounge to find their Prince Charming. Philly always had a reserved table in front of the stage where a jazz Quartet was entertaining, seated at the table were my Parents, Frenchie (head of Reservations), Jay Jayson, and his wife, Ray Parker who managed the hotel. Taking in the total environment of Concord I determined I had to get a summer job there. Being a Ballsy almost 16 years old teenager, I asked MR. Greenwald, how can I get a summer job at the hotel? "Kid please call me Philly if your mom and Dad approve you have a job starting on the last weekend of June" My parents nodded in approval. After breakfast go down to where Leo or TUMMELER in residence will be leading a game called SIMON SAYS in the Theatre. Tell him that Philly wanted me to work on the Social Staff.

That morning, I went down for breakfast with my parents. At the Concord, food was the superstar, you could order twenty dishes. After finishing my breakfast, I headed straight to the Theatre where about thirty people were on stage, standing in front of them was a heavy-set man about five feet seven inches wearing a multi-coloured Beanie, a propeller on the top of his head, a Red Sweatshirt emblazoned with LEO THE TUMMELER on the back, and a Silver Whistle around his neck.

Approaching the stage I joined the group playing SIMON SAYS. Every time a person was incapable of following Simon's instructions Leo would blow his whistle and the person left the stage. I was one of four people left standing, it was I and two women in their Thirties and a guy wearing a GOLD STAR OF DAVID. Both women were eliminated and it was just the two of us and I decided to lose so the guy could win the bottle of Champagne. It was lunchtime and all the players left except me and the TUMMELER. Introducing myself, explaining that Philly wanted me to join his staff as an assistant TUMMELER. I told Leo my plans of being a stand-up Comic, my appearance on the Gleason Show and my time spent with Milton Berle.

Walking together outside the theatre where my parents were waiting for me. I introduced the TUMMELER to my parents who told them that he was impressed and that I would make a great member of his team. We went to lunch and Leo Tummler went to Tummel.

Returning to Brooklyn and waiting for the semester to end I tried to apply myself in getting passing grades to me a straight C was the letter I was shooting for otherwise I would have to go to SUMMER SCHOOL to graduate when I was seventeen, missing Summer at the Concord. The members of REGAL HOUSE agreed to use it only on Fridays and the weekends, realizing we all had to study to become seniors.

A week after I returned from the Catskills we all decided that paying rent over the Summer made no sense. We decided to give Mrs. Schapiro notice that on May 15 we would be giving up the basement. With the warm spring weather, the sidewalk outside of the Candy Store which was directly under my apartment was the meeting spot for the older guys to hang out. Many were veterans of the Korean War which ended in 1953 as an Armistice was signed between North and South Korea. A good many of them worked as salesmen in the Garment Center, some used the GI Bill to go to college. One of the guys became a hairdresser driving a red Corvette always tan and hair sprayed that it looked like a toupee. Some worked for the city either as Firemen, Policemen or

Sanitation workers. The guys who worked for the city had their employment and pension guaranteed. None of them were married, all were in search of a lay, Many of them had cars. Saturday evenings in Manhattan were Single Dance Nights either at THE NEW YORKER HOTEL or THE PENNSYLVANIA HOTEL.

They never paid to go into the dance venue, they would go to the floor above the dance hall, take the stairway down and enter through a fire exit. Sundays were recap nights for those who struck out and came home by car leaving the winners behind. Those who found instant romance knew the desk clerks at both hotels who for a twenty-dollar tip would give them a key to an empty room. I would make sure to be on the corner to listen to their momentary conquest.

One guy who seemed to always score was a short guy whose nick-man was SLINGER. Word had it that he had a large Dick. I became their Mascot, they would buy me ice cream and Candy from Mo's Candy Store. The owner of the store was Moe Ginsberg who was a bookie on the side. The store had two phone booths, and he would take calls from people living in my building. I became his runner, going up to each tenant and telling them they had a phone call. They would either give me either fifty cents or a dollar. Across the street from the candy store, there was a Pharmacy that would have me deliver prescriptions to houses in the neighbourhood. I usually would get a dollar tip. On one of such deliveries which was at a tenement two buildings down from the Pharmacy, the tenant gave me a Bagel and Lox for a tip. At fifteen in a half, My Social and work life was split between six cultural communities, Eddie Jaffe, DA Barber, The Candy Store, Explore Scouts, Regal House, and Pharmacy.

On Memorial Day in 1956, we piled up in my Dad's Chevy and headed for the Catskills crossing into New Jersey, heading for route 17 passing the RED APPLE RESTAURANT Gateway to the BORSCHT BELT. To get to the Concord, you had to pass Kutsher's and the Nevele which was Eleven miles backwards. Both Kutsher's and the Nevele had loyal guests. Ten miles away was Grossingers which gave Arthur Winarick the impetus to build a venue bigger and better.

Checking in we were escorted to our *suite* by then it was time to eat dinner. My mother had all of her clothes custom-made and she put on a Gold Lame dress with sequins and her best jewellery. I think my father owned three suits one blue, one brown and one black.

Cordillion Room was the Night Club seating 1500 people. Buddy Hackett was the Star of the show. The opening act was the Will Masten Trio which featured Sammy Davis Jr. Ascending the elegant lobby stair we head to the dining room. Other guests were waiting in line to be seated. Everyone smoked and a haze enveloped the room. Across the room was a table set up to Photograph couples. The photographer with his lovely assistant told the smiling couples that their framed pictures would be ready after they finished their meal. No price was ever mentioned until they saw the finished product which if they wanted would be fifteen Dollars.

We were greeted by Irving Cohen the Maître De of the dining room whom regulars referred to as Irving's Dining room, a three thousand-seat dining room. His responsibilities were the kitchen staff, waiters, busboys, and most of all making the guests happy.

He had a large floor plan of the dining room with names of families written on each table. Most families came with parties of ten. Usually, people liked to sit with groups to broaden their circle of friends. My father told Irving who he was and asked for a table for four. Irving had a team of college girls escorting Guests to their tables. Usually, you would give them a five-dollar tip. After ordering five appetizers, a Beautiful blonde walked around wearing half a million dollars worth of jewellery. She was a model hired by the store owner to hawk his merchandise. Standing in the lobby I told myself this is where I belong and decided to turn myself into a college student with great hope for the future.

The Concord was a location where College kids who were ambitious went during their Summer vacation to earn money either to pay their tuition or spend on things they wanted. The jobs that made the most money were that of waiters, followed by busboys, Bellhops and parking attendants. These were jobs where you needed body strength. The Summer staff was integrated with the staff of professional full-time employees who lived in the Monticello and Liberty areas.

Time moved fast, Regal House became the place where members hooked up. Teen girls loved our sound system that played Rock and Roll, at 11 pm the music switched to Frank Sinatra, Perry Como, Patti Page Rosemary Clooney, and Dinah Shore. The final week before turning in the keys to Mrs. Shapiro we repainted the walls took the furniture we bought distributed it to each member and agreed to store them until the fall. Borrowing a cart from the local A&P I loaded the large Regal House Sign and wheeled it to my apartment to store it in my bedroom under the aged Hebrew National Salami.

The month of June was test month and I was determined to pass and become a Junior. June was a month of tests and short days. I would arrive at Jaffe's office and do my chores, my father had a Black Comedian client named NIPSY RUSSELL. Nipsy would meet us for dinner at Lindy's and discuss his career. During an early dinner, Nipsy handed me a piece of paper. "Your Father told me that you are headed to the Borscht Belt, work at The Concord. A classy man like you deserves a Black Mohair suit. The piece of paper I just gave you is the address to get your suit. Go tomorrow they expect you, ask for Roscoe." He then went on and discussed that William Morris was booking him at Grossinger's for THE FOURTH OF JULY WEEKEND and invited us to catch his act.

After school, I took the Westside IRT subway to 125 Street in Harlem. Walking down the street looking for the address I found a Dry Cleaning Store, entering the store I asked for Roscoe. Moving through the racks of suits that were waiting to be picked up, a large Black Man appeared flashing a Gold Tooth smile. "You are the kid that Nipsy told me to take care of, sit down for a minute I will be right back" I sat on the window ledge watching the action on 125 Street Even though this was part of Manhattan it felt Alien to me The only thing I knew about Harlem was the Appollo Theatre. Roscoe returned with a black suit in a plastic covering. "This is it, a Black Mohair suit. I am sure this will suit you. Go into the room with the curtain and try on the pants and jacket." Exiting the dressing room Roscoe put me in front of a mirror with chalk in hand, he adjusted the bottom of the pants. Looking at me he smiled and asked me if I wanted cuff or plain buttons. At that time everyone was wearing cuffs I decided plain buttons would be great.

Within ten minutes he came and started to wrap the suit, looking at me "I am certain you never owned a white dress shirt or tie, placing a tape measure around my neck he shouted" He shouted out to his employees that I needed a 16x30 and a Red Tie.

Wrapping the entire outfit, he placed it in a paper shopping bag. I left the store and he shouted after me "Kid, now you will look like a hip dude, give my regards to NIPSY and tell him he owes me one" Taking the Subway downtown I went back to the office. Jaffe had a Laundry bag which he wanted me to take to the Laundromat which was two long blocks away. He gave me twenty dollars to take a Taxi, I decided to walk and pocket ten dollars. The lady who took the clothes told me that they would be ready the next day. Returning from the Laundromat I climbed up the three flights of staircase, I had food trays from Zucca's which were to be delivered to Irving Hoffman, Joey Russell or Jaffe. I told Eddie that the Laundry would be ready tomorrow afternoon. I told him I would pick it up before I came into the office. He handed me a ten-dollar bill and told me to take a taxi, this one netted me twenty dollars. Every week I would deposit the money in my savings account which my Parents opened for me to deposit my Bar Mitzvah gifts. Arriving home with my suit, shirt, and tie. My Mother insisted that I model the suit for her, walking around the one-bedroom apartment modelling my Black Mohair suit. My Mother started to cry saying that I looked like a man. "You will take the suit with you to The Concord to wear when we come up for weekends." As she was serving dinner, she made a list of clothes she wanted to buy for me. The only shoes I wore were my Converse high-top Sneakers, that weekend we went to Thom McCann which had a store on Sutter Avenue two blocks away from my grandparents. I selected a pair of Black Wingtips which cost $25.00

The last week of June I received my report card straight C and one anomaly an A in history. Not that I was stupid I remembered everything that I was taught but was a poor test taker. I found no reason to excel in Geometry or Algebra, I wanted to be a Stand-Up Comic, not an Engineer. In later years taking these Math Courses was to discipline you in rational thinking, I was set my Summer was free and in September I would return as a Junior. The last week of June I put my clothes in a duffle bag and my new portable record player The Regency TR-1 which my parents gave me as a gift for passing all my tests.

July Fourth 1956 came out on Wednesday, my father made arrangements to spend the entire week at the hotel. Arriving just in time for dinner we went to the dining room Irving Cohen the Maître D greeted us and had the same beautiful blonde escort us to our table. My father told Irving that I would be joining the Social Staff starting July 1, Irving shook my hand and told me eating in the dining room was part of being a Tummeler. Meeting Leo in the Lobby who stood next to Larry the Balloon Man, was wearing a large Multi-Color Top hat and an oversized Red Vest and surrounded by guests' children. His speciality was making animals out of colourful balloons. Leo with a big smile told me to meet him at 9 a.m in front of the hotel and he would take me on a tour of the grounds. Saturday at 9 am I was standing next to the Hotel Valet and up came a Golf Cart with Leo Driving. First, he took me to the Golf Course to introduce me to Chi Chi Rodriguez, the Golf Pro at the Club, next to the courts where he introduced me to Vinny Rurac, whose wife was Magda Rurac, a Top-tier Tennis

STAR both from Romania, next it was the Soft Ball field which looked like a miniature Yankee Stadium.

We passed the outdoor pool where guests were already taking the Sun using their Suntan Reflectors. Towel boys were scurrying around making sure that the guests were comfortable and pocketing tips. Leo told me that part of the job of the social staff was to mingle with the guests and keep their teenage daughters busy but no intercourse. Steering the cart to the back of the hotel he pointed to cottages where staff lived. Part of the working summer staff had free Room and Board, stopping in front of one of the cottages Leo took me to a room with two Bunk Beds and steel lockers for your clothes and belongings.

Leo smiled and said he had to go to work, he pointed to a pair of corrugated doors and told me they led to the Hotel then drove down the road blowing his Whistle. Standing there I made a decision, there was no way I was going to spend the summer living in that dilapidated, paint-peeling employee Dormitory. Entering from the back of the hotel I found myself in one of the largest kitchens in the world. It was as long as a football field, with waiters yelling their breakfast orders and busboys bringing back dirty plates. Chefs at the grills making eggs, pancakes, waffles, and Oatmeal. By the exit of the dining room waiters picked glasses of Orange Juice, Prune Juice (called the Catskills Laxative) fresh fruit cups, small boxes of Cereals, and small boxes of milk. The wait staff had to be a great note taker, they had to write down the opening order for Breakfast for a table of ten. In addition, they had to be able to balance a tray with ten items to deliver to the guest's table.

Booking a room in any of the Borscht Belt hotels meant all meals were inclusive. Entering the dining room which was 80% filled with guests who wanted to have every meal for their money, having large Breakfasts. The Concord was Kosher, they didn't serve Bacon or any other foods that didn't make the Kosher acceptable list. Breakfast was the launching pad preparing you for the One O'clock Lunch, followed by a lavish 7 pm dinner. Followed by the main show in the Night Club which was followed by either having drinks in the Night Owl Lounge or the 24-hour Coffee Shop. Families with Children would order Sundaes, Ice Cream Sodas or the SUPER NOSH which was ten flavour scoops of ice cream, fruit nuts, chocolate syrup, and loads of real whipped cream topped by a Cherry with as many spoons as you needed. The cost was ten dollars.

Opening the door to my parent's suite they were both asleep, always missed Breakfast. I went down to the dining and had breakfast alone. It was a Glutton's paradise, there were four people at the next table ordering three of everything. The dishes just piled up in front of each plate was set a copy of the day's activities. The first event was CHA-CHA MAMBO CLASSES which were given by Tony and Marie who owned the dance studio. Tony and Marie were the epitome of what one would imagine, a Sexy Latin Couple to look like. Tony resembled silent film star Rudolph Valentino who was the Heart Throb to millions of women during the Silent Film Era. At 5'6" highly polished boots, his black hair slicked back and a pencil-thin black moustache stood out, he dressed in tight pants with a ruffle white shirt. Marie wearing heavy makeup, her shiny black hair in a bun wearing black Capri pants topped off with sequin Ballroom dancing shoes. She looked like Dolores del Rio.

Both were Silent Movie Stars before the advent of sound. They were the personification of what Latin Dancers should look like.

Latin dancing was the craze imported from Argentina, Brazil, and Cuba which was ninety miles from Miami. Watching the classes I was determined to learn the dances, what better way to keep young female Guests Happy? The class was over at noon so everybody could go to lunch. Using the house phone I called my parents telling them I would meet them in front of the dining room. They arrived at 1 pm, my mother always looked like a fashion plate even when at home she always dressed to stand in front of our apartment house. After being seated they asked me about my morning with Leo, taking them through the tour, I came to the staff housing and what a wreck it was, a fire trap with staffers smoking and drinking, mentioning that I would have to share a room. My father listened intently and said don't worry I am meeting with Philly and Frenchie later. It was a cloudy day and I wandered into the nightclub to watch Tony Bennett rehearse, the concord had two bands Marty Beck and his orchestra were resident house orchestras which according to the demand of Star Performers could expand to twenty with strings and other musicians who were not part of the resident orchestra which was twelve musicians. To satisfy the impact of Latin Dancing they had Sonny Rossi and his Latin Orchestra.

On July 1st, my father walked me to my room on the grounds of the Concord, it was nestled in a clearing not far from the back of the Nightclub I guess had the cheapest rooms on the property. It looked like an old log cabin with twenty rooms, a porch with a hanging lantern, outdoor furnishing, a couple of chairs and a swinging mini couch that fits two. My room was on the ground floor, opening the door the room had a single bed one dresser an end table, a house phone, and a bathroom with a shower. This was my room until after Labor Day and I loved it, I also was being paid fifty dollars a week. To make my mother happy I would stay with them until they left on July Fifth.

On Sunday morning after my breakfast, I met Leo who gave me two RED T-SHIRTS THAT READ TUMMELER ON THE BACK, my name ALLEN G over the front pocket on the shirt. My first assignment was to wheel out the baseball gear, gloves, bats, and balls to the Softball field and wait.

Over the loudspeaker, Leo announced THE SOFTBALL FIELD WAS OPENED. About twenty guests showed up and formed two teams, they played until lunch was announced. I packed up the gear and rolled the cart to the equipment shed here I found two towel boys smoking grass. I introduced myself and told them it was cool and that what they did was none of my business.

Finally, July 5th came, and my parents helped me bring my belongings to my room. Escorting them to the front of the hotel where the Valet brought their 1955 Chevy Bel Air. Naturally, my mother started to cry, she would cry at the opening of an egg. "You are my life, call us always…Make sure you get enough sleep" My father helped her into the front seat whispering that he plans to come to the hotel every weekend. As they drove to the exit I transformed myself into a 19-year-old college student working to pay his college tuition. I then realized that over weekends I was a guest and signed my father's name at both the Night Owl Lounge and Coffee shop. After settling in, plugging in my Elvis Presley

RCA record player stacking 15 Romantic LPS. I hung up my clothes, put on my Tummeler shirt and LEVI jeans, and went directly to what Leo was calling a Bingo Tournament where any guest who wore the silliest hat won a prize, a portable radio or free hairstyling at Mr. Marvin's beauty salon.

Putting all the Bingo Paraphernalia together I stored it in the Tummeler's game closet. Leo and I walked over to the coffee shop for iced tea, "I just want to go over the rules of being a Tummler. The most important is to keep the guest and their teenage daughters happy no matter what they look like, that means dancing with every girl that is a guest. The Lifeguards are also required to do the same. Never, never have intercourse with them, and make sure they are brought to their room by midnight. That's Mr Parker's rules" Leo smiled at me as we finished our iced tea.

As the weeks passed, I was able to discern what families were there for the entire Summer and those who were the weekenders. Realizing the dangers of having a summer romance where the girl expects you to spend the entire evening with them. I asked every girl to dance, even if they weighed two hundred pounds and had pimples on their face. By asking them to dance I made them feel pretty whereas when they were home no boy paid attention to them. I realized that by doing this I was a money maker for their parents would thank me for paying attention to their daughters. On their checkout, I made sure to say goodbye and their fathers handed me a twenty-dollar tip.

Against my code of not dating long-term Summer guests. I met Esther who was taking Tony and Marie's Latin dance class. Her family was in the Kosher Wine business, and we clicked and spent time together talking before dinner. We agreed to meet after Midnight when I finished my job of making an ordinary girl feel special. Most of the Summer guests had suites. She would sneak out of her room and meet me by the outdoor pool, we walked around the hotel under the clear Catskill sky with stars twinkling then we returned to my Cottage. The record player was used as bait to get a teen girl to my room, they were tired of listening to the sounds of Marty Beck playing dance music and Sonny Rossi* playing Mambo and Cha Cha. Entering my room, I went to my Record Player took out a Frank Sinatra Album I had a stash of, we'll sip Coca-Cola through two straws, we'll dance and sit down to LISTEN TO SPOTIFY JOE CUBA AND SONNY ROSSI, the music will transport you to the Concord 1956 bed, there was only one chair in the room. Thinking that I was in my twenties and wiser than them, they confided in me. They had everything they wanted and needed someone to talk to about their dreams and future, most of them had graduated and were heading off to college with one goal which was to please their parents, falling in love with a prospective Doctor, Lawyer or Dentist After heavy necking and ejaculating in my pants. We walked to one of the side entrances to the lobby where I told her that my parents were coming for the weekend, I had to spend time with them promising that we would get together after the weekend. I went to bed at two in the morning and woke up at 8 am All my dress pants had semen spots. Every morning, I took the pants I wore the night before, washed the crotch, and let it dry. Keeping these hours I was exhausted from working and coming seven days a week, asking myself how can intercourse be better than Heavy Petting.

My parents arrived at 6 pm complaining about the heavy traffic on route 17 which on Friday Night was backed up to The Washington Bridge, Husbands going to various Bungalow Colonies. Meeting them in the Dining room where my mother hugged me as I came back from the Moon, I had to give them a recap of my first week's experience leaving out the Girls. As I left my father handed me a package which he told me to open when I got back to my room. Passing the guest registration desk, I gave the package to the desk Clerk who was a student at Cornell. I did my usual rounds of asking teenage girls if they wanted to dance. Dancing with some girls was like driving a truck. Leo asked me to go up to the lighting booth There were twenty carpeted steps to the door of the Light booth, and with his heft, Leo slowly ascended to the booth, opening the door a balding man with glasses introduced himself as Irvin, Leo of breath, "Meet Allen he is the assistant you asked for, show him the ropes and he will take over on your days off." Exiting he turns to me, "See you tomorrow." As I stood next to the spotlight in a room that was about ninety degrees with a fan circulating hot air, as he was responding to lighting cues of the Stage Manager Irving reflected on his past life telling me that he worked at Radio City doing lighting for the Rockettes, then Carnegie Hall, a famous Concert venue in New York City handling all the lighting. He finally had it with living in Queens. Moving his family to the Monticello area he landed a job as lighting director at the Concord. Introducing The star of the show was Buddy Hackett with singer Marlyn Michaels being the opening act.

My parents were seated at the main table reserved for Senior Concord Executives, I found myself backstage introducing myself to Buddy Hackett who ignored me. Fifteen minutes before show time I had to be in the lighting booth helping Irving. After the show I joined my parents in the Night Owl Lounge sitting at Philly's table, next to my Dad was a Comic named Jackie Mason. My father pushed for Jackie to do a mid-week gig as an audition. Philly needed to book acts seven days a week during the Summer, he gave Jackie a shot for that coming Wednesday. Agent Charlie Rapp handled acts during the week. William Morris for Saturdays and major Holiday weekends. My father arranged to stay the entire week inviting Earl Wilson a columnist for THE NEW POST and Joe Cohen who was a byline writer for Variety, a major entertainment weekly newspaper. My obligation was to have lunch and dinner with my parents. Begging out of the traditional Coffee Shop Black and White ice soda. I passed the reception desk to pick up my package, entering my room I proceeded to open the gift that my father gave me. It contained 12 Durex Condoms, if I adhered to the no intercourse rule I figured it would last forever. Arriving at the dining room for an early breakfast, Leo came by telling me I had to be at the Softball field with equipment by 11 am. The hotel had a convention of New York State District Attorneys, they recruited the most talented ADA to play against the Champions of Manhattan District Attorney Frank Hogan's office. The New York DA's office was the largest in the State. When they recruited young law school graduates who passed the New York Bar and wanted to be prosecutors the best career launching pad was working for the New York DA offices. One of the major skills that Hogan was looking for in ADA was Softball skills.

Exactly at 11 am, two teams of young ADA's appeared on the field carrying their equipment. One team wore red T-shirts emblazoned HOGAN NYC, and the others wore blue T-shirts with the names of the various cities that represented New York State. Hogan's team was unbeatable, my only job was to watch the game which Hogan's team won twenty to ten. He had a thirty-year winning streak. Bringing the equipment back to the shed, I found Esther there with tears in her eyes I couldn't be seen feeling Touchie in public. Putting the softball equipment away I closed the door, she started to cry that her grandmother was very sick and the entire family would be checking out and returning to their home in Scarsdale which was a small upscale town in Westchester. "I do not think I will be back, I am starting at The University of Syracuse in the fall, visiting the Dorm and buying a new wardrobe" she blurted out while wiping her tears. Consoling her I said I would call and we could meet in New York City after Labor Day, we kissed and she went back to her room to pack up. I felt relieved that she was going home for I felt that she was too possessive.

I walked by the opened card room which had the stench of Cigar Smoke where guests were playing Gin Rummy at ten dollars a point. Heading to the hotel entrance to say goodbye to her family and wish them a safe trip. The valet pulled up a 1956 Cadillac View Master Station Wagon, placing all the luggage in the back of the car. Before they left her father shook my hand and drove off. Opening my hand, I found a hundred-dollar bill.

After viewing the new check-ins, I had to bring out the table tennis bats and balls for a 3 pm tournament, looking at the $100.00 bill this was great, his daughter gave me a blowjob and her father gives me a tip.

The week my parents were there all the entertainment was moved indoors. It rained every day, the days were filled with Bingo, Simon Sez, Latin dance lessons, water aerobics, and movies. One of the meeting rooms was turned into a Movie Theater and My job was to set up the seats, and the screen, and bring up the projector and large cans of film, suddenly Irving the lighting expert appeared and he was the projectionist. Every day was a new movie, Samson and Delilah, King Solomon's Mines, Annie Get Your Gun, Cheaper by the Dozen.

Tuesday was staff talent night some waiters were great Singers, three bus boys had a tap-dancing act, and there was an act called MR AMAZING…AMAZING was my friend who worked at the Reception desk. He was known as MR. AMAZING THE

MAGICIAN with the head of Valet parking doing stand-up comedy.

The following night my father's client Jay Jayson a standup comic was the headliner, I gave Jay a heads-up that the head Valet stole his act during the weekly hotel staff's talent show. Jay who was in the business for over ten years revamped his act using old materials from four years ago. Stealing a comics act was one of the minefields that a comic had to navigate when they worked on the CHARLIE RAPP Beach Club, Bungalow and Hotels Circuit that ran from the Hamptons to private clubs in Long Beach up Route 17 which led to the BORSCHT BELT.

This was the first week where my pants didn't have a Cum Stain. Considering myself an exceptional CHA-CHA, MAMBO dancer, teenage guests wanted to dance with me. Soon it became their mothers whose husbands were too busy Playing cards, Poker, Gin Rummy and either winning or losing large amounts of money, the players were the same every day. A new player can join if recommended by a member of the current game. I realized that if they played together for the entire season everyone broke even. Their wives displayed their wealth through their jewellery, dresses, Mink stoles, makeup, and Hairstyle.

I was dancing with both mother and daughter until showtime the only difference was that the mother was wearing Chanel Number Five. The conversation with the mother was about what college I am going to, do I want to be a Doctor, Lawyer, Attorney, Dentist, or Accountant and what profession is your father in, finally where I live. I said that I might be A Neurologist, and I lived on RIVERDALE AVENUE. Smiling, she said she had friends who lived on Riverdale Avenue, a short ride to Bronxville. I failed to mention that I lived on Riverdale Avenue in East New York Brooklyn, I realized she was interviewing me to see if I was right for her daughter.

Friday night was the new weekend check-ins, leaning on the Bell Hops station I viewed the new guests with their teenage daughters in tow. In those years very few women were size 6 exiting their car they wrapped a mink stole around them hoping they would be noticed by the other guest who were hanging around to view the procession of JAPS (Jewish American princesses) In the mid-fifties the hotel's Upper-Class families owned Packard Deluxe Clipper, Cadillac Eldorado, Chrysler Imperial, Buick Roadmaster Skylark, Lincoln Continental Mark11. Middle Class Jewish Families refused to purchase Mercedes, and Volkswagen for the horror of World War 11 was still in them. This was the Jewish community's retribution to the six million Jews who died. Twenty-five years later the children whose parents stormed the Beaches of Normandy and Iwo Jima were purchasing Mercedes, BMW's and Toyota. The parking lot was an Auto Showcase with the lowly Chevy and Ford in the back of the lot. Some guests paid extra money to have their car parked in front of the hotel.

Saturday was a big day at the pool, we were crowning the tenth Ms. Concord. My job was to convince female guests that they were Beautiful and belonged on the runway which was set up on the stage where the Judges were seated. The Judges were my Father, Philly, William Morris, Super-agent Lee Solomon, Mr. Matzah, and the King of Kosher wines. They each had paddles numbered from 1 to 10. The loudspeakers were cued to play A Pretty Girl is Like a Melody, Leo came centre stage wearing a red sequin jacket and pants. Unbeknownst to Leo, Philly the night before visited the first traveling Drag Show THE JEWEL BOX REVIEW and hired a Marilyn Monroe look-alike who happened to be a Man. Leo with a mic in hand introduced the judges to all experts in Beauty "Let's start this beauty pageant where winners would become Superstars and losers would find their future husbands, then everybody would win. From Philadelphia five feet eight inches currently a Teacher Sheila, followed by Beverly from Scarsdale New York a Student at Sarah Lawrence, Ethel from Forrest Hills Queens a Senior at Queen College, Ida a housewife from Brooklyn New York, Shirley from Lawrence New York Presently going to Syracuse University, Sophie from Greenwich Connecticut a Pharmacist, Rebecca from Newton Mass studying Art History at Vassar, Arlene from New York City studying at Cornell University to be a teacher, Eleanor from the Grand course in the Bronx studying to be a fashion designer, Finally Marlyn from New Haven Conn." As the nine other contestants lined up, Marlyn moved slowly up the runway in a one-piece White bathing suit with a black see-through, turning and blowing kisses at the audience. The crowd at the pool went crazy saying she looks like Marlyn Monroe. Each contestant walked back and forth on the runway, Leo approaching the contestants from the rear holding his mic, "Judges and audience what is your vote for Ms. Concord 1956?" Contestant one gets a nine as the audience yells and screams. All the contestants get an 8 or 9 vote, the Final Contestant is Marlyn from New Haven what do you say? All the judges give her a ten, and the crowd at the pool shout for her telephone number.

Philly arranged for all the other nine contestants to get a bouquet of roses and a bottle of Champagne which will be delivered later. Marlyn comes out as a man, the other girls step back as the crowning ceremony begins. Leo "Marlyn from New Haven you have captivated all the guests with your grace and Beauty receiving the loudest cheers on our cheer" Marlyn takes the mic "With all the films I have done and awards I have received this award means the most to my fellow contestants you are all winners." With that cue, nine towel boys deliver a bouquet of Roses and Champagne and Marlyn takes off her wig. Suddenly there was a deafening silence and then a big roar of laughter. Marlyn was escorted by hotel security to a waiting Limo, Philly walked over to Leo to apologize for his practical joke. Leo broke out in laughter and walked away saying, "I owe you one."

Every day I walked around the pool in front of one of the first-floor suites there sat a tanned man who weighed about three hundred pounds, smoking a big Havana Cigar with a huge Short Wave radio and a large yellow pad. Passing by I would say have a great day and as usual he would ignore me. I never saw his wife, his two sons were picking up tabs and buying every pretty girl at the pool drinks. Their attitude had an attitude, asking around I discovered that the man smoking cigars was one of the biggest bookmakers in the country.

Walking past the front of the hotel I saw a silver Rolls Royce which meant that ALLEN KING was the star of this Saturday night show. Allen was a big A-list stand-up comedian who entertained at Concord and Grossinger's, the crowd loved him buying into his slick routine.

The second weekend in August was Singles Weekend, where Maître De Irving Cohen was bombarded with telephone calls from Mothers pleading with him to put their daughters in their 20s at a table where she could meet a professional with a great future giving her Grandchildren. In 1950, if a girl wasn't married before she was thirty in the Jewish Community she was considered an Old Maid. Their option was to get married and buy a house in the Suburbs, the other alternative for those from a well-to-do family was to go to college and become a teacher, otherwise, she went to Katharine Gibbs a Secretarial School that taught typing and Stenography. If that didn't pan out she could always find a job working as a sales girl in a New York department store. That's where Irving Cohen's expertise comes in, my father got Irving a feature in the New York Times titled "CUPID OF THE CATSKILLS." Describing his skills Irving said that he was given a gift where he was able to read a guest placing both Males and Females at tables where their personalities would complement each other, then we have a match. "I hope that they return here as a family with kids" Singles weekend was the third weekend in August, and I made sure to hang out with the valet to watch the check-ins. The shuttle bus that brought people from the Monticello bus depot was packed, it seemed in those days few singles owned cars. I developed a rating system where one was the worst and ten was a home run. Those who were checking in had a rating of five, to be fair I would wait until dinner to re-evaluate the crowd. Three hours later leaning against the couch opposite the dining room entrance the fives became seven and eight, there were no 10s. I approached Irving who was standing next to his dining room floor plan with an X on occupied tables. My parents missed the weekend but were coming for a long Labor Day Weekend to bring me home, four young women in their early twenties introduced themselves to Irving. The only way to get a great table was to hand him a Jackson. It was obvious that these girls were Unaware of this BORSCHT BELT TRADITON. Irving summoned a busboy to escort them to their table in what was referred to as THE SINAI DESERT a football field away from the front desk. Suddenly my rating system had a true ten. One of the girls had real Red Hair, a great body, and green eyes. She was a standout, the females at the Concord either had natural dark hair or various shades of Blonde introduced by Clairol. Before sitting down with Leo and his wife I walked over to their table and introduced myself as a member of the Social Staff, I avoided telling them I was a Tummler. Looking directly at the Red Head I suggested that if she wanted to learn how to MAMBO OR CHA-CHA we could meet up at the Night Owl lounge before the Friday night show began. Usually, Sonny Rossi's band played before the show, saying I hoped to see them later I returned to Leo's table for Chopped Liver and Matzah Ball soup with Chicken and Noodles, always with Challah (a traditional Friday night bread, the Jewish version of French Brioche with oil instead of butter). These were the standard appetizers for Friday Night Dinners. The entrees were always half chicken or Brisket of beef, accompanied by a large bowl of Buckwheat and pasta Bow ties known in Yiddish as Kasha varnishkes with a side of Mushroom gravy. The guests always ordered three or four appetizers and various entrees so that the table could taste everything followed by an average of twenty desserts. The amount of food left over could feed an entire village in the SUDAN. With the ending of dinner, it was time to walk outside and breathe the fresh Catskills air and see the Stars. Walking through the lobby Larry the Balloon Man was twisting and stretching colorful balloons into animals, funny headpieces for the young children of guests. The hotel offered a babysitting service so that their parents could enjoy the show, Leo hired the fastest caricaturist in the world. He could draw in ten minutes and put them in a frame with Concord emblazoned on the top for fifteen dollars.

The four girls who were seated in the SINAI DESERT were heading for the Night Owl Lounges, I had to be aggressive but nonchalant in approaching the Red Head before she was devoured by the single guys who were there to hook up. As she was about to enter the bar I said, "Hi, would you like a private lesson in Latin Dancing?" To my surprise, she said yes and I walked her away from the bar leading her to the exterior lobby which led to the nightclub. On the dance floor, she was light on her feet with white skin, green eyes, and Red Hair. We formally introduced ourselves, her name was Kathleen O'Sullivan, and she lived in Northern Bronx in a neighbourhood called Little Ireland, worked as a teller at Manufacturers Hanover Bank, was a graduate of Katharine Gibbs, and could type three hundred words a minute. I told her I was a Junior at NYU and planned to become a lawyer. The music stopped and Marty Beck and his orchestra were setting up the show. Her friends were already seated, escorting her to their table I excused myself and said I was needed backstage. Trying to be suave I kissed her hand telling her after the show we would go to the coffee shop for dessert. She smiled and said I would like that.

Reflecting on the fifty cents I spent every weekend going to THE SUPREME Movie house on Livonia Avenue a block away from THE DA BARBER. Saturday in 1953 I accompanied my mother to a matinee called "Thunder in The East" Starring Charles Boyer. She was a Charles Boyer fan, If it was good enough for Charles Boyer to kiss a woman's hand, it was good enough for me. That night it was Henny Youngman and William Morris. Lee Solomon had Philly book Keely Smith and Louis Prima to star in the Saturday night show.

After the show, I ran from the lighting booth to the front of the nightclub, there waiting for me was Kathleen, a spitting image of Maureen O'Hara a Hollywood Movie Star who I saw starring in "The Magnificent Matador" co-starring Anthony Quinn. Guiding her through the lobby past the Night Owl Lounge where her three other roommates went, we walked towards the Coffee Shop as she took my hand. There is always a line a half block long waiting for a table, my friend Anthony one of the few non-Jews was the Maître De. Seeing me with Kathleen, he gave me a big smile. "Anthony, I need a quiet table" meaning I wanted to be seated away from Philly's table. Calling over one of the hosts, he led us to a table in the rear of the Coffee shop. Seated we gave our order, a Black and White iced soda and a Sundae. The Concord coffee shop used U BET chocolate syrup in its B&W Ice Soda.

I Knew all the waiters in the Coffee shop and they would bury the check and in return, I would leave a five-dollar tip. Kathleen dipped into sweet cream topping with a red cherry, "I have to be honest I was reluctant to come here, I usually go to the Pocono's but my friends from Catharine Gibbs wanted to go someplace new. Sandra the girl who was wearing the Blue Dress who lives in Yonkers borrowed her parent's Chevy and here I am. Why are you here?" she asked as she dug deep into the Sundae. Now it was my turn to create the greatest story ever told. "Graduating from

Thomas Jefferson High School with a 3.9 grade average I received a full Scholarship at NYU downtown, I still needed to pay my expenses. My dad was a famous publicity man, and knowing that I was interested in doing STAND UP COMEDY he reached out to one of his clients namely this hotel to hire me for the Social Staff. There were no better places where I could watch the best of the best Standup Comedians and hone my skills while getting paid."

Taking the rear door of the Coffee shop that leads to the pool, I was debating whether to invite her to my room or wait until after the Saturday night show, the nights in the Catskills were cool and if you looked hard enough you could see the outline of the Constellations and the twinkling of Mars. Placing my jacket over her shoulders we walked hand in hand to the lobby entrance pointing out the Stars as if I knew what I was talking about. Before we approached the Lobby entrance, she said she would like to see my room, this was my WOW moment. The ball was in her court, walking up the dimly lit path I pointed to various rustic two-story buildings explaining that these were the original guest houses for the Ideal House which Arthur Winarick bought in 1937. Walking up the stairs to the porch where there was some weather-beaten outdoor furniture, I opened the door to my room which was monastic except for my RCA portable record player and twenty LP albums. Reaching for my stash of Coca-Cola Cola which was placed on the window ledge. Placing Frank Sinatra's 1955 LP "We Small Hours" we both sat on the bed mesmerized by Sinatra's as the album went to the track "The-wee Small Hours of The Morning" I took her hand and we started to move slowly, kissing her face then her mouth, she pushed me away "You are kissing me as if I was your mother, how many girls have you kissed?" I figured that this was the end of my charade I looked her straight in the eye "Many and nobody complained." We were embracing and she kissed me putting her tongue in my mouth "This how you kiss a girl" As she pushed me onto the bed, I enjoyed it. We were back in bed undressing each other, amazed by her flowing Red Hair, Green eyes, and the Beauty of her breasts. Hanging between her breasts was a cross, her body was as white as porcelain which was freckled by red freckles. As I kissed her, she moved my head down to her Vagina and I felt the soft red pubic hairs. This was a different experience, all the Jewish girls I had been with had dark curly Pubic hair. As I licked her vagina and played with her nipples, her body went into spasms and suddenly went limp. The sheet was soaking wet. Moving on top of her my Star of David was hanging over her mouth, it was truly a unique experience where Moses met Jesus. This was my first Orgasm I was no longer a virgin, Kathleen got out of bed and went into the bathroom to wash up, I was laying there with my penis erect and a Durex in my hand. She sat on the bed and proceeded to give me a blow job, spitting my cum on the sheets. She looked at her watch and started to dress. As she was putting on her underwear and bra she turned to me "I do not have intercourse with a person I just met. It's just rules that I set for myself" she mumbled as she stepped into her dress and asked me to zip the back. Walking back to the main lobby we kissed and she said she would see me after lunch.

Walking back to my Cottage I convinced myself that 90% of something was better than 10% of nothing, I was still a Virgin. The linen closet was always open for clean sheets and towels, making the bed I decided that 90% of something was better than 10% of nothing. I enjoyed coming between her thighs and the GOOD

NIGHT BLOW JOB. I had five hours of sleep, then I had to be at table 18 to meet and greet nine single men and women whom Irving promised the girls' mothers that he would make a match. There were four men and five women in their mid-twenties and me. The night before I was given Index cards with a brief bio of each guest seated from left to right, In those days I had a great memory. The four men were the Gold Standard for any Jewish Mother, Larry was a lawyer from the Bronx, Sam was a Dentist from Brooklyn, Marvin was an accountant from Queens, and Murray was a General Practice from Manhattan. The five girls whose mothers married the same pedigree as the four men were at the table. My job was to jump-start the conversation and then leave when the fifth Male guest appeared at the table, his name was Stewart, and his father owned a big factory that made men's suits for various department store chains. Walking towards Siberia I noticed that Kathleen wasn't having an early breakfast. Heading across the dining room I had to say hello to everyone and remind them that they shouldn't miss Simon-Says or water aerobics in the Indoor Pool. I was seated at the SOCIAL STAFF TABLE where all the TUMMELERS SAT wearing silly headgear, taking my seat I had a large Multi-Color Top hat which I had to wear during Breakfast. Leo was wearing his Multi-Colored Beanie with Red, White, and Blue Propellers which rotated when a breeze from the air conditioner touched it.

Saturday morning was a warm August day, all the activities were scheduled outdoors. Simon Says had about Fifty participants, one of our female lifeguards did a class of Water aerobics, and Tony and Marie directed a group of Singles through their Latin Dancing steps. Before taking the softball equipment, I asked Larry the Balloon Man who was about 5'5" to Umpire and he was as blind as a bat. Now I had to run around to recruit 18 players offering them free Concord T-shirts. I had ten RED and ten blue hats. I noticed that many of them came from Various New York City Boroughs, the other male guests were from anywhere but the five Boroughs. I named the events NYC FIVE BOROUGHS AGAINST ANYWHERE ELSE SOFTBALL CHAMPIONSHIP, now I needed an audience. There was a sound system near the Softball field, and Leo approved fifty free drink coupons to give to the expected fans. Taking the microphone I announced that the Championship game between Team NYC FIVE BOROUGHS VS THE TEAM FROM ANYWHERE ELSE would begin at 11 am. Guests from the Five Boroughs and guests from anywhere else are invited to cheer their favourite team. On both sides of the field were Bleachers split the guests from the five Boroughs on one side and anywhere else on the other. I asked for four females from each side to volunteer as Cheerleaders, I had leftover New Year's Eve horns and tambourines. With that settled I played the "TAKE ME OUT TO THE BALLGAME" crowd on cue and both teams ran out onto the field Five Boroughs wore Blue T-Shirts, and Somewhere Else wore Red T-Shirts. After a brief introduction of each player, the cheers Leaders animated the crowd on each end of the field. Larry the Balloon man came out wearing a chest protection vest that fit him like a bathrobe, a Face protection mask, and a Black hat with a big U on it. Taking a coin Larry tossed it in the air it came out of heads and Somewhere Else won the toss. I had to climb up to the scoreboard and keep score, the scoreboard was facing East. I was facing the Sun getting a great tan I couldn't see the numbers. A Blond Girl teenager from New

Haven Connecticut was yelling out the runs, by the ninth inning the score was tied nine-nine with NYC and Lunch was being served. At the bottom of the Ninth Inning if NYC failed to get a run the game would go to an extra inning, and they will miss the Appetizer. It was two outs, Marvin from the upscale area of Queens called Jamaica Estates whose father was a successful Diamond Dealer was at the plate. Larry the Umpire backed away from the plate to clean his glasses and motioned to play the count which was two strikes and one ball. The crowd was screaming "We cannot miss lunch, we cannot miss lunch" The pitcher who was from Westchester threw the ball and Marvin hit a HOMERUN. The cheers lasted two minutes and everybody left for Lunch including both teams.

I was planning a great award Ceremony, but a five-course Lunch won the day, loading all my equipment I wheeled it back to the storage locker. Hurrying up to the Dining room I passed Kathleen's table and she gave me a slight smile. As I was finishing my coffee Carla who oversaw Children's activities in "Fantasy Land." A playground with swings, a jungle gym, slides, a fake horse, a Teeter Totter Board, a Giant Mushroom, and a large Princess Castle that kids can crawl through. Her job was to create entertainment for children of guests from five years old to ten years old. Asked me to help her out, It seemed the Clown she hired for Story Time was home sick with the Flu "Can you be the Clown just for an hour, here's your costume I will see you at 3:30" without waiting for an answer she headed for the exit. Leo looked at me and said I would make a great Clown, leaving the table with a Cheese Danish and my Clown costume I went to the indoor pool that had dressing rooms and lockers for guests. Opening the package, I found a White Face cream, a huge Red Wig, Red Floppy feet, Polka-Dot Clown suit which was one size too big, grabbing rolled-up towels I placed them around my body to fill out the suit. Twenty minutes later I exited the dressing room as DING DONG THE CLOWN. The only way I could get to Fantasy Land was to walk past Kathleen and her friends who had four Chaise lounges. I stopped by and said "HI ladies, I am Ding Dong the Clown and I am on my way to Fantasy Land" I handed them Ding Dong candies and sprinkled Fairy Dust over them. After an hour of reading kids' stories, and stopping them from pulling off my red Nose, and stepping on my Clown feet, Carla announced that I had to go to Clown Town. As I exited the Kid's play area I sprinkled Clown dust. Aware that I had to pass Kathleen and her friends I took an alternative route through the service road. I was skipping next to a truck bringing produce to the Kitchen. The driver looked at his rearview mirror and gave me a finger. The service door was open and I had to pass a group of ladies in the pool being instructed on how to be the AQUA ROCKETTES. The locker room was empty except for two men in their late SEVENTIES. As they started dressing, I saw that their testicles were hanging three inches below their peni, as I washed the white makeup from my face, they looked at me laughing.

I went directly to the red-carpeted runway that ended where the Beauty Pageant judges sat. This pageant would be different the CONTESTANTS Were ten-year-old girls. First Place would win a one-hundred-dollar certificate to FAO SCHWARTZ, second place a fifty-fifty certificate the other eighteen is a coupon for fifteen per cent off at La Petite Enfant a children's wear Boutique plus a bag of candy and a Coloring Book. This event was announced during Friday Night's Dinner it was open for the first twenty contestants. A registration table was set up in front of the dining room exit. Within fifteen minutes after dessert, a line of women were registering their children for the Pageant, one lady who was fifth on the line confronted me with her daughter who was six, but insisted that she looked ten. I gave my approval to register the girl and we had our twenty contestants. The lady who wanted me to make an exception handed me a twenty-dollar bill.

At 3 pm, Leo who was dressed like a fat PETER PAN introduced the judges, first there were the Barry Sisters who were the opening act for Allen King, Tony and Marie The Latin Dance Teachers, and Leslie who owned a La Petite Enfant the Children's Boutique in the hotel. After the introductions, the loudspeaker played Judy Garland's "SOMEWHERE OVER THE RAINBOW" from the 1939 Classic Film The WIZARD OF OZ. The little girls walking down the runway just walked, Three of them handled the Runway with poise acting like grown-up models looking at them floating to where the Judges Sat stopping, smiling, waving, and blowing kisses to the audience. The three were trained to do Beauty Pageants. The judges picked a little Girl from SCARSDALE, Leo handed her a bouquet of fake Roses and crowned her with a Golden Tiara, all the other little girls received SILVER Tiaras.

Mariachi Music came over the loud system, Raoul who was five feet five entered from the Indoor pool area and ran across the path leading to the outdoor pool wearing a Golden Cape headed directly to the 100-foot ladder that was set up next to the diving board, facing the audience seated around the pool as the Sun Sets in the West. Climbing to his one-hundred-foot perch with his

Golden Cape fluttering from the soft summer breeze, he lets his Golden Cape fall to the ground. Standing there he crosses himself and kisses his Star of David. As the music hits a Crescendo, he arcs his Short Brown body and dives into the deep end of the pool, popping up to screams and applause. One of our guests hands him his Golden Cape, Leo announces that Raoul Garcia has pictures of his famous dives and would be available to autograph them. With that Raoul heads for a table set up by the bar area with a stack of pictures. A line formed with about fifty people mainly women and kids. With each signature he flashed is Golden Smile, which replaced his top line of teeth that were destroyed in a diving accident. In his deal with Philly, he only worked weekends, the rest of the week he was open to hitting on the guest, and that was the reason he was wearing A Star of David. He explained in broken English that his family which was Jewish, escaped the Holocaust and migrated to Mexico before he could get Circumcised. This was the most ludicrous story ever invented but Women fell for it. Word was out that he had a very large Penis.

Working as a Social Staff had many benefits, like being friendly with Bartenders and waiters who never charged me for a drink. One of the waiters named Jeff who was in his final year at Cornell always asked if I wanted anything. I ordered a Pina Colada with a note saying I would meet you after dinner and had him bring it to Kathleen, I made it my policy that I wouldn't hang out with guests who I was having none Coitus sex with until after Dinner which ended at 9 pm. After work I usually went to the Health Club, spending time in the Steam Room where no one would find me. The showers were better than in my room, at that time I wasn't shaving, splashing on the After Shave lotion and creaming my body I went back to my Cottage to change for dinner.

The line into the dining room was now couples who met the night before insisting that Irving THE CUPID MAITRE D change tables and put the couples at the same table. Irving had a huge book of photographs of couples he introduced and married due to his placing them at the right table. Women complained they hadn't met Mr Right and Irving pointed at the Photos and calmly told them not to worry someday you will be in this book. Those who hadn't found either MS OR MR right were seated paired together at the same table, they were assigned to when they first arrived. Irving handed me blue index cards with names of unmatched guests who were now seated together, five men, and five ladies. My job was to get to the table before them and seat them in pairs. Once that was done, I had everyone introduce themselves and let the Chicken Soup create a new relationship. Completing my match-making chore I returned to the table reserved for the social staff, Leo had a surprise up his sleeve. I failed to see a small Podium and table tucked away behind a large Golden Curtain on the left side of the Dining room. He turned away from his roast chicken and pointed "Your job is to take the Trophies which are in the utility Closet next to the men's bathroom, go behind the Golden Curtain and place them on the small table next to the podium without any guest seeing you. I am going to present the Softball Champion TROPHY to the winning team before dessert, Irving will handle the lighting, Larry will play "Take Me Out To The Ball Game" and I will do the rest" After finishing my Chicken dish I left the table. Exiting the dining room, I ran to the Utility closet to grab a box of nine Baseball Trophies, reentering the dining and pushing the box of trophies behind the Curtain I placed the nine Trophies on the table. I found the opening in the curtain on the first flickering of lights I pulled out the podium, on the second flickering of lights I pulled out the table of Trophies with one hand making sure they did not fall. On the third flickering of lights TAKE ME OUT TO THE BALL GAME was played over the Dining Room sound system. Leo ran up to the Podium wearing a baseball shirt where one side was the Yankee Pinstripe, the other half was Dodger Gray Flannel with Blue lettering Dodgers, (they left Brooklyn for Los Angeles 1957) and a Red Concord Baseball cap. Leo took the Mic with a smile on his face and announced "The Five Boroughs took the Championship against our Suburban neighbours," Calling up each member of the team and handing them trophies, the guests either cheered or booed. Exiting the curtain behind Leo I went back to the table, Turning to Tony of Tony and Marie I blurted out "How can this be a Championship game when it was just one game of guests who do not know each other and I made up the names" Tony smiled, "It makes the guests happy and no one gives a fuck" It was now dessert time, I passed and headed for the front of The Night Owl Lounge waiting for Kathleen. One of our guests came over and introduced me to her Granddaughter who was about seventeen with bad skin and weighed about two hundred pounds, I excused myself saying that I had to go backstage. Taking the exterior lobby leading to the Nightclub entrance I took a detour that led me through the Night Owl Lounge standing in front was Kathleen. Taking her by the arm I navigated back through the dimly lit Lounge where guests hung out before the show. Tonight, El Machito and his Afro-Cuban Band (who with the music of Tito

Puente, and Tito Rodriguez made the Palladium Ballroom a place to go in Manhattan during the MAMBO CRAZE) had the spotlight. The dance floor was crowded, Kathleen was a fast learner, and we danced until it was showtime. Many of the Hotel Guests head for the NEVELE after the show where Tito Puente and his orchestra were in residence every weekend during the Summer. Escorting Kathleen back to her friends who were holding hands with guys they met in the afternoon, Kathleen introduced me as the entertainment director of the Social Staff. Shaking everybody's hands I excused myself and said I needed to go backstage. Heading directly to the Lighting Booth where Larry was doubled up in agony, "Take care of the lighting," he said handing the headset which was in direct communication with Norton the Stage Manager as he was running to the Men's Room. Norton worked as a Stage Manager on Broadway, he was one of those Gay people who had attitudes who in the fifties were described as feminine. Philly recruited him as the official Stage Manager in charge of lighting, his lighting cues create a mood this was done by changing the filters on the Spotlight to create various effects for the Entertainment. He would start the conversation with his slight lisp HELLO LARRY DARLING My response "Roger over and out." Norton screamed "Who the fuck is this," trying to calm him down I said I was Larry's Lighting Apprentice for the entire Summer. Larry had a Stomach FLU in the men's room and would return shortly. "Kid whatever the fuck your name is I will cut off your balls if you fuck up" With that the the curtain was raised and Marty Beck and his orchestra played TUM BALALAIKA which is a Yiddish Song that the Barry Sisters introduced on THE JEWISH CAVALCADE OF STARS a radio program presented on WEVD a radio station targeting the Yiddish Community. The Barry Sisters were the Jewish answer to the Andrew Sisters. The three sisters, Laverne, Maxene, and Patty had sold Eighty Million records in the forties through into the Sixties. The Barry Sisters in their niche market sold over a hundred thousand albums. They were the Stars of The Borscht Belt and Miami Beach. During their thirty-minute act, Norton issued fifteen lighting changes and I was able to change the lighting color filters in thirty seconds. The Barry sisters were a great opening act, the audience was of a first generation of Jewish immigrants and eighty percent of them knew Yiddish. Larry entered the booth and sat down, "You can handle King give him hot white" whispered Larry as he walked around the booth finally sitting on the stool next to me.

Marty Beck played Alan King's entrance music, Alan, a polished Standup Comic known for his dapper costume suits and sharp attire had a forty-five-minute act. One of the roles he insisted on was that waiter service cease during his act. All the times I caught his act he never bombed, as guests either went on the dance floor or to the Night Owl lounge. I moved through the crowd, Katleen was waiting for me, we hugged and I said that I had a surprise for her, then I guided her to the backstage entrance and introduced her to The Barry Sisters who pinched my cheeks and said that I was Sam's Son, my father was their press agent. Alan King was speaking to some friends of his, seeing Kathleen, he excused himself and came to say hello. Pointing to me he said that I was Philly's boy, ignoring me he took Kathleen's hand, looking at me he said she was beautiful and what is a SHIKSA doing at the Concord with that he handed her his card "If you want to see a show I will be working at the COPA early November, call me and you will be my guest" Alan excused himself, humming "DANNY BOY" I knew he was booked to do a show at Grossinger's. There was a rule, big acts had to do the Concord first.

Kathleen was impressed as we exited backstage, I planned to take her to the coffee shop, and holding my hand she navigated towards the main entrance Concord. Before we reached the door, I asked her if she wanted to go to the Coffee shop, squeezing my hand she turned to me "I feel like I've known you all my life, let's go back to your room and listen to music and talk." I looked at her and I felt my Pinus getting hard, muttering to myself "I'm finally going to get laid." Looking at me and Kissing me I said, "I am finally going to hear about your life" Entering my room I put on a Nat King Cole album Ballads of the Day the first track "A Blossom Fell," We danced through the entire album which ended with Sand and The Sea. It was a wonderful moment, the best moment I had ever had throughout my fifteen years on this earth. She excused herself and went into the bathroom. I decided to take off my pants and shirt sitting on the bed in my boxer shorts with a large erection. Kathleen returned with a towel wrapped around her and carrying her dress, looking at me with her beautiful green eyes she sat on the bed and as I was trying to unwrap the towel, she pushed my hand away and said she just wanted to cuddle. Pushing her body next to mine, I was crushed against the wall for the Mattress was a single size. "I truly want to have sex with you, but I have my monthly friend, I would rather just talk" as she moved her hand under my boxer shorts. "Let me tell you about my family, my dad is a Longshoreman. I have two younger brothers and two younger sisters, before moving to the Bronx, we lived in a walkup in Hell's

Kitchen" (Hell's Kitchen was West of Eighth Avenue going from West 57th Street to 34th Street. The houses were tenement walk-ups and railroad flats Further West was the Piers on the Hudson River waterfront. The Westies a gang of Irish Hoodlums dominated the Docks and the lives of the residents of Hell's Kitchen. Marlon Brando's film On the Waterfront was a true depiction of Hell's Kitchen and the Longshoremen who worked there.) "My parents put me in Sacred Heart of Jesus to keep me away from the neighbourhood gangs. When I was fifteen my father decided we needed a house, so we moved to Woodlawn Heights in the Northern Bronx I went to Saint Barnabas High School. After graduation, my parents wanted me to get married to a good Catholic boy, be a housewife, and have children. Instead, I enrolled in Katharine Gibbs, I can type five hundred words a minute. Now I earn two hundred dollars a week working as a cashier at Manufacturers Hanover near Rockefeller Center. Living at home is suffocating with my brothers and sister screaming and my mom and dad always fighting, I plan to move into my apartment with the two friends who brought me here. That's my life in a nutshell," tell me about yours. My mind started racing to create a biography that was half true and half fiction. Looking her straight into her deep Green Eyes, I concocted what I wished was true. "I am the only child, My family lives in Central Park South, and I went to Trinity High School. After graduation, my cousins who lived in London invited me to spend the Summer with them, returning to New York on THE Queen Mary. That was a year ago, two years ago I was entering my third Semester at NYU. My father is a Public Relations Executive (I couldn't say, Publicity Man, Public Relations created an image of Great Succes) one of his clients is the Concord Hotel. He suggested that having a job would be great for me." We were lying face to face the only thing that separated us was my hard Penis. She moved her hand down and jerked me off. With that, we both started to get dressed. As Kathleen was putting on her dress, she looked at me and asked, "Will you see me in the city?" Handing her a sheet of paper she wrote down her Telephone number. I immediately put it in my wallet. "You have my number but please don't call me, I will call you. If my father hears that I am dating a Jew Boy there will be hell to pay. For some reason, he hates Jews and Black people"

Exiting my cottage, we weren't aware of the time until we saw the Sunrise, holding her hand "I told her that she was my dream come through" This time I escorted her to the pay phone in the lobby leading to the Coffee Shop. Pick a phone she selected the very last one. Leaving her by the phone I ran to the coffee shop borrowing a pen and a sheet of paper. "Take this phone number call me this coming Wednesday at 9 pm." Leading her to the guest elevator as the door was about to close I placed my body against the door and whispered " What time are you planning to check out?" Kissing me on the cheek she said "I guess after lunch" Taking the rear exit door I walked across the dew-laden lawn to my room. I needed to change the sheet which was wet from Semen and Blood. The semen I understood, but the blood left me cold until I went into the bathroom and found a bloody Kotex pad, like the ones I found in the bathroom at home. I now put together her Best Friend and the blood. When my mother had her best friend, she was miserable for a week. Having your best friend was something no one discussed. This was the first experience I had with knowing the female body which was never discussed. Luckily,

I didn't have to start work until after lunch, entering the dining room, I navigated past the tables heading to the Sahara, finding myself in front of Kathleen's table. Now there were two couples, her two other friends met during the weekend. They were holding hands as they ate their Grapefruit appetizers. Standing next to Kathleen's chair I thanked them for spending their weekend at the Concord "By the way what time are you planning to leave" Kathleen reached out squeezing my hand, "I guess around four to beat the traffic on route 17" "Have a safe trip" I said backing away from the table, manoeuvring past waiters, bus boys, and guests. I thought to myself I couldn't show affection to her for fear of losing my job. Leo and the entire crew of Tummelers were finishing up their lunch, looking at me Leo started to laugh "The kid's in love with the only Shiksa that ever visited the hotel. Did she say you fucked me in the Country, Am I going to see you in the City." The entire table broke out in laughter. Then I realized that I wasn't in trouble, she wasn't a Jewish Guest. Leo and the rest of the Tummlers left except for Larry the Balloon Man. "Don't worry kid they were fucking with you" as he sipped his cup of Coffee. I began eating my entrée turning to Larry I asked if he could do me a favour and create the most Magnificent YELLOW AND GREEN BALLOON DOG, I needed by three O'clock, "I will do better, I will make it as you finish your lunch" Sitting there he reached into a pouch filled with various sizes and shapes of balloons that he always carries. As I was finishing my Apple Pie he was blowing and twisting a Yellow and Green Balloon forming the shape of a large Dachshund. Next to our table, a centrepiece of flowers had a red ribbon, taking a knife he cut two holes in a seating card, threading the ribbon through the card I wrote Jaffe's telephone number Press 98578. SEE YOU IN MANHATTAN tied the ribbon around the neck of the Balloon Dog and rushed to where the valet brought the cars. Kathleen and her friends were waiting for their car, handing the dog to a friend of mine who was a Bellhop I told him to deliver it to Kathleen. The dog made a big hit as she turned to me and smiled as she placed the dog in the back seat next to her and drove off.

I had a week to go to end my Virginity, my parents arrived Monday afternoon to spend the Labor Day week which was September 3rd, and to help me pack. When my Mother saw me she started to cry "You grew so big and lost a lot of weight" hugging me tight and planting a lot of kisses on my face. This greeting was unbelievable for she had seen me two weeks earlier, I was returning to Brooklyn for my third year at Thomas Jefferson High School the following Monday. My parents checked in and I had to escort them to their suite. Kissing my mom, I told her that I had work to do, I would see them at dinner. Returning to the Valet in front of the hotel watching Bellboys unloading at least ten suitcases per car, I spent an hour viewing the new Labor Day guests. Many of the families checking in had teenage daughters using my rating system from one to 10, I concluded that in my last week as an employee I would be dancing with a lot of fives. Returning to my room to shower and change, I decided to spend time in the Night Owl Lounge since I was now a guest, I ordered a Coke. There were four girls wearing tennis gear sitting at the bar as the Jazz Trio was setting up. The girls were in the range of 7 to 10 in my rating system. They were between 22 to 25 years old. My friend J who lived in Monticello was a full-time bartender. Leaning across the Bar I whispered, "How could I have missed them."

Leroy was a fan of my rating system always giving me free Coke. As he refilled my glass, wiping the top of the bar, "You didn't miss them they are guest at The Nevele. They park their car in the employee parking lot and sneak in the back door to use the tennis courts." Finishing my coke, I headed to the Ping Pong Tournament which was wrapping up. Leo always presented Trophies at every sporting event, it was almost dinner. Time for me to watch the new guests lining up to get their table assignments. The reason guests travelled with so much luggage is that the entire family packed three new outfits for every day of their stay including Fur Stoles of Mink, Chinchilla, and Persian Lamb. The women were draped in long Pearl necklaces, Brooches, Diamond rings, and Diamond earrings. Their Husbands were dressed in colourful sports jackets, Cardigan sweaters, Penny Loafers, and triple-pleated pants. Their fashion icons were Cary Grant and Frank Sinatra Bing, and Crosby Fred Astaire. Some Men's designers Copied General Eisenhower's jacket for Leisure, and Black and White loafers were all the rage. Irving Cohen the Maitre D made a thousand dollars selling tables. If the location of a table wasn't to the guests' liking, a $100.00 tip is a guarantee that you would get a ringside table. Being seated closest to the dining room entrance was an indication of how important you were, sending a message that you really made it.

My parents always arrived late due to my mother's need to always look perfect, my father's wardrobe consisted of one Black, Brown, and grey suit, for daytime to wear around the pool he owned two Cabana pool Suits. Even though I was considered a guest, Irving handed me index cards of tables where unattached guests were seated. Walking around to the Cupid tables I formally introduced each seated guest to one another. Leo was aware that I had to sit with my parents during Lunch and Dinner.

Labor Day week was Star-Studded every night at the Cotillion room, Wednesday Eddie Fisher, Friday, Phyllis Diller, Saturday, Sammy Davis Junior and the Will Maston Trio, Sunday Tony Martin and Cyd Charisse, followed by Fire Works. Monday it was softball, gathering all the softball equipment to the ballpark, a group of guys were already there. In the middle of the group, there was a guy about six feet tall talking about how the Brooklyn Dodgers were a better team than the New York Yankees unloading the gear. He looked at me and came over and grabbed me in a Bear Hug as if I was a long-lost relative. Dragging me to the crowd and Yelling this kid is one of us "This is the kid who is always selling his next at Da Barbershop, what the fuck are you doing here" Looking at him in awe, he was the famous Dennis, The Man who ran naked through the lobby of Grossinger's and let the horses out of the stable at the Nevele. Both hotels barred him forever. "I am on the Social Staff for the Summer" I replied. "You must be getting a lot of pussy," as he took the pitcher's mound and threw the first pitch which turned into a home run for the other team, looking at my watch I had to meet Leo by the outdoor pool. He already was setting up the letter blower, a machine that mixes the balls with the letters on them so the Bingo caller could announce the random numbers. My job was to sell Bingo boards for five dollars a piece, some guests bought four or five boards. The winner of the most games won the total cash prize, if there was a tie they would play one game winner-take-all. Returning to the softball field to collect the equipment, Dennis had all the players give me a five-dollar tip and he threw in an extra ten dollars to make it a

Hundred Dollars. He wasn't an Ass Hole just an adult who was a mischievous kid, tapping me on the head he invited me to join them at their table. As they headed off to the pool, I decided I cannot sit with him and his group afraid if he acted like an asshole I would lose my job. Tonight was staff talent night featuring all the talented members of The Concord Staff. A dining room waitress who sounded like Streisand received a standing ovation. From the kitchen staff, a team called the Four Chefs did a tap-dancing routine, one of the professional waiters who lived in Monticello was a Ventriloquist. Working with two Dummies one was Hasidic Rabbi ITZIK, the second Female Dummy called Rachel. Rachel would ask the Rabbi what the proper way was to make her husband happy, and what was meant by Kosher Sex. First, he would speak in Yiddish and then translate to English, his material was Biblical text, and he received a standing ovation. Leo introduced me as the newest TUMMELER. I did standup using material from all the Comics I caught working during the Summer. The biggest laugh I received was Henny Youngman's one-liner, I must admit I Bombed. At the end of the production, Leo asked the audience to pick the winner for a thousand-dollar prize, the winner was the Waiter.

After the show I visited my parents who were sitting with the General manager of the hotel, my mother proudly said I was great. That's a mother's love. I knew I was terrible, to be a great Comedian you have to know who you are at Fifteen I hardly knew who I was, proving to myself I had the balls to face five hundred people. Roaming around the Night Club I asked some guests to dance. They were all terrible, but they said I was great on stage.

Alternating between Lunch and Dinner with my parents and breakfast with the Social Staff Leo always handed out daily assignments, today I was assigned to the Shuffleboard area followed by a PING PONG EXHIBITION which was part of the New York Chinese Cultural Center. Philly offered them a free week of room and board for both them and their family one of their wives spoke perfect Yiddish which she learned as a housekeeper for a large Jewish Family who lived on Park Avenue in Manhattan. They were seated by the pool next to a family from Brooklyn who were all speaking Yiddish complaining that the Hotel allowed Chinese people to check in. At that point, the wife of one of the PING PONG PLAYERS switches from Cantonese to a perfect Yiddish saying that they should be ashamed of themselves by thinking that the Concord was built for only certain kinds of people whose food they eat every Sunday night. In New York, it was a ritual to eat Chinese food every Sunday Night. The great Chinese Immigration of 1863 to 1869 brought 15,000 Laborers recruited in China and landed in San Francisco as cheap labour to build the Transcontinental Railroad. Their offspring were inherent, and entrepreneurial and created what is known today as American Chinese food with dishes of Chow Mein, Shrimp & Lobster Sauce, and Egg rolls. These are the main dishes that you will find in Middle America and many local areas in the New York Metropolitan area. The second wave of Chinese Immigrants began in 1978 and going forward. Their arrival introduced more authentic dishes from Various regions of China in key Metropolitan Cities (eg New York, Boston, San Francisco, and Los Angeles) Those who couldn't cook started owning Dry

Cleaners, and Tailor shops and worked in the Garment Trade as sewing machine operators.

It was almost 6 pm on Wednesday, and Jackie Mason was the headliner of tonight's show. The night before I told Larry that I would be a half hour late to the lighting booth explaining that I had to spend a little time with my parents. The table conversation was always the same with my mother complaining that she didn't feel well, My Grandparents missed me and how happy they would be when I returned home. Constantly looking at my watch, timing how long it would take to go to the telephone booth next to the Coffee Shop. Taking one bite of my Apple Cobbler, I excused myself saying that I had to be at the lighting booth before the show started. Exiting the dining room I headed towards the Grand Stairway, making a right at the reception desk, taking the corridor that led to the coffee shop where the last phone was ringing. I picked up the phone on the third ring, one thing about lying was to remember the original lie. As a liar, you must believe in the lie yourself.

Kathleen:

I almost hung up I thought you were busy chasing other girls.

Me:

My parents arrived for the Labor Weekend, I couldn't rush out until I had dessert.

Kathleen:

Will I ever see you again?

Me:

If I remember you are working at the Bank at Rockefeller Center

Kathleen:

We can meet for lunch or dinner

Me:

That sounds great I must see when my I Classes start, if you recall I am working on an MBA DEGREE.

Kathleen:

You are so smart, I miss how you touch me and always make me laugh

Me:

I will be returning to New York City this coming Tuesday, Can I write to you? Here is my telephone number Crescent 5-8558

Kathleen:

I can't wait to see you

Me:

Me too

Walking back to meet my parents who were now seated in the Nightclub, I reviewed all of the negatives of my relationship with Kathleen. I did not have a place to take her, and the money I had could barely buy lunch at Chuck Fil of Nuts (a place that had great cream cheese and raisin bread sandwiches) the number I gave her was the telephone booth in MO'S candy store under my Brooklyn Apartment, I would arrange for her to call me every Wednesday at 9 pm. Arriving at my parent's ringside table my Mother stood up and hugged me. "This is my Baby someday will be a great Doctor"

Saying hello to the people at the table I excused myself, I was needed in the lighting booth.

Larry was already setting up the lights, at 9 pm Marty Beck's orchestra played their opening number and introduced the opening act Magician Carl Ballantine who wowed the audience for forty-five minutes. Then Marty introduced Rosemary Clooney whose hit record "COME ON -A MY HOUSE and starred with Bing Crosby in a movie called WHITE CHRISTMAS featuring I'm Dreaming of a White Christmas (written by Irving Berlin who was Jewish) The Backstage Manager was on the intercom, he called out for thirty lighting changes. Her act lasted 90 minutes with two ovations. Larry was sweating profusely, and the lighting booth felt like it was over a hundred degrees. We were both drenched with sweat, luckily Larry always had a change of shirts hanging in the booth. We both went to the Men's Room, washed ourselves, and dried with paper towels. Larry always left after the show to go home to his wife who was a waitress at Grossingers.

I headed directly to the entrance of the Night Club where My parents were chatting with Concord's Senior Management. After saying hello, I entered the Night Club about twenty couples were dancing to the music of Sonny Rossi's Latin orchestra. In the corner of the stage, a woman was wearing a head scarf, an ankle-length black skirt a white blouse with sleeves that ended at her wrist, and black leather shoes with a strap, dancing the Mambo alone. Walking over to her I introduced myself as Allen the Tummeler. "Where did you learn how to dance that way" As she took my hand, "I go to the Palladium Ballroom every Wednesday night" How could a woman dress like that go to the best Latin Ballroom? As we danced she introduced herself as Sophie, who works on 47th Street (which is the largest Diamond District in the country) as an office manager for her Uncle who is a big importer of Diamonds. Explaining that she lives in the Borough Park section of Brooklyn which is home to one of the largest Jewish Orthodox Communities. “My father comes here often to make sure that the Hotel adheres to the best Kosher practices.” “You are Rabbi Steinberg’s daughter, I see him every month inspecting the kitchen making sure that the dairy and meats are separate, the sinks are separate and the dishes for the diary are separated from the dishes that are used to serve meat.” “That’s my father’s business, he has almost ninety per cent of the hotels in the Catskills” After about thirty minutes of dancing I asked her if she would like to have a Sundae at the Coffee shop. Avoiding the table where my parents were seated I led her to Siberia where my friends were waiting at tables. Sophie explained that she loves Latin music, but in her neighbourhood, it was forbidden to dance with a man no less dancing the Cha-Cha or Mambo. I was fascinated by her story. “Do you go to the Palladium dressed like that?” Sophie looked at me “I feel I can confide in you. Every Wednesday after work my girlfriend Sarah who works for a Gold Refinery and I have a change of clothes in our offices. Unfortunately, we both live at home and the only excuse our family would buy is that we were catching the newest Yiddish Review on the Lower Eastside. We go to the Ladies' Room at the Algonquin Hotel to change our clothes” Leaning across the table I whispered, “How do you change back to your street Clothes” “When it was time to leave we went to the Ladies' Room where we change back to our street clothes. There are baggage lockers in the subway at TIME SQUARE for Fifty Cents we put our clothes in the locker which we pick up in the morning before we go to work, I have a safe place where I store my outfits. Every Wednesday we do the same thing."

Leaving through the rear door of the coffee shop the late nighttime August air was refreshing. The stars were twinkling. Sophie took my hand, guiding her to the outdoor pool where all the Chaise Lounges were stacked. She helped me take down one of the Chassis, placing it near the pool. The pool was reflecting the pathway lights, placing my sports jacket over her shoulders, I decided to pass on my invitation to my room and the romantic music of Sinatra. Realizing that neither she nor I had the same values I would give her a half hour of my time. As we sat there listening to a slight breeze going through the trees, she put her head on my shoulder and started discussing her dilemma. "My family believes that when a woman reaches a certain age, they should marry giving them Grandchildren. Every day they have a new match for me from this or that family who attend the same Schule. Or a cousin of a cousin has a great guy. I respect my parents and agree to meet them to talk. All they talk about is having a large family, a trip to Miami Beach and a Bungalow in the Catskills, and their father's business, there is never a conversation about what I want, my dreams, and having a career. Once I asked them if they knew who Tito Puente, Machito, Tito Rodriguez, The Mambo Kings were or if they knew how to Cha-Cha. They looked at me and thought I was from Mars" With that she turned my head and kissed me. This was unexpected, the kiss was the longest kiss I ever had. Not one to miss an opportunity, she began to explore my body. Trying to have sex on a Chaise Lounge was like walking a tightrope. Trying to unfasten her bra became a monumental task, next, she wore a girdle which was worn by women who wanted an hourglass figure. By the time this was all done I cummed, and we almost rolled off the chaise. In the distance, the flashlight of the Security guard was seen in the distance. Sophie straightened out her clothes, I placed my jacket in front of my stained pants passing the guard we walked to the side entrance and kissed good night. Following the pathway to my Cottage a deer almost hit me as she ran into woods that surrounded the hotel. Entering my room the first thing I did was try to wash the stain off my pants, the red light on the house phone was blinking and my Father's message was that my mother was very upset that I didn't kiss her goodnight. My Mother knew how to push my buttons adding to my Jewish Guilt. She would always bring up that when I did something wrong blaming me that my birth damaged her Vagina. That was guilt going back to my conception, there was nothing I could do about it. She loved me but constantly blamed me for taking pleasure out of Sex.

That morning, I was assigned to referee a teenage Basketball game which had two fifteen-minute Quarters. Opening the door to the Equipment locker I wheeled out the Basketball rack with two bags of red and green armbands, plus Concord Sweatshirts which will be awarded to the winning team. The teams comprised overweight and skinny pimply-faced kids who were totally out of shape. I had a bench of ten extra players who I could substitute if one of the original five dropped out. Using a timer, I started the first quarter within seven minutes one heavy kid dropped out, I replaced him with a tall skinny kid from Yonkers. By the end of the first quarter, the second heavy kid dropped out. Looking at the bench I saw a kid who looked like the first kid from Yonkers, I brought him in to play on the other team. I then realized that they were identical twins. Going into the second quarter the game was tied with forty seconds to go, the red team had a fifteen-year-old who was the smallest kid on the court with fifteen seconds to go he ran under the arm of the tall kid from Yonkers making a two-point layup. I told the winning team that I would present Their Concord Sweatshirts at the pool after lunch and the losing team's Concord T-shirts.

As always it was lunchtime, passing the valet station Dennis the head valet handed me a note on the envelope was a big heart "You are the lover boy of the Concord" as he drove a Cadillac Eldorado to the parking lot. My parents were already at the table, Irving the Maître de was having a family of four seated, waiting for him to finish with these new arrivals. I opened the letter "Allen you are the best dancer and listener, we had to leave early because he was doing his rounds saying hello to his clients at the other Kosher Resorts. Then returning to Brooklyn for Friday Night Sabbath. Here is my office number Diamond 7-8888 it would be great if we could meet for lunch. There is a great Kosher Restaurant on West 47th Street, I would love to meet you at THE PALLADIUM any Wednesday night. Love Sophie"

Irving the Maître De handed me a letter, "What are you doing with the Rabbi's daughter," "We were discussing the Torah" I replied Putting the letter In my pocket, Irving laughing told me to join my parents for lunch. Seated at the table was Frenchie head of reservations, being briefed by my father on an upcoming Publicity event. He arranged for the Democratic Party of New York State to have their annual Golf Outing during the last weekend in September which will be attended by Averell Harriman

Democratic Governor of New State. Handing her a comp list of reporters who would cover the cutting, sitting next to my mother who told me she would be so happy when I came home for she was lonely, The only days my father was home were during the weekends. My Mother and Father had a relationship where she was subservient to him. Her job was to cook, clean, iron his shirts and shine his shoes. He would come home any time he pleased. Occasionally, they would fight, and he would punch her. He apologized by buying her a piece of jewellery or ordering a new outfit that she only wore while standing in front of our apartment house. My mother was an abused woman without skills or awareness of herself. Looking at my watch I excused myself telling them that I had to help Leo with Bingo and I would see them by the pool. My job was to line up chairs on the outdoor patio, set up Leo's equipment, and hand out Bingo cards. The buy-in was twenty dollars for four cards, the person with the most wins is awarded a Trophy and the entire pot of cash. In case of a tie, there would be a four-card run-off winner-takes-all.

Standing on the sideline I reread Sophie's note thinking I am not even sixteen years old and caught in a dilemma with an Irish girl working in a bank at Rockefeller Center and an Orthodox Jew girl working on 47th Street, living two different lives, one to make her parents happy, the other as being a free spirit one night a week who loved LATIN MUSIC. I couldn't afford to buy lunch or dinner for either of them. Sophie's asking me to meet her at the PALLADIUM on Wednesday Nights was out of the question, I had to be 21 to get in, and of the two I was stuck on Kathleen. After each game of Bingo, I had to pick up the cards and tabulate the winner. Finally, after the fourth game, it was a tie. It was M

Katz vs L Catz they were not related Leo's blowing his whistle brought me back to reality. Both players were cigar smokers they created a cloud over the patio like a bad smog over Los Angeles. Catz with a C won the jackpot. Returning to the outdoor pool Denise from the DA BARBER SHOP was playing poker with Ally the resident bookmaker who spent the entire Summer at the hotel joining them were the Matzah King and the Jeweler who owned the concession at the hotel. The buy-in was five hundred dollars with chips valued at twenty dollars each, as I was passing the table Dennis saw me in the corner of his eye shouting "You see this kid," pointing to me "He has a business where he sells his next at Mike's BARBER SHOP for Five Dollars" He then got off his seat and hugged me. The crowd started laughing, giving me a high five. It seemed that even in the Catskills knew who DA BARBER WAS. Being one of his customers made you a celebrity with the Brooklyn hip crowd. My parents, who were part of the A list of Concord guests were seated by the pool. Among them was Robert Sylvester, a Celebrity Columnist for the Daily News who was comped for the Labor Day weekend. My father introduced me as his son. Sylvester looked at me, "I thought you were just a messenger boy who was smart enough to bypass the receptionist sneaking into the Newsroom to deliver press releases to my office. Now you can say hello" I shook his hand kissed my mother and told them I would meet them for dinner.

As usual, I spent time watching the new guests checking in for the long weekend, keeping score of the families that had teenage daughters. This was my last weekend at the Concord, if I did not get lucky I would return to Brooklyn as a Virgin who spent the Summer staining his pants.

During the Summer, Construction of a new Night Club was ongoing which would have over three thousand seats. This was Arthur Winarick's vision of having the newest and biggest venue in the Catskills. He hired architect Morris Lapidus who was known for his flamboyant modernist design. His projects in Miami Beach The Fontainebleau and The Eden Roc drew Arthur Winarick to Commission him to build the largest Night Club, the Imperial Room which seated 3,000 guests. Every day I would see him at the construction site wearing a sports jacket with a shirt and tie and a hard hat. He would pass me as I was returning to my room to change for dinner, smiling he said you are doing a great job kid.

Returning to the Dining room Irving Cohen who had a cash machine was trying to place heavy tippers at A table locations which meant moving the tables a few feet so the summer guests would still be in their acclaimed position. Watching the new guests displaying the best fashions of 1956 line up for gluttony express. Their teenage daughters wobble on their high heels trying to look sophisticated. Leo came up to me and said that there would be a 9 am staff meeting to review the events he had planned for the LABOR DAY WEEKEND. Reminding me to dance with any girl that was available no matter what they looked like. My father and mother were already at the table with Joe Cohen the entertainment editor for Variety a show business trade paper. My Mother was talking to Joe's wife, Joe looked at me playing with his eyeglasses "Sam told me that you want to do stand-up comedy" I thought for a second, I couldn't tell him that all my effort was trying to end my Virginity. Kissing my mother on the cheek I sat down. "Mr Cohen, I did a number of staff talent nights. I know what it means to bomb, I spend a lot of my time working in front of a mirror and trying to get my timing precise. I am working on the basics of Comedy" Cohen smiled as he sipped his soup "You have an intelligent approach to stand up stay with it."

This Friday was special both the furrier and Jeweler banded together to present a fashion show, which started as people began to eat their salad. Six beautiful models entered the dining room dressed in the newest fur pieces and wearing a million dollars worth of Diamonds, the girls glided between tables handing out business cards. It was a magical coordinated Ballet with the girls avoiding the bus boys who were removing the soiled soup, and appetizer dishes and the waiters bringing in either Chicken, Brisket or Salmon with fifteen entrees stacked on top of each other placed on an oval tray 27" by 30".

One of the requirements for being a waiter and busboy was strength, the ability to carry many dishes at once on a Cloche which was used to keep the dishes warm. Avoid running across the kitchen which was as large as a football field even if they forgot part of a guest's order. Excusing myself saying I had to go backstage and chat with the stage manager was a complete lie. This was the time I needed to evaluate which girls I was going to ask to dance. The area outside the dining room entrance became a Mall where every owner of a concession was displaying their wares. The table with the most action was the photography table which had photos of guests either in a Concord Frame or a small red viewer that attaches to a key chain. About ninety per cent of guests spent fifteen dollars to acquire a photo of themselves or their family as a remembrance of LABOR DAY weekend 1956. Guests and their families would geyendik around the grounds before going into the Night Club. Tonight's show was the kick-off of the Labor Day

Weekend. At 9 pm the doors to the Night Club opened, Sonny Rossi and his orchestra with musical guest Machito were playing classic Catskills Mambo and Cha-Cha music. As usual, I would visit each table and ask if their teenage daughter wanted to dance. I must have danced with a half dozen girls from Westchester and Manhattan Beach which was an upscale neighborhood boarding Brighton Beach on the very Southern part of Brooklyn facing the Atlantic Ocean. Of the six girls that I danced with not one can I relate to for they were still teenagers. On the dance floor, I was a man of the world, I wasn't a fifteen-year-old kid from Brooklyn I viewed my persona as a Senior Ivy League college student who lived on Central Park South. Looking at my watch it was time to go up to the lighting booth.

Tonight's show featured The Nicholas Brothers, a tap-dancing act who was the opening act for Comedian Myron Cohen who did his stand-up in a thick Yiddish accent.

The Nicholas Brothers had ten lighting cues, and the audience was familiar with them from their stints on The Ed Sullivan Show which was a staple Sunday Night Variety show on CBS network television running from 1948 to 1981. Larry stepped out of the booth and told me all I had to do was follow Myron with a white spot. His act ran for sixty minutes with three encores. Myron was one of those special ethnic comedians that related to the audience and the audience related to him. He was that everyday guy who was the epitome of the My phrase, My tailor, My Jeweler, My Furrier, My dentist, My Doctor, My Lawyer, My accountant. Those were the days when professionals had a relationship with their customers.

My parents were already seated at the A table in the Night Owl Lounge along with the entire executive team of Concord Management. There was an empty seat next to a very attractive tall blonde who I realized was at the hotel every weekend, always alone. I later found out that she was Philly's girlfriend, even though he was engaged to a lady from Woodmere Long Island which is part of what is called the five towns located in Nassau County home to well-to-do residents. At the end of the bar was Dennis surrounded by six beautiful women and his team from Da Barbershop including Mike who was the owner of the shop and celebrity with the Concord crowd. Seeing me he gave me a big hug and ruffled my hair. "I thought you moved out of the neighbourhood. I was wondering where you were" Turning to the Bartender "give the kid whatever he wants and put it on my tab". I ordered a Coke, Mike put his hand on my shoulder and led me outside of the bar where it was quiet to talk. I explained that my father was the Publicity man for the hotel and got me a job on the social staff for the entire Summer. Mike looked at my hair "You must have gotten a lot pussy up here, did you break your Cherry." Looking at him I said it was a learning experience. "How is Broadway Sam?" I pointed to the A table everyone in my neighborhood had a nickname and my father was Broadway Sam. Mike went back to Dennis and I went back to the table whispering in my father's ear that Mike Da Barber was at the bar. It was good timing for the group was move to the coffee shop for dessert. My father grabbed Mike to say Hello. He introduced him to the group as Broadway Sam, "he's the father of Resell the kid who always sells his next at the Barber Shop" pointing to me.

Excusing himself my father and I headed to the coffee shop where we joined the A table. I ordered a Black & White ice cream soda. The Coffee shop's staff knew how to make the best ice cream sodas' using UBET Chocolate Syrup, Seltzer Water, scoops of Vanilla Ice Cream topped with homemade whipped cream with a Cherry on top. The conversation at the table turned from Entertainment to politics General Dwight Eisenhower and America's involvement in what was then termed the Cold War. Finishing my soda I kissed my mother, telling the group I had an early morning staff meeting.

Leo's 9:30 am meeting meant that I had to wake up by 7:30 am shower, dress, and get to the dining room by 8 am to have Breakfast and meet in the Night Club by 9:30 am. It usually took me ten minutes to eat Breakfast but with the waiters having to run around the kitchen to pick up various parts of the order it took a full hour.

Leo was seated at a long table when we all took our seats, he handed out assignment sheets, and I was Leo's direct assistant. The plan was to satisfy the parents, their children, and long-term guests.

Simon Sez was the lead-off event my job was to make sure that those who failed to do Simon Sez were extracted from the game. After the game, I was to bring Baseball equipment to the ball field to refer to. After lunch, I was assigned to Potato Bag races which was an event for the entire family.

Carla who was responsible for kids under ten years old will play tag and dodgeball.

Rusty the Lifeguard will handle water volleyball, and Julius who was a Scout Leader will lead nature walks.

Leo, introduced a new event for this afternoon, A Belly Flop Contest. The contestants jump off the low diving board into the pool, and the one who makes the biggest water splatter wins a bottle of Champagne. My job was to recruit contestants, lay out the distance markers, and arrange seating for Judges. Sunday would be our final MS. Concord Beauty Pageant.

After going through the list Leo stood up and said these events would all be repeated on Sunday except The Belly Flop Contest with that he blew his Silver Whistle, "Let's make our guest happy." Following Leo to the outdoor patio there were an array of men and women all over fifty. Some women wearing net caps holding their bleached blonde hair in curlers in place so that they can comb it out hoping they resembled Marlyn Monroe. Our female guests mimicked the movie stars of the Fifties minus their bodies. Leo gave me the go-ahead to cover the softball game. I Wheeled my baseball equipment to the field which already had a crowd, half the players wore Grossinger T-shirts, and the other half Concord T-shirts. Dennis came over and told me to relax that this game was part of the Concord Tradition, an end-of-season Ball Game between the Hotels with a five-thousand-dollar prize to the winning team and approved by Philly. On the sideline sat DA BARBER and our full-time resident BOOKIE who was preparing to return to Miami with his two teenage sons.

I wasn't going to argue for Leo never told me about this tradition. Climbing up the bleachers, I placed myself next to the scoreboard, the inning went fast by the ninth inning it was tied nine to nine. In the bottom of the ninth inning, Grossner's had one man on first with two outs. Maurice who was an Afro-American Pastry chef who lived in Monticello one of the few who worked in the Catskills, not in a menial job. He was called the Jackie Robinson of Cheese Danishes. With two outs a man on first Maurice hit a home run winning the game eleven to nine. After distributing the cash, the Grossinger team put on other shirts and exited from the rear entrance.

The Concord team dejected headed for the Pool Bar, as I was loading the wagon Da Barber came over and gave me a hundred-dollar bill. "You ran a great game. I took a fifty-to-one bet that the Grossinger's team will win from Aly." Passing the pool which was deserted. It was lunchtime. My parents were already eating their appetizers. I could tell that my mother was pissed, I went to kiss her and she looked away, sitting down my father broke the ice and told my mother that I was only doing my job he loves you. I gave them a report of my morning activity. By the time I started to eat my chicken salad, my mother took my hand and kissed it. I told my father I wanted him to be a judge in THE BELLY FLOP CONTEST. He told me that Dorothy Kilgallen was an entertainment, syndicated columnist who wrote "The Voice of Broadway" for The Journal American one of New York's Major Newspapers. She also was a regular on "What's My Line" a popular television show on CBS television and was his guest for the weekend. This brought me back to my messenger boy life which will resume upon my return to New York. Once a week I would deliver exclusive column articles to her Town House where her assistant cracked the door and took the envelope. Thanks to my father I will meet the real person. Excusing myself, I went down to the pool to set up the judging area, Leo was standing there in his RED TUMMLER TEE SHIRT with the Silver whistle around his neck. Handing me three plastic rain ponchos which I will hand to the judges to keep them dry.

With that set, I had to select the guests with the biggest bellies to be contestants offering each a two-hundred-dollar gift certificate at the Capri Men's Shop with the winner getting a free weekend at the hotel. Finding men with large Bellies was easy enough they were all around me wearing their Floral and Hawaiian Pattern Cabana sets. The hard part was to convince them to enter the Contest. Most of them were playing Gin Rummy at five dollars a point. A good majority of them had their families up at the Concord for the entire Summer, joining them on weekends and long Holiday weekends. I knew their wives and Children, The best way to get a big belly to do something was either their wives or children who would nag them. Telling them that the Contest starts at 4 pm I also promised that they could take a picture with Dorothy Kilgalen who was known for being on WHAT'S MY LINE." It seemed like all the wives were slim-bleached blondes wearing heavy makeup about and the same age as their husbands. The 50s was not the decade of divorce, it was common to find couples hating each other but staying together for their children, they spent more time in the house and Summers in the Catskills.

As Leo who weighs about 250 pounds stepped on the platform 15 seconds into the opening soundtrack of the film THE TEN COMMANDENTS. Five wives with husbands in tow escorted them to the podium where Leo introduced them. Lining up and facing the crowd, guests who were sitting by the poolside started to scream and clap. Leo with the microphone in hand announced the rules, the contestant who splashes the most water wins the grand Prize, a free all-expenses paid weekend at the hotel with runners up receiving a two hundred and fifty dollar gift certificate to the men's shop, THE CAPRI. I managed to recruit one of the tall beautiful blondes who was with Denins, she was wearing Stilettos which made her over six feet tall. Her job was to take the Hawaiian print Cabana Tops from each contestant, handing them a towel as they emerged from the pool. The Judges wearing their plastic raincoats were handed cards with numbers one to ten.

Each Contestant received a kiss from their wives as they stepped on the Diving board. Four out of five just fell off the board receiving a five or six from the Judges, the fifth contestant was a sitting Judge from Brooklyn who approached the edge of the board spread his arms and glided through the air like an Albatross hunting for dinner. His splash went over the heads of the judges, as he pulled himself out of the pool he was greeted by cheers and whistles.

The judges who were now drenched awarded him five tens. The beautiful blond handed him a towel and planted a kiss on his cheek, the hotel photographer captured the moment of all four couples with the judges including Dorothy Kilgalen. The next photo was with the winner, his wife, Dorothy, and Leo, the photographer told them that they could pick up the photos after dinner as a gift from THE CONCORD. That evening began our Star-Studded weekend with movie star Tony Martin and his wife dancer Cyd Charisse who was featured in THE BAND WAGON Starring Fred Astaire. They were Hollywood Royalty, it was rumoured that Philly paid them the highest fee ever paid for a night performance in the Catskills. As the pool boys dried up the area, I was paged over the outdoor sound system to call Larry who was handling rehearsals for tonight's show. Picking up the house phone

I was connected to the lighting booth where Larry implored me to come up immediately. Larry was soaking wet from perspiration, handing me a sheet with over a hundred lighting cues for their ninety-minute act he asked me to read the cue sheet per song as Martin and Charisse finished their rehearsals. The fan in the lighting booth died, and I had to go to Housekeeping to bring up three fans.

It was a time crunch, I had to go back to my room, shower, dress up and return to the dining room to have dinner with my parents explaining to them that I had to be back in the lighting booth by nine. My Mother looked at me and kissed my cheek, she said "I am so glad that you are coming home, it's terrible how they work you" My father looked at me, "I am proud of you, Philly and Leo want you back on the team next Summer" Finishing my dessert I excused myself, heading towards the lighting booth. Proud of myself for Having lived within the employee guidelines of zero penetration of teenage daughters of hotel guests.

Passing the line of guests who were bribing the Maître de for tables closest to the stage I went up to the lighting booth where the stage intercom was buzzing with the chaos that was happening backstage before the show. At exactly nine fifteen Marty Beck played the intro of "Walk Hand in Hand" which was a big hit in 1956. Martin entered the stage with swagger and a great Suntan and the room burst with applause. He did ten songs I Get Ideas, There's No Tomorrow, Strangers in Paradise, La Vie en Rose, those were the days. Five curtain calls later Larry and I exited the booth with sweat dripping down our faces and shirts soaking wet, we had finished three large bottles of water that we filled up in the men's bathroom before we went to work. Larry went home as usual. I went down to join my parents who were already seated in The Night Owl Lounge. Taking a seat next to my mother I decided it was too much work to try to seduce a female teenage guest with just two days left before returning to Brooklyn as a Virgin.

On Sunday, we had an early Tummler meeting, Leo reviewed the activity schedule and announced that The Harlem Globe Trotters Basketball Team will be putting on an exhibition game. They were unbeatable with their antics of dribbling and ball handling. My job was keeping the scoreboard, the final score was 100 to 25. In the afternoon we were having the final Beauty Pageant of the Summer, and it will include the entire cast of The Jewel Box Review including one real woman. Arriving by bus which took the service road I greeted them at the side door to the men's locker room. I tacked on a sign closed for maintenance, waiting outside as they changed into their bathing Suits. Ten men walked in and Eleven Beautiful women in one-piece bathing suits, wearing Stiletto Heels and lavish hairdo exited the locker room. Their stage manager gave me a list of their stage names as instructed they were to mingle with the guests as normal women who were there for the Holiday Weekend. As Leo was setting up the podium I handed him a list of the contestant's names. The audience at the pool will be the judge, the one that gains the loudest approval from the Audience will be crowned Miss Concord 1956. The pool's sound system started playing THERE SHE IS MISS CONCORD. Leo came on stage wearing a tuxedo and his Converse sneakers, Leo started to sing There she is Miss Concord. I was off stage and on each pause of the song I read out the Contestant's names, Tiffany, Scarlet, Ruby, Desirree, Dilah, Sassy, Jewel, Kitty, Courtney, and Trixie, with each of their names called they stood up and walked across the pool and glided across the Red Carpet to be greeted by Leo. Each one did two turns on the Red Carpet winding up next to Leo who asked them standard questions, do you like to cook, what type of man interests you, if you only had one wish, what would it be, what is your favourite pet? Each in their Soprano's voice answered the questions, turned and lined up. All contestants were facing the audience awaiting who would be crowned Miss Concord 1956, standing next to the stage Dennis tapped me on the shoulder and said he would give me a hundred dollars if I could set him up with the Tall Blonde Kitty. He looked at me as if I was going to do him the biggest favor turning to his friends and giving them the okay sign. Standing next to me he put his hand on my shoulder telling me that I was a stand-up guy and he owed me.

Leo walked in front of each contestant and asked the audience to vote and when it came to Tiffany the Audience went wild. Tiffany in a Red Beehive hairdo, red lips, eyelashes that were about an inch long, long earrings, a yellow one-piece bathing suit, and size 14 Yellow Stiletto heels was crowned Miss Concord 1956.

Dennis whispered in my ear "Even though she didn't win I still want to be fixed up with her." Before the beauty contest Leo and I discussed whether the contestants should take off their wigs or keep the illusion of being beautiful women and we decided to go with the illusion. As they were being escorted to the men's locker I asked Kitty if he would do me a favor and say hello to Dennis. Dennis was excited and offered her a drink which she turned down, Kitty who was as tall as Dennis gave him the entire fantasy treatment stroking his face playing with his hair and offering him her telephone number in the city. With that, she said that her family had to return to New York, so she had to go back to her room and change, her stage manager was there to escort her to the bus. Watching Kitty leave Dennis came over and gave me a hundred-dollar bill saying he would bag her when he returned to the city. The Loudspeaker was Blaring Tummeler Allen, and the phone rang loudly, Picking up the house phone was Larry asking me to bring up a chicken salad sandwich and water. Larry must cover rehearsals for a negro tap dancing act The Will Masten Trio featuring Will Masten, Sammy Davis Senior and Sammy Davis Junior. Larry Auerbach of William Morris was Sammy's agent booking him at THE COPACABANA and a regular on The Ed Sullivan Show, a must-see variety show that was on CBS Television at 8 pm on Sundays. Due to Philly's relationship with Lee Solomon of the William Morris agency, he was able to book Davis over Labor Day weekend.

Entering the booth, I was introduced to Larry's Wife and his twin Sons who were about thirteen years old, the boys shook my hands and called me Sir. "I have to take a break, you handle the rest of the rehearsal" Handing me the lighting cue sheet Larry exited with his family. There were only three numbers left which meant I had to spend half an hour in the booth. At the end of the third song the House Lights came up. Reviewing the Cue sheet Will Masten Sammy Davis Senior opened the show with banter and the best tap dancing I saw. Twenty minutes into the act Sammy joined the team, it then became the Will Masten Trio with a change in lighting his father and Will Masten disappeared into the wings. Sammy's songs span from 1949 to 1956, he opened with The Way You Look Tonight, Please Don't Talk About Me When I'M Gone, You Are My Lucky Star, Dedicated To You, Laura, The Gypsy In

My Soul, Hey There, Plus tap numbers, and playing the drums with about a hundred light cues. Unlike other venues across America Sammy could not stay in venues which he entertained, the Concord gave him a suite of rooms.

Returning to my room I discovered that all the College Students who worked at the Hotel had an end of end-of-summer party that evening after midnight in the employee's Dorm, some were going back to school with between five thousand and ten thousand dollars. My Summer earnings were about seven hundred dollars. On Monday after lunch, I had to give the waiter and busboy a hundred-dollar tip which I had to ask my father for.

Walking to my room I spotted Arthur Winarick chatting with the construction manager in front of the Steel Skelton of the 5,000-seat Imperial Ballroom designed by architect Morris Lapidus. Winarick was hands-on and spent his time at the construction site wearing a hardhat viewing the creation of the largest Nightclub in the Catskills. Building this nightclub was his way of giving the finger to the Grossingers Family his main nemesis in The Borscht Belt.

I had to meet my parents in front of the Dining Room, rather than hanging out and checking out the single guests, I decided that it was a waste of time to give out free Latin Dancing lessons. My concentration was finding out where the families who spent the entire Summer at the hotel were, Irving Cohen was receiving his last tips for the Summer. Viewing his dining room seating chart, I found twenty families who spent the entire Summer at the Hotel. I planned to visit each table and thank them for being at the hotel and I look forward to seeing them next Summer. Those who had teenage daughters knew that I was entering my Junior Year at NYU, and I planned to visit them all before dessert.

My parents arrived and we were escorted to a table for eight, with two bottles of Wine, my father briefed me that the two agents and their wives from William Morris and Philly would be joining us. The conversation centred on Sammy and his extraordinary talents and how William Morris was planning to make him a superstar. The waiter was about to serve desserts, and I excused myself. Reviewing the table locations I started my Goodbye tour, all the tables were in front or three tables back of the Dining room entrance and on both sides, getting the table where everyone saw you was top of the pecking order It was the who's who of Jewish Families that of second-generation Jews that prospered in America. I started with the Shapiro family stopping at the table I thanked them for everything and wished them a healthy year. Mr. Shapiro stood up and hugged me putting something in my hand, I did the same pitch at every table, my pockets were filled with crumpled bills. Returning to my parents my father asked where I was, whispering in his ear I lied that I went to the Bathroom. None of the agents knew my age they told me that if I wanted to be an agent they would get me a job in the mailroom of William Morris, In those days the path to being an agent was through the mailroom.

My parents and the two couples from William Morris had a front-row table. The waiters were busy taking orders running back and forth with bottles of Johnnie Walker Scotch. When the house lights went down the waiters had to stop serving. Taking my seat in the lighting booth, the temperature gauge read a hundred degrees. I watched as Larry set up the color Gels which were used to turn white light into various colors. After ninety minutes Larry told me to handle the remaining lighting cues, he had to go to the men's room. The energy that Sammy generated was nothing I had ever seen over my ten weeks at the Hotel, he took five encores until the applause died down and the audience began heading for the exit. My parents were waiting for me in front of THE NIGHT OWL LOUNGE. Using the side entrance, I stepped into the fresh Catskill air where I viewed two men making out in the parking lot. At fifteen in 1956, I didn't know about Homosexuality, now I knew what my friends meant when they used the term Faggot or gay. After a few minutes, they separated, each one going in a different direction. Approaching the main entrance both men arrived by the Valet Station, I entered the lobby. The Bar was packed Dennis, and his group were drinking Champagne and making a lot of noise. Walking sideways through a packed Bar Crowd, I pushed my way to my parents' table where two large black men stopped me. Sammy was seated between the two William Morris agents and their wives, Will Masten Sammy Davis Senior, Philly, and My parents. There was one empty chair directly in front of what I assumed was Sammy's bodyguards. After finishing two Cokes the entire table decided to go to the Coffee Shop. I had a choice of my last Black and White ice cream Soda or going back to my room to pack, I chose packing, and I left telling my parents I would see them for lunch.

As I started to walk towards my room two towel boys invited me to the end of Summer Party that was being held in the dilapidated employee Dormitory. Through the Summer I was never accepted as one of the groups, they all knew that Philly was my Godfather and were afraid that I would rat on them. Following them we exited the hotel through the service road and found ourselves across the street from the Large White House where the paint was peeling off the sides and about a hundred summer employees were drinking beer, Smoking Weed, dancing to Sinatra, Perry Como, Tony Bennett, Bill Haley, and the Comets. During the entire Summer, I never saw these people in Street Clothes. They all wore uniforms, Waiters, Busboys, Valet, Bellhops, front desk, Cooks, and dishwashers. They weren't looked upon as real people, they were just people in uniforms with designated responsibilities, namely to please the guests.

Under the Starry August Night Sky, the waitresses that I saw every day were good-looking women with great bodies, makeup, jeans, print dresses, and sweaters that were styled to emphasize their Breasts. I realized that I spent the Summer with blinders on avoiding what was in front of me the entire Summer. My only close friend was Solomon who worked at the pool bar and lived in Yonker. Walking across the lawn a usual smell permeated the air, Solomon introduced me as THE TUMMELER to a group of waiters and waitresses who were on the lawn sitting on blankets drinking beer and smoking skinny cigarettes. They were all discussing how much money they made male and female waitresses were on Scholarships at top Universities in the Northeast and hated asking their parents for money. Working at the hotel gave them independence earning over ten thousand dollars for a summer's work They asked where I go to school, NYU I answered as I took a sip of beer. Solomon handed me a skinny cigarette, I puffed it, and they all chanted "INHALE" I inhaled and suddenly I felt nauseous, running to the side of the house I threw up next to a couple who were making out. The entire

Hotel service staff were either drunk or high. From that moment on I never smoked or drank beer. At 3 am those who were waiters and busboys broke off from the party, they had to be in the dining room by 7 am. I passed Solomon who was making out with one of the female servers who worked at the pool, walking back to my room I ran across one of the Hotel Security Guards who rode around in a golf cart. Shining his flashlight In my face, "I know you, you are the guy I see on the Basketball court when I am on the day Shift you are the TUMMELER, my name is Leroy what are you doing out so late? I will give you a lift to your room" I told him I went to THE NEVELE to listen to Tito Puente. My head was spinning, I fell asleep without undressing. I didn't wake until my phone rang, it was Solomon making sure that I was okay. It was 11 a m, I missed Breakfast. Realizing I never got undressed, I entirely forgot about the dollar stash in my pant pocket. Taking out crumpled bills which were mainly Jackson, and Franklins I earned five hundred dollars from my dinner table "Have a Healthy Year tour. "

My Uncle Charlie gave me his army duffle Bag, it took 10 minutes to pack, the rest of my clothes, record player, and records I would put in the trunk of my father's car. I had time to kill so I walked over to the Pool where there was a water aerobics class in session. Solomon was talking to the waitress that he was making out with, Solomon with his arm on my shoulders introduced me to the waitress Nancy who was of medium height and blonde hair. I could see through her uniform she had great breasts, "Did you hook up with one of Nancy's friends who said that you were cute? The weed that we had was great and worth every cent" I couldn't admit that it made me throw up. "If you want, I could give you the name of the local farmer who cultivates the stuff, he sells a pound for $6.00 an oz to every Valet on the Borscht Belt who then rolls them into joints and resells them to the staff for $20.00 a joint. If you want, he comes to Manhattan once a month to deliver the product which you can sell to classmates, I meet him once a month as he comes off the George Washington Bridge before he goes to Mid-Town. I make about two thousand dollars a month." Solomon writes down the number and puts it in my pocket. Some guests decided to have a late checkout and missed the Labor Day traffic on Route 17. The line to the dining room was as long as usual. I took the fire entrance and searched for the waiter and busboy who took care of me during the Summer, I gave each a fifty-dollar bill. My parents were already seated with Leo joining them, they were discussing a media schedule when Leo visited Manhattan. Leo tells my parents how great I was, and turning to me "I want you back on my staff next Summer. You are a great TUMMELER." With that he places a Silver Whistle around my neck, excusing himself he tells us that he must prepare for Tuesday's Annual Firefighters Association of New York meeting and Golf Outing.

My father peeled off two one-hundred-dollar bills handed them to both the Waiter and Busboy and headed for the table where the Manager, head of Reservation, and VP of Construction Were finishing their Lunch. Whispering in my ear he told me that I could go back to my room he would pick me up in an hour. That gave me enough time to say goodbye to all the people who worked full-time and lived in Sullivan County. Starting in the back of the hotel full-time waiters and waitresses hung out before they had to go back for dinner. Across the road, by the Summer Employees

Dorm, the lawn had scattered luggage where the summer staff wearing their School T-shirts were hugging each other. Every College in the NORTHEAST was represented allowing a certain kind of Kinship to manifest itself when they all grew older and pursued their given profession, they were part of the fraternity of former Concord waiters and waitresses. By the time I said my goodbyes my father was waiting for me in his White Chevy Bel-Air Sedan with the rear door opened in the parking lot in the back of the cottage "There is no room for your bags in the trunk, you know how your Mother packs, put your bags on the back seat." Having already packed my record play and records in a box, my clothes in the Duffle bag, and leaving my room keys on the dresser I was ready to go. As we drove out of the driveway of the Hotel heading to route 17, I reflected that my life was in Reversal from being an adult to a teenager with the closing of the rear door of the 1956 WHITE CHEVY-BEL-AIR SEDAN with air-conditioning. I would prefer my life During my ten weeks at the Concord with no days off, the most sleep I had was 6 hours. Chi-Chi Rodriguez who was the Golf Pro offered me free lessons if I showed up at 8 am, It was girls or golf the girls won. The rear seat of the Chevy was black leather, and using the Duffle Bag as a pillow, I slept during the entire trip back to Brooklyn. Luckily, we found a parking spot in front of the apartment building as usual people were sitting on the stoop and folding beach chairs. 482 Riverdale Avenue which was built in the nineteen thirties, was a five-floor walkup. The lobby was black and white marble with a huge iron door which gave you entrance to the stairway of white marble, each floor was black and white marble as the lobby. Helping my father unload the trunk he opened both doors, handing the keys to the apartment. "Bring up all the bags I have to go to the Candy Store and buy Cigarettes" My father was a two-pack-a-day smoker, his favourite brands were Lucky Strikes of Camels which cost twenty-five cents. Leaving my mother outside, I brought up the bags and opened the apartment door. I went into my room and found the Large Hebrew National Salami still hanging from a nail as hard as a rock, the smell of ageing Salami permeated my room. In the corner were cans of Tuna Fish, Salmon, Oatmeal, and Heinz Ketchup hidden behind THE REGAL Logo from our Club House. Parked under the Salami was my Schwinn bicycle with dust on it.

I opened the windows in my room to clear the air of the smell of Salami and Cigarettes. My bed was a four-poster with a matching dresser whereas my parents had two dressers, a King Size Mattress, and a television in the corner. My Mother stored her expenses in a flat box under the king-size bed. She treated her clothes as crown jewels whereas my father had three suits, black, brown and grey. As a tradition in most Jewish families, on Sundays and Holidays, they ate what was considered Chinese Food, Egg drop soup, with Wontons, dry soup noodles, Egg Rolls, Spareribs Chicken Chow Mein, Shrimp and Lobster Sauce, Fried Rice, Fortune COOKIES, none of these dishes were authentic Chinese but where designed by Chinese Immigrants to fit into what Americans surmise was real Chinese Cooking. It took me a decade to discover that by crossing the bridge into Manhattan was China Town whose menus reflected various regions of China serving authentic Chinese Food.

I had a week to hang out before returning to school, riding my bike to the playground, members of REGAL HOUSE were playing basketball. Everyone had a story to tell about how they spent their Summer. Half of them spent it in Summer School, and none of them had a summer job. They all gave recaps of their summer love which were all fictions to impress each other. It was my turn to recap the Summer, I felt like Hans Christian Andersen embellishing the big Entertainers that I met and the affairs that I had. The big question was did I get laid? "About three times a week," I had to embellish the total experience that would satisfy their fantasies of having sex. The father of One of our members owned a porn shop on West 42nd Street and brought home the latest 16-millimeter Porn film. Another member's father worked for Universal Pictures and owned a projector, together we had movie night or to better describe it JERK OFF NIGHT.

That evening around midnight Jaffe called my father asking him to tell me to come into work after 1 pm The first thing I had to do was to deposit the fifteen hundred dollars I made during the Summer at The Williamsburg Saving Bank. My mother opened an account for me with the thousand dollars in gifts I received from my Bar Mitzvah. Arriving at Jaffe's office there was a pile of laundry and a couple of black suits with a note take them to the Laundry with a fifty-dollar bill attached to the note. He always gave me the money to take a taxi and leave a deposit with Mr. Wong who owned the Laundromat/tailor shop. I never took a taxi I walked the three blocks to Ninth Avenue which was known as Hell's Kitchen. Garbage was strewn in front of the walk-up tenements, some apartments tried to bring beauty to the street with Flower Boxes in front of their apartment window to soften the view of their rusted Fire Escapes which offered egress to safety in case there was a fire. It was amazing how the landscape changed from the Great White Way to urban slums. There were some Irish Bars next to shops that were selling Porn. Along both Eighth and Ninth Avenue young street walkers were selling their wares. A few movie houses lining Eighth Avenue were offering double features of Porn Films on large screens. Rather than going back to Jaffe I figured I would surprise Kathleen for all banks closed at 3 pm Rockefeller Center was a few blocks uptown from Jaffe's office. Manufacturers Hanover was on 49th Street between 6TH Avenue and Fifth Avenue. Standing outside the bank as employees left Kathleen exited the bank heading towards Fifth Avenue Standing next to her she was oblivious to my presence, we were both waiting for the traffic light to turn RED "Pardon me You look familiar" She turned and hugged me, I handed her the flower from the Rockefeller Center Flower bed. Looking for a quiet place to talk we walked across to ST. Patrick Cathedral which was between services. Kathleen did the entire ritual when walking into her house of Worship. We found a very dark place amongst the pews. She told me she has her own telephone number which she gave to me. We started to make out as Jesus watched us from the Cross, suddenly worshippers were coming in for the evening mass. Straightening our clothes as the pews filled walking along the aisle where various Saints were displayed, simmering by the lights of candles that were lit as a tribute to their miracles. Kathleen stopped in front of Saint Patrick, lit candles and put some money in the Donation box where I contributed a dollar. Fifth Avenue was crowded with people going home from work.

Kathleen kissed me saying she had to go home to watch her baby sister telling me she was free over the weekend. Walking back to Jaffe's office with stained pants I racked my brain trying to figure out how I was going to handle this relationship. Jaffe was still sleeping and my father was writing a piece on the Concord which he asked me to deliver to Robert Sylvester who wrote a column for the Daily News. The Jewish New Year started on Wednesday, 5 September two days after Labor Day. The neighbourhood shut down for Rosh Hashanah and didn't open until after Yom Kippur. Yom Kippur is the holiest day in the Jewish Calendar and ends at Sundown September 15th. The difference between Judaism and Catholicism is that those who believe in Jesus can go every week to be absolved of their Sins, the Jews can do it in one shot on YUM KIPPUR. On Saturday afternoon I went to DA Barber Shop, about twenty guys were on the Street and five guys were pitching Quarters against the side of the Barber Shop the coin closest to the wall won the entire pot. Dennis who was pitching quarters gave me a big hello. "This kid worked the Summer as a whole at The Concord, he set me up with a beautiful Blonde named Kitty whom I took to the COPA to see Frankie Lane with that he took out a COPA Picture frame with Him Frankie Lane and his date. She is a real act I took her home and she gave me a head in the back of the taxi, it was the best I have ever had" Looking at Dennis I asked if he was planning to see her again, Dennis was looking into the mirror to make sure every hair was in place. "She told me that she was going back to Topeka Kansas to take care of her sick mother, she needed money to buy her mother's medication, so I gave her five hundred dollars to help her out. She will return in a month and promised to call me." Mike took me next and Dennis paid for my haircut. I couldn't tell him the truth, every time he saw me he thanked me for introducing him to a woman who gave the best blow job in the World.

My Mother was standing in front of our apartment house and decided that I needed clothes to start the New School year. My father went to meet friends to play Gin Rummy in a storefront called Seville Lodge which was a Burial Society. In those days many men's clubs bought plots of Burial Sites reserved for members and their families, I couldn't say no to my mother. We took the subway to Union Square (14th Street) where KLEINS was located. Kleins was the first department store to introduce discount pricing by Purchasing clothing manufacturers' excess inventory at discounted prices. My Mother was my Fashion consultant making sure that my pants were pressed and well-tailored, and that my shoes always shined. In those days the buildings didn't have laundry rooms. To save money she hand-washed the clothes using a washboard and hung them out on a clothesline that ran across the interior court of the building.

The following Monday at 9 am I reported to Thomas Jefferson High School as a Junior and viewed the girls which I thought the year before were just giggling, with pimple faces, small breasts and ugly legs. Now the girls were mimicking Marlyn Monroe wearing tight sweaters, Poodle skirts just below the knee and Bobbie Sox with their Baby Dolls or Black and white Saddle Shoes. Every class I went to I sized up the girls to have a girl more my age and closer to home. The best way to meet them is to join a club after Sox. Jefferson had a Drama Club that met on Wednesday after school, evaluating that losing a day's pay was a worthy investment towards finding a local girlfriend I skipped work on Wednesday. Ninety per cent of the call was off to Celebrate YOM KIPPUR. On

Wednesday evening the entire neighbourhood dressed up and went to various Shules for the opening prayer, Kol Nidre which kicked off with twenty-four hours of fasting and reflection. In my neighbourhood, there was only one type of Shule, Orthodox. Crossing over one of the two Bridges leading to Manhattan, Jews could choose from Orthodox, Conservative and Reformed. From Sunset to Sundown, it was mandatory to fast, we met my Bubba and my Aunt Helen at the Shule my Zayda preyed in. The Rabbi greeted the entire family and asked about my Tallis (prey shawl) Remembering that I was a kohen gadol which meant I was a decadent of Jewish High Priests. The Rabbi invited both my father and me on the stage called The Bimah next to THE TORAH to participate in the services. I was screwed by my Family, and I usually leave after Kol Nidre now I had to stand bowing and mumbling the Prayers throughout the entire service, I never felt so Jewish. On YOM KIPPUR DAY my mother handed me a list of items she needed from the A&P telling me that I should avoid being caught by our Neighbors. By the time I left for the Super Market all of them were in Shule, I had to avoid passing a Shule meaning I had to ride two blocks East passing family homes that comprised the Italian Community, My stealth trip to the A&P was just to save face, we lived in an observant Community where it was frowned upon not to follow the teaching and traditions of being Jewish, most of our neighbours were Holocaust survivors. For God to sweep away your sins of the past year you had to fast for twenty-four hours which included water. My Zayda who interpreted the bible in his way told me that if not eating makes you sick then you eat. The big event at the culmination of Yom Kippur is the breakfast dinner. That meant there were lines outside the neighbourhood Chinese Restaurants. My Bubba spent the entire day cooking breakfast where the entire family gathered except my Uncle Charlie and my Zayda.

There is something about Guilt that is inherent with being brought up in a Jewish Community, If you promised to do something and fail either and due to circumstances beyond your control you feel Guilty. This feeling of Guilt becomes part of your existence, I missed calling Kathleen because I suddenly found myself standing next to the Torah. The phone was in my Bubba's bedroom, taking the piece of paper with her number from my wallet I dialled her number, Kathleen picked up the phone, I spent ten minutes apologizing for not calling when promised. After an hour of just talking about nothing, she asked me if I was going to see her over the weekend, I said of course telling her that I would call her tomorrow and we'd agree on where to meet. I was faced with having to solve two problems, where was I going to take her and what was I going to tell my parents especially my Mother who viewed me as a child.

Taking the train into the city with my father I told him the Kathleen story, meeting her at the Concord and that she was eight years older than me and I needed his help. As we got off the subway at the 49th Street stop he bought a Variety at the newsstand and turned to me with a smile on his face "Did you have sex with her" Looking at him I said "Almost" Looking at me like I am a moron "What do you mean by almost." I then told him what happened during our forty-eight hours together as we climbed the stairway to Jaffe's office/apartment, "Dad, I really like her and we have a date tomorrow, where should I take her and what excuse can I give Mom that's taking to the city on Saturday.

Taking off his jacket, "I will tell your Mom that Jaffe needs you in the office and I will get you passes for the afternoon at Radio City" Looking in the New York Daily News there was a full-page Advertisement for the movie Tea & Sympathy starring Deborah Kerr followed by The Rockettes. That evening, I called her to meet me in front of RADIO CITY at two in the afternoon.

Kathleen was impressed with our first-class treatment at the theatre, the usher escorted us to our seats in the Orchestra. As we were about to sit down, Kathleen admitted that this was the first time she was in the theatre. Grabbing my hand, she told me that she wanted to see the show from the very last balcony in the theatre. We took the elevator to the very top of the music hall and the space was empty, we had the entire balcony to ourselves. We kissed occasionally, but every time I tried to play with her breasts, she slapped my hand. She certainly was not the same girl that I spent the weekend in the Catskills with. The movie was something that I would not pay to see the Rockettes who I have seen since I was eight years old never changed. I did it to impress her, as the curtain came down we entered the elevator with my hands clasped covering the stain on my pants. People from the Orchestra were exiting, Kathleen went to the ladies' room, and I found a Playbill to hold over my stained pants. It was 6 pm and I offered to buy her a snack. Chock Full O'Nuts was my favourite place to go. They had locations all over the city featuring Raisin Almond Cream cheese sandwiches, Donuts and coffee, the check was six dollars for both of us. We were not sitting at a table, they only had counter seating. Kathleen between bites of her raisin bread cream cheese sandwich pulled close to me and whispered, "What we had over the Summer was not me, it was my once-in-a-lifetime adventure, you were cute, funny, and someone I could talk to so why not have a fling, I hope we can still be friends." Wow, it was a relief I didn't need an apartment, or money, still being the person she thought I was since we were just friends. Exiting the Restaurant I walked her to the Eastside IRT discovering that she knows how to ice skate. Kissing her on the cheek I yelled we can meet at Wollman Ice Skating rink in Central Park as she descended to catch the train.

After the weekend I started my Junior year, my class schedule ended at various times and on Mondays, I was out at noon. Jaffe called and gave my father a list of chores. Arriving at 1 pm, I stopped at the Payphone before going to the office. It cost a dime so I called Sophie who worked on 47th St Street which is known as THE DIAMOND DISTRICT, she invited me to her office H Diamonds to have lunch, her boss was In Israel and then ANTWERP on a buying trip to purchase Diamonds. To go up to her office I had to pass through twenty showcases of vendors selling Diamonds, watches, and gold chains. An armed Security Guard was standing next to the elevator which was in the middle of the store. H Diamonds had the entire floor you had to pass three security doors to get in the office. Sophie who was dressed in her orthodox clothing with a scarf covering her brown hair with just a tiny dab of lipstick greeted me with a kiss, which was not how Orthodox ladies greet men. "I know that I look terrible, this is the game you have to play when you are part of the Community. I am ordering lunch from the Kosher Dairy, here is the menu you can order what you want, we have an account there" I ordered Blintzes and an Egg Cream. Her office walls were covered with pictures of family and a Diploma from The Gemological Institute of America. Having the GIA was a guarantee that the diamonds sold were Authentic. Sophia moved to the very corner of the room and took out a scrapbook of pictures showing her in Palladium Attire receiving a trophy for competitive dancing. Taking my hand Sophia led me to the corner of the room between three file cabinets "We are being watched by Security Cameras, I found a blind spot." I noticed four blinking red lights on the ceiling recording our every move. Her picture album and Trophy were pressed against my chest and we started to kiss. I put my tongue in her mouth and she pushed me away saying that it was gross. Kathleen was right, Jewish Girls did not know how to kiss. At the buzzer range, Sophia went to open the door and brought in our lunch. Over Blintzes and a Tuna fish sandwich Sophia opened up about the pressure she was getting from home "Constantly my mother bugs me with how difficult I made it to find the right man, nobody is good enough for you. I am only twenty-three She's afraid I will be too old to bear children. They have my entire life mapped out for me." Finishing our lunch Sophia took my hand "I like you, I am free for lunch anytime, we can meet Wednesday night at the Palladium or after Sabbath." As I entered the elevator she handed me her home telephone number "Please remember I won't answer the phone on the Sabbath".

Leaving the Diamond District I went straight to Jaffe's office, Eddie created a unique way to show his clients the results of his work. He hired a clipping service whose job was to scan every newspaper across the Country and send a packet of news articles that were printed about his clients. These stories were disseminated by major newspaper syndication and major wire services Associated Press and United Press. Every month I had a large roll of white paper, and my job was to glue every article on each client. Some clients' rolls were six feet long. Every time Jaffe had a client meeting, he would unfurl the roll of paper to display the results of his work. On the day before his meeting, he told me to dress in a suit and wear a shirt and tie. My job was to say nothing and upon his cue, I rolled out the paper. I only had two suits which was my Navy Bar Mitzvah suit which two years later fit perfectly. Exiting the taxi to go to his client's office I felt this is where I belong.

As a Junior in High School and member of the Drama Club, it was a perfect place to meet girls. I made sure that they knew I was on the Jackie Gleason Show and did a Stand-Up at the Concord. The Club was working on Tennessee Williams' A STREETCAR NAMED DESIRE was holding auditions.

Lunch in the cafeteria was a tribal gathering Jews sat with Jews, Italians with Italians, blacks with blacks, Jocks with jocks, and everybody wanted to sit with Jefferson Basketball star Leroy Ellis who went to St. Johns on a Basketball Scholarship upon graduation and was drafted by THE LA LAKERS. Ricky was part of our group and his locker smelled like a Delicatessen. He ate Salami Sandwiches every day for four straight years. We all agreed that we would Resurrect REGAL HOUSE. The sign took up too much space in my bedroom. One of our Club members moved to East Flatbush but kept his East New York Address, he wanted to hang out with us. His family was moving up in the world and bought a Single-Family home on East 98th Street in the area called Flatbush which we considered suburbia. His parents agreed to free rent as long as we keep it quiet and throw away all the garbage. As for transportation, two members of our group were 18 years old and used their parents' car. Lucky for us they screwed up on their

Regent Exam and had to take the entire year over to receive a Diploma. Having a clubhouse in Flatbush broadens our net of meeting upscale girls, the two High Schools were Erasmus and James Madison. The plan was to have a Halloween Party and distribute the invitation by hand in front of each school. Another member's father owned a printing company and agreed to print a hundred invitations, the copy was "CELEBRATE THE GREATEST HALLOWEEN PARTY OF 1956 HOSTED BY MEMBERS OF REGAL HOUSE - GREAT FOOD, MUSIC AND SURPRISES. COSTUMES OPTIONAL THE FUN STARTS AT 7 PM. We planned the party for the Night Of Halloween knowing the next day was School, the party would end by Midnight. We each agreed to contribute ten dollars to pay for food and drinks The two eighteen-year-old members who drove volunteered to skip class and hand out the invitations to only good-looking girls in front of each high school. On Monday, October 21st by the end of September, REGAL HOUSE CAME TO LIFE. All of the equipment, The Regal House Logo was hung, and the light bulbs were changed to red which we thought made the place sexy.

Kathleen and I kept in touch, now it was purely platonic, we would meet occasionally to go ice skating in Central Park or have coffee when she finished work at the bank. The conversation was about my fictional life and her life as a 23-year-old Irish Catholic girl who wanted babies. For Sophie, we met once a month when she wasn't having lunch with her Boss, we would practice Latin dancing steps and make out in the corner which lasted exactly one hour, after which I had to get back to work.

Jaffe's office apartment was like a bus terminal for people visiting from across the country, the famous Jimmy Doolittle whose team bombed Tokyo at the opening phase of War in The Pacific would tell me stories of his career. A year Jaffe went to LA to visit with John Wayne and Swifty Lazar who was a Super-agent and had his meetings in the back of his Roll-Royce. My father and I worked different hours, he would arrive at Jaffe's when I was going home and return home before Sunrise. My Mother and Father always fought at this time in my life so I always closed my bedroom door.

Staying in High School was a necessary evil, I did well in all my classes except Math which I needed to pass to graduate. I spent more time studying my classmate's breasts than the formula for a square, rectangle, Triangle, circle, or pyramid. The only way I could see the value of this course is if I could use it to estimate the size of breasts. Tuesday the night before Halloween 1956 the Club House was ready, and we discussed the rules of the Club, no Liquor, no weed, If a girl says no you back off and most of all no fighting. My costume was the clown suit I wore at the Concord with the Red Wig and floppy shoes which I carried with me, I couldn't ride my bike in floppy shoes. Isaac lived around the block, his father graduated from CCNY as an Accountant and then was drafted by The Army in 1942, after basic training and being a College Graduate he was Commissioned as a Second Lieutenant in the Third Army which was under the leadership of General George Patton. Isaac's father told him never to go into his office, one day after school Isaac found the key to the office at the bottom of a Chinese Porcelain Vase. Opening the door, the room was filled with World War 11 memorabilia. Three German Lugers, On the wall, was a burnt Nazi flag, and framed photos of inside Buchenwald, his father was part of the Battalion which Liberated the camp, and he had two mannequins one wore the entire uniform of a SS Colonel on the other was his father's U S ARMY full dress uniform with Medals. He somehow mailed it from England before he returned to Brooklyn.

I had a silver horn on my bike, Isaac came out wearing the entire SS uniform which was made for a six-foot-tall. Isaac was only five feet 8 inches the hat covered his eyes. Luckily it was dark so a Nazi SS officer and a Clown riding through a Jewish Neighborhood being illuminated by passing cars would go unnoticed. Looking closely at the Colonel's uniform the shirt had a large Blood Stain, the stain ensured that his uniform was authentic. We estimated if we were lucky ten girls out of the 100 invitations Would show up. We assigned two members Richie and Sol who were dressed as Centurion Roman Soldiers to the door. By 7 pm we had fifteen girls join the party and by 8 pm Richie shouted for me to come outside there was a line of twenty girls in costumes waiting to come in, I told Richie to let them all in. The room was packed, we had thirty-five girls and ten guys. The girls somewhat didn't care if there were only ten guys. They drank our Soda and ate our Chips. By then we were out of refreshments, luckily there was a supermarket on the corner, and Isaac volunteered to go to the store dressed as an SS Colonel. Many of the girls left by 10 pm, and eight Club members got lucky and fell temporarily in love. We all had curfews to be home before Midnight, and the older members who drove offered to take the girls home. Leaving my bike in the Club House we stood at the bus stop hoping to be home by midnight.

Time moved fast, my 16th Birthday was two days after Thanksgiving. We were invited for dinner at my aunt's Home who had married her boss after his wife died of Cancer leaving him with two young Children. My Bubba was happy that her only daughter didn't wind up as an Old Maid, you could sense the resentment of his two children one a boy and the other a girl. This table wouldn't make the Pilgrims happy.

With Christmas 1956 a few weeks away I met Kathleen at Wollman Ice Skating Ring in Central Park there she told me that she was getting engaged to her fourth Cousin. I walked her to the subway, kissed her on the cheek, and never spoke to her again. Sophie was a different story, we had lunch once a week in her office, practised how to Tango, and fooled around out of sight of the security cameras in the blind spot in her office next to the file drawers. I was practising writing short terse paragraphs for both my Fathers's and Eddie Jaffe's clients. Seeing what I wrote in Earl Wilson's column which ran in the New York Post became a high motivation. I had an idea, I would offer Publicity services to local Restaurants. My first account was a new Chinese Restaurant THE HOUSE OF MING which opened on Linden Boulevard a Large two-way street that separated East New York from Canarsie. What made this Chinese Restaurant unique was its parking lot, I showed the owner The Earl Wilson article, and he agreed to pay me a hundred dollars per mention of his restaurant. Two weeks later Earl Wilson ran a paragraph on the place. With the Column in hand, I rode my bike to collect one hundred dollars, which I and Mr. Ming agreed to. Instead of writing a check, he said he would give me a hundred dollars' worth of food. I couldn't argue with him because he suddenly forgot how to speak English, he wrote on a menu GIVE FREE FOOD UP TO ONE HUNDRED DOLLARS AND SIGNED HIS NAME. I was pissed, better food than nothing, every Sunday I would take my parents for dinner.

In May of 1957, I really screwed up by failing the Geometry Regents EXAM which I needed to graduate the next year. My Summer as a Concord TUMMLER was over, I spent the entire Summer preparing myself to retake the Regent exam. Every other weekend my father and I would drive up to Concord, this time I was a guest. The upside of the trips to the Catskills was that I had the opportunity to practice driving, at sixteen I received my learner's permit.

Just before graduation, in 1958 all members agreed to dissolve Regal House, many had girlfriends those that didn't were leaving the neighborhood to go out of town to college. Trying to get into a free City College I was rejected for I didn't have at least a B+ Average, at that stage in my life, I couldn't imagine living in any place other than New York. My alternative option was applying to NYU BUSINESS SCHOOL where tuition was around thirty-five dollars per credit. With my savings I could pay for at least 4 four Semesters, my parents agreed to pay for the rest.

On my 18th Birthday, I received my driver's license. I could only use the car when my father wasn't using it. Between my studies, working for Jaffe, and my accounts, I didn't have time to have a relationship. On weekends I would either hang out at Da Barber's or on the corner outside with older guys. Spring of 1959 My Bubba moved into my aunt's home in Laurelton Queens which was on the boundary line between Queens and Nassau County she still kept the apartment on Hinsdale Street as a security blanket, In the two-bedroom apartment, she had a Magnavox television record player combination unit with LPs the 40s late 40s, and early 50s that my aunt left when she got married.

My majors were Journalism and marketing, with a minor in Motion Picture and television production, I was lucky that NYU's Criteria for accepting students was the tuition, whereas the CITY COLLEGE OF NEW YORK was free. The subway ride from my home was about an hour door to door. As a freshman, we went through an orientation tour of the school, my class was 100% male. Half of the guys were going to college to appease their families so they could one day take over their Father's business. The other half were Veterans of The Korean War who returned in 1953 seeking a career, five years later they used the GI BILL to pay for their education. They were older than their classmates and motivated to achieve. On my first day, I needed to find the closest pay phone, every day I called Jaffe to tell him what time I finished School. I had two assignments delivering News Items to the Columnist and putting his clothes together, sometimes I would find suits missing pants. Jaffe had paying girlfriends always wearing his Burberry Raincoat, most of the time leaving without his pants either because he was in a hurry or just wanted to see if the girls brought back the pants possibly giving him a free blow job.

My father had eclectic clients, the Gaiety Burlesque which was on West 45th Street owned by AL Baker Jr whose family owned Burlesque Theatres on the Boardwalk in Atlantic City, The show consisted of erotic dancers who slowly shed their clothes until they got down to their G string underwear and pasties on their Nipple I was assigned to write bios on the Stars Stripper who was featured in the theatre for a month, I was allowed to go backstage as a member of the Publicity team. This month's show featured BUSTY RUSSELL who was five feet five inches and had a natural 50" Breasts growing up in Hagerstown Maryland. Entering her dingy dressing Room which smelled of Talcum Powder, I Introduced myself as a member of the Theatre PR team. I sat on a small stool while she was wiping the sweat off her body, she turned from the makeup mirror and faced me with her large breasts. Her act was wearing a see-through Lingerie with pastes covering her nipples and a sequin G string. During her dance routine, she covers herself in talcum powder. With one breath the talc exploded into a cloud which was enhanced by color lighting, she was two years older than me and a featured Star playing Burlesque houses across America. Finishing the interview she grabbed my hand "To tell you the truth my large breast hurt my back and I cannot sleep on my stomach. I figure I will do this act for another ten years and then go in for a breast reduction."

My father gave me a hundred dollars for doing the interview plus I used it as a project in my journalism class, and I received an A. The professor asked if the story was true, and I offered to give him an invitation to go to THE GAIETY any time he pleased. Walking around Greenwich Village I came across a men's shop called the Village Squire on West Eighth Street which featured men's clothes that I had never seen before. Entering the store, I was approached by two Gay Salesmen who I asked if the owner was around. Out of the store room, a very elegant man Introduced himself as Bill Miller the owner of the store and the designer of the clothes. He offered to show me the items he designed and showed me a scrapbook of news articles. What he designed was exciting, a White Wolf fur coat and a Harris Tweed Suit with an

Eisenhower jacket vest. Sports shirts made of vintage, men's Japanese kimonos. I told him that I would make him America's top men's fashion designer. He agreed to give me three hundred dollars a week for ninety days, after that five hundred dollars a week. This account was fascinating for I reflected on my time being a stock Clerk at SAM & Mack Haberdashers on Pitkin Avenue. All men's suits were either Black, Navy, or Brown all have structure and big shoulder pads. I learned why there were buttons on the sleeves, a tradition that went back to the late 19th Century when men would wipe their noses with the sleeves of their jackets.

As I worked with Bill, I discovered that he had a great mail-order business of Gay men across the Country who wanted to wear something different. Gay Americans were in the closet, only wearing their clothes at Special events. There was never a men's clothing designer, most of the top designers started designing women's clothes and then introduced their men's collections. With my relationship, I set up meetings with major Men's Clothes manufacturers who turned down the line saying American men were not ready to make a fashion statement they all wanted to be invisible. My relationship with Bill Miller lasted into the 80s until he died of a mysterious disease which later I realized was AIDS.

The New York Post was our bible for what single dances were going on in the City. It was difficult to sneak into all the dance venues at local clubs in Brooklyn to avoid paying admission at the door. Hotels in Manhattan were the easiest for they all had fire exits scattered around the Ballroom. On Saturday night wearing a suit and tie I would join the older guys who piled into two cars and went to Manhattan where Dances were being held with live orchestras featuring a male or female singer either at THE ASTOR

HOTEL, THE ROOSEVELT HOTEL, THE PENNSYLVANIA HOTEL which was directly across the street from Penn Station, NEW YORK Hotel. The older guys had it down pat as a military Operation with teams of four going up to the floor above the ballroom or the second floor and taking the stairs down, entering the ballroom through a fire exit. We were all on our own, the rule was that we would take the subway home. The girls ranged from twenty to thirty and most came as groups from the outer boroughs. Weaving our way through the crowd of couples dancing we searched for girls, most of the girls who weren't dancing either sat at tables or on chairs around the perimeter of the ballroom. Being a good dancer from my Summer at the Concord gave me a leg up on the competition. There sat a girl who was uneasy in this environment she had dark black hair about five feet six inches tall and she was tapping her feet to the music, I introduced myself and she agreed to dance. The Orchestra was playing a mix of Cha-Cha and Mambo interspersed with slow songs such as Frankie Avalon Venus, Paul Anka Lonely Boy, Bobby Darin Dream Lover, The Platters Smoke Gets in Your Eyes, or Connie Francis My Happiness. By the time the slow dances ended, we were a couple. We were on the floor the entire evening her name was Helen, and she lived in East Flatbush near where REGAL HOUSE had a club room. I offered to drive them home, I explained that we would have to take the subway to my Grand Mother's apartment to get to know each other better and she agreed to this plan, an hour later I opened the door to the apartment offering her a coke, We both went into the living room asking her if she liked Sinatra I put on his latest album "Only The Lonely" Excusing myself that I had to go to the bathroom I knew there was a strong possibility that before we left the apartment she would have to go. As I expected the tub was filled with roaches having their own Grand Prix, turning on the shower I killed them all. It would take Twenty-Four Hours before they were back racing. After dancing and making out we left the apartment, the Chevy was parked a couple of blocks away. By 2 am I was back in my apartment and my father was typing a Column copy.

Having access to an automobile after midnight on weekends was hampering my ability to be independent of older guys who owned cars. One Saturday night we were at the Pennsylvania hotel, and I met a cute Redhead Joanne who reminded me of Kathleen. She went along with the entire program, subway, making out, and driving her home, I left out one question before we went on this carnal journey, asking her where she lives. Leaving her in the lobby of my Bobba's apartment house I went to get the car. As I was heading for East Flatbush, I asked her what street she lived on. "You are going the wrong way, I live in Middle Village Queens" asking me to turn around and go to the Belt Parkway. I had no idea where Little Village Queens was located, sriving East on the Belt Parkway, Joanne was an ace in giving directions. About Forty-Five Minutes on the road I pulled up to a single-family home. She kissed me and gave me her telephone number, asking when she would see me again. The problem I had was how to get home, I was paying too much attention to driving. Luckily there was a 24-hour gas station open, I was told how to get to The Belt Parkway West. It was 3 am and as I turned the corner in search of a parking space my mother was standing in front of our apartment house. Seeing me she pointed her fist towards me which meant I was in deep shit. I was grounded from using the car for a month.

In the Summer of 1959, I returned to the CONCORD as a Tummler. The Summer was a repeat of my past Summers except for the opening of the 5,000-seat Imperial Ballroom, the lighting booth had all the new technology which took Larry a couple of weeks to learn. Philly's lineup Started on Memorial Day when he Booked the Movie Star Marlene Dietrich who at sixty launched her Cabaret act followed by Saturday Headliners, Paul Anka, Connie Francis, Bobby Darin, Sammy Davis Jr, Johnny Mathis, Buddy Hackett, Joey Bishop, Jackie Mason, Don Rickels Joey E Lewis Martin&Lewis, Allen&Rossi (Marty Allen would Marry Frenchie head of reservations at The Concord). I visited backstage and the entire crew was brow-beaten by Dietrich's staff. They were all refugees from Germany. She finally exited her dressing room wearing a shimmering silver gown that hugged her body. As Marty Beck played Falling In Love Again, Marlene took centre stage and received a standing ovation, the act ran ninety minutes with stories of her Hollywood experience interspersed with Songs.

I still wanted to do stand-up, One-liners didn't interest me, I wanted to create an act about the Cultural Changes of the 1950s with General Eisenhower a World War 11 hero as President unfortunately Republicans made it hard to be Funny. The Puritanical mindset of America needed to be topical but the mindset of Concord Guests was anything but topical. Talking about our Jewishness and how it sets us apart from the rest of America, which I couldn't relate to. Walking around the pool a cute girl in a one-piece bathing suit said hello don't you remember me? I could not say no. Faking it " You were on the girl's softball team" Taking off her Sunglasses, "I used to sit in the bleachers and watch the ballgame and scream every time you changed the scoreboard. I was rooting for my older sister who was a pitcher for the team that wore the Red Armbands." All I can remember was a chubby girl with Braces and bad skin, Moving a deck chair Next to her Chaise where a Penn State tote bag with the name tag Esther. Of course, I remember you Esther from Philadelphia, we started chatting and she told me she was a Sophomore at Penn State, and her older sister was about to give birth instead of spending a month my parent decided two weeks so we could be home when she gave birth"

After dinner, we met outside the Night Owl Lounge spending about an hour dancing. All this time she was sneezing, coughing, and sweating. We agreed that she should go up to her room and take aspirin, she had an adjoining room to her parents' Suite. Esther was nowhere to be seen. Skipping Lunch I called her room between coughing and sneezing she invited me up. Going into the kitchen I asked one of the Sous Chefs who was from St. Lucia for a cup of Chicken soup which was a twenty-four-hour Concord staple. Avoiding guest elevators, I took the staff elevator up to her floor, the door to her room was ajar, and there she was propped up with two pillows looking terrible. Handing her the chicken soup I sat at the foot of the bed, she was wearing a PENN STATE Sweatshirt. I had to be at the basketball courts at 2 pm with all the gear. After having her Chicken Soup, she looked at me and said "Let's make out." In the middle of making out the house phone rang her mother called asking her if she needed anything. At that moment I did not care that she had a runny nose, coughing or dripping from Sweat I just wanted to make out. I later found out that her parents called the hotel Doctor who diagnosed that she had a bad cold recommending that she stay in her room for the rest of her stay. The three days she was in her room I brought up Chicken Soup and we made out.

Not having to return to NYU until mid-September my parents allowed me to take the car to Brighton Beach which was at the Southern tip of Brooklyn. My favorite place was Bay One which was at the end of the Boardwalk separated by Jetty Barrier from Manhattan Beach an upscale neighborhood of Single-Family homes. The beach was filled with teenagers who were still working on their tans using Sun Reflectors which were the things used to get colour, without wasting time before returning to school. I was in search of my own Sandra Dee. Sitting on a blanket wearing a pair of shorts and a Madison High School tee shirt using a Sun Reflector was my Sandra Dee. Tall ash blonde hair with a pug nose small breasts and green eyes, we immediately hit it off. Her name was Marjorie Bacher and she had just graduated from James Madison High School where the girls lived in homes with finished Basements. I offered to drive her home, She lived in an apartment house on Ocean Avenue with an elevator considered an upscale neighbourhood. Somehow we connected, we spoke every day, and on weekends my father occasionally gave me the car otherwise we would meet in Manhattan. I skipped going to dances on weekends and spending time with her I feel comfortable. We just spoke constantly discussing music and movies. New Year's 1959 we met in Times Square for New Year's Eve. At 1 am 1960, we took the train back to Ocean Avenue kissing and foundling in the elevator as we wished each other a happy 1960. After three buses I arrived home at 3 am 1960.

DAIRY
MORRIS MEAT MARKET
בשר כשר
KOSHER
PROVISIONS

alamy
www.alamy.com

EBBETS FIELD

19
55
Dodgers

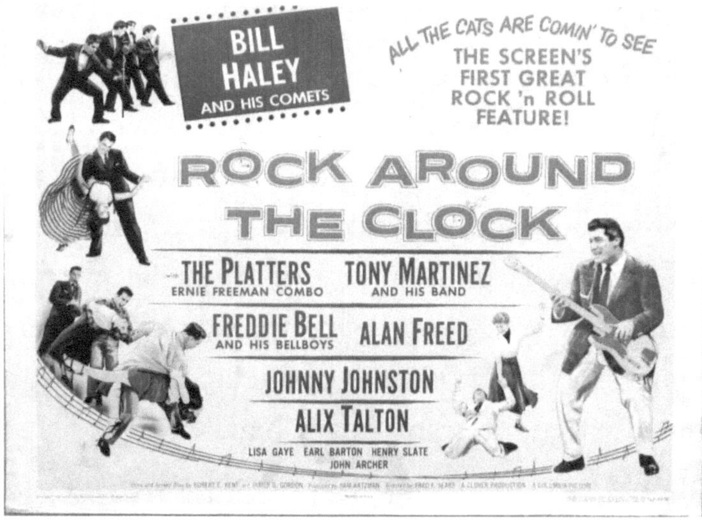
BILL HALEY
AND HIS COMETS
ALL THE CATS ARE COMIN' TO SEE
THE SCREEN'S FIRST GREAT ROCK 'n ROLL FEATURE!
ROCK AROUND THE CLOCK
THE PLATTERS
ERNIE FREEMAN COMBO
TONY MARTINEZ
AND HIS BAND
FREDDIE BELL
AND HIS BELLBOYS
ALAN FREED
JOHNNY JOHNSTON
ALIX TALTON
LISA GAYE EARL BARTON HENRY SLATE
JOHN ARCHER

DECADE TWO

Marjorie and I had a real connection, we spoke every night. On Fridays we would meet in Washington Square Park and share lunch, she started accompanying me to my classes none of the Professors suspected that she wasn't a registered student. I had a course in Public Relations, and I was listening to a Professor who didn't have hands-on experience. I would draft a feature for the fashion editor of the New York Times to do a piece on Bill Miller owner of the Village Squire. Listening partly to the lecture I decided to make myself believe that I was learning something, I needed an A to graduate in May 1962.

The Loeb Student Center just opened, and I no longer had to stay on the street to make calls. The booths with the pay phone were perfect, all I needed was a handful of Dimes, I was in business calling my press contacts. Marjorie would go and buy us lunch when the weather was bad. We agreed that we would go to my apartment and hang out, even though it was a dump compared to where she lived. Both my parents connected with her, my Mother treated her as the daughter she never had.

After dinner, we would close the door to my bedroom the smell of the ageing Salami permeated the room. For some unexplained reason when the hanging salami was finished, she would replace it with a fresh Salami. To her, it was a still life of being Jewish. We both got undressed and explored each other's bodies. She was a lousy kisser, I had to teach her the way Kathleen taught me, and she was given a midnight curfew. Week after week I would drive her home, kiss her goodnight and watch her enter the building lobby then drive off. A week before Memorial Day

1960 she told me that her parents would like me to join them for dinner with my father's approval I drove to Ocean Avenue which was a tree-lined street with buildings resembling 19th Century Village Castles with Turrets and Gargoyles decorating the exterior of the building Ringing the apartment in the lobby I took the elevator to the fourth floor. Knocking on the door my "Sandra Dee" wearing Bobby Sox a plaid skirt and a white blouse opened up and let me in. The entire apartment was decorated with traditional furniture. It was a three-bedroom apartment and sitting in the living room, her father Louie looked like Robert Taylor who starred with Vivian Leigh extended his hand welcoming me to their home. Sitting next to Louie was Pauline who was prematurely grey and her younger sister Wendy who looked as if she wasn't part of the family, Plump had black eyes with dark curly hair.

Throughout the meal, I found out that Louie was a Custom peddler and owned a black Chevy, and Pauline was a stay-at-home mom. As the evening wore on, I discovered that Pauline was from a Sephardic Jewish Family of seven sons and three girls whose roots were in Morocco. Louie's family were Ashkenazi Jews from Germany. It was unusual to see how Pauline's parents let her marry him. The custom had it that Sephardic Married Sephardic and lived on Ocean Parkway Brooklyn. Finally, Louie asked what my father did. It was a difficult question to answer, It took me twenty years to find out what my father does, I couldn't tell them that he handles strippers or that he gets up at three PM. Or he travels the country selling Souvenir programs. I finally told him that he owned a small advertising agency.

During dessert, I asked Louie about his business, leaning back in his chair he took out a piece of paper to describe what he does.

"I sell in areas where Poor People live in Bed Stuey, Brownsville, East New York. They live week to week on their Salary, they have desires to own things, and my company provides them with the opportunity. My Sales pitch is that what I am selling them is a little above wholesale always carrying inventory that I feel these customers want, upon purchasing the item I hand them a coupon book with what the monthly payment will be. Every time I go to collect the money I show them something new and different which they purchase, I am the only one who offers them credit" Taking a sip of Coffee a big smile comes on his face. "After four payments the cost of the product is paid for, and the rest is pure profit. I feel that what I do is a service to the community, helping poor people trying to live like Middle Class." I was about to discuss why exploiting poor people was a public service. Marge aware of my beliefs interrupted and said it was time to go. As I rose from the chair, she put her hand in mine whispering "Please ask them." Looking at her parents nervously "he wants to ask you something." "My parents told me to ask for permission if she could join us for the Memorial Day weekend at The Concord Hotel" After a few minutes they gave their approval. Walking to the car we kissed and planned to see each other during the week. Driving home I hoped that her father didn't have customers in my neighborhood or my building. The Memorial Day weekend was the most relaxing weekend I have ever had at Concord. I did not have to dance with ugly, needy teenagers. My parents reserved a two-bedroom suite where we could have our bedroom with privacy.

By the beginning of 1961, she began spending over the entire weekend. In 1962, my father invited me to join him in pitching for a new account, a private men's Russian Style steam bath which had eighty-four rooms Luxor Bath was built in 1925 on West 46th and predated health clubs. David Podolsky the owner agreed to meet us at 4 pm in the Steam room The attendant escorted us to the Men's locker room where we passed rooms with Masseuses working on clients and giving massages, another attendant opened two lockers handing us keys and two towels which we wrapped around our waist. Entering the pool area which had a 100% humidity.

Luxor Baths

Across the pool was the steam room, sauna, Water therapy where an attendant uses a high-pressure hose to massage your body, and Cold Plunge pool which is recommended after your Sauna. Entering the Stream Room my father asked for Fred Epstein who ran the place. "Sam Sit down" a voice echoed through the Steam, it had to be about one hundred and twenty degrees. Shaking a hand piercing through the steam my father introduced me to Fred. Let's get out of here so we can talk, with that we went from wet steam to dry heat in the Sauna. Laying across one of the ledges a man was being whipped with branches by an eighty-year-old man with a wet paper bag on his head, Fred outlined all of the services offered by LUXOR BATH to members. I was mesmerized by the old man beating a customer with twigs. Fred looked at me and explained that Platzer or in Russian Banya was a massage that used oak branches with the little man hitting your body finishing the massage by throwing a bucket of ice water over your head with the immigration of Russian Jews during the 20th Century treatment was supposed to increase circulation and blood flow.

LOBBY
SWIMMING POOL
A LUXURIOUS HOTEL ROOM
Luxor BATHS HOTEL
121 WEST 46th STREET
(East of Broadway)
TEL. BRYANT 9-3630
NEW YORK
GYMNASIUM
GARDEN SOLARIUM

Leaving the Sauna we passed a room where an attendant was placing heated glass cups on the back of a client's body which was an old-world remedy for removing the Toxins from his body. I remember my Zayda had a case of these cups in the closet.

Luxor Bath was a terrific client, I was the Cleanest Press agent in New York, and I would invite my male press contacts to join me for a Sauna and Massage. The Sauna was a great place to meet contacts. It was the only place where Mobsters, prosecutors, and Presidents of large companies were on equal footing, naked and out of shape. Local television news covered events that I created, doing features on the masseuses that worked in a 120-degree temperature beating customers with twigs.

Marjorie was a calming influence which helped in keeping my grades around a B Plus, I didn't have time to join any of the extracurricular activities. This was the time that student activists were going Down South to march with Doctor Martin Luther King, I was busy trying to pay for the remainder of my education servicing the needs of both The Village Squire and Luxor Baths. Girls like Marjorie had little motivation to have a career, all following in their Mother's footsteps of housewives, mothers and shoppers.

In 1961, the neighbourhood began to change, what used to be the Candy Store was a Bodega, and our next neighbours were from Puerto Rico, my family was one of the few Jews in the building, Many of the synagogues became Spanish Evangelist Church. During the Jewish New Year, we did not have to worry that we would be caught bringing in Groceries. On Thanksgiving one of the Bodega had a Turkey on a leash that I considered fresh meat.

January 1, 1962, after spending New Year's Eve we were taking the Subway home to my apartment when Marjorie began discussing marriage. I nodded in agreement at 21 years old I surmised that when you are a couple society expects you to be married. We weren't aware of the ramifications of getting married or having a family. We perceived it as fun and games forever. Neither one of us was aware that we didn't have real sex. I came and I doubted that she knew what an orgasm was.

Winter of 1962, we announced to our parents that we were getting married, deciding that the day was June Third which was Marge's Birthday. My parents never met her family, finally, a dinner was arranged in one of Brooklyn's legendary Sea Food restaurants Lundy in Sheep's Head Bay It was an unwritten law that the bride's family pay for everything except liquor. Over dinner, the money issues were worked out. The plan was to have a hundred and fifty couples, my parents were given a Quota of twenty-five couples My father agreed to pay for the Liquor and a Live Band. By dinner's end, neither family bonded, but they both achieved what they wanted. Wendy would finally get her room. Seeing Turkey on a leash helped my parents decide to move into a new one-bedroom apartment in a New Luxury high-rise on the sixteenth floor overlooking the Ocean in Brighton Beach. Their rent went from forty dollars a month to four hundred dollars a month which included parking. With me gone, they now had a living room. Her parents booked the Hotel St. George located in Brooklyn Heights, one of the city's largest Art Deco hotels with 2,600 rooms, an Olympic-sized swimming pool, and a Grand Ballroom.

The time we now spent together was discussing the wedding, none of us had enough friends to have Bridesmaids or ushers. Rather than being closer, we were drifting apart. One weekend we fought, and she scratched my face. With my face bleeding, my mother wanted to call off the marriage, I took the blame for the argument telling my parents that the scratches were superficial and would heal before the wedding. I avoided seeing her parents, telling anyone who asked that my cat did it. She called every day crying asking me to forgive her, she won't do it again. As I was sitting in the phone booth at the Loeb Student Center she appeared carrying lunch. We went to sit on a bench in Washington Square Park where she apologized, during our conversation, a black homeless person named George Washington Goldberg came by. The student body adopted him calling him GWG. We would spend time during our class breaks buying him lunch and discussing the current turmoil in the Country. GWG was a veteran of the Korean War Coming home with PTSD rejected by his family and the Veteran Administration he made his home in Washington Square Park when the weather was bad he would sleep under the Canopy of the NYU SCHOOL OF COMMERCE which became Stern Business School. Campus Security gave him a pass. Having resolved our issues, she apologized to my parents, using makeup to disguise my scratches when I was with her family, either they were blind or did not care never noticing the makeup on my face. Spending hours looking through Bridal Magazines she was in search of that perfect Wedding Dress, she and her mother went to Bay Ridge to Kleinfeld noted for being the place to go to find Wedding Dress. I was required to rent a formal Tuxedo with tails and a top hat. Realizing that I needed a thirty-six-inch waist I went on a Strick Sego Chocolate diet drink. I was constantly asking myself do I love her? When my friends from NYU were planning to travel after graduation, I was walking down the aisle my issue was did I want to get married.?

I had no one to talk to. My parents were self-absorbed in creating a new life for themselves, and never once asked me if I wanted to get married. A week before our marriage we went to get a blood test which was one of the requirements to get a marriage license in New York. With our Birth Certificates and the results of our blood test, we took the train to the Municipal Building located in Brooklyn's Borough Hall and were married by the County Clerk. This Civil wedding was a prelude to the real event of getting married by a Rabbi. We found a one-bedroom apartment in a new building on East Nineteenth Street off Kings Highway which was close to both our parents. Her parents brought us a bedroom set with a Mattress. The rent was three hundred dollars a month, which I knew I could cover from my current clients.

My mother had a special dress made to order for the wedding a Gold Lame dress with heels to match made of imported Italian fabric. My dad invited twenty couples who were business associates, I invited Bill Miller his boyfriend Da Barber and his wife, the owner of the Candy Store and his wife. The way the tables were set up her parents' friends and relatives were on one side of the Ballroom with my parent's friends on the opposite side of the Ballroom. The head table where the bride and groom sat was flanked by key members of each family. I introduced my Buba to her grandmother and assumed they spoke the same language, they both closely resembled each other, with overweight, grey hair and a frumpy dress. I assumed they both spoke the same language, Yiddish. As my bubba started to talk in Yiddish her grandmother looked at her and didn't understand a word. Pauline sensing that something was off spoke to her mother in Landino which was a language that Sephardic Jews who immigrated from North Africa, Turkey, Greece, and Israel spoke. My Grandmother was an Ashkenazi Jew who immigrated from, Russia only speaking Yiddish I introduced my grandmother who spoke little English as does Marjorie's Grandmother. As they said hello neither of them spoke to each other during the entire Wedding.

Throughout the entire evening, everyone gave envelopes with cash that filled both my pant pocket and Marge's small purse.

We had to end the wedding by Midnight otherwise my father had to pay each musician double overtime. We both decided to go to each table thanking everyone for attending. As we left the lights were blinking in the ballroom, and the band stopped playing. As part of the wedding package the Bridal Suite was complimentary for one night.

Finally, we were alone as Husband and wife as we scattered the gift envelopes on the bed there was a knock on the door both our parents were there to open the envelopes and make a list to send thank you notes to their guests. Separating the envelopes into two batches which indicated whose guest they were our parents were taking out either cash or checks which totaled three thousand dollars. We agreed to take five hundred dollars with us in cash with the rest being held by Louie for when we returned, we can open a joint bank account. Our parents left about two in the morning, the passion which was supposed to occur on your Wedding Night was not to be found, the only use of the Wedding Suite was to sleep.

Going to Miami Beach for our Honeymoon my father promoted a free room for a week at the Shelbourne Hotel. We booked a 4 pm flight with National Airlines leaving from La Guardia airport, and Louie agreed to take us to the airport. Neither of us has flown and National Airlines had a fleet of Boeing 707 jet passenger planes. The plane had smoking and nonsmoking sections, Marjorie's luggage was overweight, but she was ready with all contingencies. It was a four-hour trip. We arrived at Miami International Airport which was the hub for Pan American Airlines which flew Globally. Taking a taxi from MIA we arrived in front of the Art Deco Lobby of THE Shelbourne Hotel, from which I later found out that the same architect designed The Concord Hotel Morris Lapidus. My father got us an Ocean Front Suite. After Dinner we took a walk on Lincoln Road which was free of Traffic, we returned to our suite to consummate our marriage as we were about to embrace the sheet was wet with blood. Marge went into the bathroom and told me to find her Kotex. Rummaging through her luggage I couldn't find the Kotex. "Where is it?" I yelled. "Try my purse" she yelled from the bathroom, her purse was empty except for lipstick and a few dollars. "it's not there," I said through a crack in the bathroom door.

Robert Frank Grand Staircase Concord Hotel Catskills-1

"Please go down and buy me a box of Kotex." Putting on my shorts, I took the elevator down to the lobby, but the shop that sold sundries was closed. Telling the doorman what I needed, he recommended a 7-Eleven store on Lincoln Road. Miami was hot and humid, and I ran a few blocks up Lincoln Road, which was filled with tourists, finally entering the 7-Eleven and purchasing a box of Kotex. I made the entire round trip in fifteen minutes.

Entering the room, I was drenched in sweat. She was still in the bathroom, crying. After ten minutes, she came out in her pyjamas, thanked me, and went to bed. I was soaking wet from perspiration, so I showered and then went to bed. During her period, she had bad stomach aches and decided to stay in the room.

When I woke up in the morning, I couldn't breathe; I had been wheezing all night. I went down to the pool and the beach, thinking that the fresh air would help me. Finally, at dinner time, she felt better, and my wheezing subsided. The doorman recommended that we try Wolfie's, which was Miami's answer to a New York deli, for dinner. I called housekeeping, asking them to provide new pillows, vacuum the carpet, dust the drapes, and change the mattress. I thought there was something in the room I was allergic to.

During dinner, I was still having difficulty breathing. Any sensible person would have gone to Jackson Memorial ER. I was up all night, and in the morning, when my parents called to see how the trip was going, I told my mother that I thought I was having an asthma attack.

"When you were eight years old, you had whooping cough, followed by mild asthma attacks, which went away when I moved to Florida," my mother told me during our conversation. I didn't remember anything about those incidents. I asked the front desk to recommend a local doctor. The hotel had a relationship with a GP whose office was on Lincoln Road. Rather than having Marjorie join me, I decided to let her sleep. His name was Raphael Gomez, and his office was located above a bookstore. As soon as I walked in, his receptionist brought me into his office.

Listening to my chest and hearing my wheezing he asked me if anything traumatic happened to me before I arrived in Miami. Reviewing the past three days I told him that I had just gotten married and this was my Honeymoon. Scribbling on his prescription pad he told me that getting married was an emotional trigger that resulted in me getting an Asthma attack. He gave me a prescription for 15, and 25 Tofranil which was an anti-anxiety pill, and told me to start with one pill. Margie was up, wearing shorts and a Madison High School T-shirt. She asked me where I had gone. I told her that I had taken an early walk on the beach. I couldn't tell her that my asthma attack was caused by getting married; that would lead to a conversation I did not want to have.

After dinner, we were walking down Collins Avenue. A 1955 white Cadillac Eldorado pulled up alongside us. The driver leaned over and introduced himself as Carlos. Exiting the car with the engine running, he gave us a pamphlet promoting a new community on the west coast of Florida named Cape Coral, telling us that it was a great investment for young couples and a chance to drive across the Everglades, have a free lunch and a tour of the property. We looked over the brochures, and we both agreed to take the tour. Smiling, he wrote down our names, Mr and Mrs Gutwirth, promising to pick us up at 10 am in front of our hotel.

Cape Coral, Florida 1962

Yacht Club area south of Cape Coral Parkway – the first custom tailored homes were built in 1958. Source: Cape Coral Historical Museum

Putting in a call for 8:30 in the morning, the anti-anxiety pill was starting to work we still didn't have real sex. All the time we were in bed for the past two years we didn't have sex. Three days into our Honeymoon I thought it was time we should have real sex. Kissing me on the cheek she looked straight into my eyes "My Mother told me not to have sex during my period for it can create woman's problems. "We can wait until we are in our apartment and we are not going anywhere," as she rolled over on her side, I felt sticky, I took a shower and I jerked myself off.

At ten in the morning the White 1958 Eldorado Sedan pulled up in front of the hotel with another couple in the back seat. They were also newlyweds. Introducing himself as Stewart and his wife Barbera they were from Baltimore Maryland, staying at the Fontainebleau. As the Cadillac drove West, which I thought would be a short ride. Turning on US 41 with the radio blasting COUNTRY MUSIC, I asked him how long the ride to our destination was. Looking at me he said about two hours West. It was eighty degrees and muggy I put my hand on the Air Conditioner he told me not to bother it was not working, and we had no choice but to roll down the windows. With the hot wind blowing in our faces we decided to make the best of a bad situation. Stewart was about twenty-six having just graduated from John Hopkin's Medical School his wife Cathy was graduating from nursing school at the end of June. They said that they were moving to New York to do his internship at Bellevue Hospital in Manhattan at the beginning of July. Specializing in cardiology. He planned to work with his father a famous Cardiologist in Washington DC. His wife Barbara had a job lined up at Mount Sinai. The conversation came around to what we both do for a living. Now the conversation became a fantasy for neither of us knew what we wanted to do, looking at Marge she didn't know what to say. Looking at me she sat there frozen. Marge was starting to teach first grade in September, "I will be working with my father who owned a big advertising agency in Manhattan" reverting my eyes to the Landscape of the EVERGLADES.

About ninety minutes later he pulled into what appeared to be an empty restaurant with four Cessna 172 parked on a runway adjacent to the Restaurant sitting in the middle of the Everglades. Exiting the car, we were greeted by a group of men who looked like Mormon Missionaries handing lunch tickets and a promotional kit offering us an opportunity to own parcels of land in the next big Community on Florida's West Coast. The nearest town was forty-two miles away Naples Florida, a small town that became a Tourist destination until the early 70s when Interstate 75 made it easier for people from the Midwest to head South for Vacation. The room was filled with couples from Miami picked up on Collins Avenue in their early twenties. Entering the lobby there was a scale model of the prospective Community of Cape Coral sitting under a glass dome. The salesmen who greeted us pointed out the display, explaining that it was the architect's master plan for the Community. This was a choreographed sales pitch, escorting us into a large dining room with about forty young couples sitting around tables with packets in front of them. We were escorted to a table a slick film presenting a master plan of what Cape Coral would look like when the Community was finally developed. With the film presentation ending the lights came on, Out walked the head of sales who introduced himself as Orville Smith, just a simple guy from South Carolina. He was wearing a loud checkered Sports Jacket with a microphone in hand narrating a slide show, his voice sounding like a Carnival Barker outlining this unique opportunity to have your investment appreciated. The Rosen Brothers from Baltimore Maryland in 1957 purchased a hundred and three square miles of Swamp and Mangrove and Alligators for $678,000 Their new company was Gulf American (which they sold to General Acceptance Corporation for $150 million in stock) and created an interest-free payment plan to help you purchase home sites for only ten thousand dollars or three sites for twenty-four thousand dollars. This is an investment for your future, Pointing out that when they are in their mid-thirties their investments will be worth twenty times what they paid for. Everyone lined up for the buffet lunch, at the rear of the room was a table where people who were interested in taking an aerial view of the property signed a waiver. Gulf American was absolved if the plane crashed, and we all agreed to take a plane ride to survey the property. Walking up to the plane were attacked by the biggest

Mosquitoes I have ever seen. The Cessna pilot introduced himself as Yuchi an authentic Seminole Indian who learned how to fly by the end of World War 11. He guaranteed a safe flight telling us not to worry that Mosquitoes were a way of life when you live on the Gulf Coast. All four of us piled into the Cessna, Yuchi headed South flying over a Swamp with Mangroves sticking out of the water, he pointed out a few alligators and boa constrictors moving through the dark Water. It was a fifteen-minute flight touching down on the runway, Where we were ushered back into the Restaurant to a table where a sales agent wanted to close the deal. The pitch was that this was a great opportunity to create wealth for your family's future paying a monthly sum of two hundred dollars a month for ten years. As an investor of Cape Coral, your price of ten thousand dollars a home lot was locked in. We listened intently and I told him that I wanted to take the documents and discuss them with my family. Stuart was interested in his Father knew the Rosen Brothers from Baltimore and they were members of the same Country Club.

Exiting the Restaurant Carlos was leaning against the El Dorado. Returning to Miami on route 41, also known as the Tamiami Trail which cuts through the Everglades going close to a hundred miles an hour. Every fifteen minutes the sky would open pouring down torrential rain, I asked Carlos to turn on his Windshield Wipers, and looking at me he said "The Wipers like the Air Conditioning was broken. The rain was heavy, and we had to close the windows. The Windshield was fogging up and I had to take off my tee shirt to wipe the window. He told me not to worry he makes this journey six days a week. About 90 minutes later we crossed into Dade County where the speed limit was forty miles an hour with traffic lights. Arriving after 9 pm in front of the Shelbourne we exchanged telephone numbers with Stuart and his wife. Both of us had large Mosquito bites all over our body, luckily there was a drug store opened on Collins Avenue. The pharmacist recommended Calamine Lotion. Ordering two Hamburgers to go at Wolfie's we went back to our room and got undressed each one of us putting dabs of the pink lotion on each other's arms, necks back, and legs. We ate our burgers standing up so that our backs would dry. The next step was to allow the rest of our body to dry, meaning we lay nude on our backs in bed looking up at the ceiling. After fifteen minutes I had an erection turning over to my wife who still had her period just to cuddle she was fast asleep. Two days before we were to return from our Honeymoon we went to the beach together. The Ocean was always warm off Miami not like Brighton Beach where the water was freezing. Looking at her on the Chaise I wondered if this past week was an Omen of where the future of marriage was heading.

On our arrival on Sunday evening at La Guardia airport her parents and Sister Wendy were waiting to drive us to our new one-bedroom apartment six blocks from where her family lived. They had bought us everything we needed, a set of pots and pans dishes, glasses, silverware plus stocking the refrigerator with food. They also had a telephone installed, handing me an envelope of our Wedding gifts of cash and checks they invited us to dinner at Dubrow's which was a cafeteria on King's Highway. Everybody who came in got a ticket that the waiter would punch a hole in when you ordered food. Over dinner, they wanted to know everything about our Honeymoon, and we both created a fantasy of what a Honeymoon should have been. Returning to our apartment, I called my parents we both discussed our Fantasy Honeymoon. In 1962 I had three accounts including Bill Miller and a Chinese restaurant, Marge took a job as a receptionist at a local Dentist's office, and The film Cleopatra with Elizabeth Taylor and Richard Burton received Millions of Dollars worth of Publicity. It was expected to be a Box Office Blockbuster, my father told me to call his old boss Arthur Klar who owned the rights to create a souvenir program for Cleopatra. The next morning, we went to the Dime Savings Bank and opened a joint checking account. Calling Klar's office the receptionist asked how my Honeymoon was. She was a year too late. The entire office had known me since I was thirteen, putting me on hold, she returned and asked me if I could come to the office by 3 pm Since neither of us had a job, it was a struggle to pay the bills.

Klar's office was on the Northeast corner of 42nd Street and Broadway. His secretary Marci opened the door to Klar's office, Arthur was a legend in the printing and sales of Souvenir books for both Broadway and Block Buster films. He was about five feet eight inches tall with Glossy Black hair with a touch of Gray, all his suits and shirts were made to order. He said congratulations to us on our marriage. Handing me a picture book of 20th Century Fox's film Cleopatra a movie whose production cost was $31,000, 000 starring Elizabeth Taylor and Richard Burton which opened in New York on June 12, 1963. During the production of the film, the press covered them twenty-four-seven. Taylor and Burton had an ongoing romance during the production, they married in 1964, divorced in 1974 then remarried in 1975. Arthur sitting at his desk lit a Cigar "How would you like to go to Buffalo New York to sell Souvenir programs for the movie Cleopatra which is scheduled to open one week before July 4th? I will pay all your expenses plus give you One Dollar for every book sold, think about it" Looking at Marge she squeezed my hand to say yes. Taking out a wad of cash he handed me two one hundred Dollar bills to handle expenses. "I will send a thousand books directly to the Shea Theatre tell Marci to make all the travel arrangements starting June 26th," Marci called the Statler Hotel and reserved a room for us for one month. She recommended that we take a GREYHOUND BUS.

Leaving Klar's office I gave Marge a kiss saying that this would allow us to make enough money until I get a real job in the fall. Since the Greyhound Bus terminal was on West 33rd Street we walked over to get a bus schedule. The information clerk told us it takes eight to ten hours from New York City to Buffalo, arriving home Marge called her parents who weren't too pleased to hear that we were going out of town to earn money. We Called my parents to give them the news which my father knew for he discussed it with Klar. We both decided that we could shop for furniture when we came back from Buffalo. With enough money, until I got a real job, she also implied that she wanted to start a family.

Taking the ten-hour bus trip gave us a chance to see upstate New York except for the crying of a Baby for ten hours and the eventual smell of Urine from the onboard toilet, the trip wasn't that bad. Checking into the Statler Hotel which opened in 1923 whose décor was Art Nouveau we checked into a suite. Walking a few blocks, we entered the Shea Theatre which was the crown Jewel of Art Deco design with thirty-six hundred seats. Introducing ourselves to the manager of the theatre, he took us to a storage room piled high with fifty books of books, asking him for two tables to be placed in the Lobby. Unlike other movies, Cleopatra had two viewings a day in the industry it was called a hard ticket. The day that the film was opening we arrived at the theatre at 1 in the afternoon expecting to see lines outside the Shea. The film was to start at 2 pm there were only fifty people in the theatre, and we sold three books. As the days progressed the most people in the theatre was a hundred people per showing. We were selling anywhere between fifteen and twenty books a day. After the Fourth, I called Arthur to tell him we only sold a hundred books in total during the July Fourth weekend, he told me to give it another week to see if sales picked up. During our discussion, I told him that we needed more expense money to cover our meals. He told Marci to wire us a thousand dollars to cover expenses which we could pick up at Western Union. Every day I put on a suit shirt and tie, and Marge wore a Summer dress going, fifteen straight days we arrived at the theatre to sell twenty books per day at the price of three dollars a day. My Dad recommended that I sell the books for five dollars which made sense if the picture was a sellout. I decided to give Arthur a straight count for he was good to us. Our sales did not cover our expenses. Our dream of making enough money to take us through the Summer exploded in our faces.

Two days before we planned to leave, we took the two-hour Bus Ride to Niagara Falls telling Marge that this was our second Honeymoon, hopefully rekindling our passion for each other. It seemed that the worst thing we did was get married. A day before we left I put Arthur on the phone with the Manager of The Shea who he told to keep the books having a member of his staff sell them at three dollars with a sixty-cent Commission on each book that was sold. Arthur was friends of the Regional Sales Rep for Fox who will do inventory and handle the money. Returning to the apartment we have not lived in.

July August of 1963 we were inseparable. Our goal was to keep our expenses down and live on our Wedding gifts until the Fall. Luxor Baths paid me three hundred dollars a week and not a week passed without a mention in one of the major gossip columns in the three major New York Newspapers. My whole world changed in mid-September 1963 Marge told me she was pregnant and neither of us had health Benefits. I must now get a real job, I was reading the employment section of the New York Times sending out a resume where I had ten years' experience in Public Relations, with zero replies. Then I realized that the best place to find a job was in the Steam Room of Luxor Baths. All the regulars knew me, Among the regulars were Barney Balaban President of Paramount Pictures, and William Zeckdorf a major Multi-Family developer (his heirs are currently Luxury Highrise developers in Manhattan.) Judges, Lawyers, and Mobsters filled out the ranks of Habituate Luxor members who come at least four days a week. Mr. Balaban always told me to join him in his office for lunch, as we were both dressing, I asked him if he had time to meet me out of the Baths. Handing me his business card "Come up at 1 pm tomorrow, my office is across the street in the Paramount Building"

Having kept every piece of publicity that I created for clients in a scrapbook, dressing in a suit and tie with shined shoes I took the express train which stopped at 42nd Street across from the Paramount Building. Taking the elevator up to the 33rd floor. Exiting the elevator I entered a Rich Mahogany office decorated with posters of Paramount pictures greeted by a receptionist who asked me if I was Mr. Gutwirth. Nodding yes, she picked up the phone to announce that I had arrived. Within minutes a woman entered the room introducing herself as Gertude, Mr Balaban's Secretary walking down a long hallway where pictures of Paramount Studio contract actors adorn the walls. Gertrude opened double Mahogany Doors, the office was large overlooking Times Square. Barney motioned to me to sit down as he was having a heated discussion concerning the release of Elvis Presley's Fun in Acapulco which was now in Postproduction and scheduled for release that coming November. Hanging up the phone he picked up a cigar that was dripping ash on the Carpet. "I assume that any Jewish kid likes delicatessen Gertude ordered a Corn Beef and Pastrami on Rye, and two Doctor Brown Cream Sodas from the Stage.

While waiting for lunch, I gave him an overview of my talents which included taking film as a minor at NYU and working for Eddie Jaffe who Barney knew due to Eddie's relationship with John Wayne. How my wife is pregnant with our first child. He had a conference table. Gertrude entered with the sandwiches on real dishes placing them on the table. Over lunch he told me about growing up in Chicago, he and his brother-in-law Sam Katz introducing air conditioning and retrofitting movie houses with a balcony. Owning and operating 125 movie theatres in the Mid-West. In 1926 Famous Players-Lasky Corporation bought a controlling interest in the chain which later became part of United Paramount theatres. Once they went into production in 1948 the Federal Government made them divest their theatre holdings thereby Creating Paramount Studios. Looking at his watch he told me to meet him at 5 pm in the Sauna "Please call me Barney." He said before leaving.

The owners of Luxor gave me a desk with a phone and a typewriter in the Book Keeper's office which I used to pitch stories for both Luxor and The Village Squire. Entering the locker room I was greeted by Ricardo who was a Locker Room Attendant from the Dominican Republic who I figured made fifty to one hundred dollars a day in tips. Besides handing you towels he would shine your shoes or run next door to a Dry Cleaner to have your suit pressed. I had my locker this time. I was extra careful about folding my suit and placing the jacket on a hanger. Making sure that my towel was secure I entered the pool area and Barney was seated on a chaise lounge next to the Sauna drinking water, exiting the Sauna Barney called over a very Hairy man with a large Moustach wrapped in a towel asking him to joy us. They shook hands and Mr. Barney suggested that I bring over a pitcher of ice water which was located at the end of the pool. Returning with the pitcher of Ice water Barney asked me to sit down, after drinking the ice water he said calmly "Phil this is the kid I told you about. He set up the Life Magazine feature, and Eddie Jaffe has him running around to the major Gossip Columnist. Allen meet Phil Gerard of Universal Pictures." I practiced my elevator pitch, but never thought I would be doing it Naked with a Towel around my waist. Phil called over one of the Masseuse asking for a piece of paper and a pen, after writing his information on it he handed it to me. As he walked back to the Sauna he turned "Call my secretary tomorrow morning her name is Janet, tell her to put you on my schedule after lunch" I was proud of myself for the press and television exposure. LUXOR BATHS gave me the credentials I needed so that Barney

Balaban could recommend me for a job. Rather than travelling and having many girlfriends like my friends did, I opted for responsibility. Now I had to earn a living to support a wife with very little skills in earning a living, six weeks pregnant with morning sickness and a haemorrhaging bank account. Entering the apartment, I gave her an update regarding an opportunity for a job interview the following day. At 10 am, I gave Janet a call, telling her that Mr Gerard told me to tell her that she should set up a time after lunch when we could meet. Putting me on hold for a few seconds, she returned, asking, "If three this afternoon at 445 Park Avenue on the eighth floor works for you?" All I could say was, "Thank you." Looking over my wardrobe of one black mohair suit that Nipsy Russell gave me as a gift from the dry cleaner on 125th Street in Harlem, I found that the suit I wore for my Bar Mitzvah fit perfectly.

Arriving at 445 Park, I exited the elevator on the eighth floor into an Art Deco reception room, the walls were adorned with framed posters of Universal's current films in release. I was greeted by a lovely blonde receptionist, to whom I said I had an appointment with Mr Gerard. Within moments, Janet came out and escorted me into Phil Gerard's office, the windows faced 57th Street and Park Avenue. He had a large mahogany desk, two leather chairs facing the desk, and bookshelves filled with scripts and books about movies. He gestured towards me to sit down as he puffed away on a cigar, the conversation was a reiteration of the pitch I gave him when I was in a towel. We then discussed Eddie Jaffe, whom he knew, and my father, who was Eddie's partner. He was fascinated by my backstory and how I grew up in show business. Picking up the phone, he dialled an extension, He then told me he had someone he wanted me to meet. Shaking my hand, he told me to call him Phil. Hitting the intercom, he told Janet to escort me to Jerry's office. I walked through a corridor lined with framed pictures of stars who were part of the Universal Pictures Studio system. The key executives had offices facing Park Avenue. Opposite, a room was filled with members of staff assigned to each executive. At the end of the corridor was an office with the same configuration as Phil Gerard's, but facing Park Avenue and 56th Street. His secretary, Marci, escorted me into the office of Jerry Evans, VP of Marketing.

Entering, we immediately clicked. He had a cherubic face and was balding. We spent an hour chatting. At the end of the meeting, he offered me a position working for him, paying $13,000 a year plus an expense account, and wanted me to start the following Monday.

We celebrated by having a noisy dinner at Dubrow's, the cafeteria across the way from Modernage Furniture. We both felt secure enough to furnish the entire house for under a thousand dollars.

Over the weekend, I developed my vision of how to market a film, on the premise that the film should be marketed in various venues other than the entertainment pages of local print and electronic media. Before 1963, awareness of a movie was through publicity, mainly print and radio. My goal was to search through films, looking for branded products used by the cast. My goal was to create merchandising tie-ins with major companies whose products were placed in the film, dealing with their advertising agencies, corporate VPs, and major department stores (Macy's,

Bloomingdale's, JC Penney, Sears). This would translate into grassroots marketing, where local theatre managers could use the model that I Developed for their market, it was a 360-degree marketing plan. On Monday morning, after filling out some HR questions, I was told that I had to be a member of IATSE, a union that you had to join if you worked for a major Hollywood studio nearby. After all the paperwork, I was escorted into Jerry Evans's office where I made an hour-long presentation outlining my vision for the position. He listened intently, finally explaining that he was a Professor of Marketing for the Bernard Baruch School of Business, part of the City College System of New York, working three nights a week on campus. Jerry placed his pipe on an ashtray and walked towards the door. "Great presentation," he said. "You have my backing to do whatever you have to do to make it happen. My door is always open to talk, and Marci will make sure you get what you need. Now, let me introduce you to the staff." He led me into an open-plan office, called the bullpen, to a desk against the wall with a hanging corkboard. There, he introduced me to the team that worked for Paul Cami, VP of Publicity. Before lunch, I walked through the floor, introducing myself to executives who had windowed offices facing Park Avenue, realising I was the youngest person at Universal Pictures New York.

The entire fourth quarter of 1963 was spent in our fifth-floor screening rooms evaluating the products that were featured in the films to be released in 1964. Jerry Evans was more than a boss; he became my mentor. The week I started, Alfred Hitchcock's The Birds was about to open, starring Tippi Hedren, who was supposed to be the new Grace Kelly. Being part of the team that handled the press event at the Plaza Hotel, I witnessed Hitchcock surprising the audience with his disdain for actors, who, in his eyes, he considered mere props. Part of my portfolio was hiring models who would participate in window-dressing events that I created to promote a film. Placing a blurb in Showbusiness, a local paper dedicated to casting talent, would generate about fifty desiring actresses who needed a job to survive. Every day, I would interview them in the conference room. I was looking for both beauty and brains, offering them two hundred dollars a day. After a while, I viewed them as eight-by-ten glossy photographs. The idea of having sex with any one of them was a thought I never had. This was fifty years before the MeToo movement. Many of the girls had crummy photos, asking me for a reference to a photographer who wasn't expensive. I recommended Jerry Krutman, a friend of my father who had a studio on the West Side of Manhattan, hoping he could save them money. A few weeks later, one of the girls called to thank me for introducing her to such a talented photographer. I must have received twenty calls from girls with the same sentiment. Jerry finally called me to thank me for helping his sex life. It seemed that every girl I sent him went to bed with him instead of paying for their eight-by-ten composite photo. Jerry invited me to be part of the planning of openings for major film premieres. In the sixties, I could offer screen trailers, which were shown in theatres to promote coming attractions and to insert national promotional tie-ins backed up by lobby one-sheets (posters). I became the king of freebies. From soundtracks to bottles of Heinz Ketchup, items were sent directly to a list of movie critics across the country. My goal was to make every theatre manager a marketer, creating a to-do list for managers. Part of my responsibility was to hire pretty girls for promotional activities. I used Show Business, a weekly newspaper catering to aspiring actors and actresses, creating blurbs seeking models and actresses for major film studio promotional activities. This resulted in the mailroom delivering fifty envelopes of 8x10 glossy photos.

Starting my review, I selected candidates who had previously worked and finished their schooling. I arranged ten interviews a day in the corporate conference room. My criteria was brains over beauty, as they were representing the film. I offered them two hundred dollars a day plus lunch. Since I was looking for intelligence, many girls had terrible headshots. They asked if I knew any affordable photographers. My father introduced me to Jerry Krutman, whose studio was on West 53rd Street.

A few weeks later, one of the girls called to thank me for introducing her to Jerry, saying he was a nice man. By the end of two weeks, I received calls from twenty different girls with the same thank you. Jerry finally called me for lunch, something he never did, meeting at a local Italian restaurant. He thanked me for helping his sex life; it seemed the girls I sent would rather have sex than pay for the photos. I later discovered that the girls I sent, Jerry introduced me to friends who were agents and managers. Inadvertently, I was responsible for ten guys having sex with the girls I sent to be photographed. In 1964, I was the only person in New York who didn't have sex with the girls I interviewed.

We were releasing films. Universal was turning out marginal films mixed with box office successes. The two main theatres were the Palace Theatre on Broadway and Radio City Music Hall. Cary Grant's upcoming film, Father Goose, had its premiere at Radio City. When the film went into general release, each of us was assigned theatres to call at the end of opening day to get the gross numbers from theatre managers and send them to the sales office. They calculated the opening day gross figures, which were immediately incorporated into a press release to send by hand to Variety, New York newspapers, and wire services, announcing the opening weekend figures.

My life at home was a retelling of my day's activities, minus the girls' part. Marge knew how to cook basic things. She was going through a terrible pregnancy. At weekends, we would spend time with either her parents or mine. She was annoyed that I didn't call her four times a day; she couldn't agree with the idea that I was immersed in my work. I was working eight to ten hours a day; by union regulation, any time after eight hours was called 'Golden Time', which was double pay if you broke down your annual salary into an hourly rate.

Universal had a contractual agreement with Ross Hunter, who produced what was called 'four handkerchief movies': luxury lifestyle films catering to women. Ross's favourite actors were Lana Turner, Rock Hudson, and Susan Hayward, predating Dynasty, which ran on ABC from 1981-1989.

On 3 May 1964, Margie's waters broke. I was now a father of a little girl. We had to name her. Forgoing the naming tradition of the Jewish religion, we named her Julie after Julie Andrews, using the name of my grandfather, Abraham, giving her the middle name Ann. This delicate naming issue was done with Marge holding Julie Ann. Both sets of grandparents were viewing the baby because it was their first grandchild. My father handed me a hundred dollars to purchase a baby carriage. Two days later, we arrived home.

Opening the door to our apartment, we were greeted by her parents and a Jamaican nurse, who had been hired by her parents for a week. In the living room, a crib had been set up as a gift from her parents. The plan was for the baby nurse to sleep on the couch. We soon discovered that having a baby was a big task. In 1964, the only diapers available were cloth diapers from a diaper service, picked up once a week, leaving fresh diapers. We put the soiled diapers outside our doorway in a bag with baking soda, which neutralised the smell. Then there was the job of feeding the baby Marge. She wasn't breastfed; the hospital gave us a sample of Similac. That afternoon, with a shopping list, I went to purchase glass baby bottles, nipples, talcum powder formula, and a pot to sterilise the baby bottles.

Marge's mother, Pauline, was at our apartment every day to see the baby and take care of her daughter. With the premiere of Cary Grant's new film, Father Goose, opening at Radio City Music Hall, Jerry called me, asking if I could come to work. Pauline told me to go; she assured me Marge was in good hands. That Saturday morning, the cries of "Sweet Jesus, help me!" woke us up. We found the nurse carrying a baby who couldn't breathe. Within minutes of dialling zero, two police officers were at the door. One of the officers told us not to panic, taking the baby out of Marge's trembling hands. Calmly, he sat down on a chair, taking the baby, who was turning blue and gasping for breath. Placing her little body face down on his knee, gently holding her head, and tapping her back, within seconds a glob of food came out of her mouth. We sat at the back of the patrol car, with sirens blaring and lights flashing, going at forty miles an hour, we pulled into the ER of Coney Island Hospital. The officer who saved her handed the baby to a nurse, who told us to wait. Marge was hysterical; I was numb. The officer told us that he had five kids; he assured us she would be okay. An ER doctor and a nurse, carrying the baby, assured us that she would be okay, saying someone had given her solid food. Entering our apartment, we found the nurse packing her belongings, telling us she was quitting.

Now we learned how to be parents. We moved the crib into the bedroom, taking turns walking around with a crying baby. We were both sleep-deprived; my only relief was taking the subway to work in a semi-conscious state, counting how many times the doors opened until my stop.

With the opening of one of Ross Hunter's formulaic movies at the Palace Theatre, always featuring opulence in design and wardrobe, starring Sandra Dee and Maurice Chevalier, I created a promotion, giving away a box of Ritz Crackers, a fake silver spoon, and a bottle of champagne to the first hundred people. Working with one of the top furriers in New York, I had ten models walking on a runway, which ended in front of ten Rolls-Royce vehicles parked in front of the Palace Theatre. The Rolls that received the most press attention was the 1924 Silver Ghost, owned by Lord Montagu of Great Britain, an avid Rolls-Royce collector and founder Of Britain's National Motoring Museum, Montagu, a publicity hound, arrived in New York to launch his national tour of major Classic Car Shows across America, sponsored by Rolls Royce USA.

Milt Rackmil, CEO of Universal Pictures and co-founder of Decca Records, sent me a note saying, "Great job." To this day, any living veteran of the recording industry still talks about Decca's big mistake in not giving the Beatles a recording contract. Jerry now invited me to all planning meetings with sales, who handled distribution, and film producers who were visiting New York.

At home, Marge was a different woman from the girl I married. Her life revolved around her daughter, and she suddenly resented my parents visiting us, or us visiting them. In July of 1964, Julie started pulling herself up on the crib and began to crawl around. She had blonde hair and a cherubic face, always smiling and giggling. In mid-August, Marge told me that she was pregnant again; the doctor told her it would be a May baby. Realising that a one-bedroom apartment with two cribs was not workable, we both decided that we needed to buy a house. The criteria were an easy commute, near our parents, a good school district, and near the ocean. We had a choice of Seagate, which was west of Coney Island, and Manhattan Beach, east of Brighton Beach; both had an air of exclusivity, separated from the public beaches by fencing.

Our first choice was Manhattan Beach, where the streets were alphabetical. Taking my father's Chevy, we started with Pembroke, passing old ten or twenty-room mansions on tree-lined streets. The homes were guarded by six-foot-high shrubs and manicured lawns. Finally, driving up Amherst Street, there was an adobe-style stucco home with a "FOR SALE" sign on the lawn. The owner was outside trimming a huge, barren bush. Offering to give us a tour, his wife, a lady in her mid-sixties, escorted us, pointing out three bedrooms, a separate dining room, a living room, and an enclosed porch, with a full basement and enclosed garage. They were moving south, needing to close a deal as quickly as possible. Their asking price was thirty thousand dollars. Marge was excited and told them that we wanted the house. Before leaving, they promised that they would give us twenty-four hours. We both knew that we didn't have the down payment. Marge suggested that we visit her parents which we did. Handing me the baby, she disappeared with both her parents, returning with them. Her father said he would take care of the down payment.

The following day, her father picked us up, and we drove to Manhattan Beach. The entire family was escorted through the house. After a little chit-chat, Louie and the owners disappeared. Within ten minutes, they returned to congratulate us as the new owners of the home. He then suggested that we go to Lundy's, a famous seafood restaurant in Sheepshead Bay, to celebrate. He was proud of his negotiating prowess, announcing that he got the house for twenty-five thousand dollars, including the furniture. All I had to do was get a mortgage and move into the house on April 1st.

That Monday, I went to a screening of a film called The Ipcress File, which was due to be released in August of 1965, directed by Sidney Furie and introducing the British actor Michael Caine. Up until now, the film industry had never shown a leading man wearing glasses. From my point of view, the real star was the Insta-Brew, a new concept in brewing coffee. The marketing rollout was set for the summer of 1965. The office was filled with two Hundred boxes of Insta-Brew coffee makers which were sent to print media and movie critics across the country. These boxes were stored in the hallways. The studio was developing a screen trailer. To appease senior management, I gave each of them an Insta-Brew. Universal Sales picked up an animated film from Brussels, Pinocchio in Outer Space. This film gave me entrée into the toy industry, where I was able to give away rights to create Pinocchio in Outer Space toys and puzzles, which allowed me to work with major retailers. I worked closely with Arnold Stang, whose unique voice made him perfect for the animated character Nurtle the Turtle. Pinocchio was scheduled for a Christmas release. Working with Macy's, they agreed to give Pinocchio five store windows facing Broadway. Jerry gave me approval to create a Pinocchio float for Macy's traditional Thanksgiving Parade. I found myself on the Pinocchio float dressed as the Sly Fox, standing next to Arnold Stang dressed as Nurtle the Turtle, waving at the crowd.

During the summer of 1966, Jerry offered me an opportunity to showcase my marketing talents. For some reason, the studio greenlit a remake of the 1939 film Beau Geste, which had starred Gary Cooper, Ray Milland, Robert Preston, Brian Donlevy, and Susan Hayward. The 1966 version starred Guy Stockwell, Doug McClure, Leslie Nielsen, and Telly Savalas. I screened it before Christmas 1965, and, like many films, you ask yourself why the studio is wasting resources on terrible movies. One answer was that they had to fill the pipeline so that owners of movie theatres had products to sell to their customers. The adage is, "Every movie has an audience." The film would open in New York in September 1966, with a national rollout two weeks later. They wanted me to go to Detroit at the end of August, before the film's opening on 15 September 1966. The studio found two ex-Foreign Legionnaires who would meet me in Detroit to be spokespersons for the film. My job was to create a marketing and public relations campaign in key Michigan cities. Having already laid out the tour in my mind, all I had to do was tell my wife. Walking into the house, Julie was running around, and Marge was carrying Jamie to stop him from crying. She couldn't wait for me to take my coat off to hand me Jamie, who immediately stopped crying. Over dinner, I told Marjorie about the great opportunity that Jerry had given me, which was to handle the opening of a film in Detroit.

“That’s great; you’ll be gone for a few days,” she said, as we began dinner.

“It’s not a few days, but an entire month,” I answered between bites of my salad and rocking Jamie.

Marge began screaming, “I need your help.” Putting Jamie back in his crib, I explained to her that it meant more money, and she had her mother, her sister, and even my mother to help her.

With that, she said, “Never your mother.”

On 3rd May 1966, we had a family gathering celebrating Julie’s second birthday. Both sets of grandparents and Marge’s sister were there. Julie, who had begun to walk, was dressed like A Little Princess.

Every time we took her for a walk, she would scream, "Puppy! Puppy!" That afternoon, I went to a pet shop and bought her a white and brown spaniel. As they were singing 'Happy Birthday', I walked in with the puppy on a lead. She picked up the dog, and it licked her. I picked up Jamie, who would be one year old 14 days later; the puppy licked Jamie. Putting the dog back in its box, I told them we had to train the puppy. Julie was the first grandchild of both our parents. Every time my parents tried to cuddle her, Marge pulled her away. Both our parents had little in common; my father was a creative hustler.

A week later, I was on a flight to Detroit. Jerry’s secretary made all the arrangements, with two thousand dollars in my pocket to cover my expenses, which I was told would be backed up with receipts. If I needed more money, they would send it to me. It was recommended to have as many meals at the hotel as possible and sign for them. Arriving in Detroit, it was a wonderful autumn day.

The taxi pulled up to the front of the Sheraton Cadillac, which had twelve hundred rooms. Checking in, the bellhop opened the door to a one-bedroom suite. Each Legionnaire would be given a suite, which would arrive in ten days. This was a new adventure; at twenty-six years old, I had never travelled alone, always surrounded by people. After dinner at the hotel restaurant, I decided to explore what downtown Detroit was all about. Walking around the block of the hotel, I was stopped five times by girls driving Chevys, Fords, and Oldsmobiles, offering their services. No wonder they called it the Motor City! Hookers were in cars, in comparison to New York, where they were on corners and displayed their wares on Central Park South. Passing all the seedy bars, I found myself in front of an elegant restaurant, whose only inhabitants were the wait staff, bartender, and one lady at the bar. I ordered my Coke with no ice. I never did the bar scene until she mentioned joining her. After telling her I was from New York, working on marketing a film due to open in three weeks, she put her hand on mine and told me she had been stood up by a pilot who works for American Airlines, who sees her once a week, giving her five hundred dollars for her time. Explaining that she lives in Grosse Pointe, which is an upscale community ten miles away from downtown Detroit, having a great school district so she can send her daughter to a better school. The extra money helps pay her bills. About an hour later, she offered me a ride back to the hotel. Making it clear that I wasn't going to pay for sex, I invited her to join me for coffee. The valet opened the door as he drove her car; the number plate said, "Official Business, City of Detroit". Over coffee, she explained that she works in The Mayor's office and her work as an escort was needed to supplement her income.

During my stay in Detroit, she helped me obtain street permits for a Beau Geste premiere at the AMC theatre. She arranged for the Mayor to declare "Beau Geste Day," giving the Legionnaires a key to the city. She also helped me recruit models dressed as Legionnaires, creating a media tour of key cities in the Detroit metro area: Dearborn, Flint, Ann Arbor, Grand Rapids, and Lansing. She set up radio interviews and events at the local AMC Theatre. The final stop was Windsor, Ontario, which meant the Legionnaires had to show their passports at the border crossing between Canada and the USA.

There was word in the industry that MCA, a major talent agency, was negotiating to purchase Universal Pictures. MCA was the creation of Jules Stein, who, in his earlier life, was a trained ophthalmologist born in South Bend, Indiana. A talented musician, he played the violin and saxophone at weddings and bar mitzvahs. He soon discovered that he could make more money booking bands during Prohibition in Chicago speakeasies. He and two partners each contributed five thousand dollars to create the Music Corporation of America, which blossomed into a major force in the entertainment industry, representing stars like Bette Davis, Betty Grable, Joan Crawford, Frank Sinatra, and Jack Benny. Lou Wasserman started as an agent at MCA and later became CEO and Chairman of the Board. MCA introduced the concept of packaging talent for both film and television. If a studio wanted one of their stars, MCA, representing 60% of bankable talent, would put together a package of stars, writers, directors, and other talent from their roster. The concept of packaging brought in millions of dollars in commissions to MCA. Throughout the fifties and sixties, MCA acquired other talent agencies. When Wasserman made a play to purchase Decca Records, which owned Universal Pictures, the Department of Justice stepped in and charged MCA with creating a monopoly, ordering it to divest the talent agency, thereby granting permission for the Decca Records merger.

Early in March 1966, exiting the elevator, the once cheerful receptionist just nodded her head. Something was amiss; the once relaxed atmosphere had suddenly evaporated. There was an eerie silence, and everybody pretended to be working. I discovered that the DOJ had finally approved the merger of Decca Records and MCA. A tall, gaunt man in a blue suit was roaming the floor. In a whispered tone, Jerry's secretary told me that Lou Wasserman, the CEO of MCA, was on the floor, having meetings with the executive team, and I shouldn't bother Jerry that day.

Our new home was decorated in an eclectic style. The living room was contemporary, with the sectional sofa purchased for our previous apartment. For the rest of the house, we used the traditional mahogany furnishings that came with the house.

Whereas her father was a merchant with a steady income, both our mothers were from different worlds. My mother was a fashionista and a housekeeper. Pauline played cards and sewed. Her parents played Paddle Ball and were members of Brighton Beach Baths, an affordable private beach club. My parents' apartment overlooked the beach club, and my dad bought a telescope aimed at the women's showers. Fourteen days later, Marge's water broke at 3 pm. I had my father's Chevy parked on the driveway. I purchased a baby car seat and a baby carrier called a Snugli, which I placed in the boot. Marge picked up Julie, and I placed her in the car seat. I had called her obstetrician, who instructed us to go to the ER at Maimonides Hospital.

Marge gave birth at 10 pm to a boy. We now had to play the name game. A week before, we had gone to see The Greatest Story Ever Told; we always watched the credits to find a unique name. One of the actors was Jamie Farr. We both decided that Jamie was it; we now had to come up with a middle name. As the nurse brought in the baby, Marge remembered that her grandfather's name was Menahem. This was the first thing we agreed on since Julie's birth; her brother was Jamie Marc.

I now had the perfect family: a house, a lawn, a backyard, and two babies who were a year and fourteen days apart. Julie had her own room; we decided to put Jamie's cot in our bedroom. Jamie was always crying; we would take turns carrying him and checking on Julie. We learned that babies should sleep on their backs. That summer, Julie was able to sit up; we purchased a seat that was placed on the pram, which held Julie. Since we were a few blocks from the beach, we would wheel the pram to meet other couples who were letting their children run around on the sand. Marge was against getting a babysitter so that we could go out to a movie or dinner without the babies. By 1966, we were growing further apart. I was deeply involved in the release of Arabesque, starring Gregory

Peck and Sophia Loren, with a New York premiere on 5 May 1966. I was working with Icelandic Air, who wanted to promote their affordability to travellers looking for inexpensive fares to Europe. They bought the concept of screen trailers and lobby posters, which we agreed to cover in major cities. The promotion was a winner, increasing their bookings by forty per cent. As a courtesy, the head of Icelandic Air marketing gave me a special price on round-trip tickets to Paris. I had to take the trip in either early May or September. I planned to go from 4th to 11th May 1966; I was trying to recapture the romance we had before we married. In my mind, we would go to Paris, take a train to Rome, a bus to Florence, fly to Geneva, and take a train back to Paris and then back to New York. Over dinner, I discussed the trip, saying that we could leave Julie with her mother and Jamie with my mother. Marge insisted that we take Julie, who was only two years old; otherwise, she wouldn't go. No matter what I said, she wanted Julie to go. We met at the Passport Office, which was located in Rockefeller Center, applying for a family passport.

The romantic trip turned into a family disaster. Her father drove us to JFK. Now I had a pushchair, a bag of nappies, and Gerber Baby food for fourteen days, plus our luggage. Paying the added fee for overweight luggage. Boarding the plane, which allowed smoking in the rear. Our fellow passengers were young backpackers whose agenda was to visit as many European cities as possible, staying in the rough. During the eight-hour flight, we took turns holding Julie, changing her nappy over the Atlantic. We had a two-hour stopover at Shannon Airport in Ireland. Luckily, the stewardess kept the pushchair at the front of the plane. Exiting the plane, we discovered that the airport had a large duty-free shopping area.

Arriving in Paris, we took a train to Rome, where our pushchair broke down. It wasn't built for cobblestone streets. Instead of seeing the Trevi Fountain, I was in a car repair shop, explaining what I needed with hand gestures. The mechanic, in broken English, said he could fix it in ten minutes. Asking him how many Lira it would cost, he waved his hand, saying this was his gift to America.

I wanted to take a tour of Cinecitta Studios. Calling the Studio Head of Public Relations, he sent a car to pick us up for a tour, then invited us to dinner in his large apartment in the centre of Rome. The following morning, I hired a taxi driver to take us to all the tourist sites, finally dropping us off at Piazza San Pietro, the main plaza leading to Vatican City.

I needed to change dollars for Lira, but I didn't realise that all the shops closed at 1 pm and reopened at 3 pm. Arriving at the currency exchange, called 'Cambio', at five minutes to one, the clerk took my passport and two one-hundred-dollar bills and disappeared. A lady came from around the counter, motioned me to the exit, and told me to come back at three – all in Italian. Looking at my Frommer's travel guidebook, I discovered that all businesses in Italy closed from 1 pm to 3 pm.

Marge and Julie were in the centre of the plaza waiting for me. Marge, angry, told me she had been waiting for me for close to an hour. Trying to calm her down, I told her the story of the currency exchange. We had two hours to kill, so we found an outdoor café, ordered coffee and pastries, and ran after Julie, who had just started to walk. At 3 pm, Rome came to life. Returning to the exchange, the clerk handed me my passport and 125,000 Lira, which at that time was 625 Lira to one US dollar.

My friend from Cinecitta arranged a tour of the Vatican. The next day, we took the bus to Florence, where we stayed at a pensione for three days. We then bussed to Venice, used my Eurail pass to Geneva, and returned to Paris, then home to JFK. During this vacation, Julie slept between us; we never once had sex. This was the beginning of the end of our marriage.

Returning to JFK, Marge's parents were there to greet us with Jamie in their arms. Marge ignored the baby, pushing Julie towards the baggage claim. Lou handed me, Jamie. The car ride home was a recap of our entire trip; her parents had never left the United States. Jamie was starting to crawl; Julie was walking around, playing with her brother. Two days later, Jamie was a year old and began to walk.

Our next-door neighbour collected all our mail. Included with the bills was a letter from The Selective Service System, summoning me to 39 Whitehall Street for a physical. The United States needed more manpower to fight the war in Vietnam. The summons was one week after we arrived from Europe. Going through my papers in the attic, I found A letter from my neurologist at Jackson Memorial Hospital in Miami stating that I could not be exposed to any employment where there was the possibility of head trauma. The following Monday, I took the BMT, changing to the IRT, which would leave me a block away from 39 Whitehall Street, located at the very tip of Manhattan. The line of men, some with their mothers, others dressed as women, and one guy wearing winter clothes with snow boots on a 70-degree morning was quite a sight. Finally, inside, military men were taking the paperwork. Then they gave you an IQ test and a test that measured your ability to fix things. I went out of my way to try to fail all the tests. Like an assembly line, we went from doctor to doctor, where I showed my letter from Jackson Memorial. At the end of the line, they told me to sit on a bench outside the office of some Major who was a psychiatrist. After a few minutes, I was invited into his office where we had a brief discussion about my family and home life. He recommended that I seek out a psychiatrist as I had great anxiety issues, which prevented me from serving in the military. As I left his office, he stamped my application 4F, telling me to give it to the clerk. At that moment in time, I was apolitical about the Vietnam War, worried about how I could earn more money, and trying to save a marriage that was crumbling right in front of me.

Returning to work, I entered a different environment. What was relaxed was now an organisation that created fear of being fired. Jerry called me into his office for a short meeting. He was a gourmet and interested in wine. I purchased him a bottle of Latour La Mission Haut-Brion at the Duty-Free Shop at Orly.

Returning to work, Jerry scheduled two screenings. A new Ross Hunter musical, "Thoroughly Modern Millie", starring Julie Andrews, co-starring Mary Tyler Moore, Carole Channing, and John Gavin, with songs by Sammy Cahn and Jimmy Van Heusen and costumes by Jean Louis, was set for a March 1967 release. The film was laden with many opportunities for tie-ins. I arranged to tour Jean Louis's fashion, starting with a tie-in with Saks Fifth Avenue, which gave me their entire Fifth Avenue window. Decca

Records released the soundtrack, which gave me entrée to record stores across the country. The second film was a Universal Pictures distribution, "A Countess from Hong Kong", produced, written, and directed by film legend Charles Chaplin, starring Marlon Brando and Sophia Loren. The budget was three and a half million dollars. Rumours had it that one of the studio executives was setting up an interview with Life magazine, yelling across the soundstage, "Chuck, this is for you!" Chaplin thereafter barred anyone from Universal from entering the soundstage.

In July of 1966, Jerry asked me if I wanted to go to Detroit to handle the opening of "A Beau Geste", leaving on August 15th. I decided not to tell Marge until the end of July. Weekends were spent on Brighton Beach playing beach baseball. Jamie was starting to walk and talk. The first week of August, over dinner, I told Marge that I was asked to go to Detroit to open a movie. "That's great, you will be gone for a few days," she said, as we began dinner. "It's not a few days, but an entire month," I answered between bites of my salad and rocking Jamie. Marge began screaming, "I need your help!" Putting Jamie back in his crib, I explained to her that it meant more money and that she had her mother, her sister, and even my mother to help her. With that, she said, "Never your mother!"

A week later, I was on a flight to Detroit. Jerry's secretary made all the arrangements, with two thousand dollars in my pocket to cover my expenses, which I was told would be backed up with receipts. If I needed more money, they would send it to me. It was recommended to have as many meals at the hotel as possible and sign for them. Arriving in Detroit, it was a wonderful autumn day.

The taxi pulled up to the front of the Sheraton Cadillac, which had twelve hundred rooms. Checking in, the bellhop opened the door to a two-bedroom suite, which I was instructed to share with the Legionnaires who would arrive in ten days. This was a new adventure. At twenty-six years old, I had never travelled alone, always surrounded by people. After dinner at the hotel restaurant, I decided to explore what downtown Detroit was all about. Walking around the block of the hotel, I was stopped five times by girls driving Chevys, Fords, and Oldsmobiles, offering their services. No wonder they called it the Motor City! Hookers were in cars, in comparison to New York where they were on corners, displaying their wares on Central Park South. Passing all the seedy bars, I found myself in front of an elegant restaurant whose only inhabitants were the wait staff, bartender, and one lady at the bar. I ordered my Coke with no ice. I never did the bar scene. She invited me to join her. After telling her I was from New York, working on marketing a film which was due to open in three weeks, she introduced herself as Betty. She put her hand on mine and told me she had been stood up by a pilot who works for American Airlines, a steady date who saw her once a week, giving her five hundred dollars for her time. She explained that she lived in Grosse Pointe, an upscale community ten miles away from Downtown Detroit, which had a great school district so she could send her daughter to a better school. The extra money helped pay her bills. About an hour later, she offered me a ride back to the hotel. Making it clear that I wasn't going to pay for sex, I invited her to join me for coffee. The hotel valet opened the door as he drove her car; the number plate read "Official Business, City of Detroit". Over coffee, she explained that she worked for the mayor's office, and her being an escort was needed to supplement her income.

During my stay in Detroit, she helped me get street permits for a Beau Geste premiere at the AMC theatre. She had the mayor declare "Beau Geste Day", giving the Legionnaires a key to the city. She also helped me recruit models dressed as Legionnaires, creating a media tour of key cities in the Detroit metro area: Dearborn, Flint, Ann Arbor, Grand Rapids, and Lansing. She set up radio interviews at the local AMC theatre. The final stop would be Windsor, Ontario. Jerry called me to give me a heads-up that the Legionnaires would be arriving from LA that coming Monday, and I should hire a limo to pick them up.

I created a great relationship with a guy who owned the limo, always parked outside the Cadillac. On Monday morning, I went to the airport with a description to look out for two tall guys coming from LA. Waiting at the gate, out came two six-foot-tall men wearing Legionnaire uniforms with chests full of medals. Introducing myself, they replied in heavy German accents and introduced themselves as Gustave and Konrad. I was expecting French names, as the Foreign Legion was part of the French military. Over dinner, I briefed them on their press schedule, which started at 10 am the next day.

At nine in the morning, they showed up for breakfast in perfectly pressed uniforms and shoes that had a mirror polish. Each morning, we went to a different city in the Detroit metro area for radio and press interviews. As we drove back and forth from each city, I learned that they were in the Wehrmacht, part of a division taken captive during the Normandy invasion, escaping from a POW camp and joining the French Foreign Legion across the Mediterranean in Sidi-Bel-Abbes in Algeria. They were billed as consultants on the movie. Spending two weeks with them, they never realised that I was Jewish. On the final leg of the promotional tour, we crossed into Windsor, Ontario. As they showed their passports, I discovered that they were Canadian citizens and had lived in Montreal since 1958. In the back of my mind, I was wondering whether they were really who they said they were. I was on the telephone every night, talking to Marge and the kids. She started insinuating that I was unfaithful; to the contrary, I wasn't. After the first week, they asked me if I knew any women who could be their escorts for dinner.

That morning, I called Jerry, who told me he would wire me a thousand dollars and put it down on my expense account as dinner and entertainment. I didn't want to hire the girls in cars; it was too dangerous. That morning, I called Betty, my City Hall contact, inviting her and a friend for dinner at Carl's Chophouse. She was only too happy to help me if she could arrange for a babysitter. Carl's was a legendary steak house founded in 1923. Making a reservation for six, I told the maître d' who we were. Betty called back to tell me that she and a friend, Joann, would meet us for dinner; the cost was two hundred dollars for each of them. It was within my budget. That evening, Gustave and Kurt exited the lift dressed in their uniforms. I wondered if they had other clothes. During my stay, I became friendly with Gregory of hotel security; he worked the midnight to eight am shift. Handing him a twenty-dollar bill, I asked him to look the other way when Gustave and Kurt returned with their dates.

Betty arrived with her friend. Greeting her, I placed four one-hundred-dollar bills in her hand. Betty introduced her friend, a gorgeous blonde named Eleanor. Gustave and Kurt rose from their seats, clicking their heels and then kissing the hands of both women. It was my job to be a host, and I succeeded in my goal to give the two Germans a good time. Ordering two more bottles of wine, I excused myself, saying that I had work to do. Taking care of the bill, I gave the waiter a five-hundred-dollar bill, asking for a receipt. On the limo ride back to the hotel, I realised that I missed my children.

That morning, we were scheduled for a personal appearance at Hudson's Department Store. All four of them were waiting for me before ordering breakfast. The girls were clinging to them. If I didn't know better, I would say they had both found their soulmates. Gustave announced that the girls would be on their dates at the premiere of the film. I was afraid that both of them didn't realise that the girls were pay-to-play. Asking the girls to excuse us, saying that I had to review the Hudson appearance with them, I led both men to the lobby. I told them that I could not arrange another evening with the girls. Gustave told me that the girls said they were in love with both of them, telling them how great they were in bed. Gustave and Kurt thanked me for helping them in finding their soulmates, assuring me that they would take care of any additional expenses.

During my entire trip, I was working with AMC's local theatre managers, creating a template to promote the film. Two weeks before the opening of the movie, radio and print advertising began. I arranged for WKMH AM to run a free ticket giveaway for the premiere. On the night of the premiere, I ordered a red carpet and a pair of Klieg lights, replicating a Hollywood premiere. Hiring a crew to set up a sound system and a stage draped in the tricolours of France, where Rockin' Robin Seymour, the local top DJ from WKMH AM, would conduct interviews, I also worked with a local high school, giving away a hundred tickets to the premiere. I arranged to meet the students at the back door of the theatre, leading them onto the stage where there was pizza and Coke. I briefed them on how to react when guests arrived. Ten models dressed as legionnaires were used for crowd control. At 8 pm, the stretch limo pulled up to the theatre. One of the legionnaires opened the limo door as the French national anthem, 'La Marseillaise', boomed over the loudspeakers. Exiting the limo, Gustave and Kurt, accompanied by the girls I had hired the night before, were dressed in gowns with costume jewellery, draped in fox and mink stoles. Hidden from view were price tags. All of the evening television news stations covered the event. DJ Robin Seymour interviewed both Gustave and Kurt, who talked about the film shooting in Algeria and their adventures as legionnaires. Aware that Mayor Cavanagh was about to arrive, I took Betty and her friend off the stage to stand on the side until the interview and introductions were over. Mayor Cavanagh, who was a great showman, spoke about his days in France at the end of World War II, respecting the members of the Foreign Legion as great patriots.

There was a barrage of flashbulbs. Bulbs flashed from news photographers covering the event, Cavanagh flanked by Gustave and Kurt. The premiere was a success, but the film critics of both The Detroit Free Press and The Detroit Tribune panned the movie.

That evening, I called all the AMC theatres to get their opening night figures, and I phoned a telephone number that recorded box office gross for opening night. At the end of its national distribution, the film earned around three and a half million dollars and cost two and a half million to produce.

In January 1967, Ross Hunter, the producer of Millie, told us that Julie Andrews wouldn't be attending the premiere; she had a prior commitment. I came up with an idea: let's find as many Julie Andrews look-alikes as possible to use to launch the Saks Fifth Avenue promotion. Working with Show Business, a newspaper that lists casting calls from advertising agencies, film, and Broadway shows, we had a front-page announcement with a picture of Julie Andrews and the headline, "Do you look like Julie?" We held an open call two weeks before the premiere at the Drake Hotel. On the morning of the open call, we had fifty Julie Andrews look-alikes. Hiring ten girls, whom we outfitted like flappers, I contacted a vintage car collector who owned a 1920 Rolls Royce Phantom and a 1920 Packard Touring Car. He provided two chauffeurs. Working with the Saks public relations people, we arranged for Millie's "drive-up" to Saks to unveil the windows. Saks also arranged for loudspeakers to play the Millie opening number. The event was scheduled for Wednesday, 8 March 1967, at noon. Saks alerted the local precinct.

Exactly at noon, the two Packards arrived in front of Saks with ten flappers in 1920s garb, and the movie theme blaring from speakers. All New York media was alerted, guaranteeing us full coverage in the metro market. I was also working with MCA Records, who were releasing the soundtrack. Both lyricist and composer lived in New York. Sammy Cahn had a New York apartment on East 55th Street, and his composing partner, Jimmy Van Heusen, lived on 57th Street and Seventh Avenue. Sammy was a real showman; he had a Steinway in his living room, surrounded by Oscars and framed pictures of the musical composers he collaborated with. During an interview, the reporter asked him what came first, the lyrics or the music. Sammy paused and said, "The phone call." He went for the Sam Goody promotion. Goody guaranteed Thoroughly Modern Millie windows in all stores. Sammy agreed to make a personal appearance, and Goody provided the Steinway. Being the showman he was, Sammy spent two hours playing the songs he wrote.

The week before, I invited her to join me at the premiere. She told me to take my girlfriend. We had been married for five years, and her mind was set that I was having an affair. She refused to go to couples counselling, which was affecting the kids.

Five days before the premiere, I split my day between the office and working with the team at the Rainbow Room, creating a speakeasy flapper party. We hired a five-piece jazz band with both a male and female vocalist, singing the hit songs of 1922, like "My Man", "April Showers", "Toot Toot Tootsie", "I'll Build a Stairway to Paradise", "Second Hand Rose", "Do it Again", and "Sheik of Araby". All the secretaries from the office were assembling swag bags, which included a split of champagne, the Thoroughly Modern Millie album, and a Tester of Chanel No. 22 for women, Hollister cologne of California for men.

Jerry ordered ten tuxedos for the team working on the premiere, and he also reserved ten rooms at the Drake Hotel. The morning of the 21st, as I was packing an overnight bag, and as I was exiting the house, Marge shouted, "Do not bother to come home!" Stepping back in, I mentioned to her that I had invited her to the premiere, but she had declined. The only reason I was taking an overnight bag was that I knew, with all responsibility, I would be working well after midnight. Taking the subway meant I would be spending time waiting for a train and then walking a mile so that I could get up at nine am and take another ninety minutes to go to work.

A world premiere of a film in New York was like planning the Normandy invasion, except nobody dies. The only thing we had zero control over was the weather. As the entire team in tuxedos was transported to the Criterion, it started to snow. Our 7 pm premiere was in the middle of a freak snowstorm dropping nine feet nine inches on Manhattan.

In New York, everyone was a specialist, and when it came to movie premieres, it was Eddie Lazarus, whose business was movie premieres, who handled all the permits, red carpets, security, and buses to transport people to the premiere party at the Rainbow Room atop 30 Rockefeller Center in New York City. As fast as the snow came down, the Criterion crew made sure that the entrance to the red carpet was cleared. As planned, the flappers arrived in antique luxury cars, their neatly quaffed hair covered by snowflakes. The theatre played Thoroughly Modern Millie, and the girls ran up the red carpet. The owner of the cars had a flatbed auto carrier truck around the corner. No matter the weather in New York, you still get a crowd at a movie premiere. The limos pulled up with all the co-stars—Carol Channing, Beatrice Lillie, John Gavin, Pat Morita, Sammy Cahn, Jimmy Van Heusen, Lou Wasserman—except the star, Mayor John Lindsay, and every personality who was in New York. Eddie made sure that the buses were parked on West 43rd Street, right in front of the theatre fire exit. The film had a two-hour and fifteen-minute running time. As the last person to be seated in the theatre, one of the limos drove me to the Rainbow Room. Rockefeller Plaza's maintenance crew were already on the job of removing the snow from 30 Rock. My job was to make sure that all the elevators were on the lobby floor to bring the guests of the premiere up to the Art Deco entrance to the Rainbow Room, which opened in 1934. The entire restaurant was a homage to Art Deco design. Working closely with the banquet manager, we inspected the entire facility, making sure that the balloons were up, tinsel was all over the place, tables for ten were set up, and the buffet table and bars were in the right locations, and making sure that there were two girls in coat check. Many of the A-listers had drivers assigned to them for the entire evening; those who wouldn't be taken by bus to the event. Keeping tabs on the time, I took the elevator to the lobby to help expedite those who were attending the event. Timing the descent from the sixty-fifth floor to the lobby, took forty-five seconds. There were eight elevators, each capable of holding fourteen people. By 10 pm, I and five couples arrived at the entrance to The Thoroughly Modern Millie premiere party. The "Millie" girl, who was from

London and a dead ringer for Julie Andrews, wanted to meet Carole Channing. I put my hand on her shoulder to help navigate through the crowd to meet Carol Channing; Ross Hunter also sat with Carol. Introducing her, Carol invited her to join them, saying how great she was in the film. I excused myself and went to the bar for a Coke. Paul Cami, who was head of PR, invited a select group of press and film crew to document the event.

I was the first one in and the last one out, returning to the Drake Hotel and putting in a wake-up call for 9 am, only to find out Mayor Lindsay had declared a snow emergency. Calling home, Marge was crying, and the kids were crying, afraid that they would be snowed in. I was friendly with Larry, our next-door neighbour, who owned a snow blower. He was also in the media industry, owning small radio stations in Suffolk County. We both had children the same age. He was a person I could depend upon; the house had a boiler that was at least twenty years old. Even though I had converted it to gas, which didn't prevent it from making loud gurgling noises at 2 am, standing in my undershorts, turning knobs and gauges, banging it with a hammer, trying to stop it, Larry was my last resort. Calling back Marge, I told her that Larry would take care of the side entrance to the kitchen until I came home.

When it came to snowstorms, City Hall gave the Upper East Side of Manhattan priority when it came to snow removal. Phil Gerard, whom I rarely saw, called the entire office into the conference room to thank us. As everybody left the room, Phil and Jerry asked me to stay. "You know who called us first thing this morning?" Wasserman wanted to know who was the guy whose hand was on the arm of the "Millie" lookalike that was introduced to Carol Channing; he wanted them to fire him. Both Phil and Jerry knew that Wasserman was paranoid when it came to touching a person. They both replied it was one of the guests, and that they would investigate it and get back to him. Jerry gave me one piece of advice: when Wasserman was in New York, disappear. The entire office was let out early; the commute to Manhattan Beach took over an hour. Rather than walking the mile to the house, I decided to take the bus. Larry cleared the entranceway to the kitchen. Entering the door, both kids jumped on me. Marge turned her back, saying that they had already eaten. Closing the bedroom door, she shouted, "It's my time to take care of the kids!" I didn't care that she hadn't made dinner for me; I loved cooking. Julie, at three years old, was already doing two-hundred-piece puzzles; Jonathan would try to destroy Julie's work. When she pushed him away, he would cry and throw things. He was now living in his room, always climbing out of the crib. In 1967.

By mid 1967 MCA had total control of the Studio. They were the first in the Film industry to have an IBM mainframe in the basement of a thirty-five-story Black Glass Newly constructed Universal Tower at the Studio.

Marge was not a stupid person but her family didn't think that their daughters should any effort to have a career. After graduating from Madison High School they didn't make an effort for her to attend college. They did send her to Katharine Gibbs to learn how to secretary. Being a secretary or a receptionist was the career path that young women of the sixties had to take She had little motivation to work any time during our marriage. As for having sex was of little interest and whatever I tried to into anything other than the Missionary Position was disgusting. She also was afraid that Julie would come into our bedroom. I was afraid to do any repairs in the house, I was afraid if I screw up it would cost me extra. On May 3rd 1967 we had a family gathering Celebrating Julie's Third Birthday both sets of Grandparents and Marge's sister were there. Julie, who began to walk was dressed like a little Princess. Every time we took her for a walk she would scream puppy. Puppy. That afternoon I went to a pet store and bought her a White and Brown Spaniel. As they were singing Happy Birthday I walked in with a puppy on a Leash. I picked up the dog who licked her. I picked up Jamie who would be two-year-old 14 days later The puppy licked Jamie. Putting the dog back in his box I told them we must train the puppy Julie was the first Grandchild for both our parents. Every time my parents tried to cuddle her Marge pulled her away. Our parents had little in common, Her father had a 9 to five job my father woke up at three in the afternoon and came home after midnight. Both Marges' parents played paddle ball at the BRIGHTON BEACH Baths which was a private club Brooklyn's answer to the Ritzy Beach Clubs on the Eastern shores of Nassau County. My Parent's apartment overlooked the Baths where my father trained his telescope on the Women's Showers sans Roof. My Mother was a Fashionista, her mother made her clothes.

When our parents went home Marge said I should have told her saying she could not keep up with the housework and taking care of the kids, now a dog. Trying to hug her she pushed away. "I agree with you, I feel that owning a pet will give them a feeling of Responsibility. I will train, feed and take him out, That's my responsibility. The following morning the kids jump on the bed asking to play with the Puppy. Included with my Pet Shop purchase was food, a leash, two bowls, one for food the other for water and a bed. Holding him we had a naming meeting. Julie who loved CHARLIE BROWN and SNOOPY said we should call him Snoopy turning to her Brother I asked him if he liked the name Snoopy smiling he said Snoopy. The dog had already urinated on my pyjama top. They both wanted to hold him. Jamie first held him running away from his sister into his room Stopping him I told him that he had to share with his sister. Taking the dog, Jamie was hysterical banging his head on the floor. I wasn't into Tough Love, while I was holding Jamie Julie was watching the Puppy eat. Closing our bedroom door, I dressed the kids, and we took SNOOPY for a walk.

Universal Production was Green Lighting B Films to keep the pipeline of products flowing film houses across the Nation. It seems they didn't learn a lesson from the Box Office Revenue of BEAU GEST. Some genius who took film at UCLA came up with the idea of remaking the 1914 film serial produced by William Randolph Hearst Starring Pear White as Pauline. 1967 Universal took the concept and produced three shows Starring Pat Boone, Terry-Thomas and Pamela Austin as Pauline, All the television networks and Sponsors rejected the project. Rather than selling it they took all three pilots and turned it into a theatrical release spending three million dollars to produce and market. It seemed that Jerry Thought I was a miracle worker asking me if I wanted to go to New Orleans for three weeks. The film was scheduled to open the week of May 9th. Telling him that I wanted to discuss the trip with my wife. Picking up the mail there was a letter from American Express with a credit card application for a green card. Wanting to feel important I applied and received the card before my departure to New Orleans which I planned to use during the trip.

Marge looked at me and said, "Do what you think is right." To me, the right thing to do was to be a team player, knowing that if you want to get ahead in the corporate world, you do not say no. Besides, staying home would not help my marriage.

I always wondered why Jerry sent me to a city to handle the opening of a B film. Either he thought my expertise in marketing and public relations would make a difference in box office revenue, or he wanted to keep me away from Lou Wasserman, who came to New York once a month. The week before my departure, I learned that New Orleans was launching an NFL team called the Saints. Contacting Jim Henderson, the newly appointed head of public relations, I suggested setting up a cheerleading audition with Pamela, scheduled for the day of her arrival at Tulane Stadium. My next goal was to call the head of the marketing department of Maison Blanche, which was in the same category as Bloomingdale's. He agreed to promote *Perils with Four Windows* directly on Canal Street, which was the widest street in America. The Chrysler dealer group, who owned Dodge, hosted lunch the week of 17 July. On Sunday, 17 July 1967, I took the 10:00 am Eastern Airlines nonstop flight to New Orleans. Three hours later, I arrived. In those days, they didn't have jetways. After the plane landed, the airport crew rolled the stairs to the aircraft for disembarkation. Exiting the plane in New Orleans reminded me of riding the subway in August: hot and humid. The office sent me fifty press kits, which were waiting for me when I arrived. After settling into a mini-suite at the Roosevelt Hotel, I asked the concierge if he could recommend a limo service. He handed me a card that said "Luxury Limousine", telling me it was parked outside the hotel; I should just ask for Joseph. Exiting the hotel, there was a white stretch limo parked behind a line of yellow cabs. I offered Joseph fifty dollars a day, plus I paid for the petrol, starting on Wednesday at 10:00 pm With that settled, I contacted Henderson, who arranged for a car to pick me up the following day for a meeting at the Saints' new executive offices. The rest of the afternoon was spent planning the tour, with follow-up meetings with the head of public relations for ABC Interstate Theatres, who operated twenty movie theatres in key cities in Louisiana. The film was to premiere at the 2,600-seat Saenger Theatre, an Art Deco jewel owned by ABC Interstate. At noon the next day, I was in the back seat of a limo owned by the Saints. The driver immediately recognised that I was from New York, telling me that he had family in Brooklyn. He decided to be a tour guide, pointing out various landmarks as we arrived at the Saints' new offices. All the offices were decorated with original antiques, both 19th-century French Empire style and Victorian furniture, with carpets from that era. The Saints had their chef, who prepared lunch, which was served in the conference room. There were three place settings. After all the pleasantries, Jim told me that John Mecom Jr., one of the owners of the team, would join us. John was about 27 years old, six feet tall, and bought into the cheerleader event. We agreed that it was a great story. After lunch, Jim excused himself. John recognised my New York accent. Finishing his dessert, John looked at me. "I love New Yorkers," he said. "Do you have any kids?" Finishing my dessert, I realised he was wearing a wedding band. "I have a girl, three years old, and a boy, two years old." Picking up the phone, he told the person on the other end to put together a package of two children's T-shirts, two adult T-shirts, and two Saints caps. Putting down the phone, he looked me straight in the eye. "Partner, I love New York. I have an apartment in the Waldorf Towers which I use about once a month during my visit to Boonton, New Jersey. I own a company called Boontonware. Did you know anything about Formula One racing?" Saying that he had a racing team at this year's Indy 500, he escorted me to the limo and handed me a Saints t-shirt, asking me to give it to Pamela. Exchanging personal telephone numbers, I was driven back to the Roosevelt.

Pamela Austin was known as "The Dodge Rebellion Girl", having been featured in twenty television commercials, on billboards, in print, and radio spots. She became the face of all Dodge brands. The Louisiana Chrysler Dealers group were excited to do a joint promotion. Jerry sent me fifty-one sheets which measured 27" x 40" with "The Dodge Rebellion Girl" in various Dodge brands promoting the film. Over dinner, we mapped out a route which offered the dealers an opportunity to promote the Rebellion Girl. They offered a four-door sedan, the Polara, to transport us to various dealerships. After discussing this with Jerry, we both opted for a stretch limo. The Sunday Features editor of *The Times-Picayune* was scheduled for lunch with Pamela a day after her arrival.

Part of the job was picking up the film stars at the airport and briefing them on the marketing programme. Arriving on Monday, 24th July, on an American Airlines flight from LA at noon New Orleans time, Pamela was accompanied by her then-husband, Guy McElwaine. On the trip back to the hotel, Pamela introduced me to her husband, saying he would escort her during the tour. Telling them that she would be a judge of a cheerleading audition for the Saints being held at Tulane's football stadium, she admitted that as a teenager she had dreamt of being a cheerleader. The guy loved the idea. I didn't expect her to bring her husband with her; I needed a person to focus on why she was in New Orleans. Calling Jerry, saying he would take care of it, and after giving him an overview of what I had accomplished before Pamela's arrival, he asked for a favour: could I go to Brennan's, buy two quarts of seafood gumbo soup, bring it back to New York, and put it on my expense account? Checking them into their room, after half an hour they returned to the lobby. Pamela was wearing her Saints t-shirt, a short, pleated skirt, and Converse sneakers. The ride from the hotel to Tulane Stadium took about ten minutes. Walking into an eighty-thousand-seat stadium was a great experience. Mecom and the key members of the Saints executive staff were on the playing field, including TV news crews, both local and network, plus photographers from local newspapers and ten Southern beauties, all blondes with big hairdos. Pamela took control of the group; after a few minutes in a huddle with the girls, they broke into a series of cheers for the cameras.

Making reservations at Commander's Palace, which was the best restaurant in New Orleans, over dinner her husband told me that he had his own public relations firm which he had opened after leaving Rogers & Cowan. He was four years older than me, and he and Pamela had just married. Our relationship changed from when we met at the airport. As we both went back to our rooms, he told me that he would be playing tourist.

The first city on our schedule was Baton Rouge, the capital of Louisiana, where I invited the movie theatre manager to join us at a Dodge dealership, then a meet-and-greet with Louisiana Governor John McKeithen at 4 pm Dealerships received a large amount of co-op advertising money from Chrysler. They covered the entire Baton Rouge market with radio spots, offering to the first one hundred callers free tickets, and newspaper advertising. The dealership was packed with fans driving DW pickup trucks, all wanting to get Pamela's autograph.

As we headed to the state capital, four state troopers on motorcycles escorted us to the front of the building, where we were greeted by the Governor's Chief of Staff. As a guy from Brooklyn trying to muffle my obvious New York accent, I wasn't prepared for Southern charm. Governor McKeithen presented Pamela with a personal gold pen from the Governor's office and a framed proclamation making May 'Pamela Austin/Perils of Pauline Month' in Louisiana. The theatre manager gave the Governor her business card with her number, inviting him to call if he wanted to see a film. Escorting us down the marble staircase to our car, he pointed out four bullet holes on the wall, proudly telling us, "This was where Huey Long was assassinated."

Until 6 May, we covered ten towns in Louisiana, where we received the same reception as we received in Baton Rouge. The Dodge dealerships pulled out all the stops with radio advertising and print ads.

I was curious how all the Dodge dealerships surpassed their sales quotas. I discovered that in these small markets, many dealers sold cars with a handshake, mainly pick-up and muscle cars. Being such a small market, everyone knew each other, with very few defaulting on their payments.

Every day I called home. Marge would tell Julie, who was three, muttered, "I miss you, Daddy," asking her to put her brother Jamie on the phone. He would say, "Dada," and drop the phone. Marge picked up the phone, asking when I planned to come home. My response was, "This coming Thursday." I grabbed the moment to have a normal conversation with my wife, telling her that New Orleans was a beautiful city and how the entire state was still fighting integration, still calling grown Black men "boy", and how the food was great. Ending the call, Marge, for the first time, said, "I miss you." As we travelled around the state, I was coordinating the premiere of *The Perils of Pauline* with the team from ABC Interstate, who owned the Saenger Theatre with 3,000 seats.

On the day of the premiere, we had a 10 am meeting at City Hall, where Mayor Schiro gave Pamela a symbolic key to the city. The rest of the day was spent with ABC Interstate people setting up the premiere, red carpet, and Klieg lights. They had given out 100 free tickets to high schools. The New Orleans Dodge dealership went for the concept of a Dodge parade down Canal Street. Pamela and her husband were in a 1967 Dodge Coronet convertible. The dealership mustered an additional ten Coronets with newly signed players for the Saints waving to the crowd. I discovered that any event that has Klieg lights drew crowds, no matter what the event was. Pamela and her husband never saw the film, deciding to stay. I found three seats in the back of the theatre. Watching a terrible movie twice was agony. The audience laughed at unfunny scenes and cracked up during bad scenes.

Always checking in with Jerry, I asked him to wire me $2,000, which I needed to pay the limo driver, including other people who helped make the premiere a success. He also gave me approval to invite the key people who helped me during my stay in New Orleans for dinner. I was told one of the best restaurants in New Orleans was a five-star restaurant located in the Garden District: The Commander's Palace. The total tab with wine and tip was $350.

The next morning, Pam and her husband had a noon flight back to LA. Having to clean up all the loose ends, I was booked on the 2 pm flight, giving me time to put together all the press that I had created for the film. The *Times-Picayune* gave the film the worst review I have ever read. My only responsibility was to call all the cinemas that had run the film at midnight to get their box office gross, which I had to call into an answering service and give the figures. That evening, I decided to go to Antoine's, where I became friendly with the Maître D' and ordered a hundred dollars worth of seafood gumbo, which I would pick up at noon the next day. Wandering around Bourbon Street is a drag if you don't drink. I found Preservation Hall, which offered the best jazz I have ever heard.

Returning to the hotel, I started calling cinemas for their box office gross. The total of box office grosses from all the cinemas was under three thousand dollars. Rattling off the names of the cinemas and their gross receipts on the sales office answering machine, I realised that we had spent twenty times that figure on promoting the film.

On the morning of 4 August, I had breakfast. Afterwards, I began handing out twenty-dollar bills to the people who had helped me. Joseph was loading my luggage into the boot of the limo. "Where to, Boss?" he asked. I told him to swing by

Brennan's; I had to pick up gumbo soup to bring back to New York. The Maître D' handed me four quarts of seafood gumbo soup in a paper shopping bag. Arriving at the Eastern Air Lines drop-off point, he hailed a skycap to handle my luggage. During our time together, we had bonded. He was forty, with a family of four children. His wife worked as a maid for a wealthy family who lived in the Garden District. Coming from Brooklyn, I wasn't exposed to the turmoil of fighting against segregation. Joseph gave me a very personal feeling of what it meant to be Black down South. Pointing to the limo, he said that the people his wife worked for were good, and they had given him the money for the limo. Handing him a thousand dollars in his twenties, he used the back of his business card as a receipt. Before entering the terminal, I gave him my business card, telling him to call me anytime. During my time in New Orleans, I concluded that the reason society was so slow and non-aggressive was the heat, humidity, and flies. To make the trip a success, I had to become a "good ol' boy", not a twenty-seven-year-old from Brooklyn with a type A personality who wanted things done immediately, not tomorrow.

After checking my bags, I walked to the Eastern Airlines gate for my flight back to New York, carrying two shopping bags of hot gumbo soup.

Boarding the flight, I always had a bulkhead seat with my left hand on the aisle. Once seated, I placed the gumbo soup in front of me. The take-off was without incident as the plane climbed to its cruising altitude, heading to JFK. Sixty minutes into the flight, the bags in front of me started to leak, and the smell of gumbo soup permeated the aircraft. Trying to push down the lids, my hands were soaked in gumbo. The stewardess brought me towels to soak up the soup. It seemed that once the plane reached cruising altitude, the cabin became pressurised, making the hot soup in the plastic containers expand. Over the loudspeaker, the pilot announced that he was diverting the flight to Atlanta to have the plane cleaned. Arriving at the gate, I was the first to exit, with four dripping bags of gumbo soup. Eastern had a crew at the gate who immediately took the dripping shopping bags, putting them in a container as if it were a bomb. Pleading with them not to dispose of the soup, I explained that it was for my boss, who was a gourmet; if I didn't come back with the soup, I would be fired. They understood and would repackage the remaining soup in safe, airline-approved containers.

Luckily, there were a hundred people on board who were seated, ready to reboard the plane. My entire person smelled of gumbo. My dilemma: how do I get rid of my gumbo-smelling shirt and shoes? Gift shops were selling Atlanta T-shirts and booties for long flights. Purchasing those two items, I went into the men's room, took my shirt off, placed it in the sink, and soaked it. I then used a damp paper towel to wash the smell of gumbo off my body. They had hot air blowers to dry your hands. I was manoeuvring around to dry my chest. Taking my shoes off, I washed the soles. As I was wringing out my shirt, a few men came into the men's room, looking at me as if I was insane. Putting on the Atlanta T-shirt, placing my wet shirt in a bag, my booties on my feet, and carrying my wet shoes, I walked back to the gift shop, asking for another bag. I sprayed cologne on the soles of my shoes and returned to the gate as my fellow passengers were boarding the flight. Upon entering the plane, the stewardess transferred my soup into two containers of gumbo, which she would give me when we arrived at JFK. I handed her the plastic bag with my wet shirt and cologne-smelling shoes. Once the flight hit cruising altitude, I walked through the plane, apologising for the delay. I apologised to the flight crew. With a smile on her face, she thanked me for flying Eastern Airlines, then handed me two bags: one of seafood gumbo soup, my wet shirt, and shoes. With both hands full, I waved to a skycap to assist me, picking up my bags and loading them into a taxi. Forty minutes later, I was in front of 157 Amherst Street. Marge and Julie were looking out the window when I arrived. My fantasy was that when I opened the door, Marge would embrace me with both kids hugging me. It was a Norman Rockwell moment, which happened, minus the kiss and embrace. "Where is Jamie?" Julie looked at me. "Jamie was a bad boy, and mummy locked him in his room." Placing my bag on the floor, I went to Jamie's room. The door was closed. Jamie was standing in his crib, hysterical. "Mummy always puts him back in his bed when he is bad." Picking him up, he stopped crying. As the years progressed, both Julie and Jamie had their own beds. The cribs were donated to The Salvation Army.

After unpacking and handing out gifts of Saints T-shirts and caps, I suggested that we should surprise my parents and walk over to their house. Marge said she needed quiet time, and that I should go. It was still light, with the temperature at eighty degrees. Putting on their New Orleans Saints T-shirts, which hung down to their ankles, I placed Jamie in the carriage, which had a seat attached for Julie. My parents lived five blocks away. When they moved, they gave me a set of keys to their apartment. Ever since they lived there, I never went through the front of the building. I usually go through the service entrance. Leaving the carriage in front of their apartment, I opened the door and said, "Surprise, Grandpa and Grandma!" They both ran in, only to discover my parents on the couch: my mother in her robe and my dad in his undershorts, watching television with the windows wide open. They very rarely use the air conditioning due to the breeze coming off the ocean. After all the hugging and kissing, I ran around the apartment, closing windows and putting on the air conditioning, taking accessories off the shelves. My father loved playing with the kids and taking them into the bedroom. He would put them both on the bed, stretching them, tickling them, and making sounds on their bellies. He also had a box of toys, including hand puppets. Both Julie and Jamie were giggling.

My mother called me into the kitchen to prepare ice cream for the kids. "Let me ask you why your wife hates us. During the weeks you were gone, we never saw the kids. I would call to say hello, only to have her say that the kids were crying and she had to go." My mother always cries, but this was different; she was in anguish. Putting my arm on her shoulder, I tried to console her. "Mum, I do not know why she has such animosity towards you and Dad. You treated her like a daughter, always giving her gifts." Having to admit my marriage is on life support, if it wasn't for the kids, I would end it. Promising, "If I am at home, you will see them once a week." The phone rang. I picked it up. The voice on the other end asked when I was coming home. "In about an hour." My father, holding both Julie and Jamie, came back into the living room. Julie was having her ice cream, and Jamie was exploring the living room, trying to grab what he could and topple it over. The living room started to smell; Jamie was running around with a load in his nappy. Luckily, the carriage had clean cloth nappies.

Changing him, I knew that I had to wash the nappy, returning it to the bag of soiled nappies, which was picked up twice a week and replaced by clean cloth nappies.

Kissing my parents goodbye, when we returned home, Marge was outside sitting on the stoop. Picking up Julie, she turned to me, "Leave the carriage in the driveway and bring Jamie in; he has to eat," as she walked back into the house.

I tried to avoid confrontations in front of the kids. The logistics of having two children, a year and fourteen days apart, was daunting. Julie, who had a full mouth of teeth, was given real food, using phone books for her to reach the table. Jamie sat in the highchair, where I fed him a Gerber chicken dish.

It was difficult getting Jamie to bed before nine; once in the cot, he started crying. I would pick him up and walk around the property, finally falling asleep in my arms. Julie would sit on the couch watching television or working on her puzzle and sometimes fell asleep on the carpet. By the time the local television news came on, she was asleep; Marge put her in bed.

The smart thing was not to discuss her relationship with my parents. At the time, I did not have travel plans, so when I decided to bring the kids over to visit my parents, I would bring them over.

The following morning, I walked the mile to the subway, carrying the two quarts of SEAFOOD GUMBO SOUP. Boarding the express train at the last stop, I had no trouble getting a seat. With the now cold gumbo soup sitting next to me, the aroma of the soup filled the carriage; other passengers moved away from me. Leaning against the train door was a black man, about six feet tall, carrying a toolbox. Moving, standing over me, he looked down. "Hey man, is that gumbo soup between your legs?" Nodding yes, he sat down, and we started having a conversation about gumbo soup. "You know, you never forget the smell of gumbo. My mother's family lives in Saint Charles, Louisiana. Every summer, they would send me down there for two weeks. I had church on Sunday and gumbo the rest of the week. They would have those trees* that have hanging branches that looked like they were torn." "Stay cool, man, your soup brought back great memories. God bless," as he exited the train at Atlantic Avenue. What's great about buses and trains is that people open up and tell you things that they never would say in any other social setting, assured that they will never see you again. Switching to a local at Times Square, I exited the train on East 59th Street and Lexington Avenue, three blocks from the office. The smell of gumbo followed me to 445 Park Avenue. Exiting the lift, the receptionist asked where I was for three weeks. "New Orleans," as I entered the office from the reception area. Walking as fast as I could, I asked if Jerry was in. With a nod, I entered his office. He was the same affable self, smoking his pipe.

He stood up, shook my hand, and told me what a great job I did. I handed him the package with Gumbo Soup and my scrapbook, which had all the press clippings and pictures highlighting my trip. He told me that my cheerleader event hit all the Network News shows.

Jerry motioned me to sit on the couch, asking for a recap of the entire three weeks. Ninety minutes later, he told me to do my expense account. By the time I got back to my desk, the bullpen was empty; everybody was out to lunch.

I had all my receipts and called the receptionist to find out if anyone had booked the conference room. Emptying a paper bag containing my real and fake receipts, I started documenting the expenses of the trip. First, I had to justify the three thousand dollars in cash. Two hours later, I handed in my expense account, which totalled $5,950.40, not including my airfare and hotel room. Handing in my expense account, which Jerry immediately signed, I brought the report to the department that handles reimbursements; you had a choice of cheque or cash. I took the cash and immediately deposited it in my Chase Manhattan checking account.

The remaining four months of 1967 were dedicated to the screening of films that were due to be released in the first quarter of 1968.

Mid-November, the entire executive team of the New York office was summoned to LA for a meeting with their Studio counterparts, which was under the direction of David Lipton, VP of Worldwide Advertising and Publicity. A week later, the entire team returned to New York in a sombre mood.

I was assigned to be part of the team that organised the company-wide holiday party, to which wives were invited, to be held at the Rainbow Room, the same place that we had the Millie Premiere; the date was Thursday, 14 December.

Hoping that Marge would come, I offered to buy her a new dress. She answered that she had no one to watch the kids. "Ask your sister, who was doing nothing, to come over." Her reply was, "I do not trust her. How about your parents?" They were driving down to Florida. Management decided to close the office in the last week of December.

New Year's Eve 1967 was on a Sunday. As many young families with children did, we watched 1968 arrive from the comfort of our home.

Returning to work on 2 January, Jerry called me into his office. After discussing how we spent New Year's, Jerry told me that my responsibilities were being moved to the Studio in LA. Sitting there stunned, Jerry admitted that Wasserman wanted me out of the company for touching a girl and drinking while on the job. Jerry knew that I only drank Coke; my touching the Millie look-alike was to move her through the crowd. Jerry admitted that the day after the Millie Premiere, Wasserman called him to fire me, admitting that he tried to hide the fact that I was on the payroll. This moment was the saddest moment of my life; I have never been eliminated. The thing I needed was medical insurance for my family. I had two weeks to wrap things up. Word got out that Wasserman had fired me. The guys in the bullpen were a few years older than I was. One of the members of the Publicity team was the Union Shop steward, who told me any hours over forty hours a week were "golden time," which meant I would get a large severance cheque.

Constructing a timesheet of five years of employment, I came up with a figure of a thousand hours of overtime, which Jerry signed off on. HR promised that I would get health insurance for six months and keep the rate at the deductible as if I were still working there.

Marge was devastated, saying that she thought I was doing a great job. I assured her that we could make it money-wise, thinking how I could make the relationship work with us being together twenty-four hours a day.

On my last day at Universal, Jerry gave me twenty-five dollars out of his pocket to take a taxi home. We arranged to meet for lunch once a week, where he would help edit my CV.

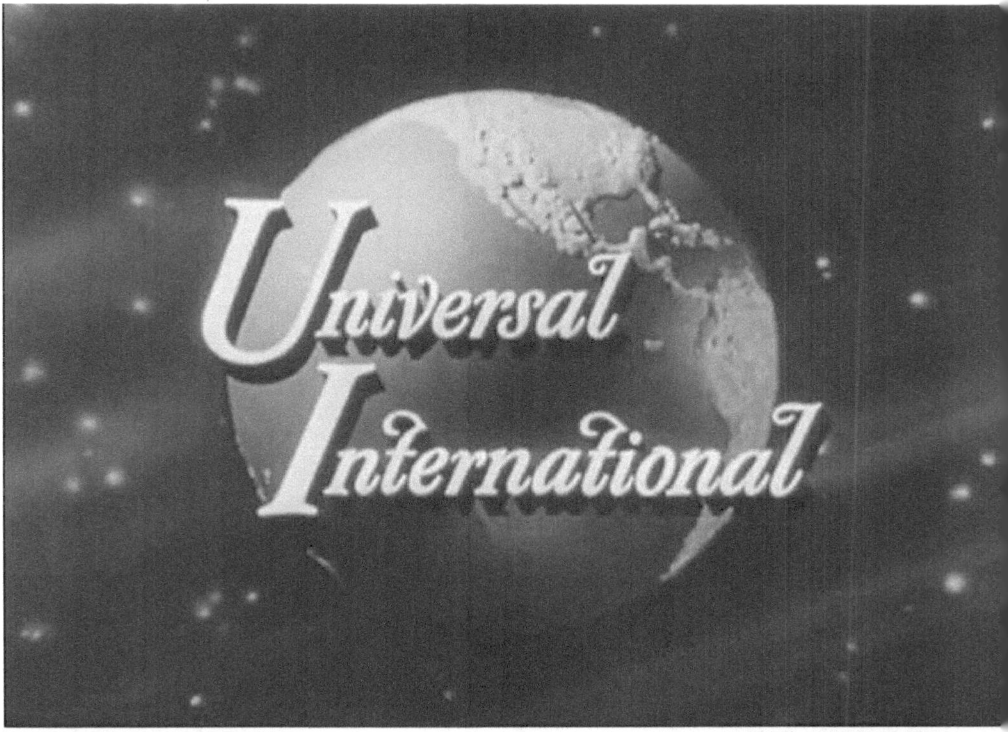
Universal
International

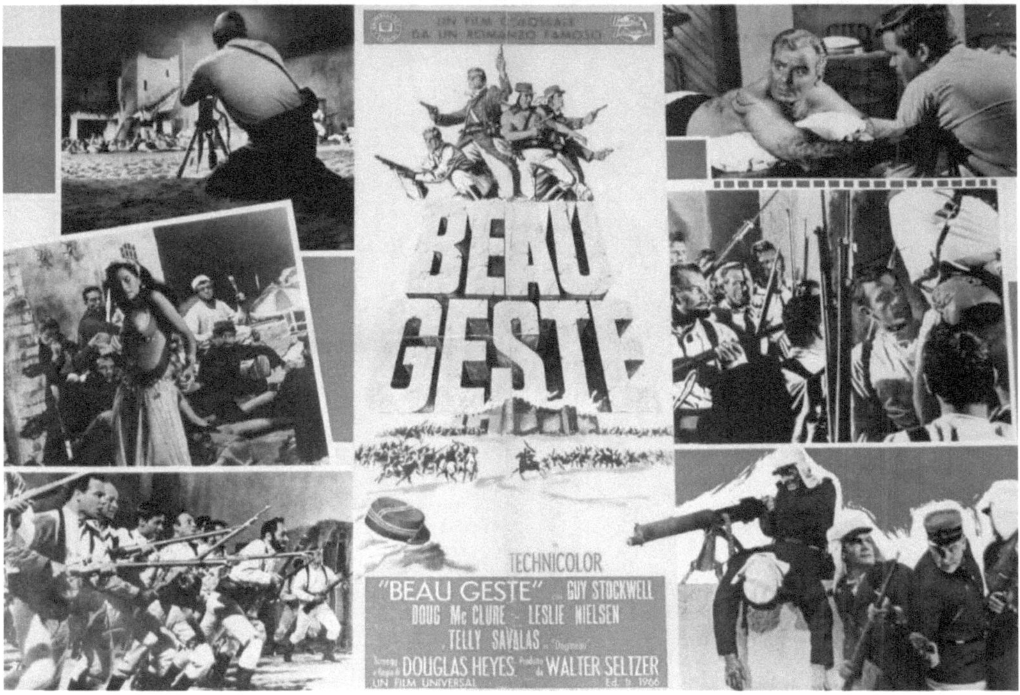
BEAU GESTE
TECHNICOLOR
"BEAU GESTE" GUY STOCKWELL
DOUG Mc CLURE LESLIE NIELSEN
TELLY SAVALAS
DOUGLAS HEYES WALTER SELTZER
UN FILM UNIVERSAL Ed. It. 1966

When in Southern California visit Universal City Studios
I want YOU
to see me
in
The Perils of Pauline
IN COLOR
SEE
Pauline
in the icy
clutches
of a mad
scientist!
SEE
Pauline
swing with
a swingin'
gorilla!
CO-STARRING
PAT BOONE
PAMELA AUSTIN
THAT REBELLION GIRL
GUEST STARS
EDWARD EVERETT HORTON
TERRY-THOMAS
SEE
Pauline
battle the love-
starved
hunter!
MUSIC BY
VIC MIZZY
WRITTEN BY
ALBERT BEICH
DIRECTED BY
HERBERT B. LEONARD
and
JOSHUA SHELLEY
PRODUCED BY
HERBERT B. LEONARD
A UNIVERSAL PICTURE
SEE
Pauline
get hung-up
by Sharks!

When in Southern California visit Universal Studios
Recapture the Happy, Crazy Fun Days of the Care-Free Twenties!
The most joyous romantic musical of the age!
Julie Andrews as MILLIE
Mary Tyler Moore
Carol Channing
in ROSS HUNTER'S PRODUCTION OF
"Thoroughly Modern Millie"
co-starring
James Fox
John Gavin
and
Beatrice Lillie
as MRS. MEERS
Music Score by ELMER BERNSTEIN · Musical Numbers Scored by ANDRE PREVIN · Musical Sequences by JOE LAYTON
Written by RICHARD MORRIS · Directed by GEORGE ROY HILL · Produced by ROSS HUNTER · A UNIVERSAL PICTURE RERELEASE · TECHNICOLOR®
ORIGINAL SOUNDTRACK ALBUM AVAILABLE EXCLUSIVELY ON DECCA RECORDS
G
R 72/358
"THOROUGHLY MODERN MILLIE"

DECADE THREE

In March 1968, I was called in for a meeting with Wally Schwartz, President of the ABC Radio Network, which had launched the four-network concept offered to affiliates: All News Radio twenty-four hours a day, Contemporary Hit Radio, Adult Contemporary, and Country Music.

With Jerry's glowing recommendation, I got the job at $30,000 a year. Working with Wally and the affiliate sales team, I created grassroots marketing plans for each concept, coordinating with the art department, in-house printing, and talking daily to the public relations manager of each affiliate station. The three music concepts' cross-promotional marketing managers of major recording companies facilitated cross-promotional tie-ins with record stores.

In June 1968, Wally introduced me to Ellis Moore, VP of Public Relations for the Television Network, who invited me to meet Dick Connelly, VP of Publicity for the Network. Twenty-four hours later, they offered me the position of Director of Special Projects for the Television Network. My promotion responsibilities crossed all day parts, from prime time, news, late night, sports, daytime, children's programming, and late night. Two years later, I was assigned to cover Dick Cavett's 6 pm studio taping so that if any news came from the show, I would call my press contacts. *The Dick Cavett Show* competed with Johnny Carson on NBC. Cavett was intellectual and probing with his guests, whereas Carson offered his audience entertainment. Cavett was a ratings flop; hence, the Network finally cancelled his show in 1974. As time progressed, I was responsible for all print media, plus wire services in the New York metro area. I would work weekends, picking up stars for upcoming television series and handling press interviews, creating cross-promotion of upcoming series. I was given a budget to create unique mailers for television reviewers and affiliate station promotion managers, being involved with Up Front presentations for advertisers.

abc

In 1971, I was assigned to create a press schedule for a young actor named James Cahn, who was starring in a *Movie of the Week* film called *Brian's Song.* It was about Brian Piccolo, a running back for the Chicago Bears football team, who was diagnosed with terminal embryonal cell carcinoma cancer. The film focused on his friendship with Gale Sayers, an African American halfback, played by actor Billy Dee Williams. Brian Piccolo passed away in 1970 at the age of 26.

Ellis Moore promoted me to the title of Vice President of Special Projects, moving me into an office with windows. That's the way corporations reward you: a title with no increase in salary. ABC programming created *The Movie of the Week* with groundbreaking subjects, which allowed me to work with both the in-house art department and print shop, which could produce four-colour posters.

With the airing of *That Certain Summer*, which dealt with homosexuality, I invited members of the Mattachine Society, the first organisation to fight for gay rights, to a screening. Hosting these screenings, I started to understand that being homosexual wasn't about the flamboyant gays I had met while doing publicity for Bill Miller, the men's clothing designer. They were people you would meet in banks, on Wall Street, or in any other business environment. As part of the screening process, I gave them cards to write their opinions on the film. The major takeaway was that the depicted couple showed no intimacy. I then invited my friend, the Monsieur of St Patrick's, to get his take on the film. After the screening, he warned me not to broadcast the movie; if the network wanted to air it, they should do so without fanfare. Many affiliates refused to air the movie. The film aired on Wednesday, 1

November 1972. The ABC switchboard lit up like a Christmas tree, with righteous Americans threatening to boycott the network.

Between meetings and spending time at the Dick Cavett taping, working with Howard Cosell and Jim McKay, and having four martini lunches with Ben Gross, who was in his early seventies and senior television writer for the *Daily News* at the Four Seasons, who wrote Sunday features on television personalities, in September of 1973, Roone Arledge, President of ABC Sports, announced that ABC Sports was going to air the "Tennis Match of the Decade": Bobby Riggs vs. Billie Jean King, which we promoted as the "Battle of the Sexes". I came up with a large green button with the male and female symbols separated by a tennis net. The press conference was held in one of our studios. Bobby Riggs was to tennis what Muhammad Ali was to boxing. Martin Starger, who was VP of Programming, had Michael Eisner and Barry Diller as members of his team.

Marge had paranoia that I was having an affair. She figured that if I left work between five and six, I would be home by 7 pm at the latest. What should have been an hour's commute sometimes turned into two hours, which included a mile's walk from the subway station. She didn't factor in train breakdowns or any MTA problems. As soon as I walked through the door, she asked me how my "whore" girlfriend was. At this point, all I could do was ignore her. When you are blamed for something you never did, you might as well do it.

I had an affair which began in February 1973. A freelance magazine writer named Natalie, who was from Chicago, was calling me every day asking to be put on the press list. Her editor wanted a profile on Susan Lucci, who starred in *All My Children*, one of ABC's top-rated daytime soap operas. I arranged for her to meet Susan on the set of *All My Children.* After a while, I put her on my press list, giving her access to all our press conferences. During a conversation over coffee, she told me that she lived in Sheepshead Bay, about a mile from my house. She was in the city three times a week and would be happy to give me a lift home. The trip on the Belt Parkway was boring; having company on the trip home would be fun. She would drop me off at Coney Island and Brighton Beach Avenue, half a mile from my house. Coming from a family of writers in Chicago, she was always under pressure to succeed. When her editor offered her an opportunity to come to New York, she jumped at the chance.

I figured it would take me ninety minutes to take the train and walk home. If the traffic was moving, I could make Brighton Beach in an hour. Looking at my watch, if the trip from the FDR to the Belt Parkway was under an hour, I would suggest she pull over at a rest stop past the Verrazano Bridge and we would talk. Talking turned to kissing, which lasted fifteen minutes. We agreed to meet at her apartment on Wednesday at 9 pm At this point, Marge paid little attention to me. That's where Snoopy comes in. I would walk him directly to my father's car and drive to her apartment, bringing Snoopy upstairs with me. I would have forty minutes of great sex, then drive back to my parent's apartment, park the car, and walk home all under ninety minutes.

In May 1973, I considered myself a loyal ABC company man, secure in my job and my future in broadcasting. I was part of the marketing team handling a week-long promotional meeting in Los Angeles to preview the Fall Network schedule.

Excited about the trip, I came home thinking Marge would be happy to join me. I laid out the entire itinerary: five days in LA, one day in San Francisco visiting KGO (which ABC owned then), and a weekend in Las Vegas where Sammy Cahn had arranged a free suite at Caesar's Palace.

Her response was, "Another trip? I have no one to watch the kids, who are nine and eight." This was expected, as she never accepted an invitation. She added one caveat: "If I go to Vegas, I want a divorce." We didn't speak for the entire week. The Sunday before I left, my parents had my itinerary. I told my father not to mention it if he saw Marge.

Since this was my first time in LA, staying at the Beverly Hilton, my room was a lanai right across from the pool. All the filming would be at the poolside. The first night was a cocktail party where all the stars of the Fall 1973 season attended. After the party, I wanted to explore Rodeo Drive. Exiting the Beverly Hilton, I discovered their "we-know" sidewalks. Walking across what I considered a park, a police cruiser stopped. The officer told me to put my hands on the car. After a body pat-down, I asked what their reason was for stopping me. Getting back into their cruiser, they simply said that no one walks in Beverly Hills.

At the end of the affiliate meetings, I spent two days in San Francisco with the KGO marketing team. The next morning, I boarded a two-hour flight to Vegas. The first thing that greeted me was slot machines. Before hailing a taxi, I put money in a slot, pulled the arm, and won fifty dollars in silver dollars. Loaded with large dollar coins, I hailed a taxi which passed The Sands, The International, The Flamingo, The Sahara, Tropicana, The

Flamingo Capri Hotel, Circus Circus, and the MGM Grand. Pulling up to Caesar's Palace, I entered the lobby and went to the registration desk. The clerk checked my reservation, welcomed me back, and gave me the key to my room. The bellboy insisted on taking my bag; the elevator took us to the top floor. Opening the door, I found myself in a two-bedroom suite whose windows overlooked the Strip. On the table was a fruit bowl with a note: "Any friend of Sammy is a friend of mine. Jay Sarno." Also attached were comps for two at any restaurant. I later found out that Jay was one of the owners of the hotel. I spent hours walking around the casino with fifty heavy silver dollars in my pocket. The casino floor was like Broadway on steroids. I walked into an environment alien to me: lights flashing, the sound of people screaming around the crap tables. The slot machines had a steel dispenser which echoed the sound of silver dollars falling into the tray. The lobby and bar area were filled with beautiful women selling their wares. Standing next to what I thought was a hot crap table where the minimum bet was five dollars, the crowd focused on the person rolling the dice, who was on a hot streak. Viewing where people were putting the most money, I turned ten dollars into chips. After spending eight hours in the casino, I had turned the fifty dollars into five thousand. Holding the chips, I went to the cage to turn them into cash. At 3 am, I returned to my suite and threw the money on the bed, placing it in neat bundles. Waking up, the sun was out; I was still dressed, with tens and twenties scattered across the unselected king-size bed. I had taken my bathing suit, tee shirt, and sneakers. It was a hundred degrees; Caesar's had a coffee shop, and I used one of my comps.

The pool was filled with beautiful women who were either with someone or working girls who had slipped past security. I never liked eating by myself or paying for sex.

If I were broke, I would have avoided the towel guys who found me a spot near the pool with an umbrella, giving the guy a five-dollar tip. My thinking was that any woman who was an eight or ten on the beauty scale was either someone's wife, girlfriend, or a working girl. I scanned the pool for the homeliest woman to talk to. The music system was playing all the Billboard top fifty hit songs like "Tie a Yellow Ribbon Round the Ole Oak Tree", "Bad, Bad Leroy Brown", "Killing Me Softly with His Song", "Let's Get it On", "My Love", "You're So Vain", and "Touch Me in the Morning", mixed with Sinatra. It reminded me of my summers at the Concord in the Catskills. At the far end of the pool was a girl with large breasts, whose name was Betty, in an ordinary one-piece bathing suit. We began talking, and she said she was from Portland, Oregon, at a banker's convention. I told her that I was from New York, spending the weekend after meetings in LA. She was a touchy-feely person, telling me how she was into nature, hiking, and camping, suggesting that I should visit Portland.

I asked her if she would like to join me for dinner at Guy Savoy, a four-star French restaurant where I could use my comp at 8 pm. Waiting outside the restaurant, the girl that I rated as a four now looked like a seven showed up. I never sat through a three-hour dinner. Walking hand in hand, I invited her up to my suite. We spent another hour talking. Looking at her watch, she got up, heading for the door. Asking her where she was going, she said, "To work." She told me that Saturday was her day off. She had a date waiting for her at the Sands. Fixing her makeup, she told me she was an escort in Portland and came to Vegas to earn money. There I was in a thousand-dollar-a-night suite with an erection. The only place to go was the casino. I had four thousand nine hundred and fifty dollars of their money to play with. By the time I checked out, I still had fifty silver dollars left. Boarding my eleven o'clock flight to JFK, I still had fifty dollars in silver dollars left. Arriving on time, I took a taxi home, paying the driver thirty-five silver dollars. "Thanks, man, you just came from Vegas," he said. I answered yes. Every time I pick up a fare from JFK and get paid in silver dollars, I know they went to Vegas. Marge was standing in the living room with a defiant look on her face. Julie, who was nine, had bought a jigsaw puzzle of San Francisco. Asking Julie where her brother was, she pointed to his room, which was missing a doorknob, which was on the Kitchen Table. Opening the door to his room, Jamie was knocking his head on the floor, crying. Sitting next to him on the floor, I rolled a toy fire engine in front of him; he stopped crying. "Does Mummy do this when you don't listen to her?" He didn't answer, going back to playing with his truck. "How was Vegas, you lying piece of shit?" she screamed, slamming the door to our bedroom. "How did you find out that I went to Vegas?" "Your fucking father, I hate your family!" As she came out of the bedroom, wiping her eyes, she shouted that she wanted a divorce. Both kids were sitting with me, calling her bluff. I said, "Great." Knowing that my parents were leaving for Greece and a twenty-one-day cruise of the Aegean this coming Friday, I would use their apartment. Changing the clothes I had travelled into shorts, I took the kids to visit their grandparents after their dinner. Not needing a stroller, the three of us walked five blocks.

My parents were not shocked when I told them what had just happened. Sitting on the couch, I asked my father, "Why did you tell her that I went to Vegas?" My father, playing with the kids, replied, "We knew you were unhappy but didn't have the guts to leave the marriage because of the kids. I spent the week at the house, and she was sleeping with my daughter. The kids sensed that something was happening between their mother and father." When my parents left on their cruise, I moved in. Since the kids were off school, I would use my father's car to pick them up for dinner or walk on the boardwalk to Coney Island. During this period, I would see Marge; suddenly, she returned to the person I had dated eleven years earlier. To be truthful, we had better sex then than when I lived at home. By the end of June, my parents returned from Greece. This relegated me to sleeping on the couch. My mother, who meant well, got up and made breakfast, treating me as if I was a teenager. I was being suffocated by her love for me. Standing on the subway platform of the Brighton Beach Station, looking east, I made a life-changing decision: I did not want to live in Brighton Beach, which was all families. This was the first time I was alone, going from my parents' home directly into being married. I had never had the opportunity to travel and meet other people except those I worked with. That's when I decided to move to Manhattan. Eddie Jaffe, who I worked for as a kid, had moved to West 55th Street, across the street from City Center, was going to Greece for two months and allowed me to use his apartment, which was a block away from ABC. I moved into Jaffe's place while I was looking for my first Manhattan apartment. I began asking people I worked with if they knew of a vacant apartment. Larry, who worked in network sales, recommended that I try 40 West 53rd Street, which was across the street from the Museum of Modern Art, where there was a four-star Chinese restaurant on the ground level. A member of the Rockefeller family owned the building; their building manager was located across the street from the building. During lunch, I went up to the management company, telling them one of my associates from ABC lived at 42 West 53rd Street and there might be an apartment available. After filling out the application, a member of their staff escorted me to view the apartment.

Climbing up three flights of stairs, the door opened into a large living room whose windows faced 53rd Street. It had high ceilings, a fireplace, one bedroom with one closet, and a small kitchen for four hundred dollars a month. Without hesitation, I asked for a two-year lease; they gave me the keys. I plan to move in on Monday, 2 July. Looking down 53rd Street, I realised that the Rockefeller family owned all the brownstones going west to Sixth Avenue. Proud of myself, I realised that my new home was built in 1882. Macy's was having their Fourth of July furniture sales. After work, I found myself on Macy's furniture floor. Within half an hour, I purchased an entire apartment with a convertible sofa, which they guaranteed to deliver on 2 July. I called Marge, telling her that I would be picking up the rest of my belongings on Saturday, 23 June, around 1 pm. One of the guys who worked in the mailroom at ABC owned a van and agreed to buy boxes and help me move. Arriving at the house, both Julie and Jamie hugged me; Marge went outside to the backyard. Julie peppered me with questions: "Why are you leaving Mummy? Will we ever see you again? Will I take Snoopy?" Assuring them that I was not taking the dog, they then asked me who was going to walk him. To get the kids' minds off what was about to happen, I had them involved in my packing. Essentially, all I took was my clothes, typewriter, stereo, records, some whisky, a wok, and a few boxes of my writing. Before leaving, I asked Marge to have her solicitor send my solicitor the divorce agreement so I could review it. As the van pulled away, I shouted that I would see the kids next weekend, reminding her, "As of now, we are still married." Driving away, I reflected on how I loved Snoopy, walking him and seeing him run on the beach, trying to mount dogs three times his size. That was my moment of relaxation. The only one. I loved the dog, determining he would have a better life staying where he was.

Sunday on West 53rd Street was pretty quiet. Carrying my belongings up three flights of stairs to my apartment felt like freedom, after spending the previous night at Jaffe's apartment. The next day, all my furniture arrived. By 6 pm, my entire apartment was set up.

That week, I discovered that several guys I worked with were going through a divorce.

On my first night there, the sound of garbage trucks and the clickety-clop of horse-drawn carriages passing under my windows kept me awake. In Manhattan Beach, the only sound was birds chirping.

By the end of June, I was served with divorce papers. After negotiations, I gave my half of the house to Marge in lieu of alimony. Child support was $300.00 per month. I would see the kids every other weekend, with a sleepover, and one month over the summer. That seemed fair. I signed the papers, and by December 1973, I was divorced.

My next-door neighbour was a classical music pianist, composer, and aspiring conductor. One floor down was a toy salesman and a hobbyist magician. Grocery shopping was at an A&P on Ninth Avenue and 54th Street, and the laundromat was on 56th Street. When I lived in Brooklyn, I would arrive at work at 10 am. Now that I lived around the corner, I would arrive at 9:30. All the VPs were in their offices. I was one of the few people who received *The New York Times*. One of the publicists would take my paper every morning and return it to me all messy. Now that I was in the office before him, I would finish the front page of the current paper and substitute a week-old *New York Times*. Everybody knew what I was doing except him.

Within my responsibilities, I worked with every segment of ABC. One morning, I was told to go to Elton Rule's office for a meeting. Elton was CEO of ABC, reporting directly to Leonard Goldenson, who was the founder of ABC. If ever I wanted to cast a CEO for a project, Elton Rule was perfect: tall, stately, always tanned, wearing a suit that looked like it was pressed before he came to 1330 Sixth Avenue. Goldenson and Rule were working with Ross Perot, who had purchased a large parcel of land, making it into a wildlife preserve and naming it The Largo Wildlife Preserve. This was a time when Warner Brothers opened a scenic attraction called Jungle Habitat, and Six Flags, a major amusement park, was opening around the country. I was to develop and create promotions for the park's opening, which required me to be at the site for a meeting the next day, and spend two weeks at the park.

The following day, I took Amtrak to Washington, D.C., rented a car, and drove 21 miles to the park. They already had signage up promoting the preserve. There were half a dozen cars parked at the Safari Ticket Office. At the meeting were the gamekeeper, head of security, people from the advertising agency, and the CEO of the park. As the meeting proceeded, I realised that the CEO knew nothing about scenic attractions. He was a buddy of Perot who had graduated from the Naval Academy and needed a job. The concept was to put paying guests in an open tram, which would complete an hour-long tour of the park, viewing the animals. They failed to realise that most animals get up in the morning and go to sleep in the afternoon. I was in a delicate situation, starting with the name of the park. People who lived on the Beltway would assume it was a government research centre.

Calling ABC New York, I was told not to go there…leave it be. I created a laundry list of promotions to do. I even worked with Washington DC Transit to stop in front of the Preserve. They suddenly wanted to put rides like Six Flags, but the governing body of Prince George's County rejected the plan. Most of the summer I was commuting between New York and Largo, Maryland, when I learned that the white residents were silently boycotting the park against having an influx of Black people come into their neighbourhood. Two years later, they closed the park and wrote off four million dollars.

Every other weekend, I would arrive from Washington, go home to 53rd Street, change, and take the subway to Brooklyn. Marge was always on the front lawn, handing over Julie and Jamie for the weekend. They both had shopping bags with their weekend clothes. I would always stop by my parents' apartment for dinner. Before we left, my mother would give me forty dollars to buy something for the kids. In those days, taking the subway any time in New York was safe. The convertible sofa was like a queen-size bed. Every morning, I found them both sleeping with me. Julie was nine and Jamie was eight. I knew the manager of one of the jazz clubs on 53rd Street; he allowed us to sit at a table in the back where we ordered Cokes. He would always send cookies. Sundays, I would take them home by 7 pm.

A year later, every call with Marge became a battle; what was once a civilised relationship became a war of words. During one of these arguments, she told me that my grandmother wasn't my real grandmother. My real grandmother recommended that I ask my mother. I always stopped by before I took the kids to Manhattan for dinner with my parents. Asking my mother to join me in the bedroom, I asked her if my grandmother was my grandmother. Apologising for not telling me earlier, she opened her dresser drawer and showed me a faded photograph of my grandfather and her real mother. Going back to the flu epidemic of 1918, there was my grandfather, an immigrant with two young children, my mother and her brother Charley, sending them both off to live with an Amish family in Lancaster, Pennsylvania, in search of a woman to take care of his two young children. That's where my grandmother came in, with whom he had my aunt and uncle. Now she admitted her biggest mistake, thinking her mother's first name was Annie. In the Jewish religion, it was custom to name a child using the first initial of a deceased relative; that's why she named me Allen. A few years later, she discovered her mother's name was Fanny. This story made no difference, for my grandmother was the one who helped bring me up.

With my travelling between New York and Largo, Maryland, it was ridiculous that on Friday night I would have to take the train to Brooklyn and back to New York. We agreed that my father would pick them up, and take them to Manhattan. After the wildlife preserve, I was summoned to a meeting where I was told that ABC was bringing in a children's circus from Spain. A Spanish priest named Jesus DeSilva opened his answer to America's Boys Town for troubled Spanish kids who would be trained to be circus performers, called Circo de Los Muchachos. ABC was booking them in large venues in key cities, opening in Madison Square Garden on 11 September 1973.

I knew the Monsignor who worked with Cardinal Cooke, aware that the Spanish Community was the lifeblood of the Catholic Church. I presented the idea of an offertory mass where the Children's Circus would perform both on the steps of St Patrick's Cathedral and, following that, by the altar. With the help of the Church, we closed off Fifth Avenue. The circus proceeded to Saint Patrick's to make their offering. I made the front page of the Metro Section of the New York Times, the front page of the New York Post, and the Daily News, and was featured on all the TV news and network news.

The marketing was a success, but the circus booked Madison Square Garden with 19,500 seats. Rather than booking a smaller venue, ABC entered another arena where they lost money. If it wasn't for the insurance covering the circus against the death of a few animals coming over by boat, it would have been a total loss.

By the end of October, I had become friends with all my neighbours. We decided to have a Halloween party. All the tenants chipped in a hundred dollars each. The Network had a large art department; one of my friends created a flyer, and then the print department took care of printing two hundred flyers. Using interoffice mail, I invited Network Sales, Affiliate Relations, Legal, Programming, Network Radio, and the entire Public Relations department. We had bars and bowls of Halloween candy, popcorn, and crisps on each floor of the brownstone. By midnight, we had a hundred people from ABC.

It was never difficult for me to connect socially, and my ABC ID card was my way of entry into the top clubs. I have never learned how to be alone. My schedule was to come home from work, take a nap, set the alarm for 9 pm, have a light meal, change my clothes, and go clubbing. After a week of hitting all the spots, I discovered Monday and Sunday nights were the worst nights to go out to meet people. Just around the corner from my apartment were the 21 Club and Jimmy's, which was owned by a member of Mayor John Lindsay's executive staff. At 21, the people at the bar were only talking about deals or were couples. Jimmy's after-work crowd was young singles in search of love. Since I didn't drink, I knew the bartender and ordered a Coke with as many refills as needed. Jimmy's was the first and last spot I would hit before going to bed at 2 am. One December evening, I went to talk to my bartender friend at Jimmy's. Seated at the bar was a good-looking woman who had had too much to drink. I offered to take her out to buy her coffee. I didn't realise that none of the coffee shops stayed open after midnight. I was in a delicate situation. I wanted to get her into a cab. Figuring that I would go around the corner towards my apartment, hoping to find a taxi. It began to snow. Instead of hailing a taxi, she followed me into the vestibule of my brownstone, hoping she could navigate the three flights to my apartment. She made it all the way. Taking off her coat, she sat on the couch. I went into the kitchen to make her coffee. As I was bringing out the cup, she was stark naked, sitting on my windowsill with her legs dangling over 53rd Street. That's all I needed – to have a naked woman falling out of my window. Luckily, I was able to pull her off the windowsill and put her on the bed. As she lay there, I saw scars on her wrists. I fell asleep on the couch. I had a 10 am staff meeting. Waking her up, I told her to get dressed, ushering her down the three flights of stairs. She told me that she was from the Poconos, her suitcase was in a locker at the Port Authority, and she wanted to stay over. I hailed a taxi, putting twenty dollars in the driver's hand, saying I had a house guest coming in from LA. As the taxi went west on 53rd Street, I realised that I never knew her name. At Christmas, I went to Brooklyn with a stack of gifts for Julie and Jamie, hanging out in what was once my home. Marge was a changed woman; we even had sex. Emotionally, I was finished with her, and the only people I cared for were my children and their well-being.

In 1974, ABC Sports, under Roone Arledge, created the concept of the *Wide World of Sports*, hosted by Jim McKay*. They also developed *Monday Night Football*, for which Roone assembled a top play-by-play team of Howard Cosell, Frank Gifford, and Don Meredith. Although ABC Sports had an entire marketing team handling NCAA Football, *Monday Night Football*, and *Wide World of Sports*, I found myself working with the *Monday Night Football* team. Howard was the most difficult person to work with: arrogant, a know-it-all, and condescending to the press.

At that time, they were televising major boxing matches in cinemas. Somehow, our engineering department was able to tap into the system that broadcast the event to theatres. I had a special list of VIPs, one of whom was Bob Tisch, CEO of Loews

Corporation, and his wife, as well as heads of security for the top discos or private clubs in Mayor Abe Beam's office. At thirty-three years old, I felt I had a bright future in broadcasting.

In 1974, Club A opened on East 61st Street. It was a popular private club selling yearly memberships. Showing my ABC ID, the doorman brought me in to meet the owner. The club was decorated in red and gold. Upon entering, there was a bar. The next room was the dining room, which flowed into the backgammon room. I had never seen such elegant-looking women. They were playing backgammon. Not only was the game interesting, but sitting opposite were women wearing low-cut dresses. After the tour, I invited him to be on my VIP list to view major pay-per-view sporting events. Standing in the corner of the room was a woman in her early thirties whose look was different from the women I was attracted to. I was always looking for a Sandra Dee type – meaning a Jewish girl who had had nose jobs and dyed her hair blonde. The giveaway that their looks were not what they were born with was their pubic hair. This woman was certainly not Jewish. After saying hello, we spent two hours talking. She told me that she was brought up in Coconut Grove, Florida. Her mother was a major politician, and her father worked for Pan Am Airlines, which was their hub in South America. It was a mild January night, and deciding to walk home, she was living in an apartment on 53rd and Eighth Avenue. Stopping by the entrance to her brownstone, I offered to put her in a taxi. Looking at me, she asked if I wanted to come up to her apartment. Entering the apartment, I had a bottle of wine from a Halloween party. Eventually, we ended up having sex. This was not my weekend with Julie and Jamie. Offering her a Coke, we sat on the couch, and she told me that she had cancer, and it was in remission. She had great breasts, and I was wondering where she had had cancer. Excusing herself, she went to the bathroom, returning with a lovely set of dentures. She explained to me that she had isolated cancer of the jaw. Would I mind if she didn't have teeth? How could I say I would mind if she went from a beautiful woman to an old lady in thirty seconds? Having sex with her was a unique experience. While I was working, she went back to her Eighth Avenue apartment to get a new set of clothes. Within a month, she had almost moved in. We would go out two or three times a week. I was drinking Coke, and she was drinking vodka. We made a deal: if she was talking to someone and I wanted to leave, it was alright with her. She would meet me at home. Usually, she would be home within an hour, drunk. I then realised she was an alcoholic. Rather than ending the relationship, I thought I could change her. Every night, she came home with a fifth of vodka. I was amazed that she was able to walk up three flights of stairs. We discussed her drinking habit, and she promised that she would stop drinking vodka and switch to wine. That made me happy, and I went out and bought a gallon of jug wine, which took her two days to finish. For some reason, I wanted to punish myself. Every weekend, she went to her apartment on Eighth Avenue. She understood that I didn't want to expose my children to another woman until we both decided it was right, and she joined us for dinner over the weekend. By the spring of 1974, I asked them both if they would mind having Jean live with me. Both Julie and Jamie said she was fun. They admitted that Marge had a man living with her. They told me that he lived down the block and worked for the sanitation department.

Jean always wore a pyjama top, which she never took off. All of our intimacy was always in the dark. Finally, I asked her why she always wore pyjama tops. Unbuttoning her top and displaying her breasts, her stomach area, like a prune, showed terrible stretch marks. Drinking her third glass of wine, she held my hand. "I feel safe with you," she said, moving eight feet to the couch. "My real name is Elizabeth Bettner. I married at sixteen to an Air Force pilot who was ten years older than me. We lived in officer's quarters, finally moving to Lakeland Air Force Base in Texas, where I had my first daughter. I was the youngest woman on the base, all alone. One day, he told me that he would be gone at the most for a week. Before he left on deployment, he admitted that he and his squadron were deployed to Vietnam – for six months. Being lonely on the base, I had an affair with a pilot who had just come back from Vietnam. I was pregnant by the time my husband returned; my second daughter was born. He assaulted me, called me a whore, and kicked me out of the house. I had no choice but to return to Coconut Grove." As our relationship ripened, she slowly opened up with more information, telling me she was never in New York but had contacts with people who ran travel clubs. These were membership clubs that offered great package deals on travel destinations. Casinos in Las Vegas would put together free flights for big gamblers. Loews Hotels opened a casino in Monte Carlo. I was offered the opportunity to run that division; unfortunately, I did not have a list of high rollers.

Jean was able to get us on the flight to Greece, leaving on 6 July and returning on 20 July. As we crossed the Atlantic, she was already drunk. Landing in Athens, the tour bus transported us to The Hotel Stanley, which was rated a four-star hotel located one square away from Syntagma Square, where many of the five-star hotels were located. After playing tourist, boarding a tour bus that took us to the ancient sites, visiting Ancient Athens and the villages outside of Athens along the Aegean Coast, and hanging out at the roof bar, I contacted a friend of Eddie Jaffe and my father, the CEO of the Epirotiki Cruise Line, picked us up for dinner. On the way back to our hotel, he ran out of gas, and we had to push the VW to the nearest gas station.

On 20 July, the day of our departure, we decided to go to the Plaka to buy a Flokati area rug. They were selling the carpet by the kilo. The hotel concierge told us not to buy a carpet that was brought up from the store's basement; the moisture of the basement would make it weigh more. After an hour of haggling, he agreed to sell us a carpet that was on the sales floor. Before he wrote the sales receipt, a sound truck passed, announcing the mobilisation of all Greek men over eighteen; the country was at war with Turkey over Cyprus. At that moment, he asked us to leave the store and go back to our hotel. Suddenly, a vibrant shopping area was a ghost town, with all the shops closed. Hurrying back to our hotel to board the bus to the airport, we were told that Athens airport was closed. Greece had what was known as the law of return. They ordered all the departed flights to return to the airport to deposit all their passengers with Greek heritage to join the army.

The following morning, 21 July, we heard the rumbling of old World War II tanks outside our hotel window. All the hotel guests were up at the roof bar, trying to figure out ways to get out of the country. The only way out was by water, going the other way.

Many found the option of taking a ferry to the Island of Brindisi, which would take fourteen hours, then a flight to Italy, to then take a flight to their home. It was a mix of couples from the UK and the USA.

We, in turn, took this as an opportunity to visit Mykonos, where Jean had a friend whose husband owned the hottest bar on the island, Pierro's. We packed a bag for five days, having the hotel concierge book us a room at a luxurious hotel on the island. In 1974, the US dollar was strong against the Greek Drachma. The ferry ride took five hours from Piraeus, which was the name of the port where you boarded a ferry to Mykonos. Enjoying a July afternoon on a ferry cutting across the Aegean, we made friends with a couple our age from London. We became instant friends while Jean was refilling her orange soda with vodka. As the ferry pulled up to the dock at Mykonos, we went down the gangplank. Searching for a taxi, I drove to the spot where I'd left her bags there; she was gone. I spent an hour looking for her; she had disappeared, figuring she would meet me at the hotel. The hotel was on top of a mountain overlooking the Aegean. As the sun started to set, she was nowhere to be found. Skipping dinner, I went down to the town centre to check at Pierro's. The owner's wife was at the reception desk in the dining room. Introducing myself as Jean Jarret's boyfriend, she was stunned; she hadn't heard from her since she left LA to marry her Greek boyfriend and move to the island. I was ashamed to mention that I'd lost my girlfriend. Walking around, I ran into the couple from London, whom I asked if they had seen her. Pointing to a person who was sitting on cobblestone steps, I thanked them and went over and sat down next to her. I didn't want to fight; I asked her what had happened.

Slurring her words, she pointed to her ankle, which was swollen. She couldn't stand. A guy pulling a watermelon cart passed, and I asked him if he could help us. Agreeing to pay him twenty US dollars, he loaded her onto the back of his cart, bringing her to the hotel. Luckily, they had a wheelchair. I asked the desk clerk if he knew of a doctor, looking at me as if I was crazy, saying they all went off to the war. The only person who was around was an eighty-year-old veterinarian who was too old to join the army; he took care of all the livestock on the island. I had no choice; I needed someone to handle her swollen ankle. Fifty dollars later, he gave her a shot of painkiller, wrapped her ankle, and told me that I should go back to Athens to take her to a hospital; it's free for tourists. The next morning, I left early to buy return tickets to Athens. My plan was three days on the island; now it was twenty-four hours. Purchasing the ferry tickets, I roamed the retail shops and bought Julie and Jamie gifts from Mykonos.

Returning to the hotel ninety minutes later, Jean accused me of having sex with another woman. Total insanity. Finding another guy with a watermelon cart, who brought her down to the ferry landing, which cost twenty US dollars. Luckily, the ferry had a wheelchair; they placed us on the stern of the boat. Cruising back to Athens, the Aegean was sparkling, with the sun reflecting off the water. Next to us was a family wearing NYU caps; leaning over, I asked him what year he graduated. In broken English, he explained that he was a janitor at the business school, living in Astoria, Queens. They offered to share feta cheese flatbread and wine. As he sliced the cheese, putting down his knife, he looked at me. "America is a great country; if you are sick, they do not charge for medical treatment. In Greece, the citizens must pay if they go to the emergency room or the city hospital. Tourists, if they get sick, do not get charged." Looking at Jean's foot, he told me to take her to the General Hospital of Athens.

Helping Jean down the gangplank in Athens, I told the taxi driver to take us to the General Hospital. Looking at Jean's bandaged ankle, he asked what hotel we were staying at. He told me that first, I had to go to a satellite EMS, who would examine her; if necessary, they would transport her to the General Hospital. Dropping us off at a storefront with a sign saying EMS, a couple of blocks away from the Stanley Hotel, we sat in the waiting room. She was in pain; the nurse at the desk said it would be soon. Looking at Jean, I told her that I would bring our overnight bags back to our hotel, which was a couple of blocks away. Jogging to the hotel with two bags on my shoulder, I handed them to the desk clerk, who asked me where my wife was. "EMS," I said, running back to the storefront. Jean was still in the waiting room. An hour later, a young doctor examined her, immediately ordering an ambulance to take us to the General Hospital. It seems that there is a universality with EMS all over the world: sick people waiting for hours.

After a series of X-rays, the young doctor wrapped her ankle, giving her a bottle of painkillers which he said shouldn't be mixed with alcohol. Returning to The Stanley Hotel, I bought food and hung out with people on the rooftop bar. On the 23rd, I told Jean that I wanted to go to the ABC Athens Bureau and have them send a message to both ABC and my parents that we were okay. Passing through Syntagma Square, the only living thing was a pigeon; it was empty. Finding the ABC Bureau, which was a fifteen-minute walk from the square, I introduced myself to the staff and asked them to send a message to New York saying I was safe. Could they call my parents?

Returning to the square, there were now a million people jumping for joy, some waving the Greek flag, others banging on pots, car horns honking. Pushing myself through the crowd, I asked if anyone spoke English. A person wearing a beret told me that he spoke English. "This is a great day for Greece; we are returning to where democracy was created," he said, asking me if I was American and screaming that the Junta was overthrown, and Constantine Karamanlis had just landed from Paris to build a new government. The war with Turkey was over in two days.

Returning to the hotel, the desk clerk gave me a message from the tour company saying that a charter bus would pick us up for a 7 pm Pan Am flight to JFK. She was stoned from the painkillers the doctor gave her. The Pan Am ticket office was a couple of blocks from the hotel. Grabbing our tickets, I went to the office to make arrangements for bulkhead seats, telling them that my wife had had an accident while visiting Mykonos and needed special treatment, asking them to have a wheelchair to take us through passport control and onto the plane. Our bulkhead seats were the next section from first class, giving her room to stretch out her feet. The flight back to JFK was eleven and a half hours.

Two hours into the flight, our fellow passengers, rather than take the aisle to the bathroom, started taking shortcuts, using the space between our seats to cross over to the other aisle. Passengers crossing in front of us as their right. Jean, having had enough of people encroaching on her space, put her legs on the wall in front of us, blocking their passage. There became a shouting match between her and the other passengers. A stewardess had to contain the situation; passengers were on the verge of being physical. Suddenly, Jean started screaming; she had chest pains. The other passengers who sat in our row were moved to vacant seats in the back. One of the passengers, who was a doctor, volunteered to treat her. They pulled up the armrests of the adjoining seats, lying her down across the row with a pillow behind her head and an oxygen mask on her face. The entire plane was quiet for the rest of the flight.

Landing at JFK, they asked us if we wanted an ambulance to meet us at the gate. Jean thanked them, asking for only a wheelchair. Customer service took us through customs, wheeling us to baggage claim. The skycap picked up our luggage, taking us to the front of the taxi line. Helping her out of the wheelchair, and taking back the oxygen mask, I directed the taxi to our apartment. Placing her head on my shoulder, she began to laugh. "Wasn't I great? I had those bastards feeling sorry for giving me a heart attack."

Looking at her, "You scared me; why didn't you tell me?"

Moving towards the taxi window, she smiled. "If I told you, I couldn't count on you having a straight face. You had to believe that I had a heart attack."

The taxi dropped us off in front of 40 West 53rd Street. I had to make two round trips to the apartment, leaving Jean leaning against a parked car. After living there for a while, I started counting the steps. It was a hundred steps, holding onto a mahogany wood bannister almost a century old. Reaching my apartment with one suitcase, I opened the door that had three locks. Running down two flights, I brought up the second suitcase. Now I ran down to help Jean hobble one hundred steps, stopping on each floor. It took a week for the swelling to go down.

While I was away, my father did some detective work to gather evidence that I should get rid of her. Knowing how children are, you don't always listen to your parents. On my first day back, I was greeted as if I had returned from a war zone. My schedule was fairly open after the meeting, catching up on screening new programming for airing this coming September. ABC was so used to being number three. Most producers left ABC for last. Dick Clark's *American Bandstand* was a long-time staple for ABC. When *Bandstand* came to an end, DCCP produced music award specials and *Rocklin New Year's Eve.* Aaron Spelling was also one of ABC's major producers, responsible for *The Mod Squad*, *Starsky & Hutch*, *Charlie's Angels*, *The Rookies*, and *S.W.A.T.*

Julie told Marge that I had a girlfriend who was a famous actress and that she was nice. On many of my alternative weekends, my father escorted only Jamie to the city. Jean agreed to lay off the liquor while my children stayed over.

Spending hours together, her life remained a mystery to me. She told me about her Hollywood years, where she dated major studio heads and famous scriptwriters. She had a long-term relationship with the star of a major crime series on NBC that ran from 1967 to 1970, telling me that he was into kinky sex. One morning, a housekeeper at the Sherry Netherland found her handcuffed to a bed. She was eventually released when her lover came back to take her out to lunch and shopping at Bergdorf Goodman.

I avoided taking her to network events because I couldn't control her drinking. I told her I had late phone meetings with ABC's West Coast PR team. After the event, I would rush around the corner to our favourite bar, where she was drunk. We discovered that she was hypoglycemic, and taking two drinks of vodka made her drunk and unbearable.

Jean was obsessed with finding her birth mother. She was adopted by her family in Coconut Grove. She constantly said she was the daughter of Marilyn Monroe. In those days, DNA testing was in its infancy.

Marge began making it difficult for me to see Julie and Jamie. She now refused to give the children to my father, making it so I would have to take the subway after work, making two round trips on Friday, again on the subway. Julie was always busy.

In 1975, they took away my office window, moving me to an office that once housed the copier. In those days, street hawkers would hand out leaflets advertising topless clubs.

Rebelling against their taking away my window, I decorated my office walls with various coloured leaflets promoting topless bars.

Jean introduced me to her New York friends. A Polish Jew who escaped from Birkenau, a German death camp, joined a partisan group, blowing up munition trains. Immigrating in 1946, he now lived in Central South, owning a big Chevy dealership in Brooklyn and a partnership in a Long Island Savings and Loan. He always had three girls living with him, owning a house in West Hampton and a large cabin cruiser docked in front of his 15-room house. He also had a chauffeur who drove him around in a stretch limo. He treated the girls who lived with him like objects. In Club

A, we became friends with the owner of a chain of Japanese restaurants who had a penchant for collecting Rolls Royce and keeping blondes. He was also the publisher of a magazine that tried to be another *Hustler.* His other claim to fame was his skill at playing backgammon. Her doctor was a Polish doctor who was always pitching hair restoration formulas, working out of a second-floor office on lower Fifth Avenue.

Our relationship revolved around her drinking and her returning home at three in the morning. My goal was to get her to an AA meeting, which she resisted, saying she wasn't an alcoholic.

When she was drunk, she became Elizabeth Bettner. She bragged about being one of a dozen girls on Bebe Robozo's yacht during a fundraising event for Richard Nixon. A Coconut Grove activist, she'd had a long-term affair with the then-governor of Florida. She ran against Charles Snowden in 1972, losing by a small margin for the Florida House of Representatives. As an aside, she told me that when she lived in Florida, she always had a gun under her car seat, killing two Cuban hitmen who came at her as she was parking her car.

These were great stories coming out of the mouth of a drunk woman. By 1975, my relationship with Marge was constant fighting. I threatened to cut off child support. I am a person who doesn't hide his emotions. Threats and cursing were part of my day at work.

Jean, or Elizabeth – I didn't know which person I was living with – arranged for a long weekend at the Hotel Xanadu in Freeport, in the Bahamas. I had vacation time coming to me. We spent a week drinking. I took the sun, walking past a hotel newsstand. There was a front-page story in the *Miami Herald* about an IRS undercover sting operation called Operation Leprechaun, to root out corruption of Miami politicians. Her mother, whose name was also Elizabeth, outed her daughter in the *Miami Herald* story.

It was all in print, and all the stories she told me were true. Returning to New York, there were six calls from Walter Cronkite. CBS News wanted to interview her.

https://www.youtube.com/watch?v=q-Q8eAabuvU&t=890s

I did something that I would regret for the rest of my life. Calling Av Westin, President of ABC News, he told me that Geraldo Rivera had already booked Elsa Guttierze, who outed the IRS. Transferring me to his producer, who was eager to book Elizabeth as a guest. I was a company man and loyal to ABC. Now that she was on ABC, I called Stan, with whom I played beach baseball on Bay One at Brighton Beach, a VP at Hill & Knowlton, a major public relations agency. Being friendly with the manager of the Warwick Hotel, where I booked all our visiting celebrities, he gave me a conference room for free. We decided that we had to move quickly and set up our press conference for the next day. Elizabeth wanted her story out there, wanting to set the record straight on behalf of the IRS.

The following morning, at about 9 am, I received a telephone call. The voice on the other end introduced himself from the Criminal Investigation Division of the IRS, asking me if Elizabeth Bettner was available to come to the phone. Giving her the phone, she took it, and the conversation consisted of "yes," "no," and "certainly." Within two hours, two men in dark suits showed up at the apartment, flashing their badges. They asked her to get dressed, escorting her out of the apartment. She told me not to worry; they were taking her to be debriefed at their offices located at Federal Plaza. I was astounded to realise that all of her stories were true. I had called the office, telling them I would be in late. The big event was the release of the programming schedule for Q4 of 1975. ABC would rent the Ziegfeld Theatre and invite advertisers and the press. Gaining insight into the programming strategy of both CBS and NBC was like looking at a crystal ball. The decisions were made on the material that the research department dealt with: demographics and psychographics of the television viewer. Prime time was from 8 pm to 11 pm. The success of the affiliates' local news in their market, which is from 5 pm to 6:30 pm, leads into the network news feed, followed by syndicated game shows. The key to prime-time success hinged on which local affiliates had the largest viewing audience in their market leading into prime time. The research discovered that viewers rarely changed channels once on their local news shows.

In the industry, networks guarded their schedules like the CIA handled classified documents. The concept was counter-programming: creating a block of programs that would flow together until local news came on. The sales department would sell advertising spots, guaranteeing that the programmes would attain the ratings that were promised. If this didn't happen, sales would give them spots for free to make up for their projected share of the audience. Fred Pierce was assigned to turn the network around. Eight to nine was the family hour, followed by a block of shows. I felt accepted by all the senior management. Not one thanked me for giving ABC News an exclusive on Operation Leprechaun. Elizabeth called me to meet her and one of the CID agents for a drink at the Warwick. He shook my hand and told me how lucky I was to have Elizabeth as a significant other. He then gave me the process: Elizabeth would be picked up by agents and taken to the federal office for a series of debriefs. He cautioned me not to open packages or to report any unusual activity on my block. There was some intelligence that Santo Trafficante Jr, a Mafia boss who controlled South Florida, had a contract out on Elizabeth, offering us twenty-four hours of protection. Elizabeth thanked him, saying she didn't need it. Paying the tab, he shook my hand, leaving the bar; he never told me his name.

Walking home, I always managed to trail her. After that meeting at the Warwick, she was picked up every day and driven down to Federal Plaza. There was only one entrance from my building to the street. Before leaving for work, I opened the window to scan the street. This was difficult, as 53rd Street was a busy street full of office workers and tourists visiting the Museum of Modern Art. I never wore hats or sunglasses. Now, when I left the apartment, I wore a hat, sunglasses, and a raincoat. I would wait until a crowd of people going west passed by, trying to blend in.

Not only was I walking behind Elizabeth, I was at war with Marjorie, who worked hard at keeping me and my parents away from the children. It was impossible to have a civilised conversation with her. Suddenly, her muscle-bound sanitation worker boyfriend started to get involved with the issue of seeing my children. He threatened to kick the shit out of me if I came near the house. Marge would bring them to the corner. Jamie was happy to go with me; Julie was non-existent, always with an excuse that she had something to do over the weekend.

Elizabeth's IRS debriefing came to an end. I was tired of fighting to see my children. Doing some research, I discovered Attorney Doris Sassower, whose main office was in Westchester. She was a pioneer in the field of family law and was particularly known for her expertise in child custody cases. As a founding member of the American Academy of Matrimonial Lawyers, and serving as president of the New York State Bar Association's Family Law Section, she had a great track record of attaining custody for her clients. Calling her Westchester office, she offered a free consultation meeting in her New York office in the Pan Am building. After a thirty-minute conversation, she told me her initial fee was five thousand dollars upfront. Thanking her, I said I would call her when I had amassed that amount of money.

A month after *The Geraldo Rivera Show*, I received a call from Human Resources requesting a meeting. They told me that I was being terminated. Curious as to the reason, he said, "Bad judgement. Management requested that you terminate your relationship with Elizabeth if you wanted to keep your job." I told him I would give him my decision in twenty-four hours. In the seventies, employees who weren't part of a union, especially senior management, had zero protection. I thought I would be promoted for bringing ABC an exclusive national story; instead, I was fired. Thinking I was the best in the industry, I thought I would find a position within.

Sitting in front of the HR director, I was asked what my decision was regarding Elizabeth Bettner working for ABC. I asked him why a corporation would even think of interfering in my personal life. I had two more years before I was fully vested in ABC Corporation. I had to show them that I was not intimidated. He offered me a package of one year's salary. I laughed, for I knew people who thought they were important received two or three years of severance, threatening that I would go to my contacts at the *NEW YORK TIMES*, *VARIETY*, *BROADCASTING MAGAZINE*, and any other media outlet, who would be only too happy to run a piece on how Walter Cronkite of CBS NEWS called my apartment numerous times and was the first to contact Elizabeth. Feeling loyal to ABC, I contacted AV Westin, who was the executive producer of *ABC World News Tonight.* He told me that Geraldo Rivera had booked Elsa Gutierrez, who ousted the IRS in an exclusive interview. AV put me on hold, calling the producer of the show, who jumped at the idea of booking

Elizabeth on the same show, springing her on Elsa to discuss the Leprechaun affair.

I went through the entire scenario, talking to AV and discussing corporate loyalty, then my demands for eight years of severance and doubled my health insurance, which I got free for six months. To sweeten my resignation, they would hire an out-placement agency to create a CV, do a mailing to various heads of companies where I felt my talents could flourish, requesting that he put the entire package in writing, realising that what they offered was a package that only senior department heads received when they were terminated without cause.

Returning to my office, I reached out to every major executive I worked with, from Roone Arledge, Fred Pierce, Michael Eisner, Barry Diller, Jim McKay, Marvin Mord, Mark Cohen, and Sy Amlin—no one was there to help me. Both Ellis Moore and Dick Connelly avoided me. By Friday of that week, I received my exit package. Packing up my office, two security guards escorted me out of 1330 Sixth Avenue. They forgot one thing: having me sign an NDA. I never mentioned what happened, saying only that they transferred my work to the West Coast. Owning about five hundred shares, I was sent an invitation to the annual stockholder meeting being held at New York's Waldorf Astoria on 18 May 1976. The only close friend I had was Rick Giacalone, who oversaw hiring photographers at the Network.

I told him of my plans to bring up my dismissal at the meeting. He warned me that if I did this, I would be blackballed from working at another Network for life. Taking his advice, I went the safe route, keeping quiet. Right before the stockholder meeting,

Rick called me, recommending that I apply for a position as head of marketing for affiliate relations. I called the president of that division, who knew me, setting up a meeting for the following week. The morning of the meeting, he called to cancel, saying that I would never be hired by ABC, and suggesting who to call at the other Networks. Marge was getting more antagonistic.

I had more money than I ever had. Having lunch with Jerry Evans of Universal, he offered me an opportunity to work on *Midway*, which was due to open in June. He told me to set up a PR firm with Universal as my client.

I had arranged to take both Julie and Jamie to Acapulco for a month, renting an apartment in a condo right on the beach next to the El Presidente Hotel. Called Marge to give the kids a letter that authorised me to take the children out of the country, even though I was their father, I needed a letter from the parent who had custody allowing me to take them out of the country. I was stupid; I should never have told her. I could have written the letter, and Elizabeth would have signed it. I figured this was a simple request, so why lie? Exiting the train on Brighton Beach Avenue, I walked to pick up my children. Marge was on the corner, standing next to my eleven-year-old son, who was holding a paper shopping bag. She let his hand go, and he ran to me. I asked him where his sister was. He said that Julie had decided she didn't want to go. Looking at his shopping bag, I asked where his clothes were for a month. "Mummy said that you should buy me new clothes." My last question was where the letter was that his mother had promised to give him. "She doesn't want me to leave the country," was his reply. Returning to Manhattan, I had to cancel my reservations with Aero Mexico and the Mexican condo owner. The moment I walked into the apartment, the telephone started ringing. Marge demanded that I return my son, saying that she would be by with her boyfriend, Joel, to pick up Jamie tonight. We both packed what we needed for two weeks anywhere but New York City.

During my time at ABC, I began a friendship with Allen, who was the manager of the Warwick Hotel and happened to live with his family in the hotel. He was aware of the problems I had with my ex. He recommended that we go to Puerto Rico. He called his contact at El San Juan in Puerto Rico, who comped us for two weeks. I made a reservation for three on a non-stop Eastern Airlines flight leaving from La Guardia to San Juan. Over the weekend, I took Jamie to Alexander's discount department store for clothes. After midnight, we returned to 53rd Street to pick up clothes for our trip. During our vacation, building sandcastles on the beach, Jamie told me that he was always locked in his room, either by Mummy or Joel. "Sometimes Mummy, Julie, and Joel would take showers together." On the flight back to New York, I told him that he was going back to his mother. He asked, "Can I live with you? I do not want to go home." We couldn't go back to the apartment; we had nowhere to go. I called Allen at the Warwick. He said he had a convention the following week, but rooms were available now for a week.

After checking in at the Warwick Hotel, I decided to go for custody now that I had Jamie, which would make it easier rather than returning him to his mother to start the process. I called Doris Sassower to set up a meeting ASAP and called my parents, who both agreed with my decision, saying they would join me for the meeting with my attorney. Jean agreed that this meeting was inappropriate for her to attend.

We met Sassower in the conference room of her office in the Pan Am building. Joining her was Richard Kurtz, who I later found out was an expert on Orthodox Jewish divorce. After an hour-long meeting, we agreed on a fee of no more than ten thousand dollars. Doris asked us to leave the room; she wanted to talk to Jamie about what he wanted. Taking Jamie's hand, she said that before she filed and served papers, she wanted to make sure that Jamie's decision was not based on his having fun in Puerto Rico, giving me the telephone number of a psychiatrist who specialises in children for an evaluation. That afternoon, I called to set up an appointment with the head of psychiatry at Albert Einstein School of Medicine in the Bronx. The next morning, I was seated in the waiting room as the director of adolescent psychiatry at Einstein School of Medicine. Exiting his office, I asked the doctor what his evaluation of Jamie was. Patting Jamie on his head, he said, "I will send my evaluation to your attorney."

Marjorie reported that I had kidnapped Jamie. All my time on the run, I wore sunglasses and a hat with a camera around my neck so that I would look like a tourist. Jamie wore a New York Yankees baseball cap. It was difficult avoiding the police, for the Summit was around the corner from the 17th Precinct, which we passed almost every day.

The following morning, the attorney called, telling me, "Marge will be served by the end of the week," recommending that I go somewhere with Jamie, staying there until a court date was set.

Jean made plans for us to join Rocky Aoki* on his cabin cruiser to watch the 4th of July fireworks celebration of our nation's Bicentennial in New York Harbour. I never knew that the Statue of Liberty was green. Returning to the Summit, Alan arranged for me to stay at the Colony Motel in Atlantic City. In 1976, the New Jersey Legislature approved gambling in Atlantic City. Across from the motel, the Resorts Casino and Hotel were renovating two old hotels, the Chalfont House and Haddon House. Both hotels were built in the 1920s when Atlantic City and its boardwalk were the domain of the wealthy during the Prohibition era. I was eating up my money from the ABC severance. We all shared one room. Atlantic City was a city in need of urban renewal, which the state hoped would happen when casinos opened on the boardwalk. On 6th August, Elizabeth gave me an ultimatum: we get married, or she will return to New York. Discussing this with Jamie, he gave his approval. The process was simple: get a licence from the City Clerk, who escorted us to the Judge's Chambers, who married us. Elizabeth excused herself; she had to go to the ladies' room, telling us to wait for her. After fifteen minutes, I knocked on the bathroom door, receiving no answer. I opened the door; she was gone. Jamie asked where she was. I dismissed the question. We headed to McDonald's for a wedding dinner minus the bride. She returned at 4 am, totally soused, falling asleep in her clothes. The next morning, 8th August, we received an evacuation notice that Hurricane Bella was bearing down on Atlantic City. Buses were filled with people, and we were transported to a large brick building, which was an armoury on high ground. The people in the centre were mainly poor black people who lived in low-lying areas prone to flooding. The air conditioning was hardly working, and the smell of human sweat permeated the air. By 2 am, the all-clear was given, and the buses returned us to our location.

The Colony Motel was badly damaged. Our room had water on the floor; whatever we brought from New York was either wet or soiled by ocean salt water. We had nowhere to sleep. Taking whatever was left, we walked to the Greyhound terminal to catch the first bus to New York. We purchased the last three tickets for the 9 am bus, which was cancelled until the Garden State Parkway opened to travel. I always made up stories to help him fall asleep. At 9 am, the terminal loudspeaker announced that the bus to New York would depart at noon. Calling Alan at the Warwick to report what damage had occurred at the Colony Motel, he told me not to worry; he would call the manager of the Summit and reserve a room for us.

Checking into our room at the Summit Hotel with only the clothes on our backs, at midnight, I walked over to my apartment to pick up clothes for the three of us. That morning, I contacted Sassower, who told me the good news: the custody hearing was set for Monday, 16th August, at the Brooklyn Supreme Court at 10 am before Judge Carson. Her strategy was not to go to family court for custody but to the Brooklyn Supreme Court.

Entering the courtroom with my parents and Jamie, Marge was there with an attorney friend of her father. We called the psychiatrist, Albert Einstein, as an expert witness. After his testimony, the judge called a recess until Monday, 26 August 1976, so that Marge could arrange a meeting with a child psychiatrist. My attorney asked for a temporary restraining order against Marge and her boyfriend.

Ducking out of the courthouse with my parents, they asked how Jean was – they didn't know her real name, and I wanted to keep it that way. My parents weren't happy about the relationship and recommended that I break it off. They didn't know that we'd married in Atlantic City; they were both shocked. My mother had an old saying: "How you make your bed, you must lie in it." The Star Delicatessen was one of his clients. Jean met us there; I was worried that she would be drunk before noon. My parents adored Jamie, but my mother missed Julie. The conversation around the table saw my parents congratulate us on our marriage. Asking Jamie if he missed his sister, he said no.

We had to make a decision: did we still stay in the hotel or go back to our apartment? I decided to rent a car and drive up to The Concord Hotel for a week. Ray Parker, who knew me as a kid, gave me a complimentary room and meals for a week.

We left Concord on Saturday, 24 August, deciding to go back to our apartment and return the rental car to Avis.

Jamie was an oddity; he was the only eleven-year-old kid living on West 53rd Street between Fifth and Sixth Avenues. The following morning, Jamie and I took a taxi which dropped us off in front of the courthouse building, which was located in Boro Hall, a section in downtown Brooklyn where all municipal offices were located. My parents didn't come; it was me, Jamie, my attorney, Marge, and her boyfriend, Joel, Judge Carson, the court stenographer, and the bailiff.

The judge brought the court to a session, asking Marge's attorney for the psychiatric evaluation of Jamie. The attorney answered that his client couldn't afford one. Marge hated me, accusing me of stealing her son. She wouldn't believe that Jamie had decided on his own.

My attorney immediately asked for temporary custody of Jamie. He had to be registered in grade school. The judge immediately consented to my lawyer's request.

Ending the hearing, he said that he would make a final decision in January 1977, telling Sassower to call his clerk to set up a date.

I already had a grammar school in mind; there was one on East 57th Street between Second and Third Avenues. One of my friends owned a condo down the block from the school.

Now it was my responsibility to create a new life for my son. Enrolling him in grade school, I walked him there at eight in the morning, picking him up at three. I still harboured the fear that Marge would pick him up. He was eleven. Being respectful of my faith, I enrolled Jamie in Temple Emanu-El, a Reformed synagogue located on Upper Fifth Avenue, to prepare him for his Bar Mitzvah, a coming-of-age ritual in the Jewish faith for boys who turn thirteen. He was also enrolled in Sunday school. I found a Boy Scout troop operating from a church located on the Upper West Side of Manhattan. Jamie was supposed to sleep on the convertible sofa; after a while, I moved him into the bedroom, afraid that he would be exposed to Elizabeth's drunken bouts. I never understood how she made it up the three flights of stairs.

Professionally, I became a gig worker before there were gig workers. I worked per assignment for Universal Pictures, United Artists, and of course, my father and Eddie Jaffe.

In January of 1977, my attorney called me to say that we were due in court on Friday, 6 January, at 10:00 am for the final court verdict on who had custody of Jamie.

The day before the hearing, I booked three tickets to Los Angeles. I had a friend parked outside to take us to JFK if the verdict went against us. Jamie, my parents, and I were on one side; Marge and her attorney were on the other. After a ten-minute speech about the happiness of children, the judge asked the bailiff to escort Jamie into his chambers. Fifteen minutes later, the judge ruled that she, as a loving mother, had failed to pay for psychiatric consultation to retain custodial power over her minor child, and awarded total custody to his birth father. Exiting the courtroom surrounded by my parents, Marge came over, screaming at Jamie, "You will feel sorry for choosing your fucking father and his alcoholic girlfriend over me. I will make sure that you never see or hear from my daughter again your mother is a witch!" Her parents, who had accompanied her to court, pulled her away as she was about to lunge at me, leaving the courthouse.

I was told that this verdict would go down as case law: that a minor of eleven years old has the right to choose which parent he wants to live with. Neither Marge nor I were called to testify on why we would be a better parent; it was all in the hands of the child. His ruling did not designate visitation rights. He said that the attorneys would work it out. This was a half-victory. I hadn't seen or talked to my twelve-year-old daughter since 1976. It seemed that there was no way that the court could enforce visitation rights that were laid out in the original divorce document, which stipulated the rights of the non-custodial parent to see his child while undergoing daily psychological pressure from the parent who has custodial powers over the child.

Discussing this issue with my attorney, she told me to still pay child support, promising to take care of it by the end of the summer.

Elizabeth became obsessed with the stretch marks on her stomach due to childbirth, seeking a doctor who could prescribe creams to hide the marks. When sober, she would work with Jamie on his homework. When he went to bed, she went out; six hours later, she returned home. I didn't worry about her cheating; all she was interested in was talking to strangers. She carried a flask filled with vodka, always buying one drink and nursing it all night. Realising that you cannot help an alcoholic unless she wants help, and figuring that by reducing the alcohol content I went back to bringing home jug wine, which she finished in two days.

In August of 1977, Elizabeth arranged for a trip to Southern Spain with her friend, who operated the same charter company that took us to Greece. Arriving in Malaga, we took the bus to Fuengirola, a small beach resort, staying in the Hotel IPV Palace and Spa. This trip was different from Greece; we became a family. Most of the time, we spent time on the beach, hanging out with gypsy families who lived in caravans overlooking the beach. They spent a good part of the day hunting for sea urchins to serve during dinner. All the beach bars were playing Sinatra's "Strangers in the Night", which was startling; I worked on that film while at Universal Pictures. A year later, the score was being played over loudspeakers on the beaches of Costa del Sol. We decided on taking a side trip to Tangier, boarding a bus to the port of Algeciras for the hour ferry ride across the Straits of Gibraltar to Tangier. Exiting the ferry, we entered an alien society, which was Islamic. The port overlooked Gibraltar, which was a British Overseas

Territory. Roaming around the city, I was approached a dozen times to buy hash; being a tourist in Tangier, everyone was out to hustle. We finally decided to have lunch at a French/Moroccan café located in Grand Socco, lunch being hummus, flatbread, and skewered lamb. The American dollar went a long way; some shops refused to sell to us, saying we were Zionists. My first purchase for Jamie was a mother-of-pearl Berber rifle; I settled for a camel-hide sun hat, which smelled like a camel. Jean stopped by a stall that made custom perfume, taking fifteen minutes to blend the oils, handing her jasmine perfume.

Boarding the ferry back to Spain, all the tourists were in tears. Standing next to a couple from London, I asked why everybody was so glum. "Haven't you heard? Elvis just died."

By 1978, I had not spoken to my daughter for going on 18 months. My mother would run into them, and Marge would pull her away.

In May 1978, my parents and Jean had a cordial relationship, planning Jamie's Bar Mitzvah. We decided that Jamie should join a youth group from Temple Emanu-El, going to Israel for a month. Again, my friend Allen arranged for a penthouse suite at the Summit Hotel; all we had to pay for was a bartender and the food. To create goodwill, I invited Marge, her boyfriend, and Julie to Jamie's Bar Mitzvah at the Temple. They didn't show up.

I remember that Jamie told me that Julie was taking showers with his mother and boyfriend. I taped every conversation with Marge in preparation for going for custody of my daughter, who was fourteen.

A smarter me should have walked away from the entire situation. Having discussions with my attorney on strategy, we decided that I should sue for custody of my daughter; the only way was to have the courts mandate that my daughter see me. My case became something special for my attorney, who was an avowed feminist who resented mothers who used their children as pawns to get even on their ex-spouse. I only wanted to be part of my daughter's life. I was open to having Jamie spend time with his mother, and me with Julie. Within a week, she was served with papers to appear for a custody hearing before the same judge that awarded custody of Jamie. Sassower made an impassioned plea to the judge as to why I would make a better parent, still paying my monthly child support cheques, which were entered into evidence, and bringing up the shower episode that Jamie described. Neither Marge nor her attorney showed up. Rather than holding her in contempt, he recommended that the attorneys find a solution.

Returning to her office in the Pan Am building, we collaborated on an agreement. Ending the payment of child support or funding for higher education for Julie, since both children were teenagers, and no parent should obstruct either child from in-person or telephone communication with said parent. My only goal was to see my daughter and have a relationship with her. I didn't end the child support to save money; I knew it wasn't going to her. If there was a mechanism that would ensure that my daughter would receive the money, I would pay. As a parent, you cannot control who your teenager can talk to. It was up to them.

Jean's daughter suddenly came to New York to audition for the Metropolitan Opera. Heather was a big girl with a great voice. She and her younger sister, Cindy, were brought up by their grandmother, whose name was also Elizabeth. Talking to Heather, she hadn't spoken to her mother since 1973. The interaction between Jean and her daughter was strained. After dinner, Heather said he had to go; I would never see her again.

1979 was a pivotal year. I realised that broadcasting spends more time in meetings than getting things done. From a management point of view, you cannot own your accomplishments; the guy above you wants to take all the credit. Their reward was making me a VP with an increase in pay to massage your ego. For eight years, ABC defined who I was as a person. Entering the 21 Club, Sadri's, The Four Seasons, you were respected as Mr. ABC, not as the person you were.

In June of 1979, I had a power breakfast meeting with Hank Schwartz, who owned many patents on satellite technology. He was responsible for producing many pay-per-view fights, including "Rumble in the Jungle", televised live from Zaire, featuring Muhammad Ali versus George Foreman. Don King, the legendary boxing promoter, also joined us for breakfast and offered me a freelance opportunity. Excusing myself, I had a noon meeting with NBC. Hailing a taxi, my suit jacket got stuck in the door. Trying to dislodge the jacket, I tore the seams. I had the taxi drop me off on 53rd Street and Fifth Avenue and ran up three flights of stairs to change suits. Opening the door, I discovered that the apartment was missing a coffee table, accessories that had been purchased during our overseas trips, and three large paintings. My first reaction was that someone had broken into our apartment. Going into the bedroom, all of Elizabeth's clothes were gone. It suddenly dawned on me that she had moved out while I was at my breakfast meeting.

Like a fool, I had given her a credit card and opened a joint checking account at Apple Bank, which was around the corner. Immediately, I went to the bank to discover that she had withdrawn two thousand dollars. My goal was always to protect Jamie. His school year was coming to an end, and I discovered that the Temple was planning another trip to Israel, following the Israeli and Egyptian signing of the Camp David Accords in 1978. I suggested that he take the trip again, and he liked the idea. The trip was to leave at the end of June and return before Labor Day 1979. When Jamie asked me where Jean was, I told him she had gone to Florida to visit her family.

The charter bus was parked outside Temple Eman-El, taking the group of 50 teenagers to JFK, from where they would depart on EL AL Airlines to Tel Aviv.

Elizabeth (aka Jean) had disappeared, changing the locks on the apartment. I went about my life. I wanted to put up a sign that read, "Please remove the hit on Elizabeth Bettner, aka Jean Jarret; she no longer lives here."

My neighbour, Bob Rossi, who lived on the second floor, asked if I had heard anything about the Rockefeller family selling their five brownstones plus a parking lot that abutted the CBS office building on 53rd Street and Sixth Avenue to a commercial real estate developer. The developer planned to assemble the property and build a large office building. Bob mentioned that this could be a big payday for us, as they had to buy out all the tenants of the building to get their project off the ground. Some of the tenants had lived there for twenty years and were paying only one hundred dollars for their apartments.

With Jamie gone, this was the first time I had lived alone, absorbing the energy of the city. In mid-July, as I exited the brownstone, a man about six feet tall and weighing close to three hundred pounds approached me, his hand tucked inside his suit jacket. He asked me if I was Allen Gutwirth, and when I nodded yes, my mind started racing. Was this the hit meant for Elizabeth? Closing my eyes, I waited for the gun to be fired. There was no click of a firing pin. Slowly opening my eyes, the large person asked if I had ever been served before. From his jacket pocket, he handed me an envelope, saying, "Now you are served," and walked away.

Handing my attorney a signed, uncontested divorce paper, I began a new chapter in my life. As a member of The World Zionist Organization, which was planning a trip to Israel partly sponsored by the Israeli Government, I boarded an EL AL flight to Tel Aviv. The process of boarding the flight to Israel, after a rigorous security check, involved boarding a shuttle bus which took us to the aircraft parked a mile away from the terminal. The flight crew greeted us and directed us to our seats. At that time, airlines allowed smoking, even though they closed the curtain separating the smoking section from the non-smoking area of the plane. After ten hours in the air, you could still smell the smoke. As soon as the plane approached sunrise, all the seated passengers rose from their seats, praying in unison the Jewish morning prayer, the Shema.

Boarding a tour bus that took us to the Tel Aviv Hilton Hotel overlooking the Mediterranean, I checked in. I planned to play tourist and have Jamie join me at the end of his second Israeli experience after he attended a cocktail reception and fundraising pitch. Leaving the hotel and walking on the promenade, I asked passers-by if they knew the location of a kosher delicatessen.

People I asked, who spoke only Hebrew, didn't understand the meaning of "delicatessen". I later found out that corned beef, pastrami, and knishes were a manifestation of Eastern European Jews who immigrated to America.

I grabbed a bite at an outdoor café on Dizengoff Street, which was described as the Champs-Élysées of Israel. Upon returning to the Hilton, I was approached a dozen times by street walkers; some were Palestinians, and many were Jews from North Africa. Coming from New York, where I lived in the middle of key tourist hotels where streetwalkers congregated in search of clients, I assumed that none of them was Jewish. I realised that selling sex was ecumenical; women of all faiths, when in need of money and lacking skills, find it easier to sell their bodies to survive. I was never into buying sex.

The next morning, my hotel phone rang. It was Jamie on the other end. Asking him how he discovered that I was in Israel, his reply was, "Grandpa, I wanted to hang out by myself."

"Jamie, we can go back to New York together," I said.

"I'll see you in an hour," he replied and hung up the phone. An hour later, there was a knock on my door. There stood Jamie, carrying his duffle bag. Jamie was a big kid who weighed over two hundred pounds. One of my goals in sending him back to Israel was to get him to lose weight.

Hanging out on the beach, I started talking to a woman who introduced herself as Sarah, claiming to be a tourist guide on holiday. Inviting her to join us for dinner, she became affectionate, always sticking up for Jamie and approving of the food he ate.

After a week in Tel Aviv, I booked a ride in a sherut, which was a shared taxi between Tel Aviv and Jerusalem. Jamie asked that I invite Sarah; he liked her. I thought it was a great idea; I would have my tourist guide and a woman with a great body. Checking into the Hilton in Jerusalem, we had a room with two queen-size beds. Entering the room, she put her stuff on one bed and told me that Jamie and I should share the other bed.

The next morning, I asked her if she could take us on a tour of the Old City. She took a map and outlined where we should go, saying she was going to hang out by the pool. I realised I had made a terrible decision; I had to get rid of her without making a scene. I told her that the Israeli Broadcasting System was having a cocktail party after sundown.

Saturday in Jerusalem is Sabbath, and everything shuts down. Walking a few blocks, we found ourselves by the Wailing Wall. Jamie told me that he'd got Bar Mitzvah again. I must admit, the Old City had a magic about it. Hundreds of people were praying and stuffing notes into what is called the Wailing Wall. The country was always on full alert. Above the wall was the Al-Aqsa Mosque, one of the holiest places in Islam.

Returning to the Hilton, there were dishes piled in front of the door. On the tray was a receipt – a room service bill for fifty dollars.

Going down to the pool, there was a group of executives from the Israeli Broadcasting System playing backgammon. Jamie went into the water. I said hello to Sarah, leaving her to say hello. I was introduced to them in Tel Aviv; one guy was named Asher. Explaining what was happening with Sarah, he went over to her, telling her something in Hebrew. She got up and left. Going back to our room, all of her stuff was gone.

The next afternoon, we went back to explore the Old City with its ancient cobblestone streets. Finding ourselves in the Christian Quarter, walking down the Via Dolorosa, a Greek Orthodox priest took us on a tour of the Church of the Holy Sepulchre. His English was great, and he told me that he grew up in Astoria, Queens. "In my twenties, I suddenly found out what I wanted to do. I came to Jerusalem, studied, and I am part of a team that rotates to secure our holiest of holy sites," he explained to Jamie, telling him what happened 1979 years ago. Before leaving, I asked my priest friend where I could find the best lamb in Jerusalem. He directed me to a restaurant beyond the Flower Gate, which leads you into the Muslim Quarter. Exiting the restaurant, we returned to the Hilton, where my friend from the IBS asked where we had gone. I told him about a great restaurant I found past the Flower Gate. He looked at me as if I was crazy. "That's the Muslim Quarter. It's dangerous for Jews," he said. I reminded him that I came from New York City, which was dangerous any time you left your apartment.

The next morning, we boarded a tour bus which was escorted by two jeeps filled with IDF members carrying automatic weapons. Our first stop was Masada, an ancient fort overlooking the Dead Sea where Jews fought back against the Romans in 72-73 CE. Exiting the bus, I decided to walk up to Masada in ninety-degree heat. There we were, two fat, overweight father and son ascending to the top of the mountain, 1,424 feet above the Dead Sea. The rest of the tour group took the cable car up. The tour guide luckily brought bottled water with him. The plan was to spend two hours at the site. After fifteen minutes of taking in the landscape, we took the cable car down. I always wanted to float in the Dead Sea. Jamie decided to sit in the shade while I changed into my bathing suit. The facility had lockers for tourists. Thinking that I was in Brighton Beach, Brooklyn, I ran into the water and floated. On the other side of the Dead Sea was Israel's border with Jordan. I remember that caking your body in Dead Sea mud was great for your skin. I rolled around in the mud like a pig. The attendant directed me to an enclosed pool area to rinse off the mud. Walking into the pool, the area smelled like rotten eggs. Thinking it was my imagination, I waded into the pool, rinsing off the mud. After ten minutes, I couldn't stand the smell, and the tour bus was about to leave. The attendant gave me a towel, recommending that I take a shower. Handing Jamie my shorts, I turned on the shower which was on the rocky beach of the Dead Sea. Standing under the shower, expecting cool water, I was hit with hot water.

Ninety per cent of my body was caked in Dead Sea mud, and I smelled of sulphuric acid. Putting on my camel hat, I boarded the tour bus. Luckily, the bus was half-filled, and the people around me went to the rear. The tour guide apologised that he had failed to tell me that the soaking pool was filled with well water that had a high sulphuric acid content, and the lines that fed water to the showers were above ground and baked by the sun. Arriving at the Hilton, I was the first one off the bus, caked in dripping mud, wearing a stinky camel hat, walking through the elegant lobby, and taking the lift up to our room.

Two days later, we flew back to JFK. Jamie received notification that he had been accepted at The High School of Music and Art. He gained acceptance based on a saxophone audition. The first week in high school, they transferred him to oboe, which he hated. On Open School Day, where parents meet the teachers, Jamie refused to accompany me. The teachers all loved him, but he wasn't applying himself. I taped every meeting I had and played it back over the stereo. Taking his history books and writing silly things over the paragraphs, I would ask him if he saw anything unusual in what he was reading. I warned him that if he messed up, they would throw him out of the school, which was one of New York's elite high schools. It has been three years since I have spoken to my daughter. I would call her every week, and Marge told me that she didn't want to speak to me. Marge never reached out to speak to Jamie. Being Jewish was very important to me. Jamie continued his Hebrew Sunday School, for in the Reform Movement, they believed in confirmation. Walking home from Emanu-El, he passed a pet store on Madison Avenue, where the owner gave him a male kitten. Arriving home with a new pet, I couldn't refuse him, for he had lost Snoopy when he decided to live with me. Jamie agreed to take care of him. We discussed names; every pet had a name. The kitten was dubbed Cat. After the naming ceremony, we went to a pet store on Ninth Avenue, buying a litter box, a large bag of litter, toys, and a scratching post.

Universal
International

LOBBY
SWIMMING POOL
A LUXURIOUS HOTEL ROOM
GYMNASIUM
Luxor BATHS HOTEL
121 WEST 46th STREET
(East of Broadway)
TEL. BRYANT 9-3630
NEW YORK
GARDEN SOLARIUM

The World's Immortal Adventure!
BEAU GESTE
In TECHNICOLOR
"BEAU GESTE"—GUY STOCKWELL
DOUG McCLURE · LESLIE NIELSEN
TELLY SAVALAS
DOUGLAS HEYES · WALTER SELTZER
A UNIVERSAL PICTURE
FOR GENERAL EXHIBITION

I want YOU
to see me
in
The Perils of Pauline
IN COLOR
See Pauline in the icy clutches of a mad scientist!
See Pauline swing with a swingin' gorilla!
See Pauline battle the love-starved hunter!
See Pauline get hung-up by Sharks!
PAT BOONE
PAMELA AUSTIN
EDWARD EVERETT HORTON
TERRY-THOMAS
ALBERT BEICH
HERBERT B. LEONARD
JOSHUA SHELLEY
HERBERT B. LEONARD
A UNIVERSAL PICTURE

Recapture the Happy, Crazy Fun Days of the Care-Free Twenties!
The most joyous romantic musical of the age!
Julie Andrews
Mary Tyler Moore
Carol Channing
in ROSS HUNTER'S PRODUCTION OF
"Thoroughly Modern Millie"
James Fox
John Gavin
Beatrice Lillie
"THOROUGHLY MODERN MILLIE"

DECADE FOUR

In 1979, My Father landed a new account PLATO'S RETREATMENT where the owners wanted to promote the Club as an alternative to STUDIO 54 as a place where free thinkers and couples with the same likes opened in the Basement of the Ansonia Hotel whose prior tenant was the Continental Baths a Gay Bathhouse

https://www.youtube.com/watch?v=17yRrNnsBVo&t=531s

My father, who was the last of the Broadway publicists, invited me to visit one of his new accounts. I was introduced as an account executive for what I discovered was a swing club, Plato's Retreat, located in the basement of the Ansonia Hotel on West 72nd Street, a New York landmark and protected property. Plato's leased the space that had been home to the Continental Baths, a gay bathhouse with its entrance on West 73rd Street. Bette Midler was a regular entertainer there.

We were greeted by a 300-pound doorman/security guard and waited in the dimly lit lobby, where the cashier/bookkeeper called downstairs for the owner, Larry Levenson, to escort us down to the club. Walking down a spiral staircase, we found ourselves in an adult Disneyland. Everybody was a club member, having signed a waiver and paid an admission fee of fifty dollars. The only rule was that all men must be accompanied by a female. Joining the club was seen by some as the answer to the concept of an open marriage. In the mind of a married male member, he was not cheating because his wife was with him. Most wives, however, were the victims of their mates' coercion, opening a Pandora's Box. Their male counterparts didn't factor in the physical difference between men's and women's performance. Men were relegated to the sideline as their spouses experienced multiple orgasms.

We saw members in all forms of nudity, having sex around the pool, and gathering by a buffet of assorted meats and salads. Realising they could not get a liquor licence, they served soft drinks and lemonade.

In the middle of the space was a spacious room called the Orgy Room, guarded by a staff member checking that people entering were couples.

The club had a great disco and a steam room. At the rear were lockers for members to disrobe and lock their valuables. Long-term members had their own lockers. The lockers led through a warren of small rooms with mats on the floor for couples to have private sex, and if they wanted company, they would leave the door open.

My dad and I followed Larry to his large, personal swing room in the rear. It was dimly lit, with red-painted walls, many mats, and a telephone.

Larry explained that swinging was his life. Before opening Plato's, he and his followers would rent loft space, bring in mats and food, and invite his followers. His significant other, Mary, sat there monitoring the meeting, and he would both be spokespersons for the concept of a swinging lifestyle. He was an advocate for an open lifestyle and against monogamous relationships.

My father got the account, and I was the account executive tasked with visiting the club several times a week, escorting press, and bringing friends and dates. I was allowed to enter the club without a date. Having Plato's as an account, I received daily calls from journalists representing major newspapers in countries like Great Britain, Germany, Japan, Norway, and Sweden. All were asked to interview Larry and his partner, Marie, to discuss their views on monogamy. I laid out the ground rules for all media outlet representatives: if they came, they could have dinner at the buffets and interview any members who agreed to discuss their alternative lifestyle; without a female date, they could not participate.

As the weeks went by, I noticed streetwalkers selling themselves as escorts for single men. Once inside, they sat around the club as their date went to change into a towel. After an hour, the girls would leave. The club was so busy with customers that security did not notice that one female was leaving without her date.

My visits were strictly business unless I brought a date. Many nights, I would invite women for dinner at the club, telling them it would be a unique experience. Before entering the club, I told them that I was there purely for business. Escorting them down the dimly lit stairway, I took them on a tour of the club. My strategy was simply to have dinner at the smorgasbord, then dance at the disco among members where the men were just wearing towels and the women in fantasy lingerie that they purchased from

Frederick's of Hollywood, who specialised in creating sexy women's lingerie.

Ninety per cent of the women I took to Plato's wanted to have sex. Some women were in town for business meetings from the Midwest; they would thank me for the experience. This was the first time I was thanked by a woman with whom I had sex. There were club protocols: people who wanted to have sex in the privacy of their cubicle could keep the door closed. If they decided they wanted company, they would leave the door open.

Passing the integrated locker room, I ran into a six-foot club member with a large moustache whose name was Rick the Prick. He was slipping into a silver low-cut gown, inserting padding to create breasts, and putting on a size fourteen silver pumps, which made him at least six and a half feet tall. After adjusting a black hat with a veil, he exited the locker room. Looking at him in wonder, I asked him if he was gay. Lifting his veil, he looked at me as if I was crazy. "Are you off your fucking mind? This is a fantasy trip for my girlfriend to see if she is into women." With that, he picked up his silver purse and headed towards the disco.

Running into Charlie, who was the club's co-manager, with his wife Gloria, I asked him if he knew what business Rick the Prick was in. "That asshole has a big product distribution business in New Jersey."

I became an observer, joining a well-dressed club member who he and his wife would visit the club every Friday. He was wearing Gucci loafers and a Rolex watch. Exiting the locker room was his wife, Diane, wearing red bikini underwear with a Hermès scarf covering her breasts and wearing black high heels. She kissed him on the cheek, telling him she would be back in fifteen minutes. As Stuart was finishing his salad, Diane returned, holding hands with a woman. He told me that he would see me later; the trio went towards the private swing rooms.

Walking around, I stopped to say hello to Seymour, who is in control of who enters the community swing room. Only couples were allowed in. Talking to Seymour, he told me in confidence that he is married; his wife works in the office as a bookkeeper, admitting that he was a draft dodger who crossed the border with Canada rather than serve in Vietnam.

The jacuzzi, as usual, was crowded; the steam of the one-hundred-degree water created a haze. As the water was bubbling, a woman seated in the pool had a great orgasm. I figured that she was playing with her G-spot. Popping out of the water was a head who was embraced by the woman.

The major event in 1979 was the Halloween party, where members vied for the best costume, with the winner getting a free weekend at the Swingers Dude Ranch located outside of Monticello. The club was decked out in spider webs, large pumpkins, and skeletons; two members were dressed like witches stirring a large pot filled with dry ice. Larry, with his pot belly, and Mary were dressed as Adam and Eve. Couples that didn't have costumes were given Venetian carnival face masks, which were sent by a club member living in Milan. By 10 pm, the place was filled with couples in fantasy outfits, S&M paraphernalia, and sexy nurses. One guy came as a mummy with an erection. Historical outfits like Mark Antony and Cleopatra, Asian girls all dressed like teenagers, Hercules and Medusa, harem slaves. Two couples came as Siamese twins. At midnight, the couples paraded before the audience; the winners were the Siamese twins.

One night, a friend accompanied me who was very handsome, even studying for the priesthood. In the real world, he always scored. He had a problem talking to a naked lady. His game was to romance and then have sex. Plato's eliminated the romance part of the equation.

Imagine taking a divorcee from Westchester or a female tourist from Cleveland for dinner at Plato's Retreat. I even invited my friend from ABC Television, who later became CEO of Disney.

Leaving Plato's at midnight, I would go to Studio 54, which was located around the corner from my apartment. Rather than going home, I went to Studio 54. At midnight, the crowd waiting to be selected spiled into 54th Street, stopping traffic. Pushing through the crowd, I was immediately let in by the head of security, whom I had invited to Plato's, either with or without a date. The job of the guys behind the red rope was to pick the best-looking and wealthiest people, eliminating the "bridge and tunnel" crowd – namely, ordinary people – from entering the club, with a few exceptions, allowing couples in who palmed them a twenty-dollar bill.

Before I passed through the rope line, I noticed an old friend of mine, Huntington Hartford, scion of the A&P Super Market fortune, fighting to get in. Grabbing him by the arm, I pushed him in front of me. Everybody at the bar knew him. The reason why he needed me to get in was that he was too plain-looking, wearing a dark suit and tie. The same crowd of celebrities who were hanging out at the bar greeted him. Most of them were his guests at his Beekman Place duplex facing the East River. Hunt introduced me to Andy Warhol. Halston invited me to his showroom at Olympic Towers, which was across the street from St Patrick's. Ordering my Coke and refusing a hit of marijuana, I observed the dance floor with its light show and compared it to where I had just come from. The couples on the dance floor at Studio 54 were simulating sex, whereas the couples on the disco floor at Plato's were already undressed, ready, willing, and able to have sex. I began thinking of the concept between "nude" and "naked". Both connote the same thing, but the imagery is quite different: a nude woman is someone wearing a beautiful negligee, whereas a naked woman is wearing a housecoat. There were always single women at Studio. I was a pretty good dancer. Searching for mature women, I asked a blonde lady, who was surrounded by three young gay men, if she wanted to dance. Exchanging names, she introduced herself as Selma, who was ten years older than me. Two hours later, we left the club. Her driver was waiting for her. We kissed each other on the cheek, exchanging telephone numbers. She offered to drive me home. I told her that I lived around the corner. I had no interest in her because she drank. Exchanging telephone numbers was a courtesy, knowing that I would never follow up. I never realised that she came to the Studio at least three times a week with her gay friends. Selma would call me after midnight, complaining about her life. One day, Selma invited me for lunch. She owned a condo at the Galleria on East 57th Street. Entering the apartment, her housekeeper led me into the dining room. During lunch, she told me that she lived in the Five Towns, an enclave in Nassau County. She had two children, a boy and an adopted girl. Her husband, Sidney, was running a heavy machinery moving company, which was founded by her father. Taking me on a tour of the apartment, which was designed by Mario Buatta, she showed me her bedroom, which had floor-to-ceiling windows. Passing a room that I imagined was a study, she told me that it was where her husband, Sidney, slept. As I was leaving, her husband, Sidney, entered the apartment. Sidney, who was over six feet tall and weighed about two hundred pounds, shook my hand. Selma made me her psychiatrist, calling me every night and keeping me on the phone. Owning an apartment at the Galleria, she offered to leave my name at the private club so I could use their facilities – pool, steam room, sauna, and gym. Being single in New York in the late seventies and into the eighties, the best way to meet women was either at house parties or single dances that were promoted by a few resourceful women. Making a deal with a restaurant where they kept the bar sales and she the door takings. These promoters would hang out in upper-class bars during cocktail hour, promoting their events. They usually had more women than men, who were in short supply and always in need of men. The entire bar of the Sherry Netherland received invitations.

The parties reminded me of the old days when I was eighteen, sneaking in through the fire exits at the Statler Hilton. The difference was, that I became a much sought-after commodity as more women got divorced, seeking a new romance.

The event started at 8 pm. If I didn't meet someone with whom I had mutual monetary magic, I was doomed, for my deal with Jamie was that he had to be home by midnight. My philosophy was that the woman was in charge of how far she would go sexually. All the women came with friends. Those from Westchester, New

Jersey, Long Island, and the five boroughs would either come with friends in their car or, if they were serious about meeting someone, they drove in alone, paying for parking, then taking taxis to various singles hangouts. This was the first piece of intelligence I had to gather during the first dance: did they live in Manhattan, and where? My parameters in dating were their zip code: 10019 (where I lived), 10021 (East 72nd Street), 10023 (West 72nd Street), and 10016 (East 34th Street). If the answer to all these questions was negative, there was never a second dance. As for women from suburbia, I would suggest showing them a great view of Manhattan. Taking a taxi or their car, we would drive up to my apartment building, leaving the car with my doorman, Ramon. Taking the elevator up to the roof deck on the thirty-first floor, which overlooked Broadway, if what I called a magical experience led to heavy kissing, I would invite her down to my apartment for a glass of wine. The apartment was always messy; the bed that turned into a couch was unmade. Acting as if I was annoyed, I shouted, "The damn cleaning lady didn't come in again!" Immediately, Cat came out to sniff the woman I was with. Dancing to Sinatra, we both agreed to have sex. The cat was running around the living room. Picking him up, I placed him in Jamie's bedroom and closed the door. As we were caressing each other, Cat started to meow, but in stereo, scratching the door. Interrupting our lovemaking, I filled his bowl with cat food, putting it in the bathroom, figuring that by the time we both had orgasms, the cat would still be eating his food. As we were about to climax, a pair of green eyes was staring down at us; if that wasn't enough, his tail was stroking my arse.

Whatever her name was, she went into the bathroom to freshen up, got dressed, and we exchanged telephone numbers. As we went down, Jamie came up. Ramon, the doorman, handed her the keys, we kissed goodnight, and we never saw each other again. On New Year's Eve, 1979, I found myself without a date. Larry Levenson sent out an invitation inviting Plato club members to the greatest New Year's Eve party; a black tie was required. At the bottom of the invite was "BYOB".

We decided to invite both mainstream media and all the pornographic publications, including *Tit* and *Ass* magazines, *Playboy*, *Penthouse*, and *Hustler*, to cover the most unusual New Year's Eve party. I had to go out and buy a tuxedo. Arriving at the club, Larry rented two Klieg lights with red filters that shot up to the sky. I arrived at the club at 8:30 pm, not expecting any coverage from mainstream media. Suddenly, five news vans pulled up in front of Plato's, with their local news reporters interviewing couples in black tie and evening gowns. I stood outside with red carnations on my lapel. Many reporters wanted to film inside the club; I turned them all down, promising a media day where they could film inside and interview Larry and Mary about their concept of an alternative lifestyle. Avoiding the news camera crews were members of the pornographic and *Tit* and *Ass* media. Al Goldstein, who was the publisher of *Screw* magazine and producer of *Midnight Blue*, a sex talk show viewed on Manhattan Cable's public access channels, rolled up to the front door of Plato's in his stretch limo. Taking the spiral staircase down, Bacco, the club's DJ, had an innate feeling for what music turned club members on. He knew the pulse of the crowd. An hour before midnight, Larry took the mic and introduced Solara. With that introduction, Bacco played "The Dance of the Seven Veils". A tall woman appeared, clad in seven veils. Moving gracefully across the floor in ballet slippers, she removed all but one veil, exposing herself with wondrous breasts and a tight stomach. Two more veils remained: one covering her face and hair. She was one of the most beautiful women I had ever seen. There was one more veil left around her waist. With the lights pulsating and the music hitting its crescendo, she pulled off the last veil, exposing a ten-inch dick. The audience went wild. Taking a bow, he removed his wig and put on a bathrobe. Ten minutes to midnight, sparklers, which were placed on the perimeter of the pool, were lit. Placed on the ceiling in the middle of the pool, covered with a black tarp, the room went pitch black. Suddenly, a large penis was lowered from the ceiling as the seconds counted down. When it hit midnight, a spray of what I found out was milk hit the pool.

At one minute after midnight, 1 January 1980, the room became deserted as all members went to change into towels. Wishing everyone a Happy New Year, I hailed a taxi, going to Studio 54 in my tuxedo. Paparazzi surrounded the entrance. I was let in immediately and wished Steve Rubell, the owner of the club, a Happy New Year. He hugged me and kissed me on the cheek. All the beautiful young models were mingling with the in-crowd, hoping to be discovered. I said hello to everybody at the bar, who was already stoned. I always made it a point to go up to the balcony at Studio, where people were snorting cocaine, getting high, popping Quaaludes, fucking, getting a blow job, and drinking champagne. I had to go to the bathroom, which was down two levels, dimly lit with couches all around. Everybody was snorting coke or smoking marijuana. Went into the men's room, where all the stalls were taken by gay couples getting it on.

In 1980, my father was paying me just enough to survive. All my creative projects didn't pan out. My father also represented Chandler Steakhouse. Part of his deal was free dinners. Both myself, Jamie, and my mother, would meet him for dinner after she visited her dermatologist, Norman Orentreich, who treated her for hair loss by injecting his formula into her scalp to help regrow hair. She always went to a superstar doctor. Doctor Orentreich, whose offices were on 72nd Street and Fifth Avenue, was the creator of the Clinique line of skin care products marketed by Estée Lauder and the formula for Head and Shoulders. One of the owners took a liking to Jamie, confiding in him. I explained that I was looking to join a restaurant group as head of marketing. After a short conversation, he picked up the phone and handed it to me, introducing me to Larry Elliman, a famous New York restaurateur who owned The Cattleman and Beefsteak Charlie. After a five-minute conversation, he invited me to meet him at his office at 3 pm, which was located on East 25th Street.

After an hour-long meeting, Larry offered me $40,000 a year with the title of VP of Marketing. Accepting his offer, he then called the Head of Operations, the Master Chef who developed the menus, and the VP of Franchising to meet me, learning that there were one hundred and fifty units up and down the I-95 corridor. Part of my responsibility was handling the advertising budget and all grassroots marketing for the owners of Beefsteak Charlie's franchises. Elliman created an all-you-can-eat concept, offering a free salad bar, beer, wine, and Sangria. The rationale was that the sales of sides such as appetisers, soup, and desserts would generate profit. This concept would work if the price of baby back ribs and the price of no-roll beef (beef not graded by the FDA) were favourable. Being involved with both operations and purchasing, I reached out to a friend who was a purveyor of beef products, selling large quantities of beef, lamb, and pork products at great prices and keeping them in cold storage. That idea was killed because Elliman had a piece of the company that supplied the franchisees with products. Since many of the franchisees were in malls or strip malls, I created a marketing plan that covered a ten-mile radius of the restaurant. Meeting with the agency that purchased television time, I discovered that the actor who played Beefsteak Charlie was a union member of AFTRA and that Elliman had failed to pay residuals. We couldn't use the television spots until Elliman paid the actor.

Elliman was a health freak, taking over a hundred vitamins a day. Part of the job was visiting store managers, training them to be marketers, and representing themselves as Beefsteak Charlie. Patrons always wanted a personality attached to where they were dining. By day, I was promoting steaks; in the evening, I was marketing sex.

On the third Sunday in August, when club members' children returned from summer camp, we had a family day at Plato's. Jamie was almost fifteen years old. I took him to Plato's. Many of the members' children went swimming; Jamie was at the buffet, which was serving fried chicken, hamburgers, hot dogs, French fries, and Good Humor ice cream. One night, a distraught woman called the club to ask if her husband, Simon Baron, was at the club. The club's cashier, also the Director of Membership, answered her politely, saying, "We have John Smith, Frank Smith, and Sam Smith, but no Simon Baron."

The club was always closed on Monday nights. Larry was always looking for events, and working with other people in the industry. Monday nights were usually S&M night, which was produced by two overweight grandmothers who lived around the corner from the house I gave my wife. It was truly a spectator sport, with all the dominatrixes bringing their submissive clients. It was a big draw, with Larry splitting the door takings. With a crowd of a hundred people, submissives were searching for a master. I became friendly with a tall, beautiful master named Shana, who had migrated to New York from Oberlin, Ohio, which was thirty-four miles from Cleveland. Dressed in leather, with spiked patent leather boots that went past her knee, she carried a whip. During our conversation, a guy in a business suit, shirt, and tie interrupted us. Turning to him, she said, "Shut the fuck up and lick my boots." She then put a dog collar on him and disappeared into the back room. Shana and I had an unusual relationship. She lived in a walk-up on 55th Street and Ninth Avenue. After every S&M night, she would come by anywhere between 2 and 3 am to talk and play Scrabble. She would discuss all the freaks who paid her money to abuse them, paying her one hundred dollars for a session. She made it clear that she never had intercourse with her clients. I respected her honesty, never making a move on her. I respected her professionalism.

Another instance of women creating the ground rules involved a lady I met at a popular hangout on Park Avenue. If she met a guy she liked who was visiting from out of town and he invited her for dinner, she immediately asked him how much he planned to spend. He would think for a minute, offering a figure from one to two hundred dollars. She would tell him to skip dinner and give her the cash, explaining that she resented being put in an expense account.

Since I was very social, I introduced people who hung out at various hot spots in mid-town Manhattan, which were within walking distance of each other. Going south from the Sherry was a new Italian restaurant called Bici on 53rd Street. Around the corner was the Rendezvous Room in the Berkshire Hotel. Many of them were ten years older than me—lawyers, accountants, doctors, dentists, insurance salesmen—all had children, leaving marriages that had happened too soon.

One night, I met Doreen, a woman from Mobile, Alabama, now living in New York. After fifteen minutes, I suggested we go somewhere quieter to talk. The St. Regis Hotel had a trio playing in one of their new venues during cocktail hour. We were seated at one of their red banquette tables overlooking the dance floor. I ordered a Diet Coke; she, a white wine. Sitting opposite each other, illuminated by a single candle on the table, I asked her if she would like to dance. She nodded yes. The trio was playing one of Sinatra's love songs. Snuggling up to me, I reacted with an erection.

After the set, we were seated opposite each other. It seemed natural that we held each other's hands across the table. Squeezing both my hands, Doreen looked straight into my eyes. "Do you know what it is to be born again?"

Squeezing her hands, I replied, "I doubt if my mother would do it a second time; she blames me for ripping her vagina."

Doreen laughed. "That's not what I meant. Spiritually giving your life to Jesus. Eliminating lust. Job 31:11–12: 'For it is a heinous crime; yea, it is an iniquity to be punished by the judges. For it is a fire that consumeth unto destruction, and rooteth out all mine increase.'" Instinctively, I looked at my watch, asking the waiter for the cheque, claiming that I had a business meeting. I didn't take her dancing to give my life to Jesus; all I wanted was to get laid.

Exiting the hotel, I opened the door to a parked taxi. As she slipped into the rear seat, Doreen tugged my jacket sleeve, saying, "Come home with me. Miss your stupid meeting." She lived in a high-rise on East 31st Street. We had two hours of great sex. Thank God she was intent on bending the rules of the New Testament.

The New York Post was the bible for single dancers; it was our Wall Street Journal. Some of the ladies we met recommended that we go to the Palace Stadium Apartments, which was just over the George Washington Bridge in Fort Lee, New Jersey. It offered live music and a perfect spot to instantaneously fall in love. The car park was filled with people making out against cars.

In the summer of 1981, my father took Jamie to Cartagena, Colombia. He was into boom boxes. With his luggage, he carried a fifty-pound boom box. On passing customs in Colombia, he was told that he had to return with it; otherwise, he would be arrested. My father always warned him to leave the boom box in the room. He carried it on tour buses. When he went into town, all the kids offered to buy it. The morning before the day they were to leave while sitting by the hotel pool, he went to the bathroom. Upon his return, the boombox was gone. They wound up wasting a day at the police station making a report. Luckily, hotel security had CCTV by the pool. The entire theft was on camera. The police gave my father a document that declared his boombox stolen. I would talk to my mother, who refused to go to the beach, explaining that she was ashamed that my ex-daughter-in-law was lying on a blanket making out with her boyfriend, with her sixteen-year-old granddaughter ignoring her. She would then break down and cry, asking why she hated her so much. Explaining to her that this was beyond my control, telling her that's the way she is, reminding her I have not seen or spoken to my daughter in four years.

Just after Labor Day, 1980, Al Goldstein, publisher of *Screw Magazine* and *Midnight Blue*, created a Monday night event: a Spermathon, featuring Tara Alexander; her husband, accompanied by a nurse to inspect the participants. The goal was to have 100 men ejaculate. Arriving at the club to meet my press contacts, I found a line of men in suits carrying attaché cases. Shocked at the crowd, I asked a participant why he was there. He told me this was history and he never in his life expected to have sex with a porn star.

Entering the club, I found Goldstein and Levenson laying out the ground rules. Levenson would go first. I was offered the opportunity to be number two. I turned down the offer. Then they read the ground rules of the Spermathon:

1. Inspection of genitals by the nurse, who forgot her glasses.
2. Four men every four minutes.
3. The goal is to have sex with 200 men.

My most unusual birthday gift took place on 24 November 1980, the evening of my fortieth birthday. I arrived at midnight on 23 November to view the action. I was hungry and decided to have some chicken and salad at the open buffet. Having dinner with naked people around you was surrealistic. I met a lady wrapped in a towel, and we started to talk. She told me that she had just arrived from La Guardia airport and had come directly to the club. When I asked her where she was from, she told me Bangor, Maine, and planned to catch the 8:00 am flight back to Maine. I asked her why she made the trip, she told me, "Where can I have sex with twenty to thirty men in one night but Plato's?" She left the buffet in search of her tenth partner.

Charlie, the club manager, came over with a message that Larry wanted to see me in his room right now. (Charlie and his wife had an apartment in the club as part of their employment perk.) Walking through the warren of private rooms, hearing moans and groans of orgasms, I knocked at the closed door of Larry's private swing room. A beautiful, nude Russian girl opened the door and said, "Happy Birthday. Take your clothes off." Larry was involved with two ladies in various sexual positions. The Russian immediately gave me fellatio. I came quickly. She immediately joined the group sex. I found myself sitting in a corner, figuring out ways to leave without insulting my host. Looking at my watch, I excused myself, saying that I expected a writer from *Time Magazine* to meet me in the lobby.

My father would arrive home at 4 pm on a Wednesday, dressed in a shirt and tie, an outfit he never usually wore, carrying cooked chicken from the Carnegie Deli. Curious about where he was going, I asked him. He told me he went to Roseland, a dance hall a few blocks away. I asked if my mother knew. He told me to keep it between us. Three times a week, he would bring home Carnegie Deli chicken. Soon, I was giving chicken to the neighbours. Very rarely did I have dinner at home; as a group, we would go out to dinner and try to chat up the women dining together, or invite them to join us. Many men in my group were business owners, always picking up the bill, as it was a business event. It's hard to have close friends in the Manhattan single scene, as most of the men were living double lives: single during the week and dads on weekends. Ray, known as the Coffee Man owned a company that provided total packages of coffee, brewers, cups, water coolers and other amenities for corporations. His major business was with women's fashion manufacturers' showrooms in New York's Garment Centre. He was the only person I knew who asked for your astrological sign on employment applications. Living on 57th Street on Central Park South, he would throw large parties where the entire crew was expected to invite ten women. His apartment was packed with older singles looking to meet the man of their dreams. Some parties had ten women for every guy.

Ray was obsessed with blondes. One day, we were driving up Third Avenue when he spotted a blonde. Double-parking, he ran up to the woman to introduce himself. It turned out that it was a man. He would date wonderful, successful women whom he asked to become blonde. He also saw himself as an operatic tenor. He would go once a week for singing lessons. The big event of the year was when Ray hired a piano accompanist. He would book one of the small auditoriums at Carnegie Hall, inviting everyone he knew. After a two-hour recital and a standing ovation, while mingling with friends in the lobby waiting for Ray, we all agreed that he should not give up his day job.

In May of 1981, my mother called me, saying she had run into my daughter, who told her that she was graduating from high school. She asked my mother if she would ask me to get her and four of her friends into a disco that coming Friday. The head of security at Studio 54, Chuck Garelick, told me that I could bring them in using the 53rd Street fire exit. I hoped that this gesture would bring us together. I called Marge, and she immediately answered the phone, not even asking how her son was. "Your father is on the phone." The conversation lacked any warmth from her; she did not even ask how her brother was. After giving her instructions on what time and where the limo should drop them off, without even saying thank you, she hung up the phone.

That Friday, I began fantasising that my daughter would step out of her limo and hug me, promising that we would see each other and be as close as we were when she was seven years old. A big white stretch limo pulled up, and five women exited the car. Which one was my daughter? They all looked so old; where was my little girl? An ash blonde wearing gold high heels stepped in front, saying, "Hi, Dad," wearing an above-the-knee, form-fitting, backless golden dress. Knocking on the door, Chuck opened it, introducing her as my daughter. Julie looked back and said, "Thank you," before she disappeared. I told her I would be at the bar with Andy Warhol if she wanted to talk. The five of them disappeared into the crowd of frenzied disco dancers. Around midnight, I walked through the club looking for her, but she and her friends had disappeared. I never had the conversation I had planned to have.

In the summer of 1981, Jamie and I would go out to Southampton, where we would sleep on a friend's boat. Jamie suddenly became aware of his weight and became addicted to bodybuilding. After school, rather than coming home, he would go to Better Bodies, a gym on West 18th Street, where he would work on various parts of his body, prompting me to buy him weights and a bench to do chest presses. In 1982, Jamie was supposed to graduate from City-as-a-School. His receiving a diploma came with one caveat: he had to finish two years of college. Since he liked hotel and restaurant management, I enrolled him in a school based in Brooklyn, New York Technical College, which offered a course in hospitality management. I found myself lucky that Jamie hung out with a great group of guys who neither smoked, drank, nor took drugs. I had one problem: everyone who loved him treated him like shit. Jewish Family and Children's Services were around the corner. I felt he was in pain because of rejection from his mother, which would follow him into adulthood. They offered free psychological services for children and teenagers. Jamie turned down the concept.

Living in a luxury building offered many opportunities to meet ladies. Entering the lift one day, I was accompanied by an overweight woman with a Chihuahua who lived two floors below me. As I said hello to everyone, she invited me into her apartment. The apartment looked like a garbage dump furnished with expensive pieces. Sitting on the couch, she introduced herself as Alexis. Having grown up in Oak Park, Illinois, she had moved to New York ten years previously. I told her that I had won custody of my son and that I did marketing for Plato's Retreat. She broke out in laughter, explaining that she and her boyfriend owned The Zoo, which was a pseudo-swing club on Broadway between 48th and 47th Street, its entrance being on Broadway. In essence, they were not part of the swinging lifestyle. The club allowed men in without escorts. There was a rule that male customers had to get undressed first, thus avoiding a bust by the New York Police Department vice squad, and it also had a juice bar called Ecstasy. She explained that she was in business with her boyfriend, who was twenty years older than her.

The first time she came to my apartment, we played Scrabble, which ended with us having sex. From then on, we were just friends, coming up to my apartment after midnight to cuddle. She was a true slob, eating out of cans in her bedroom. Fred had given her a cheque for $100,000, which was lying on her bedroom floor with stains of dog urine and tomato sauce. At least once a week, I took her to Studio 54, where we sat in the VIP section. The waiter immediately brought us Dom Perignon. Suddenly, all the young gay guys were at our table, drinking champagne and making her feel needed. While Jamie was at school, she would come up to straighten the house. She was like the sister I never had. We would share Carnegie Deli chicken. She joined Weight Watchers and started to carry a small scale in her purse.

In six months, she went from a size sixteen to a size eight. When I told her that I was proud of her, she got undressed, showing me her body. Her large breasts were sagging, and all the excess skin on her body looked like it was pasted onto her skeleton. By mid-June, she announced that she was going to move to Paris, where she had rented an apartment on the Champs-Élysées. During her absence, she would call me once a week to give me a run-down on what she was doing. With her new body, she went on a buying spree, spending close to a quarter of a million dollars on designer clothes. She told me that she had fallen in love with her French teacher and might bring him home with her. Before Labor Day 1983, the doorman called, telling me that he had someone who wanted to talk to me. The voice on the other end shouted, "I am back!" and asked me to meet her in front of her apartment. Taking the stairs down two flights, there she was with Yves, her French teacher. She immediately started to unpack, showing me the clothes she had bought from Chanel, Hermès, Laurent, and Dior. She sadly admitted that she had regained all the weight she had lost. Welcoming Yves to New York, he admitted that it was a shock. He had thought Paris was big. He explained that he had grown up in Yvoire, a small town on the French side of Lake Geneva with a population of twelve hundred, and had moved to Paris to teach French.

He proudly told me that all his clothes were second-hand. She went out every night of the week with Yves, sending him down to the liquor store to buy a Bordeaux. I asked her what she saw in him. Looking at me, she replied, "He's a great fuck."

Conversations with Yves became more political. He put down our lifestyle and how we wasted money, speaking about how great Communism was compared to our "phoney" lifestyle. The incident that was long in coming occurred when she gave him five hundred dollars to buy orchestra tickets for *Cats*. That evening, they both went to the Wintergarden Theatre. It was a packed house; everyone was seated, and the usher escorted them to a spot for a standing room. Asking him why he did such a stupid thing, he explained that he could go to the Follies in Paris for fifteen dollars, so why pay more?

The following morning, Alexis bought him a one-way ticket to Paris, telling him to keep the four hundred dollars and get out of her life. Before Yves left, he called me from the lobby, asking me what he had done to deserve such treatment. I simply told him that he and she were from two different societies, wishing him a safe trip home.

Alexis went back to counting calories using her small scales. We made each other a promise that we would introduce and discuss any person who came into our lives.

Being single in New York City, the types of women you would meet were angry that their husbands had left them for a younger woman. The divorce settlement was not enough to support the lifestyle they were used to. These women were my peers; they got married in their late teens or early twenties, many of them with teenage children, a large house, and trapped in a community where they couldn't meet anyone. The other type of woman was in her late twenties to early thirties, with a career, and being annoyed by her mother wanting her to get married and give her grandchildren. I became aware of how these women felt when they were first exposed to the single bar scene. A good majority of them had adult children, and having realised that their past suburban lifestyle was over, they moved into Manhattan, buying an apartment. They all had stories to tell; if you had the patience to listen to their never-ending saga about kids, husbands, and gardening, nine times out of ten, you would wind up in bed with them in their apartment. One relationship I had was out of my zip code. She owned a three-bedroom apartment on lower Fifth Avenue near Washington Square. The sex was very… Jewish. She was sweet but boring; all she spoke about was tennis and golf, neither of which I played.

Jamie would ride his bike to the Sherry Bar, knock on the window, and the head of security for the Sherry and a couple of my friends would go to spend time with him.

My father and I turned Plato's and Larry Levenson's lifestyles into an acceptable business. In the spring of 1980, we ran a press tour for editors of college newspapers. *The Harvard Crimson* featured us on the front page, and *The Yale Daily News* ran a full spread of pictures. David Susskind, who had a syndicated television show, did a complete show on Larry and Mary. *Psychology Today* did a ten-page spread with photos. I arranged for top movie personalities to visit the club to play pool.

In 1981, the walls collapsed in on Plato's Retreat. The onset of Herpes, followed by the report of AIDS in both the gay and heterosexual communities, made members think twice about swinging. Word was out that men in suits were counting towels and scrutinising laundry bills. These bills mainly dated from the late seventies, when they sent out towels to be laundered. In the mid-1980s, they purchased industrial-size laundry machines and clothes dryers. Then the men in suits measured detergent. By early 1981, Larry Levenson, the public face of Plato's, Hy (a pleasant-looking guy who looked like he worked on Wall Street), Frank (an owner of a disco on Ocean Parkway in Brooklyn), and their accountant, Alan, were indicted by the IRS for skimming $2.3 million. Club members only paid in cash; credit cards were not a dominant form of payment in the eighties. During the proceedings of their federal trial, new owners of the Ansonia offered them a seven-figure sum to end their lease. Accepting this offer, they bought an empty warehouse with a parking lot on West 34th Street, near the new convention centre named after New York Senator Jacob Javits.

The story of two sets of books emerged. One of the partners was having an affair with the cashier/bookkeeper. She caught him cheating on her and went to the Feds to get even. The IRS came to the club to count laundry receipts and calculated that close to 1,000 people came each week in 1980. It seemed that the federal government was intent on closing venues that offered people an opportunity to release their pent-up endorphins by either dancing and taking drugs, or plain fucking without wasting time romancing someone. The IRS indicted the owners of Studio 54 for tax evasion, which was celebrated by a star-studded going-away party before reporting to a federal prison camp in Montgomery, Alabama, for twenty months. Studio 54 lost its glamour and closed in 1980.

Plato's attorneys were working with the federal prosecutors on a plea deal. They offered to send them the account books on earnings. Calling the club, they told an employee to send over the books. They kept two sets of books, and the real books were sent. Their sentence was eight years, starting in the spring of 1981, whereas Steve Rubell and Ian Schrager received a lighter sentence for the same crime under the presidency of Jimmy Carter. Plato's indictment was under the conservative presidency of Ronald Reagan. They messed up by sending the real set of books, destroying the plea deal and pissing off the US Attorney for the Southern District, who now tacked on organised crime as the real owners of the club, demanding the maximum sentence. The night before he was to report for his eight-year stint in Allenwood Federal Prison, Larry decided to go out with a bang, announcing that he would come fifty times. Mary was the official scorekeeper. Fifty wives and girlfriends of members lined up outside his private swing room, offering their bodies to the King of Swing. None of the members left by 8 am. Larry exited his swing room wearing a black bathrobe with Plato's logo, walking with Mary to the main room to deafening applause and whistles. He was ordered to report by noon to White Deer, Pennsylvania, home of Allenwood.

With Larry, Hy, and Frank behind bars, Mary took the reins to create a more exciting club on the Westside. Applying for building permits, they listed the place as a Health Club with a January opening in 1982. My assignment was to send out monthly updates to members, which included Larry's letter to members.

AIDS was also a wake-up call to the heterosexual community; the joy of unprotected sex had come to an end. Never did I spend so much time in Walgreens in search of the ultimate condom. Latex, non-latex, lambskin, flavoured – they even made condoms that glowed in the dark! During sexual gymnastics, in the throes of great passion with a partner who could place it on your *penis* while it was still erect, if my partner wasn't sexually savvy (which most Jewish women were not), you were taking a chance. Dismounting, opening the package, and slipping it on, your erection might not last; if not, you have to start over again. Now, trying to get laid became like a job interview, with each one delving into the other's life before you even kissed.

After a year of renovations and buying off building inspectors, The New Plato's Retreat was ready for its grand opening. It was a red-carpet event with celebrities from the world of porn and any other luminaries, in addition to press (both print and electronic) that I and my father could bring to the club. Viewing the new club with its disco, jacuzzi, swimming pool, buffet table, and chaise longues circling the pool, the most revered lounges were the ones facing the orgy room. I noticed that the lounges were the same as in the old place. Asking Mary why she didn't buy new furniture, she told me that Larry explicitly told her to take the old chaises; members liked them, and anything new would turn them off.

The threesome behind bars, those who pulled the strings, relegated Mary to be a figurehead. The new caretaker of Plato's Retreat was Moshe, a gruff Israeli who operated a car towing company. Unlike Larry and his significant other, Mary, who espoused an alternate lifestyle movement, attending swinger conventions and weekend getaways at a dude ranch where fifty rooms could house 200 swingers, Moshe, an Israeli who was supposed to be a high-ranking officer in the Israeli Defence Force, wasn't into sex; he did it for the money. Being gruff and unpleasant, I worked on avoiding him and getting my cheque from the new cashier/bookkeeper.

Opening night was a red carpet event; all the characters showed up. Rick the Prick from Jersey City arrived wheeling a suitcase containing his woman's outfit. A woman who dressed as a nurse, sometimes wearing a fake cast, played on male members' sympathy to have sex with a woman in a cast. One week the cast was on her arm, the next on her leg.

Going to Plato's on West 34th Street was a pain; I needed two buses to get there, and the new manager took the fun out of the place. July 1982 was a hot month, and the air conditioning broke down; the indoor air must have been over a hundred degrees. I asked Moshe why he didn't fix the air conditioning; he said, "I give them Italian ice, isn't that enough?"

Moshe didn't have to wait for a members' revolt. In 1981, the first case of the AIDS virus was recorded by the CDC. The straight world thought the disease was only transmitted during homosexual sex. We discovered that heterosexual unprotected sex was exposed to the virus. Slowly, all the regulars stopped coming to the club. Swinging became self-contained in people's homes with the couples they met at Plato's. They developed rigorous testing requirements and pledged to contain their swinging to the members of the group.

Plato's hung on until 1985, closing its doors on West 34th Street.

During the demise of Plato's Retreat, Ray and I would travel out of Manhattan to meet women. Women who lived in suburbia were all willing to drive into the city. Since they all had cars, I would take them to my favourite inexpensive restaurant in Chinatown. If they passed my test over dinner, I would either bring them up to my apartment or tell them I had an early morning meeting. I became bored with casual sex. I thought of it as unemotional fucking; my goal was to have a long-term relationship. Wednesdays and Fridays were the prime nights to score, running back and forth between the Sherry, the Rendezvous, and Bice, a new chic Italian restaurant imported from Milan. They were the top spots to meet a woman. If I struck out, there was a piano bar, La Camilla, on East 58th Street, which was packed after 11 pm. Helping the bottom line was John Gotti, who appeared wearing his wrap-around camel hair coat, groomed to perfection, accompanied by five associates, escorted by Tony, the Maître D', to a table in the rear of the restaurant which was always reserved for him. Returning to the front, he greeted four men in dark suits; they were investigators from the U.S. Attorney's office, the Southern District office. They were seated at a table across from Gotti. Then members of the NYPD organised crime task force were seated on the opposite side of the room, all dining on taxpayers' money.

In September of 1984, while having my coke with my friends at the Sherry, Gloria walked in and she ticked all the boxes. She spoke as if she was raised in Boston. Two dates later, we had sex. I later learned that she grew up in Yonkers, not Boston. She lived in Scarsdale and had two teenage children, separated for the last three years, fighting over child support and alimony from her husband, a successful men's wear manufacturer with a large contract with the Department of Defence for military uniforms. We started spending every weekend together. Jamie, who was nineteen years old, accepted Gloria into our household. Keeping to our plan, I introduced Alexis to Gloria; they became immediate friends. To make extra money, she would make costume jewellery by going down to Orchard Street on the Lower East Side to buy fleece sweat suits wholesale. She would decorate the sweatshirts with various designs, selling them to boutiques. Finally, she invited me to Scarsdale to spend a weekend at her house. Taking Metro North, she met me at the station. Her house was ordinary; in the garage, there sat a 1932 Jaguar convertible which she told me that her husband bought for her as a birthday gift. Introducing me to her kids, who immediately hated me. Having to go to the bathroom, she told me to use the one in the basement. After three hours of feeling unwanted, I had her call a taxi to take me back to New York. That incident should have ended our relationship. Later, she called to apologise, saying her children still had not accepted the break-up. One weekend, she decided to use a new product which was like a Tampax with a spermicide, inserting it in the vagina with a cord for easy extraction after sex. I didn't use a condom; making love to Gloria became a job; emotionally, she was holding back. As usual, she would go to the bathroom. Coming out holding a washcloth, she started to cry, explaining that she couldn't find the string. Taking a flashlight, I also searched for the string. Reading the instructions on the box, we found they had a twenty-four-hour nurse hotline, who worked with Gloria to remove the product. Every month, Gloria would go to a row of brownstones off Madison Avenue called The Foundation. We would meet for coffee before returning to Scarsdale to have dinner with her children.

In 1986, she arrived at my apartment telling me she needed an abortion. It was the only option we had; she wasn't divorced, and I didn't need a second family. The cost at that time was about three hundred dollars. She told me that her gynaecologist, who was a superstar, would do the procedure, admitting her to New York Presbyterian with a diagnosis that she needed a D&C so that her husband's insurance would pay for it. Explaining that the out-of-pocket cost would be fifteen hundred dollars, which she expected me to pay, she spent two days in the hospital rather than being released the same day. She never offered to pick up a cheque; we would walk on Columbus Avenue, and she spotted a men's linen suit with a price tag of five hundred dollars, insisting that I would look great in it.

For those men who have affairs when married, the excitement is in not getting caught. I would see a couple who were regulars at the Sherry Bar; she always had a tan and was about twenty-eight years old, and he seemed ten years older. I perceived them as newlyweds.

Thanksgiving of 1986, Gloria invited me to her friend Judy's home for dinner. Judy came to the door, escorting us to the dining room. There, seated, was her husband, Bob, who happened to be the male half of the couple who were always making out at the Sherry. As Judy formally introduced us, the blood drained from his face; I thought he was going to have a stroke. With a firm grasp of his hand, I whispered, "We're cool."

Men who cheated on their spouses did it for the thrill of the game, with the object never to get caught. I had a wealthy friend from Los Angeles who rented his girlfriend a studio apartment in the same luxury high-rise in Manhattan, three floors below his. Stuart, an insurance broker, used his wife's Nissan Z, to have an affair with a woman in Forest Hills. After wine and sex, he went out to go home only to discover someone had stolen his wife's Z. By the time he made a police report, taking a taxi home to Merrick, Long Island, it was close to three am His wife, meeting him at the front door as he exited the taxi, explained that he was writing up a big policy when he left the client, and the car was gone. Between spending time filling out a police report, making a finding a taxi driver who would take me to Merrick.

Jamie finally received his high school diploma after finishing two years at New York Technical College. He could have gone an extra two years for a BS degree. That meant he had to take regular college courses; he opted for a certificate. My only option was to get him an assistant manager's job at Beefsteak Charlie's, which opened a few blocks from our apartment.

1986 was a big year for Jamie; he was to be twenty-one years old. We invited all his friends to join us for dinner. We told Jamie to meet us at 7 pm After an hour, I called him at home; he had forgotten about the dinner. Twenty minutes later, he showed up. I presented him with the "ASSHOLE OF THE YEAR" award. Over the weekend, Jamie went out and purchased a red Yamaha V motorcycle. Calling me, he asked that I meet him in the driveway of our apartment building. Within minutes, he arrived on his shiny new bike. He gave me every reason why the motorcycle made sense, then he rolled the bike into the lobby to park it in our apartment. That evening, Jamie slept with his motorcycle in his bedroom. The next day, he went down to ask the guy who worked in the garage in our building the cost. It was $50.00 per month. I asked him if he had purchased insurance. He told me he bought the most secure lock on the market and would secure it to a gate next to a parking garage on 54th Street. Saturday morning, Jamie walked out of the apartment with his helmet to take a spin down to lower Manhattan. Fifteen minutes later, he returned with part of the steel fence and his most expensive secure lock. The bike was gone. Trying to stay in touch with my daughter, Marge, I told her that she was away at college. Before I could ask what school, she slammed down the phone.

Beef Steak Charlie's earnings were decreasing, especially as the cost of produce and shrimp increased at the wholesale level. Rather than making products like potato salad and coleslaw, store operators were buying ready-made items. My job was to retrain wait staff to sell sides, which were marked up by as much as 500%.

Larry Elliman always wanted to go public, but the numbers that he presented to prospective bankers did not reflect real figures. In late 1987, an opportunity was presented to him. A Sikh who owned a restaurant in London and Montreal was looking for a foothold in the United States and an opportunity to go public. A merger was made in the winter of 1987. Bombay Palace now owned the company.

The new president of the company, Sant Chatwal, was a brilliant marketer. The shares in the newly public company were sold to Sikhs in both the USA and Canada as a conglomerate that owned various restaurants and budget hotels. Sant's main play was real estate that was turned into hotels. I felt secure in the job and put all my efforts into promoting his real estate ventures.

My father was a very big part of my life. His weekly visits with Carnegie Chickens and dressing to go dancing in Roseland were diminished. He refused to discuss his medical condition. My mother, whose entire life was my father, told me that he was "drowning in his water"; the skin on his legs became brittle, and touching his legs, water would seep out.

I was close to Jules Bergman, the science reporter for ABC Network News. I recommended a top cardiologist at Lenox Hill Hospital. The diagnosis was cardiomyopathy, which meant his heart was not pumping blood through his system. The doctor set up a follow-up appointment for a week later. My father told me to forget it. "My dick doesn't get hard, so why should I spend money on treatment when I can leave it all to your mother?" This was an argument I couldn't win. He was dead set on dying and, at sixty-eight years old, told me that his father and brother both died before they were seventy.

Gloria was always discussing how her husband refused to give her a divorce. I met Roy Cohn at Studio 54. He represented Steve Rubell, and she was considering hiring him to put an end to the Westchester attorneys who were handling her divorce without getting results. A meeting at his East Side townhouse, where he lived and worked, took twenty minutes. His fee was ten thousand dollars up front, just to write a letter to her husband's attorney. If that didn't work, he would recommend another attorney. I couldn't in good conscience advise her to pay Cohn the upfront money.

In the summer of 1987, my father promoted a free airfare deal to Ixtapa, plus a travel agent rate at Club Med. He wanted to discuss his funeral arrangements. He failed to mention that the flight to Mexico was departing from Philadelphia at noon. Renting a car from Avis, we drove to Brighton Beach and directly to Philly. Arriving in Mexico City, we had a two-hour layover, during which my father had trouble breathing. Arriving at Club Med at 6 pm, he reserved two rooms. My father and Jamie shared one room; I had my own. Wanting to discuss the purpose of our trip, my father avoided the conversation.

It was a mixed group, both singles and couples. The singles were either from the West Coast or the Midwest and had saved all year for a budget vacation. Every minute of the day there were planned activities. Before dinner, they invited all the guests to dance The Macarena, which was used as an ice-breaker between the guests so they could bond. Jamie hung out with the club DJ. Meeting a teacher from LA, we talked and walked down the moonlit beach. She told me that she was going through a long and depressing divorce. That ended the walk; I wasn't looking for a clone of Gloria.

My father met a lady who was a correction officer at the Joliet Correctional Center in Illinois. A muscular woman, well-tanned, about forty-five. Jamie and I went back to our rooms around midnight. At two in the morning, there was a knock on the door. Jamie was standing there in his shorts. "Grandpa wanted to be alone with the lady and told me to go to your room to sleep," he said, as he fell asleep sharing my queen-size bed.

That morning, we met my father for breakfast. Jamie forgot his snorkel gear in the room, leaving me and my father alone. I asked him how it went. Sadly, he looked at me and said, "It just didn't work. I apologised and asked her to leave at three this morning." Jamie returned, and after finishing our breakfast, the three of us walked on the beach. Wading into the water, my father held both my and Jamie's hands. "The reason for the trip," he began, "I want to discuss how I want to be buried. It should be Orthodox. I own a burial plot where your grandparents are buried, which I purchased when I was a member of Seville Lodge when you were a baby, reserved for me, your mother, and you. I want a plain pine box, dressed in a linen shroud. I and your mother have a Do Not Resuscitate order on both of our medical records. They must be followed to the letter. My burial must be the day after my death. Mummy has all this in writing on the nightstand on my side of the bed. I do not want you to waste your time getting me a specialist. Go about your life; let God handle it."

Jamie started to cry. Looking at him, I blew my top. "You flew us three thousand miles to discuss this bullshit? I never thought of you as a quitter. You are sixty-seven years old. Why the fuck do you want to die, because your dick doesn't work? It's not like you go to sleep and never get up. You are going to suffer and make my mother suffer!" Jamie and I both walked away. The rest of the week at Club Med was like a funeral; all the fun was gone.

Checking out of the hotel, we had a three-hour layover in Mexico City. Sitting at the gate for the flight back to Philadelphia, I asked a ground attendant to bring him a tank of oxygen, losing my temper. This was the first time I spoke back to my father. "You are a cheap fucking fool! We are stuck for three hours in a place you cannot breathe just because you like deals rather than flying into JFK so you can save a couple of hundred dollars, making me drive an extra three hours from Philly to Brooklyn." Telling Jamie to take care of his grandfather, all this gave me an anxiety attack.

Exiting the terminal, a limo driver approached me, offering him twenty dollars and settling for forty. He took me on a three-hour tour of Mexico City. The first stop was The Cathedral of the Assumption of the Most Blessed Virgin Mary into Heaven. It's one of the largest cathedrals in Latin America. The square had people holding up signs looking for work. As he drove around the city, he pointed out top tourist destinations, which were all a blur, and I kept thinking of how I could save my father's life.

We arrived in Brooklyn at about 8 pm, after spending an hour with my mother, who wanted to know how our trip was. Wanting to spare her the reality she was about to face, I made up a fairy tale.

Arriving in Manhattan, I dropped Jamie and the luggage at our apartment, returning the rental to Avis. The answering machine had messages from Selma, Gloria, and other women I was dating and seeing during the week. My relationship with Gloria returned to the three-day weekend together, travelling to Atlantic City. Suddenly, her mother joined us. Her mum turned out to be a regular person, knowing who the real Gloria was, confiding in me that she had suddenly changed once her husband became successful, admitting that her daughter initiated the separation.

I finally had a conversation with my mother about what we discussed during our trip to Mexico. She told me that he had joined an HMO called Elderplan to save money. Whereas she had the best supplemental medical coverage offered by AARP, unlike her custom-made clothes, he wanted the best in doctors. Maimonides Hospital in Bensonhurst became his hospital of choice. He didn't have an assigned doctor; he went to the clinic. Doctors told him not to eat hot dogs, yet he rode his bike on the Boardwalk to Nathan's in Coney Island. It was useless to try to help him.

Beefsteak Charlie was slowly changing. One morning, as I was entering the building, Larry Elliman arrived by taxi. As we both entered the lift, he admitted that, under the new agreement, his limo and driver were cut from the operating budget. After the Labour Day weekend, as always, I would stop by Betty's desk to say good morning. She was gone, and a beautiful Indian lady sat at her desk, peering into the office. Sant, wearing a red turban, was unpacking his belongings in Larry's office.

Christmas week 1987: Gloria's husband took his children on a ski vacation. One of the issues of the divorce was ownership of the apartment on South Ocean Drive, Palm Beach. Picking me up at the Palm Beach airport, as we were driving to her apartment, a parade of senior citizens, all wearing white, was doing a power walk on the side of A1A. We spent New Year's Eve welcoming in 1988 at a party at the Colony Hotel. The crowd was the same people I knew from Club A, The Westhampton Bath and Tennis Club, and the chic restaurants on Madison Avenue. After the first of the year, we flew back to La Guardia. She had a Westchester car service waiting for her; I hailed a taxi to Manhattan. The following Friday, she arrived at my apartment for the weekend. She was a changed woman. Pacing around as we spoke, she went from one thought to another in rapid fire. Having kept me up all night, she became uncontrollable. Jamie was in the bedroom, oblivious to what was happening beyond his closed bedroom door. I was never confronted with a situation like this. Handing me her phone, she told me to call her husband. He happened to live at 245 East 63rd Street. Picking up the phone, I dialled his number, playing around in my mind about how I was going to handle this conversation. The person on the other end picked up the phone. Before he introduced himself, deciding to cut to the chase, I said, "Bernie, this is Allen, and I am dating Gloria. She is in my apartment in a bad way." He knew immediately what I was talking about, instructing me to drive her to Gracie Square Hospital on East 76th Street, between First and York Avenue. He would meet me there, then bring back her car to the garage in his building. I then called the doorman, asking if they had a wheelchair. She never got undressed. Telling him that she was ill, we brought her down to the lobby of my building while I pulled her Oldsmobile out of the garage. At 8 am on Saturday, the traffic was light. Arriving in front of Gracie Square, two orderlies placed her in a wheelchair, disappearing beyond the glass doors. With her safely in the hospital, I drove her car to the garage in her husband's building. Needing to clear my head, I decided to walk up Second Avenue to the hospital. Going up to her room, she was sleeping. The nurse asked me if I was family. "No, I am a concerned friend." The nurse, looking at her chart, recommended that I return after six pm Going into her room and kissing her goodbye, her chart was by the foot of the bed. Under her name and address was the word "Maniac Episode". By the end of the week, she was transferred to New York-Presbyterian Behavioral Health Center in White Plains. Curious to find out what a "Maniac Episode" was, I went to the Donnell Library on West 53rd Street to research the subject. I discovered that Gloria was bipolar, which can be treated by injections of lithium. Realising that all the gifts she bought me were during her "Maniac Episodes", that was why we met on Madison Avenue once a month when she visited a brownstone called The Foundation for treatment. Jamie told me that his sister was getting married this coming June. At Beefsteak Charlie, I was the only non-Indian in the office. The smell of curry wafted through the entire floor; some of the employees had hot plates in their offices. I was juggling between visiting my father, who had lost twenty-five pounds, and Gloria, who was going through treatment in White Plains. By telling the staff that she was my significant other, they revealed information about the nature of her disorder and that this was not the first time she had been hospitalised. Part of her recovery was classes in creating costume jewellery, which was part of her therapy, turning it into a business.

Having a girlfriend who was bipolar, and a father you loved and respected slowly committing suicide because his DICK wasn't working, was the reality. Every time I spoke to him, he took pleasure in reminding me that he wouldn't be alive by his 69th birthday, which was on New Year's Eve.

As the last remaining executive, I had to create a reason not to get fired by the new CEO. By February 1988, he had assembled three properties in Manhattan that were perfect for budget-minded European tourists. I put together a marketing plan to reach European travel wholesalers who created travel packages including airfare, hotel, guided tours, and coupons for dining. I sold them on the idea of attending two travel trade shows which were being held in Amsterdam and West Berlin in mid-March. Every other weekend, I took Metro North to White Plains to visit Gloria, who couldn't stop grilling me about who I was sleeping with. The other weekends, I visited my father, who was now sleeping in the living room, threatening to throw my mother out the window. Jamie, who was twenty-three, found a job as an Assistant Manager at PJ Clarke's, a legendary New York saloon where Sinatra would hold court, opening a two-hundred-and-fifty-seat restaurant in Macy's flagship store on 34th Street and Broadway. Jamie started to learn how to be a DJ, spending his money on sound equipment and turntables, and turning his bedroom into a mini studio.

Gloria was released the day I left for Amsterdam for the International Travel Bourse, which lasted three days, to promote our budget hotels. During the evening, I visited the Red-Light District, where partially nude prostitutes displayed their wares like Tiffany displayed their diamonds. Each woman paid rent to one person who owned all the storefronts; on the exterior was a red light. Under their bed was an alarm button that the girls activated if they had violent clients. Three days later, as I was waiting to board my KLM flight, I visited the duty-free area where they were selling single-polished diamonds. The Netherlands, with the city of Rotterdam, was the diamond capital of the world; why not sell single diamonds? It was a great way to bring in money without paying taxes. Boarding a turbo-prop to Tempelhof airport in West Berlin, at that time, Berlin was two cities. Geographically, Berlin was in the Eastern zone, which was a communist regime, dividing the country by a thirteen-foot-high brick wall running ninety-six miles, dividing Germany. West Berlin was governed by the three Allied powers from the Second World War (the United States, Great Britain, and France). Checking into the Intercontinental, I was met by a six-foot-three-inch Sikh in a yellow leather coat and a red turban named Gil. Gil was a friend of Sant's and worked for

Lufthansa (West Germany's national airline). He was in shock that he was staying at the Intercontinental Hotel, explaining that Indian companies usually put their employees in a Holiday Inn. For three business days, I met with the largest travel packagers in Europe. It seemed every woman I met was a tour guide offering a tour of her body for two hundred US dollars. The Intercontinental had a cocktail lounge overlooking the city. To the right were the bright lights of West Berlin; to the left was pitch darkness, which was East Berlin.

Rather than spending the third day at ITB, I decided to visit East Berlin. In my mind, I was making a sequel to Orson Welles' *The Third Man*. Ennio Morricone would compose the score.

DECADE SIX

BEFORE THE WALL CRUMBLED

Opening of the film in colour. Light snow was falling. The camera follows an overweight man in a Burberry raincoat, wearing a black wool cap, walking along Budapester Strasse. Slipping through the subway turnstile, he boards the U2 train, viewing his fellow passengers with suspicion. The sound of the train making whooshing sounds is interrupted by an announcement in German of the upcoming stops. Nineteen minutes later, the conductor announced the final stop, Bahnhof Kochstrasse, which was a two-minute walk to Checkpoint Charlie, the last stop on the subway.

Approaching the American military checkpoint, I presented my passport. Panning to the right and left, I saw the bleachers facing No Man's Land, the area which is a graveyard for people trying to escape into the West. Getting an okay to cross into East Germany, the film turned to black and white the moment I was greeted by a two-hundred-and-fifty-pound East German border guard who looked at my passport, eager to find something wrong. Finally, I was told that I had to pay to get across the border and buy East German (GDR) currency, which had zero value in the West. I peeled off five ten-dollar bills. The camera did a close-up of the customs agent pocketing two ten-dollar bills before he stamped my passport. He asked how long I planned to stay. The camera pulls back, and there is a six-foot Negro wearing a leather coat and speaking fluent German. Exiting passport control, I waited for the man in the black leather coat. The camera pulls back, revealing both men standing outside the customs office in an area that looked like a construction site but was, in reality, a street in East Berlin. The man in the leather coat takes out a large cigar and flips his Zippo lighter.

Allen: "You speak great German. Are you from the US?"

Negro: "Originally from Chicago, now living in Berlin."

Allen (shaking hands): "Allen from Manhattan, originally from Brooklyn, New York."

Negro: "Humphrey. I served twenty-five years in the US Air Force. When it came time to quit, I retired as a Chief Master Sergeant. My kin all passed on. I liked living here, so when I got discharged, I found myself an apartment and put down roots. There is an awful lot of money to be made. Eventually, the country will be one. If you want to hang out, I will take you on a tour of this fucked-up Communist-controlled part of a great city."

Allen: "How do you make your money?"

Humphrey: "I am lucky…I play a pretty good guitar. I am the only blues singer in this part of the world. The people love me, and I convert my worthless GDR money into merchandise which I bring over to the West to sell."

The camera follows them as they walk past shuttered buildings facing the Wall, finally stopping in front of what seemed a vacant building.

Humphrey: "This is where my booking agent has his offices, and he would be happy to meet an American."

Opening the door, the camera follows the two men as they ascend three floors until they get to a glass door: Gustave Talent

Agency. Upon opening the door, the walls are decorated with various pictures of talent that Gustave books. At the reception desk was a grey-haired lady in her late sixties wearing steel-rimmed glasses who greeted us. She gets up and hugs Humphrey. "My son is waiting for you." The walls of Gustave's office were decorated with old movie posters and a framed picture of Erich Honecker, who was the President of East Germany. His office directly overlooked the Wall. Humphrey introduced me as an American from New York City. Putting me in a bear hug, Gustave said, "Gut, gut," in German. After handing Humphrey an envelope of money, Humphrey said he would be back before he headed across the border. Descending three stories on a stairway that was badly in need of repair, the piles of dirt were covered with patches of snow.

Humphrey: "I will take you for lunch in The Grand Hotel, one of the most luxurious hotels in East Berlin, where a lot of blondes hang out for lunch."

Walking up a tree-lined street called Unter den Linden, which was compared to the Champs-Élysées in Paris, we passed an antique shop. Humphrey suggested we go in. He asked the owner to show him a tray of old watches. After ten minutes of negotiation, he handed him $50.00 US, dropping it down his left cowboy boot. Back on Unter den Linden, the snow had now turned to rain, coming down in big flakes that melted as they hit the ground. A block away, on Friedrichstrasse, was a huge white building that resembled a mausoleum with windows.

"This big, ugly mother has almost eleven hundred rooms and is open to visitors from the East," Humphrey said.

Entering the lobby reminded me of one of the hotels in Manhattan that rented out rooms by the hour. The Maître D', dressed in a black tailcoat, greeted Humphrey as an old friend, taking us past a line of people waiting to be seated, at a table that said 'Reserved', adjacent to the bar. Two beautiful blondes, in their late twenties, were in the midst of a conversation. Before the waiter asked to take our order, Humphrey rose from his seat, telling him to wait a few minutes. Moving through the crowd at the bar, he approached the two blondes, who knew who he was, inviting them to join us. The entire lunch was like a foreign movie with subtitles. He introduced me as an important movie producer visiting Berlin, scouting locations for my next films. Suddenly, the girls knew how to speak English. They were excited to learn who I knew, rattling off names like Tom Cruise, Arnold Schwarzenegger, Tom Hanks, Julia Roberts, and Meryl Streep, weaving interesting stories of people I had never met. As we left the dining room, each girl held our hand. Taking out her lipstick, she wrote her telephone number in the palm of my hand, saying that we could meet at 8 pm on Friedrichstrasse and go for some drinks. Kissing me on the cheek, they left. We took a taxi back to Gustave's office.

This entire scene was filmed in black and white. I paid for the taxi. My new friend told me that I should wait for him; he had to pick up the packages that Gustave was holding for him. Standing outside the dilapidated building, Humphrey exited, holding what seemed like a painting wrapped in newspaper, and a large shopping bag filled with books. Offering to help him carry the bag, it suddenly dawned on me that I didn't know what was in it. About fifty feet from the customs shack to leave East Berlin, I handed him back the package. He told me to go in first; he would meet me at Checkpoint Charlie, driving me back to the hotel. As I entered, he ducked into a building to smoke a Marlboro. The same guy who stamped my passport was there, telling me he was a New York Yankees fan. Walking back through the passageway that led to the West, I could hear raised voices in German. Exiting, an American soldier checked my passport and welcomed me back to West Berlin; my film was in colour again. A few minutes later, Humphrey appeared, holding both packages. Asking what the shouting was about, he explained that he was given a letter from the Ministry of Trade, giving him carte blanche to bring out consumer goods. All that "asshole" had to do was call the number on the paper. His Mercedes was parked a block away. Driving down Budapester Strasse.

ALLEN: I am curious as to why you didn't move back to the States.

HUMPHREY: "In America, I was still considered a Nigger. In this country, however fucked up it is, I am not just a Black man. I am a Star, a Celebrity; the people respect me. I am married to a beautiful blonde German girl with two kids. I have a shit load of money that's worthless on this side of the wall. I have arrangements with both East and West to bring cameras, feather quilts, Meissen porcelain from Dresden, typewriters, watches, and optical products from Zeiss. In small quantities, under the radar. This could never happen to me if I lived in the States."

As the car pulled into the driveway of the Intercontinental, we exchanged telephone numbers. Before I opened the door, he told me that someday, when the wall comes down, he and a group of investors will be millionaires, owning a large chunk of residential property whose owners were deceased. As the Mercedes sped away, the camera followed me past the bar, where the beautiful tour guides were chatting up a new set of out-of-town businessmen.

The house phone message light was red. Gil had left me a message that Kuoni, a major tour packager based out of Zurich, Switzerland, was throwing a farewell cocktail party at a landmark restaurant, Ganymed Brasserie, whose family had operated the business since 1931, restoring it to its original site, which was destroyed by Allied bombing raids on Berlin. In its heyday, before the war, it had hosted Marlene Dietrich, Albert Einstein, Charlie Chaplin, Kurt Weill, and Arnold Schoenberg. A ten-minute taxi ride from the hotel. Feeling unclean from my trip to East Berlin, I stepped into a hot shower. Soaping my body, red was flowing down into the drain. I realised that the writing on my hand, with Helga's name and telephone number, was disappearing. This was the first time my brain superseded my dick. Gazing up at the shower head, my mind raced to scenes where Jews would look up at the shower head, rather than having water cleanse their bodies. Zyklon B eradicated their lives with that thought.

THE LAST TITLE: DAS ENDE. My film was over.

U ARMY CHECKPOINT
YOU ARE LEAVING
THE AMERICAN SECTOR
ВЫ ВЫЕЗЖАЕТЕ ИЗ
АМЕРИКАНСКОГО СЕКТОРА
VOUS SORTEZ
SECTEUR AMERICAIN
VERLASSEN DEN AMERIKANISCHEN SEKTOR

I was back to reality. Gil got smashed, and I had to hold him up to get him into the taxi. Three doormen brought him up to his room.

After asking for a late check-out, I took a taxi to the Holocaust Memorial. The hotel concierge recommended that I visit KaDeWe. I spent the rest of the day walking around what I considered the greatest food court in the world, with over a hundred vendors. Each vendor had counter seats where you could eat or buy food by the kilo. By the time I was ready to go back to the hotel, I had spent twenty DM, which was about $33.00. The week I spent in West Berlin, the US dollar was very weak.

I was booked on PAN AM FLIGHT 110. It was a seven-hour flight to JFK, arriving at 1:25 am EST.

Spending all my time walking across the Atlantic, I couldn't sleep. I spent time talking to flight attendants. The "Fasten your seat belt" sign was my signal to return to my seat. As the plane descended, the lights of the street grid of Canarsie were like sparkling diamonds, acting as a beacon guiding us to JFK.

Opening the door to my apartment, I found Jamie asleep. The only greeting I received was from Cat. The living room was how I had left it two weeks ago, with the unmade queen-size bed – Jamie was too lazy to turn it back into a couch. He was twenty-four years old and a true loner. He had gone from an overweight teen to a person who turned his body into pure muscle, drinking protein drinks and spending most of his free time in the gym or honing his skills as a DJ. When we were at Club Med with my father, he became friends with the person who hired DJs for Club Med resorts in the Caribbean. He spent the entire summer of 1984

DJing at the Resorts St. Lucia Village. Returning to New York, I asked him how many girlfriends he had. His answer was: "None. All they wanted was somebody with money." Part of his job involved receiving beads for drinks to spend on guests. In his room was a bottle with a hundred beads on his dresser. He told me that they offered him a contract to DJ at various clubs throughout the Caribbean. I viewed this opportunity as a dream job for a young person who was not sure what he wanted to do with his life. I gave him all the reasons why he should sign the contract, from doing something he enjoyed to saving money, great weather, and meeting girls. I saw him as an older version of myself when I worked at the Concord Hotel. All he could say was that working there, he couldn't see his future. My response was: "Do what makes you happy." Opening his bedroom door, I found him fast asleep, not knowing that I had returned home.

Not bothering to unpack, I fell asleep with Cat next to me. Jamie, seeing I was asleep, didn't bother waking me, going off to work at Macy's PJ Clarke's, where he was assistant manager, opening the restaurant for lunch.

Gloria had no idea when I was returning. Being an only child, my first responsibility was to my parents.

Entering the BMT subway, whose entrance was half a block from my apartment, I caught the express train to Brighton Beach. I had bought my mother a gift of Chanel No. 5 at the duty-free shop at Tempelhof. I always liked surprising my parents, asking the doorman not to announce me. I took the Sabbath elevator, which opened on each floor until it reached the sixteenth floor. Using my key, I opened the apartment door, surprising my mother, who always walked around wearing her underwear and bra. The apartment had the smell of death. My father, who now slept on the couch, was as always. She smothered me with kisses and started to cry. She was always a drama queen. Between the tears, she asked me if I was hungry. Wiping away the tears, she left the room to put on a housecoat. Approaching the couch, I saw a man who was determined to die. Kissing him on the forehead, I asked him how he felt. Looking up at me without his dentures, he grabbed my sleeve and whispered: "Your fucking mother is driving me crazy. If she doesn't stop, I am going to throw her out the window." My eyes moved down his body until I reached his legs. They were crusty and swollen; the skin was like rice paper, and one touch of water would make it ooze. Coaxing him to stand up, I took him for a walk in the hallway, discussing my trips to Amsterdam and West Berlin. He wanted to know if I got laid. Looking at him, I created the fantasy of going to East Berlin, visiting Helga in her apartment, and having great sex, then taking a taxi back to Checkpoint Charlie and back to the hotel. Before returning to the couch, with tears swelling up, he asked if I had heard from Julie. Keeping him steady, I told him not since 1976, except for the time I arranged for her and her friends to enter Studio 54; even then, we didn't speak. As I helped him get back on the couch, he asked how Jamie was. That shocked me. I thought Jamie was talking to his grandfather, who took him on trips and had fart contests in my apartment. Looking at my watch, I was ready to go back to Manhattan. As my mother walked me to the elevator, I pleaded with her: "I know that you love him, but just do what he wants." The subway ride back to Manhattan brought back memories of 1972, going through twenty steno pads, and writing my first novel,

The Agony of Larry Altman. It was a fictional novel of my life before my divorce. An editor at Simon and Schuster liked the book and gave me a twenty-five thousand dollar advance. It went to galleys, and I was on a real high. Before it went to press, my editor got canned. The new team pulled the book.

Arriving in Manhattan, Jamie was in his room with earphones on, oblivious to his surroundings. I hated confrontation, and Jamie was emotionally fragile. Walking up behind him, I lifted his earphones. "I yelled, 'Stop what the fuck you are doing! Have a little respect. Ask me how my trip was. Say that you spoke to or visited your grandfather while I was gone.'"

He turned and hugged me, saying he was sorry. "Gloria called to say hello, asking when you would be coming back from Berlin."

I spent the rest of the weekend writing a report on my activities in Amsterdam and Berlin. At both conferences, we were featured on the front page of the show's daily newsletters, which were distributed to all attendees.

On Sunday, I called Gloria. This was the first time we had spoken since she was released from the Mental Health Facility in White Plains. She sounded upbeat and happy, and we made plans to spend the weekend together.

On Monday morning, I arrived at the office with the familiar smell of curry. Knocking on his door, I saw Sant, a picture of elegance in a blue turban, who added another six inches to his six-foot-four frame. Rumour had it that he was one of the first pilots to fly off an Indian aircraft carrier. Motioning me to join him for tea, we spent almost an hour discussing my trip. After presenting him with the presentation, he discussed his plans to purchase more properties. He was looking at a rundown hotel called THE TUDOR on East 42nd Street. His real estate portfolio was expanding, thanks to his Indian investors.

Gloria and I went back to dating. It wasn't the same; she was not the same person I had dated, resenting her husband for having a younger live-in girlfriend. Sexually, she was inhibited. I never asked her to be monogamous. On Sunday night, as she was going to the FDR on her journey back to Westchester, she dropped me off at a singles hangout on Eighty-third Street and Second Avenue as she headed to the entrance to the FDR. Walking over to the apartment of a woman named Michelle, who was in the sales department of *New York Magazine*, I found her to be a chess master and an expert in needlework. People paid her hundreds of dollars for a sweater, and she owned two German Shepherds. During the week, she would take me out for dinner on her magazine expense account; she had to show that she was spending money on clients. After dinner, we would have sex. I had a problem with both Shepherds; they slept in front of the bedroom. The first time we had sex, she fell asleep. Opening the bedroom door, I almost got mauled. Slamming the door, I had to wake her up to control the dogs. She asked me why I always had to leave. My excuse was that my eleven-year-old son was living with me, and I had to make breakfast, making sure he went to school. Jamie would also stay eleven as long as I had one-nighters. The other reason was that Gloria always called me at eleven am If I didn't answer, I would have to spend the entire weekend discussing where I was at eleven am No matter in whose apartment I was having sex, I had to be home. I had this stupid sense of loyalty.

My mother called me every day, telling me my father was threatening to harm her. I found myself on the subway, going to their apartment to make peace. Asking my father for the name of his doctor, he told me not to bother. Finally, I picked up the phone and called Elder Plan, where I found out he had no specific doctor. I asked for the last doctor he saw. They put me on hold for fifteen minutes. The voice on the other end introduced himself as Doctor Elliott. He sounded young, and I surmised he was in his residency at Maimonides. Elliott went through a litany of what was wrong with him: "Slight Alzheimer's, cardiomyopathy, on warm days he entered the clinic wearing a down jacket, complaining that he's always freezing." Controlling my temper, I asked the doctor what he thought was wrong with him. "I would assume it's overactive thyroid," he replied. Getting pissed off, I retorted, "How could you assume? Are you his doctor?" "Mr Gutwirth, I am part of a team who treats your father; no single doctor handles a patient on an Elder Plan," he explained. Realising that this wasn't Elliott's fault, but rather my father wanting to go the cheap way, I now offered sympathy for his dilemma. "His legs are full of water," I said. Elliott put me on hold. Five minutes later, he came back. "I am reviewing his chart. I see he was prescribed diuretics to take daily, which will help eliminate excess water in his system. On one of his visits, I was on my lunch break, and there was your father eating a hot dog. He has to change his diet; otherwise, as doctors, there is nothing we can do to help." Disconnecting the call, I got the total picture of a person who wants to die, and there is nothing I can do to stop it.

As an executive of Beefsteak Charlie, my job was visiting various locations unannounced for dinner. Either I had a date, or my buddy Ray, the Coffee Man, or Operatic Diva joined me for dinner at various locations, and I would write up a summary of each location. All the Beefsteak Charlies in Manhattan and the five boroughs were company-owned; their monthly numbers were down. One of our Manhattan restaurants, on Third Avenue and 58th Street, where I went to dinner with Lenny the Attorney, reminded me of how I associated all my friends by their profession rather than using their last names: Stuie Insurance refused, Nat Real Estate, Simon Westchester, Lenny the Greek, Larry the Accountant. Most of the men I befriended had been married for twenty years or more. Having dinner with Lenny the Attorney, who wore five-thousand-dollar custom-made suits, reminded me of how he left his partnership in a Long Island law firm when one of his clients, based in Switzerland, whose products were manufacturing special ink sold to government treasuries to use in printing their currency, made him chief legal counsel, bought a townhouse on East 61st Street off Park Avenue, and paid for a luxury apartment in Museum Tower next to the Museum of Modern Art. Falling in love with a thirty-something American Airlines attendant who naturally worked first class, he left his wife of thirty years in their lavish home on the North Shore of Long Island. With his adult children hating him, he decided to file for divorce and marry Ms American Airlines. He had one dilemma: should he give his wife the house, or sell it and split the money made through the sale of the home? I couldn't believe how a man so smart could think so stupidly. After ordering dessert, I looked at him. "My solution is simple," I said. "You lived with your wife for thirty years; no matter how much you screwed around, you came home. You have enough money to give her the house." As the waiter brought us coffee, four couples were trying to get in; the manager waved them off, saying the restaurant was closed. Using my corporate credit card and leaving a tip, we left. The next morning, I had a meeting with the head of Restaurant Operations, who sent out a memo that all units must stay open Wednesday, Friday, and Saturday until 11 pm. After dinner, we regrouped at the closest piano bar, where Nat Real Estate was looking for another wife; he was afraid of dying alone.

Gloria was still my weekend date when she had an opportunity to unload her problems at home, recapping why, after four years, her husband had refused to give her a divorce.

The second week in April, my mother called, crying that my father had tried to commit suicide. She explained that she had gone out shopping. Returning home, she found my father had taken Valium and Johnny Walker and was sprawled on the couch. Screaming, one of her neighbours called 911, and she was going in the ambulance with him to Coney Island Hospital. It was 5 pm. Taking a taxi to Brooklyn would take at least ninety minutes. The express train was faster. Making record time, I arrived at Stillwell Avenue, which was the last stop on the BMT. The hospital was about half a mile from the station. Suddenly, there was a downpour. Ducking into a building, I found myself next to a beautiful blonde Russian woman in her mid-twenties. Across the building was a church. As the blonde offered a blow job for fifty dollars, there was a rainbow right behind the cross. Turning down the blow job, I felt that the rainbow was a message from God that my father wasn't ready to die. Running into the ER, I found my mother hysterical, waiting for word on my father. Coney Island Hospital was city-run and mainly served the minority community that comprised the various neighbourhoods near the hospital. One of the nurses came out and told us he was alive and being transferred to a room for an overnight stay. Thirty minutes later, we were up in his room that he shared with three other patients. It was sad to see that my mother was so fragile. As my father lay there, she smothered him with kisses, tears running down her face. We stayed watching over him until the nursing staff asked us to leave. In the taxi ride to their apartment, my mother vividly recreated, step by step, the total scenario of her day. "I try not to leave him, only to go shopping. He was on the couch watching television, finishing his breakfast. I was gone no longer than thirty minutes. Opening the door, I dropped my shopping bag. I was so afraid that I ran into the hall screaming. Thank God my next-door neighbour was home, and he dialled 911." Analysing my mother's retelling of what happened, I realised that my father didn't want to commit suicide. If he did, there were three locks on the door which he could have closed; by the time they opened the door, he would be dead. He never closed the door, making sure my mother would find him and save his life. I decided not to tell her what I believed would happen. Let her believe she saved my father's life.

Calling Jamie, I told him what happened, telling him that I would spend the night with my mother. The next morning, we took my father home. I decided not to confront him, exposing him to the devious thing he pulled off just for attention.

The last week of March, I received a promotional letter from the New York Post. They were creating a special section saluting Israel's fortieth anniversary, to coincide with the Israel Day Parade up Fifth Avenue on 18 April 1988. Since we had sixty units in the New York Metro area, which was home to the largest Jewish population in the United States, it made sense to buy a full-page advertisement. With a circulation of six hundred thousand readers, a good majority being Jewish, I set up a meeting with Sant, who had to approve all marketing expenditures. Making my pitch, he looked at me as if I was stupid, handing back the paperwork. "India has no diplomatic relations with the Nation of Israel." Rather than walking out of his office, I faced him, saying his decision was wrong, ticking off the following reasons why it made good marketing sense. Again, he said no diplomatic relations. He went back to what he was doing. I thanked him for his time, quietly shutting the door behind me.

Three weeks later, I was terminated. Chopra, his CFO, handed me a cheque which was sixteen weeks' salary. Packing my belongings, I hailed a taxi going uptown. Unpacking my eight years of memos, purchase orders, franchise marketing plans, and barter contracts, I decided to dump everything. I placed them in black garbage bags and placed them in the trash room.

Between my severance and unemployment, I had enough money to survive the summer. That coming summer, Gloria and her husband agreed that he would take the children; they still weren't divorced. Now that she was free, she and her newly divorced friends rented a house in Westhampton for the summer. None of them had relationships, so they agreed that no man would stay over. Gloria was the only person who decided to spend the entire summer in the Hamptons. Some mid-weeks, I would take the Long Island Railroad to Westhampton, spending three days with her, having Ray pick me up on Friday nights, where we became guests of friends who owned houses in Westhampton, making Westhampton's Bath and Tennis Club Marina our base of operations. Many of the summer regulars were founders of major brands of both men's and women's fashion lines which were manufactured in the U.S. before big box stores dictated lower price points. Domestic contractors whose employees were members of the ILGW, a union which negotiated liveable wages for its members. Unable to compete, American brands outsourced to third-world countries, where mainland China was the leading beneficiary, leading to the destruction of American-made clothes. This was the beginning of outsourcing to China and other third-world countries, destroying the made-in-America garment industry. The owners of these companies were mainly Jewish, owning homes in Westhampton on Dune Road. They all hung out together; many of them I knew from Club A, Studio 54, The Sherry Netherland's Bar, or recognised wearing a towel at Plato's Retreat. Hanging out at the pool bar, their wives were bedecked in jewellery, the men with gold chains and Rolex watches. None of them walked out on the beach, seeking safety in numbers behind the dunes. You could tell who was single; they would lie on their chaise, taking the sun, or in the saltwater swimming pool. Meeting them was simple: just hanging out in the pool, inviting them to take a walk on the beach, creating stories that made them feel good, and asking about their hopes and dreams. A good percentage of the time, I would have sex before dinner.

The weekends I didn't go to the Hamptons, I went to Brooklyn, trying to take my father to the beach where he always spent his summers with a group of guys in their early forties and late fifties, hanging out against the jetty that separated Brighton Beach from Manhattan Beach. They would smoke joints and play bongos, looking like remnants of Woodstock, always interested in how Broadway Sam was doing. Jason, who was a licensed psychiatrist, would play his bongos across the way from the Westside Highway to ward off evil spirits. Natalie, a well-tanned woman, would sit for hours on the shoreline in a meditative state. Their conversation was about how to attain inner light, as believed in Buddhism and the Zohar. They were all New Age thinkers whose source of income always baffled me. They were all on the beach, even in the winter. The second weekend of August, my father was grasping for breath. My mother and I decided that he would be better off in the hospital. Calling Maimonides Hospital, the ambulance arrived. My mother and I accompanied him to the ER. By 10 pm on Sunday, 21 August 1988, he was admitted to a room which was shared by three other patients. During the taxi ride back to my parents' apartment, my mother sat with tears going down her face, asking me what she was going to do if he died. I didn't have the answer, saying, "It's in God's hands." Ordering Chinese food, she discussed the good times, reverting to being a child. I asked my mother's permission to go away for the Labour Day weekend. She never said no to me. Wiping the tears from her face, she suddenly became a strong woman. "Go," she said, "you deserve to have fun." Leaving Brooklyn, I arrived in Manhattan. Jamie was in the apartment.

The summer flew by, and Gloria and I hadn't slept together for six weeks. The truth is, I didn't miss her. One of our friends owned a large commercial real estate agency and a large yacht berthed at a marina in Sag Harbor. Jerry, who owned the boat, had a chauffeured limo and a duplex on the East River. He would throw great parties with beautiful women. The weekend was a duplication of his Manhattan events, with more drugs and more women under thirty, all in bikinis, for some reason. I felt guilty hanging out in Sag Harbor, not being at my mother's side. That part of the weekend I spent using the pay phone at the end of the pier, the curse of being an only child, not having a sibling to share the pain of losing a parent. With a pocket full of quarters, I would spend time using the pay phone at the end of the wharf, checking in with both the hospital and my mother for updates on my father.

Driving back on the LIE, Ray raved about the weekend, having had sex with two women. I, for one, neither met nor had sex. I would think that waiting for the expected death of one's parent would have a major effect on one's libido.

Jamie supplemented his Macy's salary by doing DJ gigs. He was devoid of any emotions. I expected him to care for me as I cared for my father. Being in his world, he skirted the issue of death. There was a lack of humanity in him, avoiding visiting his grandfather in the hospital.

From the 6th of September 1988, I took the two-hour D train to the hospital, coaxing him to walk around the floor with his oxygen mask on. On Thursday, the 8th of September, I arrived at about noon. Helping him out of his bed, we walked around the entire floor twice. Saying to myself, "This is progress, hopefully, he may survive." Placing him in a wheelchair, I took him down to the hospital cafeteria, ordering him apple pie and a chocolate milkshake. At that point, he weighed one hundred and sixty-five pounds, down from his high of two hundred and fifteen pounds. For the first time, he started to cry. Wiping the tears from his eyes, he grabbed my hand. "I am sorry for putting you and Mommy through this. It was selfish of me wanting to die; I never thought it would be so difficult. My reason for wanting to save the money I had left was so your mother wouldn't have to ask people for help." Wheeling him back to his room, he took off his pinky ring, white gold, two diamonds and a ruby, slipping it on my pinky, saying in a low voice, "Where I am going, I doubt if anybody wears rings." Helping him into his bed, I kissed him on the forehead. As I was about to take the elevator, letting the door close, I went back to his room, kissing him on the cheek as he dozed off. "Dad, I will see you tomorrow. I am certain if we put our heads together, we can get you out of this mess. I will call the cardiologist that we met to arrange to have you transferred to Lenox Hill Hospital." Leaving the hospital, I felt a glimmer of hope that he would not die.

On the ninety-minute train ride back to Manhattan, the subway car was empty. Once we crossed the Manhattan Bridge, it was bodies against bodies. At that point, the train went express to 57th Street, only stopping at stations where passengers could transfer to other lines for their homebound journey. Rather than going home, I walked over to the Rendezvous, which was in the Berkshire Hotel on East 52nd Street, which became our gathering place. From there, we migrated to Bici, the Italian restaurant on East 53rd Street, winding up at PJ Clarke's. Entering the dining room, at the first table sat Frank Sinatra, his wife Barbara, Dennis Stein, Jilly Rizzo and his wife. Dennis Stein greeted me as if I were his long-lost brother, bringing up Mike Da Barbar and Philly Greenwald of the Concord Hotel. Sinatra looked up for a moment, "Hi, kid," shaking my hand without missing a beat, and went back to his meal. The Maître D' gave us a table in the back. I explained to my friends my relationship with Dennis Stein.

At about midnight, Ray dropped me off in front of my building. Jamie was in his bedroom playing DJ. For the first time, he asked me how his grandfather was. I told him he seemed to be getting better, also agreeing that I should transfer him to Lenox Hill over the weekend. At 2:00 am, the phone rang. The voice on the other end introduced himself as the doctor on call, informing me that my father was on life support and that a family member must make a decision according to his DNR. It made no sense calling my mother at 3:00 am to announce that her husband of FIFTY YEARS was on life support. It was impossible to fall asleep. As I closed my eyes, the movie of my forty-eight years with my father flashed by, with all the good times and bad times. At about 11:00 am, I called my mother to tell her that I would pick her up around noon to go to the hospital. There was silence on the other end of the line. Then she screamed that Sammy had died. I assured her that he hadn't, but that we both had to go to Maimonides, asking her to bring her chequebook.

There was a car service that spent money on television advertising, promoting the brand CARMEL with a jingle: 212-666-6666. It picked up my mother, who was dressed in black.

Entering his room, the curtain was drawn; the other three beds were empty. My father was hooked up to machines that beeped and constantly flickered from red to green. The young resident brought my mother, who stood frozen for a few seconds next to her husband. We both decided to leave her alone for a few minutes, putting a chair next to the bed. After a few minutes, I escorted her out of the room. They had a small lounge on his floor. Wiping my mother's tears, we discussed my father's options. The young resident introduced himself as Doctor Sherman. He then explained that my father was drowning in his fluids. Asking how old my father was, I replied that he would be sixty-nine years old this coming New Year's Eve. Holding my mother's hands, Doctor Sherman said, "If he had the proper treatment, he would survive another ten years." I couldn't tell him that he resisted medical treatment because his *dick* wasn't working. Asking the doctor what his quality of life would be if we let the machines do their work for a few more days, Doctor Sherman looked at both of us. "He will have to live his entire life on machines until his heart stops beating," he said. Handing us a paper to sign that would allow the hospital to remove life support, Doctor Sherman left the room. We both sat there staring at the document. My mother was saying, "What if?" My reply was, "There are no 'what ifs'." Both of us signed the release, handing it to Doctor Sherman. As he was consoling her, he recommended that I go down to the Rabbi's office, saying that he was an expert in grief management. As the nurses removed all the life support machinery, my mother sat completely silent, holding his hand and stroking his brow. Rather than having the nurse call, I went down to the lobby where there was a synagogue. Luckily, I met Rabbi Twerski, who agreed to spend time with my mother. Doctor Sherman came by, wondering why the doctors hadn't tried dialysis, which could have extended his life. I couldn't answer his question; he never had a doctor who was his point man.

By 3 pm on 9 September 1988, my father accomplished what he set his mind to do…DIE. The Rabbi escorted my mother from the room. After signing some documents, I had to arrange for a funeral home to collect the body. As he was a member of Seville Lodge, all their funeral arrangements were pre-made. All I had to do was call I.J. Morris, a funeral home located in Brooklyn; they would handle the rest. I set up a meeting with the Funeral Director for 5 pm that very day.

The funeral home was a sombre place. The salesman was cordial; he explained his job was to handle the entire process, leaving us to think about our loved ones. He asked what cemetery the deceased was to be interred in. My mother suddenly perked up. "Beth Moses in Long Island," she said, continuing to give the salesman the backstory of the cemetery, who was buried there, and Seville Lodge, saying that she had already ordered the headstone; all she had to do was call the monument store and give the time and date of her husband's death.

He then explained that the burial could not take place on the Sabbath. Rosh Hashanah 5749 started this coming Sunday, 11 September, ending on Tuesday, 13 September. After explaining the adherence to religious dogma, we agreed to the burial date of 14 September.

He then took us to the casket showroom. There were several simple wooden caskets, constructed without nails or hinges. The concept was eco-friendly, with the body and casket decomposing at the same time.

Back in his office, he went over the price list: five thousand dollars for refrigeration, and two thousand dollars for the Chevra Kadisha. These are the people who prepare the body for burial. This ancient ritual, where they wash the body with warm water while reciting prayers and psalms, then dress the deceased in a one hundred per cent white linen shroud, costs five hundred dollars. While they were reciting prayers and psalms, my mother asked to see the linen shroud, inspecting it, running her hand against the fabric, checking the stitching, finally declaring that it was well made, one hundred per cent linen, comparing it to a black costume made of linen she owned.

Finally, the cheerful funeral director discussed whether we needed the chapel for a memorial service and how many limousines would be needed. My mother and I stepped aside to discuss the Tuesday memorial service and the limousines, both deciding they were unnecessary. All we wanted was a hearse to deliver the body to Beth Moses at 2 pm on Tuesday, the fourteenth of September. My mother removed her cheque book from her purse; I filled out the cheque for five thousand dollars as a deposit, paying the balance after the body was delivered.

On the car ride back to her apartment, the thought of not getting three bids from other funeral homes annoyed me. Funeral homes can be shopped around for the best prices if you pre-plan your demise. Very few of us admit that we are going to die, leaving the surviving spouse or children to handle it. You cannot pre-plan your Emergency Room visits, lying on a gurney being wheeled into an MRI or CT scan; you are not thinking to ask ChatGPT for the best prices for MRIs or CT scans in your zip code.

Entering the apartment, the first call she made was to the Rabbi, who was a close family friend. The moment the voice on the other end said hello, she became hysterical, handing the phone to me. After wishing each other a Happy Holiday, I laid out the timeframe for the funeral. Most of our family lived in Miami. There are rules laid out in the Jewish religion, such as covering mirrors and wearing a black torn piece of fabric on your outer garment.

After the burial, the immediate family, which was my mother and I, had to sit shiva for seven days, accepting condolences from visiting friends and family. My parents had no friends; all their neighbours had either died or moved to South Florida.

Staying overnight, I went through my father's papers. Stacks of Reader's Digest magazines, an unfinished novel, posters from when he co-produced a play that ran for seven days, a picture of him with the winner of the "Largest Breasts in America" beauty pageant (with only one contestant, a stripper who was the featured star at The Gaiety Burlesque), communications with the White House where he arranged for one of his clients, the musical group THE BT EXPRESS, to do a concert on the White House lawn (with Jamie on stage), and newspaper clippings from when he sued his next-door neighbour for snoring like a freight train (who refused to move his bed to the opposite wall). In court, his lawyer entered into evidence a tape of the neighbour snoring. The outcome was that the court ordered the snorer to move his bed; the building then ripped down the sheetrock in their bedroom and added soundproofing.

Spending the weekend with my mother, going through my father's clothes, I realised he hadn't bought anything new since he made up his mind to die. On Sunday, my aunt and her two daughters arrived. My uncle also flew in with them, heading for Oceanside to stay with his friends. None of my father's family were invited; his brother had passed away, and the rest of his family I didn't know how to contact.

With the entire family bedded down in a one-bedroom apartment, I left Brighton Beach for Manhattan. Jamie was hanging out at the bodega across the street. Taking the lift up to our apartment, he turned to me. "Is Grandpa really dead?"

Opening the apartment door, I pushed him against the wall. "You should be ashamed of yourself for never once visiting him in the hospital."

In tears, he replied, "Grandpa always played games; I thought he was faking it." With that, he put his hand through the bathroom door. "You will have to call your boss, telling him that your grandfather's funeral is this coming Tuesday."

Gloria called and asked me how my father was. After a few seconds, I replied, "He is dead."

"I am so sorry. How is Ida taking the loss?"

"It was almost a fifty-year marriage; she has nothing else in her life."

Silence on the other end. "When is the funeral?"

"Tuesday at 2 pm, Beth Moses in Farmingdale, Long Island."

"When did he die?" she asked. My reply was, "Friday. Because of the Sabbath and Rosh Hashanah, we could not bury him earlier, Gloria."

"What time should I pick you up?"

"I am renting a car from Hertz. It's faster for you to go direct from Scarsdale to Farmingdale." Hanging up the phone, she never once said, 'I love you.' That's what I needed.

Taking a chance on some humanity, I called Julie. Marge picked up the phone. "Can I please speak to Julie?"

"She's not in," Marge replied.

"Tell her that her grandfather passed away. If she wants to come to the funeral this coming Tuesday, call me to make arrangements." I didn't know whether Julie was married or had children; she simply disappeared from my life.

On Tuesday, both Jamie and I, dressed in suits, picked up a Hertz rental and drove ninety minutes to Farmingdale, Long Island, a town of twenty-five thousand with a population of over half a million below ground. By 1:30 pm, we passed under the gate that said 'Beth Moses'. The gravel entrance led to the administration building. There were half a dozen rabbis dressed in black walking around, reading the Old Testament, in the hope that grieving families who didn't have a personal rabbi would hire them to pray over the coffin of the deceased.

Pulling into the car park, twenty people were surrounding my mother, who wore a black linen suit, which was her yardstick for how my father's white linen shroud was made. At 2 pm sharp, the hearse transporting my father's body rolled in, stopping directly in front of my mother. The chauffeur, dressed in black, opened the rear door and lifted the top of my father's kosher pine coffin. Nodding, it was him. The immediate family kissed his forehead. Closing the coffin, the driver handed me an envelope with the balance due. Then, a member of the office staff joined the chauffeur, leading him to the entrance of the Seville Lodge burial plots. Workmen were finishing preparing the grave site. I was surrounded by my family, thinking this was the only investment my father made in real estate. As they began lowering the coffin, the rabbi chanted the Jewish prayer for the dead. As custom had it, everyone threw a handful of earth onto the coffin. My mother let out a scream: "Sammy, what will I do without him?"

As my mother composed herself, she pointed out where she would be buried, and a place reserved for me. Looking through the crowd, Gloria never showed up.

After the services, all the people I didn't know or remember offered me their condolences and left. To me, a funeral is like a Bar Mitzvah where you know no one, but they give you envelopes with cash. I leaned against the hearse; the chauffeur was waiting for his cheque and tip. Reviewing the final bill, the balance was $7,000. I decided to write the cheque without questioning certain charges, like paying for gas for the hearse that already cost $1,000. I thought if my father knew his no-frills funeral cost $12,500, which included the Rabbi's fee, he would never have died.

My Uncle Mike, the youngest of the remaining family, had to catch a flight back to Miami and drive off to JFK. My Aunt, her two grown daughters, Abbie and Charlene, and my mother drove back to Brighton Beach. Giving Jamie the wheel of the rental car, he asked how to get back to the city. Looking at him, I said, "We are not going back to the city. You and I will spend time with Grandma, and order Chinese food. If you want to take the subway back to the city, be my guest."

Entering the lobby of Sea Coast Towers, where my parents were original tenants, all the doormen offered their condolences, handing me a fresh fruit basket with a note from Gloria. Over dinner, the girls told stories of my father popping their blackheads. My father had a habit of leaving my mother in search of a new life, going down to Miami, and spending time with my aunt and her daughters. Three weeks later, he would return, saying he was sorry to my mother.

The death of my father ended my thought of immortality. Not only was he my father, but he was also a friend. A man who set his own path in life, never as an employee. He was a true survivor, making sure he could always cover the family expenses, doing things he enjoyed doing. My mother was a unique woman who took his nonsense. Either she truly loved him or was fearful of an existence without him. She always played the victim card.

With his death, I started analysing my life. It was empty, having sex with people I didn't care about, currently in a relationship with a woman who would not allow me to use her bathroom; her kids hated me. This had to change. I needed a person who cared about me, with no baggage, who could add to my life. I concluded that Gloria and I were finished. The following Tuesday, 20th September, Jews around the world celebrated Yom Kippur, which ended at sundown on Wednesday, 21st September. Out of respect for my father, Jamie and I went to Temple Emanu-El, where he was Bar Mitzvah and confirmed. Emanu-El was to Reformed Jews as St. Patrick's was to Catholics; both were on Fifth Avenue. There were a lot of rules around Yom Kippur: fasting from sundown to sundown, not using transportation, working, or carrying money. I followed none of those rules. Whereas Orthodox Jews started at sundown, Emanu-El would start later so their congregants could finish their dinner. Most took taxis or their chauffeured limos to services. Since I didn't expect my father to die during the holidays, you needed to purchase a ticket to sit in the main sanctuary. Being community-minded, they piped in the services to seating in their basement. Opening services begin with Kol Nidre; during the twenty-four hours, you have an opportunity to renounce your sins. By the time the services are over, you are sin-free. Unlike Catholics, they can go to confession every Sunday, being absolved of their sins by a priest behind a mesh screen. Essentially, Jews believe in having a good life on Earth, whereas the other religions send you to a place you cannot send postcards, deemed a United Nations World Heritage site.

My mother adjusted to living alone, no longer waiting for him to walk through the door. This time, she realised he was never coming back. I was living with the illusion that she would make a new life for herself. She was a good-looking, seventy-two-year-old woman who, I discovered, was totally insecure. Her only outing was to visit her doctors in Manhattan.

Being absorbed with anger towards my father's death, I felt he could have lived another five to ten years if he had listened to the cardiologist who examined him at Lenox Hill.

I ignored Cat. He wasn't eating or jumping on the table to share my food, or swishing his tail on my backside while I was having sex. Looking at him, I realised that he was very sick. Wrapping Cat in his favourite blanket, I made an appointment with a nearby vet, who diagnosed him with a deadly kidney ailment. He gave me a choice: an operation for fifteen hundred dollars, which might extend his life by six months, or euthanise him to take him out of his misery. This was a decision I could not make alone. Telling the vet that I needed a day to think about what direction we wanted to go, I placed Cat back in his blanket and brought him back to my apartment. Jamie was oblivious to Cat's medical condition. That evening, we had dinner together, discussing Cat's medical condition. In reality, Cat was Jamie's pet, whom he had acquired when he was twelve years old. We both agreed that it was stupid to extend Cat's life. The next morning, we went back to the vet. Sitting in the waiting room, an hour later he brought a box containing Cat's remains, which cost us a hundred dollars. Holding a box with a dead feline, we now had to give him a dignified funeral. Jamie had the option of opening PJ Clarke's at Macy's and burying him in Central Park. I needed a shovel; I decided to bury Cat at sea. Returning home, we passed a construction site, finding a split brick, all his toys in the burial box, which fitted perfectly into a Bloomingdale's brown shopping bag. Carrying a dead cat, taking two subways, I found myself boarding the Staten Island Ferry, which at that time allowed automobiles across the harbour. Taking the stairway down to where the cars were parked, as the ferry approached mid-way in New York Harbour, I said the Jewish prayer for the dead, tossing the brown Bloomingdale's shopping bag overboard, hoping the current would take Cat to the open sea.

DECADE SEVEN

1988 TWO DEATHS AND A PARTY WHICH CHANGED MY LIFE,

All relationships have a beginning and End. The Middle is for you to fill in. The end is usually written by either both of your actions or by a higher power that controls our destinies, you cannot rewind the video of your life. It is THE FINAL EDIT.

THE FOLLOWING IS ABOUT US AND WE

On Friday, 28th October, one of the women I knew was throwing a Halloween party at The Park Avenue Pavilion. At these events, people weren't mingling but staying together with people they knew. Spotting a very elegant woman with dark hair, and deep-set eyes, wearing a black jumpsuit with red designs and no bra, I interrupted their conversation, asking her to dance. After an hour on the floor, we sat at a table. She had a five-carat diamond on her finger. Introducing herself as Elaine Lewis, she told me that she owned a space planning and interior design firm. I didn't know how much was real and how much of it was fantasy. After two hours, I asked if she wanted to leave and go to a piano bar on East 58th Street. Exiting on Lexington Avenue, I started to hail a taxi. She squeezed my hand and told me she had a car waiting. The town car drove us to La Camelia, one of my hangouts. As usual, a few of my friends were at the bar. An hour later, she lived on East 63rd Street. Kissing me goodnight, she handed me her business card, telling the driver to take me home.

Over the weekend, Gloria, her mother, and I drove to Atlantic City, reserving two rooms at Bally's. Never winning, just breaking even; I guess I can call it winning.

That Monday, I called Elaine at her office, which was on East 61st Street. After five minutes, she picked up the phone. Our conversation was business-like, finally inviting her to dinner, saying she would love to, "Let me check my calendar. I am available Friday, 11th November." This was the first time I called a woman for dinner and she said, "I must check my calendar." "Great, meet me at the bar in the Berkshire Hotel at 8 pm" I was hedging my bets; if she didn't show up, I would be with my friends heading out to New Jersey. The bar at the Rendezvous was four deep, filled with single women from the suburbs or hotel guests who were visiting Manhattan. At 8 pm sharp, Elaine walks in, with a cashmere poncho covering a shimmering silver halter, black slacks, perfect makeup, and well-coiffed hair. Compared to the other women at the bar, she was a standout. Escorting her to meet my friends, I could see from her body language that she was uncomfortable in this environment.

Walking out on East 52nd Street to hail a taxi, a town car pulled up. The driver exited the vehicle and opened the rear door. Remember, I didn't know anything about this lady except she had great cleavage and wonderful breasts. The driver turned and asked me where we were going. Without thinking about where she would like to eat, I directed him to go to Wo Hop, located on Mott Street in Chinatown. Turning to Elaine, I gave her a quick overview of the restaurant, failing to say that it was inexpensive. Placing her hand on mine, she said, "I never went to Chinatown. I would go to Bruce Ho on East 57th Street." Bruce Ho had tablecloths, waiters wearing dark jackets and ties, plus, they accepted credit cards. On the other hand, Wo Hop's tables were covered by paper rather than cotton tablecloths, and the silverware was wrapped in a paper napkin. We ate for two hours, discussing what I did, where I was born, and if I had children. I briefed her on how I went into a custody battle for my son, who lived with me. She gave me little information about herself, only that she never had kids and her husband died during a vacation at a spa outside Mexico City. Asking for the cheque, which came to thirty dollars including a tip.

Elaine Lewis and John Kerry

Elaine Lewis and Donald Trump

We left the restaurant to cross the street to the only arcade, which mimicked those in Coney Island, complete with a dancing chicken. In front of the entrance stood a majestic, real white chicken. It would dance if you deposited fifty cents. I was always fascinated by the dancing chicken. Watching tourists drop coins into the machine, I discovered that electric wires ran into the glass-enclosed vending machine. These wires gave the chicken a small electrical shock, making it appear to dance.

As the car headed back uptown, I told him to drop us off at Regine's, which was on Park Avenue. The Maître D', a friend of mine, seated us at a table where we ordered two cokes. By 1:00 am, we were dancing, kissing, and holding hands. When the music slowed down, it was a turn-on, having her breast against my chest and my hands moving up and down her silky back.

Leaving Regine's, we acted like kids, making out in the back of my father's car. As the car pulled up to 245 East 63rd Street, she told the driver to take me home. As she exited the Town Car, she hesitated for a minute, turning back to give me a goodnight kiss. As the doorman opened the lobby door, I yelled out, "Are you free this evening?" mouthing, "Call me!" as the car headed to the Westside.

LESS IS MORE
A PRACTICAL GUIDE TO
MAXIMIZING THE SPACE
IN YOUR HOME
ELAINE LEWIS

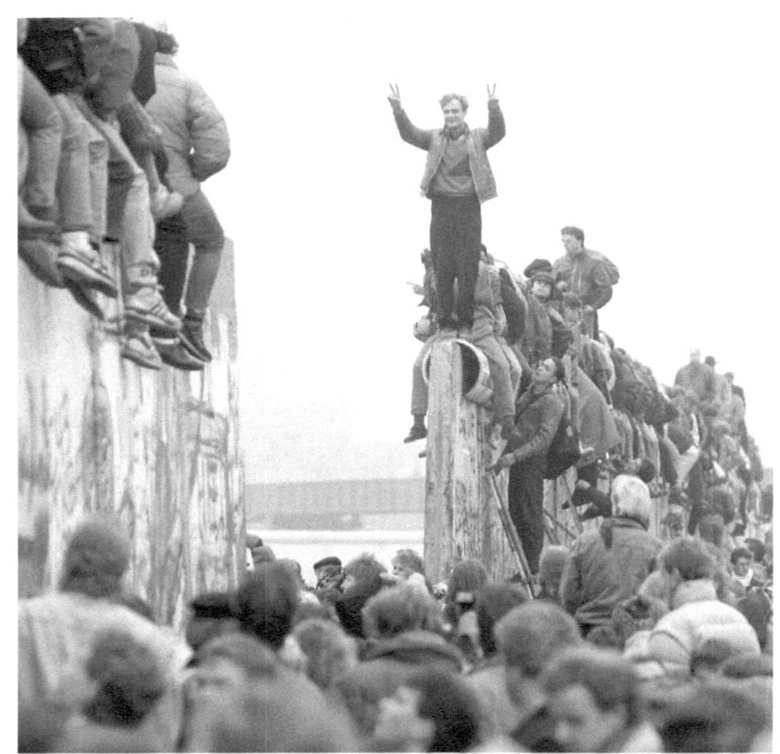

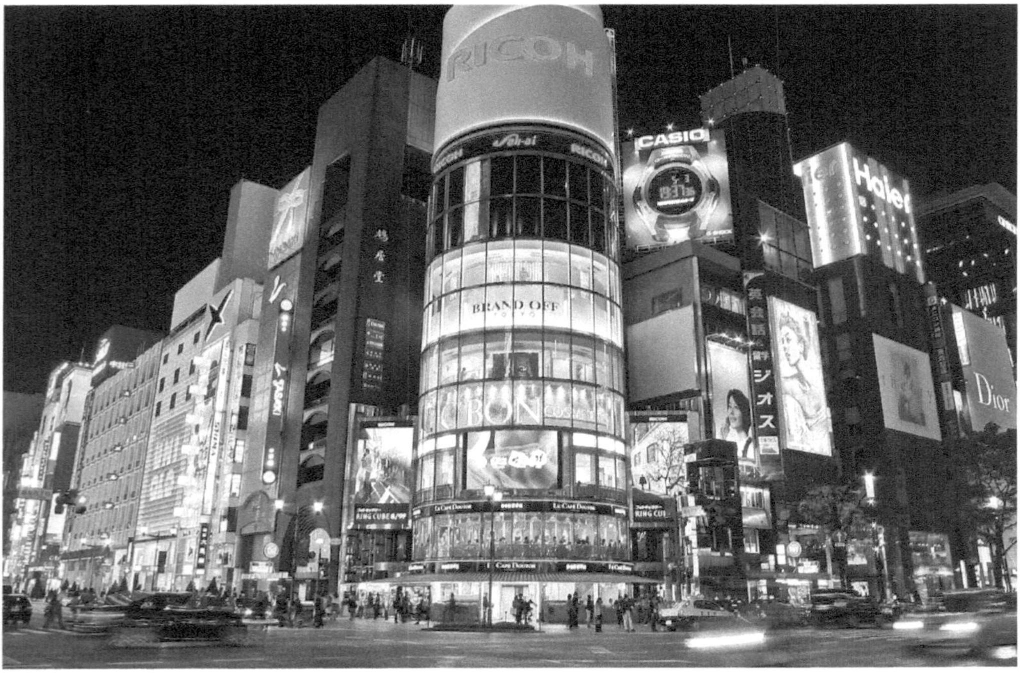
RICOH
CASIO
BRAND OFF
Dior

I cancelled my weekend with Gloria around noon. I called Elaine, and we decided to see the new Nicole Kidman film, *Emerald City*. We were both dressed casually and had dinner at Fiorello's, an Italian restaurant around the corner from her apartment. During the two hours, she told me that she grew up on Ocean Avenue, which happened to be a block away from where the mother of my children lived. She got married when she was sixteen, a marriage that lasted a year. I asked her why she got married so young. Looking at me, she said, "I couldn't take my father; all he wanted me to do was live by his rules." Her second husband's family owned a large furniture store near Brooklyn College called Harrison Interiors. He wanted her to work with his mother to learn the business. Within a year, she was on the sales floor, and within six months, she became the buyer, going to trade shows. "I hated his mother," she said. "So, I found a location on Kings Highway, between East Seventeenth Street and Sixteenth Street, which was perfect for a furniture store. I opened the second Harrison Interiors in 1963."

While she was talking, I drew an Elaine Lewis timeline with stick figures on Fiorello's paper tablecloth, using the box of crayons. Curious, she asked, "What are you doing?" Putting down my crayon, I replied, "I'm just doodling. Please go on." Squeezing my hand, she continued with the story of her life. "In 1973, I was bored living in Brooklyn. Howard and I agreed that we should open a store in Manhattan. I found a ten-thousand-square-foot store on Second Avenue at a great rent. Having created relationships with all the key furniture manufacturers, they supplied us with products on consignment, offering free interior design, which was unusual in home furnishings at that time. My marriage to Howard lasted five years. A persistent accessories salesman named Eli was bugging me for a date. I divorced Howard, and Eli and I got married, a marriage that lasted for about three years. Eli was a pothead, always stoned. Now I was totally alone, living in a one-bedroom apartment on East Fifty-seventh Street and Third Avenue. Howard closed the Manhattan showroom."

Having had enough of her marriages, I began laughing. "It's funny how, in a city of fifteen million people, I would meet a person whose life intersected with mine but whom I never met. First, you lived a block away from my first wife; then you owned a store two blocks away from my first apartment, which I passed every day for three years. One last thing: when is your birthday?"

She took a yellow crayon and, in big numbers, wrote 11/18. I took a green crayon and, underneath her birthday, I wrote 11/24. After paying the bill, we walked around the corner to 245 East 63rd Street. As the doorman opened the door, I leaned over to kiss her goodnight. Instead, she invited me up to her apartment. Opening the door into a large living room with floor-to-ceiling mirrors, she led me into her bedroom and put her finger to my mouth, whispering that her housekeeper was asleep. The lovemaking was a meeting of two bodies. Her body was like alabaster—no stretch marks, firm, silky skin. I experienced making love, not fucking. I decided not to sleep over and took a taxi home. We saw each other almost every night; the only night we didn't see each other was on her birthday. I wanted to buy her a birthday gift. Going to Saks, I thought about a neutral gift, and a lovely belt seemed the most sensible choice. I brought the gift over to her apartment and left it with the doorman, who struck up a conversation, telling me that she is a famous interior designer who has an office a couple of blocks away. I walked back to the Berkshire Hotel. In the world of interior design, I had only one reference point: James Mont, the interior designer of the Mob, who would visit Christian Science Reading Rooms to persuade women to fund one of his design concepts, like a highly polished grandfather clock with a stereo player and speakers built in.

Gloria suspected something was wrong. I made myself unavailable with outlandish excuses.

We had dinner the night after her birthday, with her picking me up in front of my building. She directed the driver to Bello's on Ninth Avenue and kissed me on the cheek. "My firm did the model interiors, the lobby and hallways of your building. I know the exact size of your apartment," she said, looking at me. "I remember the people in the rental office took me on a walk-through." During dinner, she told me that her husband, David Lewis, had passed away two years ago. He was fifteen years older than her and the owner of a big menswear company. "David and I lived in the penthouse when he died. I decided to downsize. The owners of the building, for whom I did work, had a vacant two-bedroom with a huge terrace at a lower rent, where I could start over, leaving my memories behind." From that dinner on, we saw each other almost every day. She had plans to see *The Phantom of the Opera* and agreed to meet me in the lobby of the Parker Meridian Hotel. We went to Regine's. On the day of my birthday, the doorman brought up a bouquet; the card was from Elaine.

At the end of November, I had to come clean with Gloria. We arranged to meet at a coffee shop on the ground floor of her hair stylist's salon. I apologised for not being open with her. As she stirred the cream in her coffee, she said, "I heard that you are seeing a famous interior designer." Reaching over to hold her hand, she pulled it away. "I didn't know how famous she was; all I knew was that she filled a void in my life. A widow, she didn't have children, unlike Gloria, who was always angry." Before I could pay the cheque, she walked out of the coffee shop.

In early December 1988, she invited me to a staff Christmas party at the Water Club, a restaurant on East Thirty-First Street, directly on the East River. Greeting me, she took me around the room, introducing me to each member of her staff and their spouses. She seated me next to her at the dinner table, while her African American secretary, Denise, handed out Christmas bonuses. Before dinner was served, Elaine got up and thanked her team for the great job they did on all the furnished models and sales office at the new Belaire Condo on East 72nd Street. She also announced that she had just signed Jeffrey Koo, a Taiwanese banker and owner of the China Trust Bank; he had purchased an entire floor as a corporate apartment. This was the first time I realised that she was for real. Going back to her apartment, she told me that she had made reservations for two weeks at the Safety Harbor Spa, a twenty-minute drive from the Tampa/St. Pete airport. Having never been to a spa – all the vacations I took were either in Acapulco or Jamaica – I was intrigued. The night before the trip, I packed my luggage, telling Jamie that I would be back after New Year's. My American Express card had the funds to cover expenses if needed. The morning of our departure, the doorman came up and picked up eight suitcases and a large Louis Vuitton bag and loaded them into the back of the Town Car; two were placed on the front seat with the driver. During the ride to La Guardia, I asked her why she had so many bags. Her answer was, "That's how I travel." We hailed a skycap, who wheeled the luggage to the Eastern Airlines ticket counter. After weighing the luggage, it cost a hundred dollars overweight, which she paid with her Amex. Landing at the Tampa/St. Pete airport, we decided to rent a car at Avis for two weeks. I needed an upgrade to a car with a large trunk. Checking in, it seemed the spa employees knew Elaine. In the dining room, you had an option for either a spa diet or regular food. She bought a spa package every day; she had massages. By the end of the week, I had had enough of the spa. Wanting to surprise her, I called my friend Mike Eisner, who at that time was CEO of Disney, and had his secretary set up a three-day pass at the park and a discounted room at Disney's Grand

Floridian Resort and Spa. Elaine loved the idea, suggesting that we spend New Year's Eve with friends who lived in West Palm Beach. Calling Avis, I arranged for the car to be dropped off at Palm Beach Airport, changing our return flight to Palm Beach for 2 January 1989. The spa week ended; Elaine decided to pare down items in her luggage, taking what she needed for the rest of the week. Calling New York for her UPS account, we arranged for the spa to send the suitcases with clothes to her home. The trip to Orlando was an hour and a half. We were like kids; the pass gave us full access to the park. The night before we were to leave for Palm Beach, we took the free ferry across the lagoon, with Cinderella's Castle and fireworks. Standing in front of the castle, we both knew that we belonged to each other. After three days at the Magic Kingdom, Elaine called her old friend Tina, who lived in West Palm Beach, and who invited us to celebrate New Year's as her house guests. As we drove to West Palm, Elaine told me that Tina was her manicurist who had moved from New York to set up her own manicure studio, where she had guaranteed business from her wealthy New York clients who spent the winter in their Palm Beach homes. In the afternoon, we would drive over the bridge from West Palm to Palm Beach. Elaine was my tour guide, pointing out the condo apartment where she and David Lewis had owned an apartment, which she sold upon his death. We passed a 17-room mansion on the Intercoastal with a large iron gate surrounding the property; at the main entrance, in large letters, was CASA TOVA. We celebrated New Year's with two large pizzas.

During the flight back to New York, she had every weekend planned for us; she had leased a townhouse in Southampton yearly.

I still wasn't aware of who Elaine Lewis was. My measurement of real success was having my television series or a leading role in a film. Suddenly, she suggested that we live together. To me, living together was an evolutionary process, something I had to think about, discussing it with my son who, in 1988, was twenty-three years old. I still used the teenager ruse to avoid waking up and having breakfast with someone. Arriving at her apartment, I left my luggage with the doorman. Stephanie, her live-in housekeeper, was in the living room viewing a large-screen Magnavox colour television housed in a large wooden cabinet. We were connected, speaking every day, with my calls always being screened by her secretary, Denise, who, in the beginning, would say, "I do not have her right now," after a minute of silence, Elaine was on the phone. We usually met for drinks at the Regency Hotel or out to dinner, alternating on who picked up the cheque. Some evenings, Stephanie would make us dinner. A couple of weeks into 1989, she invited me to meet at her office. Her office was located next to Vertical Club, one of the first health clubs in New York. Taking the elevator, I exited into a reception area with lettering that read "Elaine Lewis Design Space Planning, Interior Designs". I was greeted by the receptionist. The walls of the reception room were covered by framed pictures of major luxury multi-family buildings. Within minutes, a Black girl entered the reception area, introducing herself as Denise, Elaine's assistant, escorting me to her office. There she sat behind a large desk stacked with purchase orders and floor plans. After a few minutes, she took me on a tour of her office. There were fifty desks in a large room with product catalogues, paint chips, a ring of wood finishes, and a rack of upholstery fabrics. That weekend, she suggested that I rent a car and drive out to her townhouse in Southampton. As we pulled into the driveway of a community called Southampton Common, we drove up to a two-storey attached townhouse which she leased on an annual basis. She announced that she was going to cook dinner for us. One problem was that there was no food in the house. Asked her where the supermarket was, and she looked at me and said, "I do not know. Denise calls, and they deliver it, leaving it at the door." After unpacking, we stopped at a petrol station, asking for directions to the nearest supermarket. He said, "Two lights, make a left, and you will see Gristedes."

Entering the store, which was empty, I looked at Elaine as if she were a kid visiting Disneyland for the first time. As I pushed the cart, she just began filling it with groceries. The total amount of groceries was over a hundred dollars. Taking out my Amex to pay the bill, she told the cashier to put it on her tab. Saturday, after breakfast, we drove to the beach, which was deserted. The weekend was for relaxing; gone was the makeup, the high heels, the designer clothes. The stillness that surrounded us offered her tranquillity, while I had an anxiety attack; my psyche was the street noise of mid-town Manhattan. That evening, she attempted what I gathered was the first time she had cooked dinner: Chicken Parmigiana and pasta. Observing her attempt to prepare dinner, with the tomato sauce and breadcrumbs splattered all over the kitchen walls and floor, I gave her credit for trying. This was the first and last dinner she ever cooked. By the end of March, while driving home from the Hamptons between Exit 70 and Exit 52 on the Long Island Expressway, we both concluded that I should move in. Returning to Manhattan, Elaine's building doorman took her luggage. Deciding it was time for Jamie to meet Elaine, we arrived at La Premiere, which had a curved driveway and parked the car. Entering the lobby, Omar, the doorman, gave Elaine a big, "Hello, Ms Lewis." She stopped at the desk and told me what a big help he was when she was finishing off the models. Jamie wasn't home yet from his job at Macy's. The apartment was spotless; everything was in order. At 8 PM, Jamie walked through the door, finally meeting Elaine. Inviting him to join us for dinner, we went to our favourite restaurant on Ninth Avenue called Bello. After a two-hour dinner, I told Jamie that Elaine and I had decided to live together. Jamie, eating his pasta, looked at both of us and said, "I was hoping that this would happen. It made no sense that you came home at 3 AM every night of the week." Paying the cheque, Jamie whispered in my ear that he couldn't afford to pay the rent. I told him that I would pay the rent for the remainder of the lease. The next day, she ordered a car service to help me move my clothes. Since Jamie was staying in the apartment, I planned to give it time, realising that spending a long vacation and weekends was really getting to know the person.

The first few weeks were about getting used to her regime, which started at 11 AM with a personal trainer, and then a makeup artist. Once a week, she had a hairstylist. The housekeeper, who was from Northfield, Minnesota, a town with a population of under twenty thousand people, always made breakfast, did the shopping and straightened the house. Once a week, she had a meeting with her attorney to draft new contracts and go over financials. At this point in our relationship, I felt her financials were none of my business.

Living and working with her, my goal was to establish Elaine Lewis Designs as the go-to firm for model interiors, both domestically and globally. A key player in creating and implementing these interiors was a Czech designer named Wolfie. He came from the world of window displays for Lord & Taylor, a New York department store, and specialised in creating renderings of apartments so developers could visualise the model interiors. Assisting with the renderings were two talented designers from the Middle East. One, Nabeel, considered himself a Palestinian whose upper-class family had sent him to the United States to study architecture and interior design. His friend, Chablis, from Beirut, implemented the interiors. Elaine's personal assistant, Walter, was both her personal shopper and tasked with visiting home furnishing showrooms to select merchandise for the design team. Elaine had met Walter at the age of eighteen at The Harbor Island Spa in New Jersey, where he was a dance instructor. Then there was Denise, Elaine's gatekeeper, responsible for managing her appointments and communications, and essentially in charge when Elaine was away. She also kept track of all the employees. Elaine was averse to technology. Having little concern for saving money, she would send a member of her team to a store on Second Avenue to send and receive faxes. Only after realising the cost of sending faxes from Second Avenue did she agree to purchase a fax machine.

During the summer of 1989, we spent long weekends in the Hamptons. We played a game where I had to follow her footsteps in the sand. She had a perfect stride, while my feet were all over the place. One Saturday in August, she looked at me and said, "Let's get married this coming November, on my birthday." After six months of living together, I had learned it was easier to say yes. As we headed towards Manhattan, I suggested a detour to

Brighton Beach to surprise my mother. "Let's do it," she said. After forty minutes, we were about to pull into the driveway of Seacoast Towers. We passed a store selling flowers. Elaine asked me to stop, and within minutes, she returned with a bouquet. Usually, I would find parking and go through the service entrance. This time, I wanted the doorman to announce us so my mother would have time to put on her house dress. When she was alone, Elaine would wear a huge bra and panties. She had large breasts and wore a custom-made brassiere. I knew that my mother had a close relationship with Gloria, with whom she connected regarding family and children. I was about to introduce her to a successful woman who had never had children; their only common ground was designer clothes. Exiting the elevator on the sixteenth floor, we found my mother in front of the door in her housecoat. As usual, she asked why I hadn't called to let her know we were coming so she could make dinner. From a previous conversation, my mother knew that Elaine was an interior designer. After putting the flowers in a vase, she gave Elaine a tour of her James Mont furniture. Sitting in the living room was a large portrait of my mother. My mother's conversation focused on my father. Two hours later, we kissed goodbye and drove back to Manhattan. That first meeting with my mother established a schedule for our visits: once a month in Brooklyn after returning from the Hamptons, or lunch and dinner in Manhattan after her doctor's or tailor's appointments. Crossing the Williamsburg Bridge from Brooklyn to Manhattan, Elaine was busy drawing up a list of wedding guests, suggesting the wedding be held at the Friars Club. I remembered her showing me pictures of her wedding with her deceased husband at the Friars Club. I went along with everything, indulging her fantasy. On the Tuesday before Labor Day, she called me to meet her at Tiffany's to discuss wedding invitations. Her personal shopper in the Wedding Department was ready to close the sale. After requesting samples of invitations, I suggested we place the order after the holiday weekend.

We always went to the beach at sunset. Elaine was obsessed with keeping her skin milky white. Picking up perfectly shaped seashells, we both faced the crashing waves. Putting my arms around her, I decided it was time for my argument against getting married. "I see our relationship as long-term. You've been married four times and widowed once. We both don't want children. I feel our bond is stronger than any legal document that proclaims our love for each other." Kissing me, she replied, "I guess I'm a marriage junkie. My first marriage was to escape my father, who was a German disciplinarian. In my other three marriages, they expected me to be a homemaker without a career, a duplication of their mothers. I'm ready to try it your way." During the summer, her team was busy working on the China Trust corporate apartment and a new community in Jersey City built by the Lefrak Organization, Newport Center, which was opening one of its residential high rises. It was a large job, encompassing model floors, lobbies, and public areas.

After Labour Day, we would stop by to inspect the progress of the job. Nabeel was the project manager during the final weeks. Walter went out to buy accessories, which included everything needed to make it ready for occupancy. Usually, model interiors were created on floors that would be difficult to sell. By the end of October, it was time for the final walk-through with the owners. This was Elaine's opening night. Assembled in the apartment was her executive assistant, Walter, who was over six feet tall and always had a smile on his face; Den, her make-up artist; and Helio, a Brazilian hair stylist – all assembling to create Elaine Lewis, the diva of interior design, for a client walk-through.

We planned to meet her in front of the Belaire at 4:00 pm Wearing a suit and tie, at 4:00 pm a town car stopped in front of the building. Out stepped Walter and Elaine; all that was missing was a red carpet. Taking the lift up to the sales office, which she also designed, she was greeted by a team of in-house salespeople. Elaine, who always had great cleavage, would throw her chest out, creating the illusion that she had large breasts. Ten minutes later, the developers, the Zeckendorf brothers, entered, and there was a big round of hugs and kisses. Elaine introduced me to both of the brothers, Arthur and Lie, the grandsons of William Zeckendorf Senior, with whom I spent time when I was doing public relations for Luxor. I realised that everyone around her was window-dressing. She took the brothers around each model, explaining the rationale behind each design feature; she was the teacher, and they were her students. After the tour, they gave her another commission: a new project on East Eighty-Seventh Street.

Living with Elaine meant putting my ego on the back burner. For years, I saw myself as part of a major corporation. I knew I was the best at what I did; unfortunately, those who interviewed me had a set budget, which was below my expectations. I decided that working for a large corporation was more about whose backside you kissed. Corporate politics was more important than talent. Elaine Lewis Design was a perfect small company, offering a proven track record to real estate developers who needed furnished interiors to sell or rent their properties. Marketing was business-to-business. Elaine was not interested in doing residential interiors for private individuals unless they were famous, or the budget was over £500,000. Manhattan, an island separated from the other boroughs by nine bridges, in 1980 was a decade where developers were assembling empty lots and walk-up tenements to build luxury multi-family high-rises on both the East and West Side. Fifth Avenue was the major shopping area in Manhattan, dividing the city between both rivers: the Hudson River and the East River. Elaine had the foresight to create a niche interior design business, which created furnished interiors to enhance the properties' footprint. She could make a 500-square-foot apartment look like it was twice the size, having furnished showcases in every major new luxury high-rise in Manhattan. Her company never had to go out and solicit business; developers would come to her, offering new projects.

During the first meeting with the developer, she would discuss who the potential renters or buyers of the property were. This meeting was not a bidding situation; Elaine Lewis Design automatically had the project. Developers would give her £50,000 on signing the contract that her lawyer, Jack Rosen, would create. They would then give Elaine their budget for the model apartments. Her design group would then work on creating a floor plan using the architect's drawings. All apartments were the same square footage. During the design process, Elaine would meet with the architects to select apartment finishes: flooring, kitchen hardware, countertops, cabinets, appliances, bathroom hardware and finishes.

She was a master at making money, which came into play after making the final presentation with sample boards representing every element of the apartment, including fabric selections pasted on large blackboards. This meeting was usually in the client's conference room. Attending the meeting were the owners, their construction team, members of either their in-house real estate team or outside real estate consultants who were hired to market the property. Our team was Elaine, Wolfie, Nabeel and Walter, who would take notes of the meeting. Our site was highly choreographed, with Elaine starting her pitch, followed by Wolfie, who went through the floor plan. Nabeel, with his elegant Middle Eastern accent, went slowly through the presentation boards and the motivation behind each selection. I followed Nabeel with a marketing analysis. After two hours, the client signed off on the project, and Elaine was given the second payment on the contract. She was a master at making money, which came into play after making the final presentation with sample boards representing every element of the apartment, including fabric selections pasted on large blackboards. Now that all the selections were approved by her team, she reached out to furniture factories in High Point, North Carolina, to create knock-offs of both upholstered and case goods, giving her a 60% profit on the entire interior package. She always had five to ten jobs in-house to create constant cash flow.

As the months went on, the relationship suffered from headwinds, and people were telling her I was with her for her money. They didn't realise what I was doing behind the scenes. We were constantly going to real estate events; Walter always joined us. Her entrance was choreographed to maximise the impact, to show that she was special. Before entering a room, she would stand there in her six-inch heels, wearing a floor-length mink coat – an expensive outfit with elegant accessories used to create a dramatic presentation. After a few seconds, Walter would help her take off her coat and take it to the cloakroom. She never moved, waiting for people to come to her; she was perceived as a diva. Even though she would rather stay home, she was aware that visibility was good for business. Sensing that it was best that I let her and Walter do their thing, I would hang out and meet young real estate brokers and small real estate developers. I made a bogus business card: "Allen Gutwirth, VP of Business Development and Marketing." Every man in the room wanted to sleep with Elaine; I never cared about it. I knew it wouldn't happen.

The Koo project was to create a common entertainment and dining area, like an elegant Chinese restaurant, with four small bedrooms with bunk beds which opened into three full bathrooms. Every six months, a new team of bankers would come to New York to take special courses at NYU Stern School of Business. It seemed that Jeffrey was a graduate of NYU when I attended. At least once a month, we would meet his lawyer, the chief of staff's wife, expecting *yongjin* (commission). If we paid all the people with handouts, we would be broke. Every time we met, she would take them out to a five-star restaurant. Koo, who had ordered a personal jet, invited Elaine to design the interiors. By the end of the summer of 1989, the corporate apartment was completed. At this point, Koo took one more shot at making Elaine his New York mistress, inviting her to Taipei to remodel several apartments he owned, where he would invite his global golf buddies. China Trust sponsored a golf tournament in Taiwan.

On 1 November 1989, she told me that we were going to Taiwan to design five apartments for Koo, and he was paying all expenses. On the return home, we would stop in Tokyo for a week and celebrate our birthdays. Not being a person to miss out on press opportunities, I arranged interviews with the Taiwan News Agency and Kyodo News Service.

Always on the lookout for new business opportunities, I arranged, through the offices of Taiwanese and Japanese bureaus based in New York, for television appearances in both countries when we arrived. Finally, on 15 November, we were heading to JFK in a van. Elaine had a dozen pieces of luggage; I had one suitcase, flying JAL business class to Taiwan. On checking in, she was charged three hundred dollars in overweight charges. Since I and my father were handling the marketing for a travel wholesaler, I had an IATA number; we were bumped up to first class without charge. With one stopover in Tokyo, waiting two hours for a connecting flight, we spent over twenty hours in the air. Finally arriving at Taoyuan International Airport, we were greeted by Koo's chief of staff and his wife, Yalli. Naturally, they were surprised to see me. Elaine read their body language and introduced me as her husband. Ushering us past passport control into a parked limo, they asked where our luggage was. I slowly pointed to a small Chinese skycap pushing a cart piled high with her luggage. Reacting like a person who has gone through this before, Bob hailed two taxis, giving them instructions to take the luggage to the Caesars Park Hotel. Casually, Bob mentioned Elizabeth Taylor was a hotel guest. Travelling to the hotel, reminded me of taking the Van Wyck Expressway from JFK, and travelling through Queens, but all the signs were in Chinese. Arriving at the hotel, Elaine was greeted like a movie star by the hotel manager. The other two taxis pulled up in the back of the limo; three bellhops loaded the luggage. With great flourish, the general manager took us up to our suite, which overlooked the entire city, introducing himself as Chin, and mentioning that he went to hotel school in Switzerland. Running around the suite, Chin turned on all the lights, showing all the features of the suite. On a table were a large bowl of fruit and cheese and a bottle of champagne. Chin opened the bottle, explaining how important the Koo family was to the building and growth of Taiwan. Before leaving, Bob gave Elaine a copy of her itinerary and meeting schedule with selected general contractors, which would begin in just twelve hours. As we finally relaxed, a bellboy brought up a large DHL box with floor plans, finishes, and furniture selections.

These were the finished interior design plans for Koo's apartments that the team had worked on during October. We were scheduled every day to be driven around by contractors, with Yalli, Koo's Chief of Staff's wife, acting as an interpreter. We never once met with Koo; I guess Elaine deflated his ego as a man who got whatever he wanted. Deciding to appease Yalli, we offered to host a dinner for the top designers, journalists, and interior designers in Taipei. Yalli reserved a private banquet room in one of the city's most luxurious restaurants. We had a long table for fifteen. When we arrived, Elaine was seated at the head of the table, and I was at the other end. Next to me was an American woman of about seventy. She introduced herself as Margaret. I asked her if she was an interior designer who lived in Taipei. As she sipped a glass of wine, she told me that she lived in Hollywood, Florida, and was a member of the Bahá'í Faith, whose global members let other members stay with them for free. The airlines offer senior fares, and on her Social Security and pension, she was able to travel the globe. Only arriving a week ago, she was the house guest of Andy.

He was one of the top interior designers in Taipei. Leaning over to shake my hand, Andy, who was gay like everyone else at the table, told me how beautiful Elaine was, and how impressed he was with my wife's work. The dinner lasted almost three hours, with the servers pouring wine and placing dishes on four lazy Susans. As a lover of Chinese cuisine, none of the dishes served was like anything I had ever eaten. All Elaine ate was vegetables. Finally, I asked for the cheque. I carried Elaine's AMEX. The cheque, with tip, came to three thousand US dollars; the bill was entirely in Chinese. Curious, I asked why the bill was so high. The waiter looked at me, passing his hand over a wine glass, and said, in broken English, "The wine." Exiting the restaurant, our driver was waiting for us. I told Elaine that I would meet her back at the hotel and decided to walk. It was a five-block walk back to the hotel. Within those five blocks, I was offered every sexual experience in broken English by cute young Chinese girls who wore mini-skirts and six-inch heels. The evening before we departed, we were invited to have dinner at Koo's mansion. Jeffrey Koo was one of a handful of billionaires whose forefathers were involved in Chiang Kai-shek's ability to form another country off the Chinese mainland, defying the communist mainland with a democratic government. Generations of the Koo family were deeply involved in the growth and prosperity of Taiwan. That afternoon, Elaine went for a massage, and a bevvy of make-up artists and hair stylists arrived at our suite. I was working on planning our flight back to Tokyo. During the Eighties, Japan had a financial boom, and its major corporations were investing heavily in purchasing real estate in the US. The Yen was king. I planned to research major trading companies that were involved in buying or building residential properties in key cities across the United States, using the Kyodo News story to set up meetings. It was like flying blind; luckily, there was an American Express office not too far from the hotel. The travel agent typed out the names of major real estate companies and their CEOs and booked us into a new hotel, The Prince, which was right across the street from the main bus terminal. The agent suggested that whatever airport we landed at, either Haneda International Airport or Narita, we should take the bus into Tokyo, for taxis or limos were very expensive. Returning to the hotel, Elaine looked like she had just stepped out of Vogue.

The limo arrived at 6 pm and drove for about thirty minutes outside of the city. Usually, when you visit very wealthy people's homes, you pass gated communities with lawns and trees. This ride took us past slums and garbage dumps until we came to a ten-foot grey wall with a large gate. Stopping by the security guard, the driver told him, in Chinese, that it was Ms Lewis. Within seconds, the gate opened. We travelled up a driveway lined with trees to the Fujian-style mansion, which had about forty rooms. Greeting us was Jeffrey Koo and a beautiful Japanese woman whom he introduced as his wife, Mitzi. Leading us past millions of dollars' worth of art and a large display of ancient Chinese hand-crafted porcelain vases from the Ming Dynasty and Qing Dynasty, into a large book-lined study where twenty people were mingling around, drinking cocktails. Koo escorted Elaine around the room, introducing her to the other guests. After an hour of drinks, a large sliding mahogany door opened, and an elegantly dressed waiter announced that dinner was served. As you entered the dining room, a large, glistening crystal chandelier hung from a twenty-foot ceiling, illuminating three tables with seating for ten. I was seated next to Mitzi Koo, and Elaine next to Jeffrey. As the soup was being served, a butler came over and whispered in his ear. Koo rose and apologised that he had to go; President Lee Teng-hui had just summoned him to the Presidential Palace. Mitzi leaned over to me and whispered, "Don't be insulted; he is probably visiting one of his girlfriends." She then explained that she lived in Yokohama, Japan, and was starting a foundation for young, talented musicians. The next hour and a half they discussed interior design. Telling her that we were going to Tokyo, I brought up my concept of creating a furniture line designed for Japanese apartments. Loving the concept, she recommended that I contact Seiji Tsutsumi, CEO of Seibu Department Stores, mentioning Jeffrey's name. The traditional Chinese dinner isn't about eating; it's about dining and having long discussions. The people at our table spoke English, were all well-travelled, and many owned apartments in New York.

Returning to the hotel, I suggested that Elaine consolidate what she needed into two bags, leaving the rest in storage at JAL. She laid out five outfits and accessories.

Checking out of the hotel, we were told that the bill had been paid for by the China Trust. Seven hours later, we were on the bus from Tokyo International, which cost $60 rather than $150 by private car. Wheeling a luggage cart to the exit of the terminal, I ran across the street to The Prince Hotel, giving a bellhop $5. He ran across the street to relieve Elaine of our three suitcases.

As soon as we checked in, Elaine immediately booked a day of beauty package lasting the entire day. I went to the business centre to hire an interpreter to help me create a cover sheet for my fax campaign of setting up meetings, using the Kyoto feature story to set up meetings with real estate developers. As suggested by Mitzi Koo, I took a taxi to Seibu Department Store and shopped the furniture floor. All of their upholstery and case goods were imported from Scandinavia, which, in my opinion, was too large for Japanese apartments. Returning to the hotel, I asked the girl to call the CEO of Seibu, telling his admin that I was a friend of Jeffrey Koo, asking for his direct fax number. Within an hour, I created "THE NEW YORK LOOK" business summary, translated into Japanese, including the Kyodo News story, requesting an immediate meeting. A good part of my luggage was an Elaine Lewis press kit. I packed two suits, a pair of Levi's and twenty press kits. I went over my plan for the rest of the week. Japan was the picture of efficiency, with taxis whose rear doors opened automatically; their yellow pages had fax numbers of every company listed. It was still early. I went down to the business centre where I had the girl do research on who was the CEO of Haseko, one of our clients, having just finished a floor of model apartments which they developed on East 40th Street in Manhattan.

By the end of the day, I had six meetings set, which was a record time for an American businessman to arrange meetings.

I had heard great things about the ritual of bathing in Japan; my only point of reference was the Luxor Bath and the steam room at Plato's Retreat. I went to explore the Onsen (a name for a Japanese bathhouse). Entering, I was greeted by an attendant who took my clothes, handing me a towel and a wristband with a number. He spoke little English but pointed to a large sign outlining the steps for bathing. Rather than showering for five minutes, the shower lasted fifteen minutes, lathering every part of my body, and finishing with dumping a wooden bucket of cold water over my head. Next, I went to the communal pool where about twenty naked men were relaxing; it was a solemn experience, and no one spoke. Not one person had hair on their body. As if a bell rang, the entire pool emptied; I followed them into the steam room where I lasted ten minutes. Part of our travels is to have bottled spring water. Rather than going up to the room, I went to a grocery store a block away from the hotel, purchasing two gallons of spring water.

Back in the room, Elaine was asleep; she always fell asleep after a massage. The house phone was blinking red. Several messages were asking me to confirm meetings in broken English, watching CNN International.

Over dinner, I discussed the meetings that I had set up. She looked at me, "I thought we were on vacation?" I knew if I explained the reasoning behind the meeting, she would buy into it. "Japan is on a buying spree; their main target is Manhattan residential development. We are meeting with builders of the Highpoint, Haseko, and other potential developers of New York residential real estate. I am also waiting for the CEO of Seibu Department Stores to set up a meeting with his home furnishing buyers to talk about creating a collection called 'The New York Look' using your space planning talents."

The following morning, I received a call that the Seibu meeting was set for Thursday at noon. I thought it was a good idea to have one of the news bureaus of major USA television networks cover the meeting. The CBS Tokyo Bureau loved the idea, planning to cover the meeting, and contacting Seibu who loved the idea. Since dinner was an opportunity to get a wire service story, I called the Associated Press Tokyo Bureau, using my New York AP contact. I spoke to the bureau chief who assigned a reporter to meet us for cocktails at the hotel. A two-hour interview ensued, and an AP photographer showed up to shoot Elaine. Over a hundred newspapers picked up the story with a headline: **"ELAINE LEWIS, NEW YORK SPACE PLANNER, INTERIOR DESIGNER, TACKLES SMALL APARTMENTS IN TOKYO."** On the morning of 9 November 1989, as we were having great sex, Elaine was the most orgasmic woman I had ever encountered. CNN International was reporting that the Berlin Wall was coming down, creating a unified Germany. At that point, I rushed to have an orgasm. Elaine asked me what was happening that was so important that I stopped fucking. Sitting on the edge of the bed, "This is monumental, that the wall was coming down." Propping her against the pillow, looking at me as if I was out of my mind, "What wall?" I then recapped my visit to Berlin in 1988, Checkpoint Charlie, No Man's Land, East Berlin and HUMPHRY, the black blues singer who was a star in East Germany. I realised that politics and sex did not work together unless you were a spy. Over dinner, I explained the historic events of the day.

The next afternoon, Elaine, the translator, and I took a taxi for our noon presentation to the team of home furnishing buyers at Seibu. As we took the elevator to the executive office floor, we were met by a woman dressed in a black skirt, a white blouse under a black jacket, and heels, who escorted us to where the meeting was being held. A CBS camera crew was setting up by the entrance.

After a five-minute interview with Elaine, we entered a mahogany-panelled conference room with a fifteen-foot-long conference table. Seated around it were eleven young men and a greying older man, all wearing the same black suits, white shirts, and black ties. Each man rose, bowed, and handed us their business card. I circled the table, bowing and giving each one our press kit with the Kyodo feature. Elaine and I were used to dog and pony shows. After five minutes, I took over the presentation, outlining my vision and the capabilities of our design team to create furnishings for the modern Japanese home. The older man at the table rose and walked over to a large blackboard and started drawing an organisation chart. He turned to us and, in perfect English, announced that what we were presenting did not fit within the organisation chart. Thanking us, they all rose and bowed, leaving the room. One thing was consistent in all the meetings we had: they never said NO, only "we will let you know". Over the weekend, we took the train to Hakone, a town famous for hot springs, which offered traditional Japanese cottages called *Minka.*

It was the total Japanese experience: dining on the floor, on futons which were placed behind a *shoji* screen and rolled out every evening. Elaine, who had ordered a series of shiatsu massages, was the catalyst for my fantasy about a young, beautiful Japanese girl working on me. In came two women of sixty, weighing about two hundred pounds. After fifteen minutes of deep tissue massage, I turned to the lady, pleading, "Not so hard." Bowing, she walked backwards out of the room. The rest of my day I spent watching carp of every colour swimming through lush ponds that encircled the hotel.

Upon our return to New York, we spent New Year's Eve at the Friars Club. The Friars were a private club whose membership comprised entertainers and executives of various media and film companies, mixed with wealthy people who could pay the membership fee, in addition to spending a set monthly fee on dining. I felt right at home because a good number of entertainers knew me, either from when I was a kid working at the Concord Hotel, Universal Pictures, or ABC. Milton Berle was a regular with a big, unlit cigar in his mouth; we would sit and talk about me hanging out in his office, wanting to know what I was doing with my life. Liz Minnelli and then Elaine was the first woman to become a member. That meant taking clients for either lunch or dinner and being invited to their annual roasts, which were a black-tie affair. The roasts were held in the Grand Ballroom of the New York Hilton. The dais was filled with comics and politicians. The targets of the roast were people like Hugh Hefner, George Burns, and Johnny Carson, to name just a few. Elaine was in search of a new housekeeper, working with an agency that screens domestic workers. They sent up a woman whose credentials were impressive; her past employers were verified wealthy families. We ate at home two or three times a week; the dinner table was set like a four-star Michelin restaurant. She lasted a month. Dinner became a battle between my right and left hand. Finally, she got pissed when I told her to serve me on the left rather than the right side. I told her she works for us. In a huff, she put down the tray, packed her stuff, and left. A few weeks later, Elaine hired Amy from Jamaica, who showed up at the apartment with one suitcase. She was recommended by a friend of a friend of Denise, Elaine's admin. This was a perfect match for Elaine, who called her every ten minutes to do something. Elaine was a person who never did anything like an ordinary person. She never brought up the mail, did the laundry, boiled an egg, or went grocery shopping. Her clothes, always a size six, were selected by a personal shopper at Bloomingdale's or Walter. They would lay out the clothes; Elaine would review them, pick out what she wanted, take them into the bedroom, try on the clothes, and come back into the living room for Walter and the shopper to concur.

By spring, I was finished with the proposal for an interior design book on Elaine's work, spending time browsing the aisles at Barnes & Noble and Borders, which featured 'How to' books on interior design. One publisher that had published interior design books was Viking Studio Books. Not wanting the run-around that publishers usually give, with various editors whose deal-making decision was above their pay grade, I believed in working directly with the decision-maker. At that time, Michael Fragnito was an editor-in-chief at Viking Studio Books. With one phone call, I was put through to his office. Dropping the names of some of our important clients, within seconds I was put through, delivering my elevator pitch which summed everything up in thirty seconds. He was intrigued. He asked if I had photos of the work. My answer was "hundreds of photos taken by one of the best interior photographers in America, Peter Paige." This conversation was followed by a visit to Viking's offices in Tribeca, where Elaine performed HER ELAINE LEWIS TO PERFECTION. At the meeting were the head of marketing and the editor who would work on the book. They asked if we had an agent. I immediately said, "William Morris." The only agent I was close to was William Morris's Lee Solomon, who I knew from my days at the Concord.

In the town car back to the office, Elaine asked if she really had an agent. My answer was, "You will by the end of the week."

In my opinion, working with agents if you are not already a star is for lazy people. Most of the agents were mainly Jewish, starting in the mailroom before the turn of the century. Having a college degree wasn't required. All that you needed was street smarts and balls to get ahead. The following morning, I called Lee, who immediately recognised Elaine as the designer of the Friars Club. He transferred me to Mel Berger, who was one of the agents in the Literary Department. I handed Mel the complete package; all he had to do was work with Viking's business affairs people on the contract. The deal was a $100,000 advance, and we had to find a ghost writer whom they must approve. We had to pay them out of our advance. Needing to find an interior design writer who had no ego, I reached out to Monica Gerron, Editor-in-Chief of *Interior Design Magazine*, who recommended a writer named Judith Davidson. I was responsible for getting the design team to work on the book while working on projects. Nabeel became the book's project manager.

My lease on my Westside apartment was up. Jamie left P.J. Clarke's restaurant, which was located in the basement at Macy's, going up to the furniture floor where he joined the sales team. Now I was faced with getting rid of my furniture, paintings, two hundred acetate albums, and other stuff that I had accumulated from 1973 to the present. Moving in with a person who had everything, there wasn't anything that I had that would fit in her apartment. Through Elaine's real estate contacts, we were able to get Jamie a studio apartment at the just-completed residential conversion of the McAlpin Hotel, a block away from Macy's on

34th Street. Not certain of what the future held for Elaine and me, I put things that were important to me in storage, donating big stuff to The Salvation Army.

The summer of 1990 was spent with weekends in Southampton. Judith Davidson and Elaine spent hours working on the book. Judith became attached to her Jamaican housekeeper, Amy, who came out with us. During our beach walks, Amy walked beside her with an umbrella to shield her from the sun.

Having spent the last two weeks of August in Southampton, we returned home after Labor Day only to discover that our home phone was shut off. New York Telephone was our service provider. That evening, I walked over to the office, calling the phone company's customer service, who told me that the phone bill had not been paid in three months and the total owed was $4,000. I requested that they send the entire bill to our office.

Returning to the apartment, I took Elaine into the bedroom and explained that she owed $4,000 to New York Telephone, and they were sending copies of the bills to the office.

Two days later, I received an envelope with fifty pages of international long-distance calls to Jamaica, two minutes to five minutes in duration. Confronting Amy with the bills, she started to cry and ran out of the apartment. Looking at Elaine, I asked, "Do you look at any of the mail that comes to the apartment?"

"That's the job of the housekeeper," she replied. "She brings up the mail; any bills she puts in the bill folder at the beginning of the month. Allen, our bookkeeper, handles both accounts payable and receivable, writes out the cheques, I sign them, that's it." Her attorney convinced New York Telephone that it was theft of services. All she had to pay was for local calls. Going into the bedroom that was reserved for housekeepers, we found Amy's clothes and passport. Something wasn't right; no one leaves a passport. We brought it down and left it with the doorman.

While in the bedroom, I came across Elaine's passport and discovered that she was born in nineteen thirty-two, making her eight years older than me. Seeing me holding her passport, she went ballistic, accusing me of sneaking around her stuff. That afternoon, I went out and rented a studio in a third-floor walk-up on East 54th Street. Two days later, I had all the stuff I had in storage moved into the apartment. Collecting plastic milk crates, I set them up as dresser drawers. As I was leaving her apartment, I told her, "If we are going to live together, I expect that we trust each other." New York is a small town. Each demographic had their favourite place. Returning to the places I hung out with before I met Elaine, I was greeted as a long-lost friend by the same people I was going to invite to my wedding. We did the same circuit of hot new restaurants, starting at Bice. Ending up at Regine's, it seemed that our paths always crossed; Elaine was always with a date. I was jealous, of course, I was. Deciding that it was her move, or fuck it, a month later she left a message on my answering machine that she was going to a spa outside of London.

I called Gloria for dinner. If she said no, I would understand; she was happy to hear from me. It was meeting an old friend whose life was full of bullshit and who didn't know how to get out of it. Ending with us having sex at seven in the morning, the phone rang; it was Elaine calling from England. Asking me what I was doing, I told her the truth: I was having sex with Gloria. During the three weeks I was alone, which was the first time since 1989, Jamie had little time to spend with me between working at Macy's and DJing. As I walked up the three flights to my studio, it was déjà vu of 1973. This time it was different; after two years living with the largest ego I have ever seen, it was time to put my ego on the shelf. I have always known I was the best at what I do; unfortunately, I was the only one who knew it.

A few days later, returning from London, she invited me for dinner, apologising for her outburst when I discovered how old she was. Holding hands across the table, I told her I could not live and work with her. I didn't want to be on her payroll, and any publicity I did for her was because I loved her. As for getting her work, I wanted a ten per cent commission on gross sales, which she agreed to. She had never seen my studio; trekking up three flights of stairs, we wound up making love. That was the last time I slept in my apartment I used as an office. One of my contacts was a publisher of graduation yearbooks for all the military academies (West Point, Naval and Air Force Academy, National War College). The cost of a full page was ten thousand dollars; my commission was fifteen per cent. The advertisers were any company that sold to the military. It was a fast and easy sale. My window for sales was the last week of April, a month before graduation. The lease on Elaine's apartment was up at the end of September, and all of her advisors recommended that she buy an apartment. As she searched for an apartment, I would go to various stores that sold unique, cutting-edge products, like the Sharper Image, a store on West 57th Street. I discovered the perfect product: gel soles, which you insert in your shoe to cushion your walk, which sold for twenty-five dollars a pair. I discovered from the packaging that they had an office in San Diego. Within a week, I had a hundred pairs of different sizes for both men and women, even for high heels. My next investment was a cheap folding table that people use to eat while watching television. Within a week, I was in business, selling gel soles for fifteen dollars a pair, wearing a suit with a shirt and tie. The first week, I ran into all the people I knew, who thought it was a gag. When a patrol car passed, I hid the table and a bag with gel soles. 61st Street and Madison Avenue were great; I would go to the Regency Hotel, check my table and inventory, and meet Elaine in the bar, where we counted my daily sales.

Analyzing the market, I visited places where people were constantly on their feet. Rather than standing in a corner, I would go to all the topless bars, selling to the entertainers. I would pay off security with a free pair of soles so they would let me into the girls' dressing room. Exhausting this market, I moved uptown to New York Presbyterian Hospital, selling to nurses and doctors. Then downtown to the NYU Medical Center.

During this time, Elaine purchased a duplex loft apartment at 350 East 62nd Street with twenty-foot ceilings. Discovering that the ceiling when entering the apartment was dropped, by eliminating it, we were able to extend the loft another thirty feet. This had five racks of clothing shelves to put almost one hundred pairs of shoes. She even had a small private bathroom all to herself, which neither the building nor the city approved.

All the general contracting, millwork, and a twenty-foot floor-to-ceiling mirror covered the wall facing the couch. The apartment overlooked a large tree which separated the rear of the tenements facing 62nd Street. We installed floodlights to illuminate the tree at night, which was also without the permission of the condo board.

As for our bedroom, the design Team mirrored all of the walls, creating an optical illusion of a large bedroom. In reality, it was big enough for a king-size mattress. In order to go to sleep, I had to crawl into the bed.

The construction of the loft finished a week before signing a new lease, leaving the new tenants with design upgrades, mirrored walls, built-in cabinets, outdoor furniture, a built-in barbecue, plus weatherproofed storage closets on the huge terrace facing Second Avenue. By that time, she had given up on a live-in housekeeper. Since the loft had a kitchenette with small appliances, we built an island which separated the cooking area from the living area.

The near-death of the sole business occurred when I saw a full-page colour advertising insert in the *Daily News* offering three pairs for fifteen dollars. I continued to sell them; if a customer mentioned three pairs for fifteen dollars, my response was that my soles were developed with superior technology.

Real estate development changed before the business was in the hands of the owners. Their children were now running the show, giving the marketing/real estate company working on the project a significant say in which designers were selected for the model units and public areas.

Over the years, as these women decision-makers were growing their careers, Elaine treated them appallingly. They felt intimidated by her and ignored her, as she only worked with the owners, making her grand entrance when the sales or rental offices opened. If the women were overweight or not elegant enough, she treated them as inferior creatures. Now, these same women were deciding who to hire. Discovering which projects were either on the drawing board or going into the ground required a lot of research. My apartment, which was now my office, had various trade papers and newspapers strewn across the floor and the bed. Now I had to placate the same women whom Elaine had always talked down to to hire her.

The foundation of who Elaine Lewis is stems from her interest in spirituality. Every Sunday, she would turn on TV services from the Crystal Cathedral, hosted by televangelist Robert Schuller. When Pastor Schuller passed away in 2015, Elaine discovered Joel Osteen and his wealth doctrine. She subscribed to *The Daily Word*, published by Unity Church. *The Daily Word* offered pages of affirmations and inspirational messages for every day of the week. Whenever we travelled, we would find Unity Church services. The concept of Unity was open to people of all faiths, offering them spiritual grounding.

Like every niche industry, the New York real estate community had various organisations that held dinners and cocktail parties throughout the year. They created all sorts of awards for different segments of the industry. One was a dinner for women in marketing and sales. By the end of the night, Elaine was presented with the Emma Lazarus Award, which was a block of crystal embossed with Emma Lazarus's image. As Elaine rose to receive the award, I asked myself what the lady who wrote an inspirational message on the base of the Statue of Liberty had to do with New York real estate. I assumed that the inference was to all the immigrants who arrived in New York, whose families became successful, and those who would construct the actual buildings.

In 1992, she decided to have her face done by the most sought-after plastic surgeon in the United States, Doctor Daniel Baker. Twenty-four hours later, I picked her up at the doctor's office; he had recovery facilities on the premises. For the rest of the week, she had nurses take care of her.

Immediately after Hurricane Andrew devastated South Florida, we took an exploratory trip to Miami, finding an apartment in South Beach where we spent three weeks living in a single room in search of a furnished apartment. Elaine remembered that her third husband had lived in Turnberry in North Miami. We found a one-bedroom apartment with one and a half bathrooms. In September, I subleased my apartment; she found a tenement for the condo. After a few weeks, I discovered that the North Tower in Turnberry was *the* place where single women would hang out at the bar in search of a husband, even if he was already married. I thought, with her track record in creating model apartments, it would be our entrée into creating models during the building boom in both single and multi-family homes in Southern Florida. We learned a lesson: local designers, who also stocked furniture, would provide the service free to developers, which would make them exclusive designers for their developments. Renting an office and leasing my first car, we were determined to conquer the market in two years. We only completed two single-family communities after having her New York staff do the layouts and purchasing, and flying in Nabeel to be project manager. She had a knack for duplicating all the services she had in New York: masseuse, hairstylist, and makeup artists, all on call to service her. I had my gel soles sent to Florida, where in the evenings we would visit topless bars where I would sell my gel soles. In the *Miami Herald*, there was a story in the business section that the International Book Fair was being held at the Miami Beach Convention Center. The galleys of *Less is More – A Practical Guide to Maximizing the Space in Your Home* was approved and sitting on our editor's desk. We arranged a dinner with the publisher of Viking Studio books, who scheduled the book to be on bookstore shelves before Christmas 1995.

One evening, the telephone rang, and the voice on the other end told me he was her brother, Howard. We always had two business phones, one in the living room and the other in the bedroom. Motioning me to put him on hold, she disappeared into the bedroom for an hour. Elaine would never have a phone conversation with other people listening; that's why we had five lines in our New York apartment. During the summer, she told me that her brother, Howard, was driving across the country and would be in Miami in three days and would like to see her. We had been together for four years, and she had never mentioned her brother, who lived in San Diego with his wife and three children and who was disowned by her father, Jack. Three days later, we were in front of our building when a 1980 Oldsmobile pulled up. Howard exited the car, giving the valet the keys. He was a replica of his father, Jack, who came once a month and slept upstairs in the loft area. Jack was about five feet six inches tall, balding, with a prominent nose. He, along with his eight siblings, was a first-generation German Jew, born on the Lower East Side in 1909, whose father opened a bakery on Clinton Street where all new Jewish arrivals escaping from European anti-Semitism found a home in the tenements of the Lower East Side of Manhattan, along with the tide of Italian immigrants. He was enlisted by his father to give out Challah on the Sabbath to help his fellow Jews. Jack went on to become a Supervisor in the United States Post Office, investing in the stock market after the Depression of 1929. At home, he was a disciplinarian, one of the reasons that Elaine got married when she was sixteen; she wanted her freedom. Jack expected Howard to be successful, which became the biggest disappointment in his life. Elaine's mother, Rose, was the love of her life. The animosity between father and daughter was palpable, where Elaine called him Jack, not Dad. Once he realised that Elaine was the success, not his son, he became proud of her; suddenly all the anger was swept away. Elaine finally called him Dad. Now accepted into the world of money and power, she painted a picture of a girl who grew up on Park Avenue with maids and servants, including a degree from Parsons School of Design. Parsons was the only truth in her résumé; instead of graduating, she left after two years. One thing Interior Design School didn't teach is how to get business, close the deal, and make a large profit.

The difference was that Howard was six feet three inches tall, weighing about a hundred and seventy pounds, with skinny legs and balding. Elaine was six years older; they hadn't seen each other for almost twenty years. She made reservations for three in the Dining Room, which was off the lobby of the building, facing the Intercoastal Waterway that separated Miami Beach from Greater Miami. After sitting there for half an hour, I realised how much he hated his father and the gulf between brother and sister. Leaving the table, I excused myself, saying that I had work. Turnberry was on the Intercoastal, having a great marina with enough room for large yachts. Moored there was a large mahogany yacht owned by the Kennedy family, with "Honey Fitz" painted across the cabin.

Elaine didn't invite her brother to be our house guest. We had two dinners before he drove west.

After Labour Day, she wanted to test if we still liked big cities, as an experiment, booking a two-week trip to London. After returning to Miami, we decided to move back to Manhattan. I leased my car on a thirty-six-month contract. If we returned it before the end of the lease, there would be a penalty. Reviewing the contract, she told me not to worry about it; she would handle it.

The two years in Florida had cemented our relationship. All her friends and advisors were set on destroying us, whispering in her ear that I was a loser, an opportunist and that she should find a wealthy man. Nabeel picked us up at Newark Airport at 6 pm on New Year's Eve, 1994. Her tenants were out of the apartment. We changed and met Nabeel and his Middle Eastern friends, who adored her. It was a unique party, with his American wife at the table and his Egyptian girlfriend across the room. Every fifteen minutes, he would excuse himself, saying that he had a urinary tract infection, and needed to go to the men's room. As his American wife's focus was on the belly dancers, Nabeel was in a dark corner, making out with his girlfriend. We settled back into our loft apartment, where I had to climb into bed. Walking up a staircase with brass railing, leading to the loft, there was a giant steel beam running the length of the loft. We set up a desk, typewriter, and telephone; this was going to be my work area. If I wasn't careful, I would bang my head.

Within a month, we were out looking for an office. Both she and I agreed that we could not work in the same location. We found a small office about ten blocks from where we lived, to pitch for business and coordinate the marketing with the Viking Studio Public Relations department. Her book was going to be released after Labour Day, 1995, as a Christmas gift. Jamie had moved to his new apartment between Ninth and Tenth Avenue. Even though we lived a mile apart, he never once came to our apartment. If I wanted to see him, I had to go to Macy's furniture floor. One afternoon, he showed up at my office with a beautiful, tall Chinese girl called Jenny, who worked as a cocktail waitress at the Marriott Marquis. Within three months, he bought her an engagement ring and a dog. By the summer of 1995, she disappeared, taking the dog and leaving him the engagement ring.

That spring, it seemed that Elaine and her brother were trying to renew their relationship after twenty years of not talking to each other. He invited us to San Diego to be his house guests. He had decided to separate from his wife after thirty years of marriage. There he was in the baggage area, smoking a joint. He looked like Rumpelstiltskin in Bermuda shorts, reeking of alcohol, loading our luggage into the boot of his car. I had to move aside empty soda cans and beer bottles settling in the back seat. Howard was driving seventy-five miles per hour, tailgating the car in front of us. Tapping Elaine on the shoulder, making sure she was wearing her seat belt, Howard drove with one hand, holding a large plastic cup of vodka and orange juice. He was doing an amazing juggling act: smoking a joint, sipping his drink, and taking his eyes off the road, saying that the seat belts weren't working. Finally, we arrived at the apartment he had just rented at the behest of his wife of thirty years, having been kicked out of their home. You must realise that Elaine had cleaning ladies twice a week. Entering his apartment, the living room had restaurant discount coupons scattered around. With a grand gesture, he gave us his bedroom, saying he would sleep on the living room floor. He then announced that he only eats one meal a day at a restaurant that has discount coupons. The arguments started immediately, telling us that he hated their father. After two days, Elaine had had enough. I called a taxi which took me to Avis. She called The Hotel del Coronado, which was the hotel used in the film *Some Like It Hot.* The day before we left, Elaine invited Howard, his wife Sandy, and their two children, David and Lisa, who still lived at home, for dinner. It was a dysfunctional family gathering. Sensing the body language of his teenage daughter whenever her father touched her, she pushed his arm away. His wife, Sandy, started discussing her oldest son, Jerry, who lived in New York, working on a PhD at NYU. Sandy was an enabler who, for thirty years, had taken Howard's abuse. The following morning, we were on a flight back to New York. The dream of uniting with her brother was just that – a dream. Returning to the apartment, I called Jamie, who told me that his sister had called; they rarely spoke. Julie was about to turn thirty-five that coming May. The last time I saw her was when I arranged for her and her classmates to enter Studio 54 on her prom night. Meeting at a coffee shop on West Fifty-Fifth Street, I sat in a booth facing the door with my mother. A woman entered, looking around. I realised that it was my daughter. The image I had of her was when she was eleven years old. We hugged, and my mother started crying and showering her with kisses. It's difficult to catch up on a lifetime during a forty-five-minute coffee. She told us she and her husband had bought a house in Staten Island. Her husband, Bruce, was now working for AMC Theatres, and she drives a BMW. Looking at her watch, she gave me her direct line, explaining that she had left her cards in the office. My response was nothing. It was as if I had met a stranger. My mother, wiping the tears from her eyes, said, "That's not the child I remember; she's an impostor." Walking my mother to the subway, she apologised for being so emotional. My response was, "Thank God you have Jamie." That was bullshit. Jamie never went out of his way to see his grandmother. She would have to go to Macy's to see him. He was kind enough to use his employee discount to save her money when she bought something.

In 1990, the US economy was still in the Saving and Loan Crisis, where developers were defaulting on their loans and handing their properties back to the banks. Some developers were even buying the same buildings at fire-sale prices, having a relative bid for them at auction. Sitting in my office, I realised that the development of luxury multi-family properties was on hold.

One day, I received an invitation to a showroom on East 57th Street to view the Mezzanine. I discovered it was a bed that, with the touch of a remote, would go up to the ceiling, turning the space from a bedroom to a work area – unlike the Murphy bed, which at that time took up floor space. Both principals were in the showroom: one of Indian descent named Shiva, a Francophile whose money came from metal trading, and his partner, a retired airline pilot who flew chartered jets. From their conversation, I discovered that they knew nothing about home furnishings. They agreed to pay me £500 per week and 15% on every sale.

After two and a half months and a half-page story in the *New York Times*, not one unit was sold. It was too expensive for people who needed it; those who could afford it didn't need it. There was a big chain of mattress stores called Sleepy's. Figuring there was a synergy between them and the Mezzanine, I offered to put the bed in their Eastside showroom. The deal was closed until their attorneys wanted to make sure that there was a UL safety seal attached to the product. The cost was £15,000, which neither Shiva nor Tony had thought of doing before opening the showroom. The bed had a European Union safety certificate, but they still needed a UL seal to sell in the United States.

At that time, everyone was discussing Omega 3 for better heart health. Shiva, who was always looking for a way to make money, was in negotiation with a processing plant in Brittany that made salmon patties and burgers. For exclusive rights to sell the product in the United States, as a sign of good faith, he purchased 100,000 pounds of burgers and patties, put in cold storage in New Jersey and Maryland, without one item being sold. Looking back at my Beefsteak Charlie days, I knew we had to get a food distributor to sell the product. The logic was to sell salmon to finance the Mezzanine.

Elaine spent her days being pampered, showing up at the showroom with a flourish. Tony and Shiva were impressed by the presence of such an icon visiting their showroom.

Our first introduction to the restaurant and food service industry was at the Javits Center. We hired a chef and two models to hand out samples and sales material. As the burgers were being made, the entire Javits Center smelled of salmon. Not only did we not get distributors, but we also made many enemies. The results were about fifty leads, which resulted in fifty demos at their corporate offices, where just cooking the salmon drifted through the air conditioning vents and filled their offices with the smell of salmon. The bottom line: not one company wanted to buy the salmon for its smell while cooking. Coming home from Javits, my clothes and body smelled of salmon.

Out of desperation, Shiva called Brittany, putting me on the phone with the owner, who spoke English. After all the niceties, I explained that no chef wanted to cook it because it smelled awful. Could he readjust the processing so that the salmon didn't smell like salmon? The voice on the other end went ballistic: "You Americans want food to smell like perfume! In France, we want our food to smell like food!" slamming down the phone.

My next effort was to sell to nursing homes – Jewish nursing homes. They needed me to guarantee a Circle K seal, which meant Kosher. The only place to get the Kosher seal was an office located on the basement level of a multi-story apartment building in the Crown Heights section of Brooklyn. This area had one of the largest communities of Hassidic Jews in the United States. They certified coconuts for macaroons, and small bars of Kosher soap distributed by Rokeach, a New Jersey company that specialises in the Jewish Kosher market. The process was simple: a large upfront payment and the covering of expenses for a rabbi from England or France to visit the plant three times a year, certifying that manufacturing met all the stringent rules governing the Kosher seal.

Then I looked at both state and federal prison systems. Those in charge of purchasing made me aware that they spend £3 a day on feeding prisoners, which includes paper goods. I never realised that salmon was on the commodity exchange and selling for under £3 a pound.

Aware that this business venture was about to implode, admitting whatever I did was unsustainable to keep the business afloat, I learned that you get more respect if you are honest with people. I would rather have their friendship than their money.

Elaine, even though there wasn't any business, was still the Diva. This time, we took buses and trains with the other people. Once a month, she would have meetings with her financial advisers, which I avoided. The internet was in its infancy. During a lunch meeting with the Vice President of Public Relations for Viking Studio Books, the conversation at the table was about a start-up called Amazon and how it would change how books were sold.

My perception of marketing was window displays in Barnes & Noble and television appearances on talk shows, which would take place after the summer.

Sitting alone in my office on East 56th Street, I realised my dream of landing a corporate job paying me six figures was unattainable. Elaine's mindset was not to work unless the job came to her. As for money, I would contribute fifteen hundred dollars a month towards rent. For eating out, we would alternate picking up the cheque. Now, my job was finding a job. Searching Craigslist, I found a decorative lighting store located on the Bowery, near Chinatown, which was looking for a salesman for fifteen dollars an hour and a seven per cent commission. Never having paid attention to what was called the Decorative Lighting Centre of America, I realised that within two blocks there were twenty lighting stores owned by three people. Most of their customers came from the suburbs or were out-of-towners. These stores sold chandeliers and furniture for owners of single-family homes whose entryways were anywhere from sixteen to twenty feet high. All the stores were selling the same type of large fixtures, mostly from Spain and Italy, buying them before the Euro was introduced and the dollar was strong. Until the middle of 1990, none of them accepted credit cards. The owner of Bowery Lighting and two other stores was an Egyptian Jew who grew up in Milan. His mother ran one of the stores. I was a duck out of water, discovering that working on the Bowery was their career. All the support and help was either from Guyana or the Dominican Republic. Every salesperson fought over who walked through the door, discovering that certain ethnic groups – Italian, Chinese, Russian, Indian – loved crystal chandeliers. The markup was five hundred per cent. The fixture was built and dressed by the support staff. The job was from 10:00 am to 6:00 pm. Lunch was buying noodles from a cart for a dollar or from a Chinese coffee shop, which was a gathering place for Chinese senior citizens. My days off were Wednesday and Thursday. Working on the Bowery, the dress code was very relaxed. On the nights we had black-tie affairs, Walter would bring my tuxedo, where I would change from a lighting salesman on the Bowery to an executive at Elaine Lewis Designs, working in the banquet room in search of projects. During the summer, many of her contacts either owned or rented homes in the Hamptons, especially East Hampton. Since the house was empty during the week, we would drive out Tuesday night, returning Thursday evening. On Tuesday evening, she called me at the store, asking me to meet her at The Regency Hotel Bar.

She was seated at our favourite table, facing Park Avenue. Henry, whom we considered like a son, was serving her coffee. We always sat together. Across the room, there was a woman at a table who had wonderful breasts. Elaine was attuned to every move I made. Kissing my cheek, she said, "You like those breasts? Tomorrow, Daniel Baker will give you a pair." Looking directly at her cleavage, I asked, "Are you fucking crazy? How are you going to sleep with those big boobs?" "I thought you would be happy." "How long are you going to be in the hospital?" "It's a one-day procedure. Baker's nurse will call with the time to pick me up. I already have a nurse booked for two weeks." Within a month, she was like a kid with a pair of new toys. Selfishly, I was hoping that her nipples were as sensitive as they were before the procedure. As the months passed, Elaine would go braless. Whenever we were together, my hand brushed across her new breasts. She relished being an author. I had the flexibility to take time off. Viking scheduled a book tour to Toronto for five days of press and TV appearances.

In 1997, Elaine threw a big birthday party at the Friars Club to celebrate her father's NINETIETH birthday. In the summer of 1998, we received a call that her father was acting strangely. We explored options for when he would be incapable of taking care of himself. On West 72nd Street and West End Avenue, she found a luxury living senior citizen's residence, The Esplanade, where a one-bedroom apartment costs $4,500 a month, including meals and entertainment. Elaine's financial advisor, who also handled her father's money, calculated that what he received monthly in pension and Social Security would cover the monthly cost. We immediately moved him in. Whenever he asked Elaine what he was paying a month for the apartment, her answer was, "Don't worry, she and Vincent (financial advisor) are handling it."

Knowing her father, there was one thing he remembered: money. His rent was about four hundred dollars per month; he lived in the same apartment for fifty years. When he came once a month, he would take the subway, which was $1.25. A select bus was $3.25, which stopped in front of his apartment. For five of the seven years he visited, he never once picked up a dinner check. Paying $4,500 a month was inconceivable to Jack.

Before the turn of the millennium, technology changed how business functioned. Gone were typewriters; in came desktop computers – the beginning of a new learning curve for thousands of employees. The first thing I had to do was get a domain name. I realised that we couldn't use the name "Elaine Lewis Designs" as a domain name, for it was used by another Elaine Lewis. The Internet Registry accepted www.elainelewisinternational.com. That meant changing voicemail, brochures, and any other marketing tools. Since the internet was in its infancy, Nabil, a young Egyptian techie, handled our transition to the digital age. My first introduction to cell phones was when I was walking up Park Avenue. A woman was gesticulating, screaming into the air. As I was walking next to her, she was talking on a cell phone.

With the birth of the internet, venture capital firms were financing projects that were written on napkins, and the goal was to sell online to consumers. A company called furniture.com raised seventy million dollars for a company that didn't have a name attached to it. We developed a business-to-consumer company called Celebrity Interior Design. Raising a million dollars, we had

BDO Seidman do the business plan, which was finished in March of 2000. We had our first VC meeting with Chase Capital Partners, who had funded Furniture.com. By the time this meeting was over, the dot-com bubble had burst. Two months later, we gave our investors back their money.

By 2001, Jack was getting frailer. My mother withdrew into her shell. Most of her friends in the building either died or moved to Florida.

On 11 September 2001, every New Yorker had what they were doing seared into their memory. My early morning bus ride downtown to NYU Medical Center for a doctor's appointment: the entire hospital was being mobilised. On Lexington Avenue, people walking uptown seemed shocked, covered in white dust. Jet fighters were circling Manhattan, sirens blaring. The Bowery, where I worked, was closed for a week. Out of the pile of rubbish that was once the World Trade Center, a cloud of carcinogens was swallowing up the air in Manhattan and the adjoining boroughs, which in twenty years saw the rise of various cancers. The Department of Health kept their air sampling to a two-mile radius of the Trade Center, rather than giving results for the entire metro area.

The lighting stores on the Bowery opened but hardly had any buyers. Eighty per cent of the time, I would take the city bus which ran north on Allen Street, which turned into First Avenue. Passing three city blocks of pictures of the dead or missing, attached to fences, which ended a block away from the New York Medical Examiner's office. Parked on a dead-end street were four sixteen-wheel refrigerated trailers with the remains of victims that were extracted from what was known as "the pile".

Jack, who always listened to the news and read *The New York Times*, was now oblivious to his surroundings. We never mentioned what happened at The World Trade Center. A month later, Jack died at the age of ninety-four. Elaine's brother, Howard, flew in with his Vietnamese girlfriend for the funeral. Jack's body was taken to the Riverside Funeral Home, which was a few blocks away. The services were held at 11:00 am, followed by a trip to Mt. Ararat Cemetery in Farmingdale, Long Island. The room was packed by all of Elaine's friends and Jack's youngest sister, who was in her mid-eighties. One by one, ten people praised Jack for his accomplishments and charitable giving. The man that they were talking about wasn't the man I knew. Three days later, Elaine had a party to celebrate her father's life at a chic, members-only club, The Town Private Club, on East Eighty-Sixth Street. Howard had too much to drink, smoked a joint, and got into a heated argument with Elaine concerning the reading of the will. It took her attorney to give a date, which was two weeks. He was told he could go back to San Diego or stay in New York. After a brief discussion with her attorney, she offered to pay the airfare from San Diego to New York for the reading of the will. From the time Jack was at the Esplanade, Elaine paid the rent on her father's apartment on Ocean Avenue in Brooklyn. Howard was given the option of staying in the apartment he grew up in. Howard opted for Brooklyn. During the two weeks before the reading of the will, she avoided seeing her brother. On the day of the reading, Elaine asked me to take the day off, escorting her to the attorney's office, which was a block away from Macy's on West 34th Street. All arriving at the same time, I sat with Howard's Vietnamese girlfriend, Monique, who I found out was married to an American officer who was stationed in Saigon. The days before the North Vietnamese Army were to arrive in Saigon, she was part of the Embassy personnel evacuated by helicopter, lifting off from the Embassy roof. She settled in San Diego, where she and her husband brought up six daughters. After a thirty-year marriage, she was a widow. Her daughters recommended that she place an advertisement in one of the local papers. Howard answered the advertisement; that's why she was sitting next to me in the reception room of an attorney's office. You could hear Howard's angry voice as he exited the door, motioning to Monique to go. Elaine was followed by her attorney, who she kissed on the cheek, thanking him for all he did for the family.

Howard and Monique were standing in front of the building on Thirty-Fourth Street with their luggage. Approaching Elaine, he called her a "cunt" who turned their father against him. Elaine walked past him, shaking and crying. Hailing a taxi, Howard instructed the driver to take them to JFK. His last words were, "I will see you in court."

Composing herself, she suggested that since we were near Macy's, we should visit the furniture department where Jamie worked. She needed this shot of adulation from the salespeople in the furniture department, whom Jamie always introduced her to as his mother, "one of the most famous Interior Designers in New York City". This moment was like giving her a shot of oxygen.

Over dinner, she told me about the reading of the will. "The estate was close to four million dollars. I received three-quarters of the money. My father gave Howard twenty-five per cent, his three grandchildren nothing. Do you remember when I told you Vincent and I were going to Brooklyn? My father had three savings accounts which were not included in the will. He made me the beneficiary of the accounts, which was another half million dollars. Vince deposited it in my JP Morgan Chase investment account."

We only had one parent left, my mother, whom we either met in the city when she finished visiting her doctors, or we would take the subway to Brighton Beach. Every time we met, she asked how Jack was. We both agreed not to tell my mother of Jack's passing. My mother, who now dressed like a Sicilian woman in mourning, would meet us for an early dinner at her favourite Italian restaurant, ordering the same gnocchi dish, eating only half and taking the rest home. In the spring of 2002, we met, and her face was yellow. A conversation with my mother always started: "Mom, you look yellow." Looking at me, "That's my natural colour, it's from the sun." "You never sit in the sun." "Don't worry, I am fine. It could be my blood pressure or my rosacea." That was the end of the conversation. I could never win. A week later, a neighbour called to say he found my mother on the floor. EMS was taking her to Coney Island Hospital's Emergency Room. It took ten minutes for the car to arrive, another forty minutes to go to Coney Island Hospital, and an hour to get her released, transferring her records to St Luke's Roosevelt Hospital on West 59th Street in Manhattan. The emergency room staff, upon undressing her, discovered that the entire back of her body was bruised. Looking at me, they asked if I abused my mother. She must have fallen several times, never telling me. After four hours in the ER, they transported her to a private room where she told the doctor that she was falling on the hard wooden floors of her living room. After two days of tests, they told me that her bile ducts were clogged for many months, over time becoming toxic, leading to death.

Every day I would visit my mother after work. Elaine either met me at the hospital or the Regency Hotel. By the second week of May, they transferred her to a nursing home a couple of blocks north of the Islamic Cultural Center, which was one of the largest mosques in the Northeast. Visiting her every day, she seemed to be getting better. Ten days before Memorial Day, I purchased flowers. Entering her room, she usually smiled at me. Thinking she was taking a nap, I kissed her; she was unresponsive. Going over to the nurses' station, and asking if anyone checked in to see how she was doing, they told me at noon when they brought her lunch. Taking one of the nurses back to her room, my mother had shallow breathing. I asked her to call the doctor. She explained that they didn't have a doctor on the premises. Asking, "If you find one of your patients in this state, what do you do?" her answer was to call an ambulance. Within five minutes, she and I were taken to Lenox Hill Hospital Emergency Room. As you are all aware, sitting in the ER waiting for a resident to start the process of moving the patient along to various tests. The immediate diagnosis was: that my mother had pneumonia. After what felt like an eternity, they wheeled her up to a room with three other patients. This was a week before Memorial Day, and we planned to drive out to East Hampton that coming Tuesday. We went every day to see her. That Monday, I took the subway to Lenox Hill. Sitting at her bedside, holding her hand, after an hour I went to the nurses' station, asking their opinion if I should go to East Hampton. One of the nurses looked at me, "If that was my mother, I would not go." Taking the elevator to the lobby, I decided to walk home. After two blocks, I realised that I had not kissed my mother, saying I would see her tomorrow. Taking the elevator up to her floor, and walking past the nurse's station, I muttered that I forgot to kiss my mother goodnight. It took me fifteen minutes to reach our apartment. Elaine was sitting on the couch as the phone rang. The voice on the other end told me that my mother had died.

My parents, who were always spontaneous about making decisions, made a concerted effort to ensure their last days on this earth were well planned. My mother handed me a note after my father's death and told me to put it in a safe place. That was fourteen years ago. I always keep important documents with the Tallit (prayer shawl) and Tefillin, which are leather straps that you wrap around your arm and place in the middle of your forehead daily, as dictated by Deuteronomy 28:10. The set was given to me in 1953 at my Bar Mitzvah. They came with a velvet pouch, and this is where I keep my important papers. The instructions were clear: call the Funeral Home, IJ Morris in Brooklyn, to pick up the body, and they would take care of everything. Since she died on Thursday, she couldn't be buried until Sunday because the cemetery was closed for the Sabbath on Friday and Saturday. This was the long Memorial Day weekend. I arranged the funeral for the following Tuesday, giving my aunt, uncle, her two adult daughters (who lived in Fort Lauderdale, Florida), a cousin who lived in Queens, and the Rabbi who would conduct the services, time to buy airline tickets. Elaine and I were both orphans. The sad thing about my mother was that she was given an extra fourteen years to enjoy life, but the insecurity of being her own person, and her dependence on my father (no matter how badly he treated her), did not allow her to be independent.

Death has a process; it's either immediate or a long-drawn-out affair where the family still has a glimmer of hope that their loved one will get better. I imagine the agony a person experiences when the home they grew up in, a place where they had fond memories, is suddenly lifeless. If they have siblings, it's the distribution of assets among them. Money is negotiable; memories are not. That's when people get into disputes over possessions.

Arriving at my mother's apartment with Elaine, my aunt and her two daughters, who were planning to stay overnight until their flight back to Florida, I had no sense of ownership, for I had never lived there. While in the apartment, the girls went through my mother's clothes, all custom-made with the finest materials. My mother's belongings were from a bygone era; they belonged in the Met's American Clothes Gallery. After saying our farewells, we drove back to Manhattan. The rent on the apartment was paid through June.

During those thirty days, I tried to do the impossible: selling the furniture for the value that Elaine and I thought was a fair price. The furniture was created by James Mont, whose designs became collectables for people who were in search of original Art Deco designs. The price we were looking for was fifteen thousand dollars for the entire apartment. By the middle of June, there were no takers. I agreed to sell the entire package for five thousand dollars. My mother's jewellery, which I had kept during her first stay with me, she asked me to return, as the pieces made her feel more secure. Now that she was deceased, I found the velvet purse where she kept all her jewellery, discovering that major pieces were missing. Recalling that one of her neighbours had spent time in the apartment with her five-year-old daughter, I suspected they had probably taken some pieces. Giving Elaine the rest of the jewellery, she decided to take the cashmere and vicuña coats, mink fur coats, and a couple of other pieces that she felt could be converted into the "New Look" style. Confronted by a large portrait of my mother, which was hanging in the living room, Elaine decided to put it in one of three storage rooms where she paid to house her mother's clothing – four racks of it.

The apartment was emptied by the end of the month. I refused to throw out what remained of her wardrobe. I had a large piece of luggage with wheels, loading it with as many outfits as I could without breaking the zipper, leaving the apartment door open, and placing it in the boot of my Avis rental. I drove back to Manhattan on 25 June 2002, which was the last time I went to Brighton Beach.

That experience made me think it would be a great business for a company to make an offer for the entire home, thereby eliminating the emotional difficulties of saying one last goodbye.

At the suggestion of her advisors, she decided to sell the condo. Working with one of the top real estate brokerage firms, prospective buyers were constantly walking through the apartment, with not one making an offer. I concluded that any buyer close to six feet tall was not going to make an offer, recommending to our broker to look at the Asian market. In early 2023, the apartment was sold. We moved into a forty-storey luxury high-rise with a black tinted glass exterior wall, on East 61st Street, called Sutton Place North. The real estate salesperson showed us a bedroom and one and a half bathrooms on the fourth floor, facing east, for four thousand dollars a month.

Elaine's goal was to set up the apartment as a model home. Realising she needed more closet space, she went back to vendors she had helped make wealthy. One put mirrors across a long living room wall. The cabinet maker created a custom wall unit in the bedroom, across a fifteen-foot wall, wall to wall. You must realise that this apartment was a rental. Every year, she would have an infusion to prevent osteoporosis. She was on the Mediterranean diet before it became chic. We never changed our lifestyle. By 2004, I needed a hip replacement. Searching for an alternative heat solution, I would go for massages, acupuncture, and jogging in the pool.

None of them worked. Our two-year lease was about to expire. Elaine decided that dry heat was the answer; either we move to Tucson or Las Vegas. We both loved the action, so Las Vegas was the answer. That's when she told me that her deceased husband was part of a group that owned the Flamingo Hotel on the Vegas strip. The decision was made. Vincent, Elaine's financial advisor, was able to get us a casino rate at The Paris Hotel, which opened in 1999. The move date was 18 August 2005. Searching for an inexpensive mover that went across the country, we discovered U-Pack, owned by a national long-haul trucking company, ABF. Spending one month at The Paris Hotel, which became a haven for tourists who lived in New Orleans, and whose lives were shattered by Katrina. Elaine, who always kept out of the sun, fell in love with the Toyota Solara Convertible. We rented a three-bedroom penthouse with a wraparound balcony, overlooking the lights of the Strip and the mountain range. Hiring the team who handled audio at The Paris, we had speakers in every room. U-Pack unloaded the furniture. She flew in her assistant to help set up the apartment.

Jamie was emotionally destroyed by Jenny's disappearance and his mother's total absence from his life. While we were living in New York, he told me he was dating another Chinese girl. One of his colleagues at Macy's took them for a weekend in Atlantic City. Jamie, who had moved to a large L-shaped studio apartment on West 57th Street between Ninth and Tenth Avenue, was essentially a loner who didn't smoke, take drugs, or drink alcohol. That weekend trip turned him and his girlfriend, who would later be his wife, into slot addicts. Every weekend, they would rent a car. All I asked was if he had seen her Green Card; he replied that it wasn't important. We offered to arrange a wedding for them at the Chapel of the Bells, a Vegas landmark known for quickie weddings, offering a wedding package just inside the gate. I began inviting strangers to the wedding, wanting to fill the chapel. My pitch was to offer them the chance to witness a true Las Vegas wedding. By the time Jamie arrived at the chapel, he had ten friends in the limo. The bride's sister and mother were there, but her father and three brothers were missing. The minister entered the chapel from a side door, standing in her robes with a weather-worn face, and motioned for us to rise over the sound system's organ music – Judy Garland's "Somewhere Over the Rainbow" from *The Wizard of Oz*. The entire ceremony took under ten minutes. As everyone exited the chapel, I thanked the minister, who was expecting a tip. Shaking her hand, I told her what a great job she did and left. The wedding dinner was held in a private room at the Barbary Coast, which was across the street from Paris. As I walked around the table, I whispered in each person's ear, "Please do not give them a cash gift. They will blow it on slot machines." The bride's mother could only speak Cantonese; her sister spoke English and interpreted what I was saying. It was a one-way conversation, with her mother just nodding her head. They left before the dinner started; it seemed they only ate Chinese food. Jamie, who had to be at work the following Monday, was ready to leave. Before saying goodnight, I offered to pick them up and bring them to the apartment. Looking me straight in the face, he said, "Why should I bother? You will be back in New York within a month." I called him an asshole and wished him a safe flight back to New York.

Elaine never did any of the physical work; she only directed. While adjusting a picture, the glass shattered, cutting her foot. Refusing to go to the ER, we went to a 24-hour medical clinic, where they cleaned and bandaged the wound; she didn't need stitches. Twenty-four hours later, Elaine announced that she wanted to go back to New York; she didn't trust the medical care offered in Las Vegas. Our lease where we were living was month-to-month. Contacting U-Pack, we hired a team of people who worked at the Paris, to whom we gave the extra furniture purchased for the two extra bedrooms. Again, we went to the Toyota dealer to return the Solara with only five hundred miles on the odometer. She never worried about where we were going to live. She picked up the phone and called the rental office from where we had come. After two days staying at the Las Vegas Hilton, which was at the northern end of the Strip, we boarded Jet Blue back to New York, staying in a new hotel, the Bentley, which was four blocks from where we had lived before, this time on a lower floor. Three days later, the furniture arrived. There she goes again, setting up our new apartment. I always avoided talking about money, but this time it was different. I had a ballpark figure in my head of what the rent was, which was unacceptable. Letting her do her stuff, I left the apartment and went down to the rental office to find out if they had a one-bedroom available. The answer was yes, on a lower floor facing west.

Going back upstairs, I asked Elaine to join me in the bathroom. This was the first time I spoke to her about money. "Could you please tell me how much money we are paying for this apartment?"

Looking at me as if I was crazy, she answered that the rent was five thousand five hundred dollars a month, but she would use the extra bedroom to store her stuff instead of paying for a storage locker. This time she agreed with me. Telling the movers to take a break, we went to the rental office to sign a new lease on a one-bedroom apartment on a lower floor for four thousand dollars a month. We went back upstairs and had the movers bring everything down to the new apartment. This entire episode was insane. We had an entire penthouse for two thousand dollars a month, plus free cable and parking, and because of one accident, we were back where we started.

Two years later, Jamie's wife gave birth to a boy. Since New York real estate developers were not aware that Elaine had left New York, we were called in to do a floor of model interiors for The Durst Organization, which was building the second environmentally friendly multi-family high-rise on West 57th Street. After the contract was signed, Elaine assembled her old team. The job was to be finished by two thousand and six. Flying in one of her trusted designers, who had relocated to Aman,

Jordan, to handle the apartment set-up and installation, we needed housing. She rented a studio apartment two floors below our apartment. Returning to Bowery Lighting, was the beginning of our odyssey of travelling back and forth across the country.

It seemed every two years we were moving. In 2007, Elaine came to the realisation that the only person left in her family was her brother. Deciding she would, she gave him a cheque for half a million dollars from her father's estate. We were moving to La Jolla, about fourteen miles from San Diego. New York-California Express picked up our furniture and stored it in Los Angeles until we found an apartment. Checking into a room at the Best Western La Jolla Village became our headquarters for a month. Neither of us could relate to living in a single-family home. San Diego was a military city with a large naval shipyard, a Marine Corps museum, and a SEAL training facility across the bay on Coronado. With the growth of the region in biotech, healthcare, and tech companies servicing the Department of Defence, the city of San Diego was also in the midst of a multi-family high-rise construction boom overlooking the harbour. The rents were close to Manhattan, with more space. Viewing the luxury high-rises, she was ready to sign a lease. Never saying no, I said that we would think about it. Before the end of the week, we discovered that there were high-rises about a mile from the Torre Pines Golf Club, Scripps Medical Center, and two miles away from the Miramar Naval Base. Having found our new home on the ninth floor – two bedrooms, two baths, free parking, cable, and a health club for eighteen hundred dollars a month – I congratulated Elaine on finding a new home we could afford, which offered the luxury that we were accustomed to. Turning in the rental, we leased a Mazda for three years.

The bonding of sister and brother would never happen. Her brother was either stoned or drunk; neither of us could take his erratic behaviour.

In early 2008, her financial advisor visited us in San Diego. Before he went back to New York, he told Elaine to make La Jolla our home. In March of 2008, a member of Chase's Private Client team, based in LA, called to tell her that she was broke. They would be driving down to visit her with a cheque for one hundred thousand dollars, never explaining what happened to her portfolio of four million dollars. We later found out that they were investing in emerging markets rather than ring-fencing her account to consider her age. Chase ignored their fiduciary responsibilities to protect her investments.

Thinking that La Jolla was now my permanent home, I was in search of a job. When Elaine's book was published, I was pitching Home Depot to create a home décor line curated by Elaine. Finally, we had a meeting with the CEO, Craig Menear. Explaining that the timing wasn't right, and aware that the most important rooms of the home were the kitchen and bathrooms, after a half-hour conversation, he asked me if I had ever worked in a big box store. Life is about learning. The employment process involved three weeks' training on all the computer programmes. Home Depot had a large pyramid in the training room with "THE CUSTOMER IS ALWAYS RIGHT" at the top. The process ended with donning an orange apron and proceeding to the sales floor. I felt so confident that this was our last move that I reached out to friends in Las Vegas to get Jamie a job at the Wynn Hotel. My thinking was that it would be closer so I could visit my grandson, hopefully curing Jamie of his slot addiction since he was inside gaming, learning the stupidity of blowing your money on slots. As for living, Vegas was 50% cheaper than New York. As Jamie was moving to Las Vegas, Elaine announced that she wanted to move back to New York. She had it all planned out. She knew the owners of a luxury high-rise on West 56th Street off Eighth Avenue called Symphony House, who would not bother with a credit application. We would stay in Jamie's apartment until the furniture arrived. Ten days passed, and we still didn't get our household goods, which included corporate files. Calling the movers, the girl on the other end told me that there was an accident when a cement truck fell through the roof of the garage in LA, landing on the truck that was transporting everything we owned. She texted me a photo that was in the *LA Times*. The building department closed the garage, checking for structural damage to the property. It would be ten days before the authorities would allow me or my representative to inspect the damage. I was not flying to LA to visit a garage. I had an attorney in LA who volunteered to assess the damage. One question he asked me was whether I had bought insurance. With all the moving we did, I calculated the odds of a sixteen-wheeler having an accident as close to zero. I never factored in that a cement truck fell through the roof. Immediately, I contacted The Federal Motor Carrier Safety Administration, who informed me that without insurance, the carrier is obligated to give you sixty cents per pound. I involved the Los Angeles DA in search of a remedy for our pain and suffering. In the meantime, we had an apartment to furnish. This wasn't a situation where we could go to suppliers who had a very limited inventory. The first call we made was to a cabinet shop where we purchased eight mirrored wardrobes that were in the van where the cement truck landed, supposedly destroying all of the units. We ordered four units that were delivered the next day. As for the other furniture, we had to go to retail. Elaine was a fan of West Elm. Within three hours and spending $10,000, we furnished our apartment. Within a week, we had the entire apartment furnished with new computers, new televisions, and a new king-size mattress. Four days into the Jewish New Year, my mobile phone rang. It was Moshe, a representative of New York California Express, who I put on speaker. "Mr. Lewis, after inspecting the moving van, your belongings were not damaged. If you want your merchandise, the owners want an extra £3,250." Our agreement was £3,500, of which we gave you half a deposit. "I would like to talk to the owner," I said. Moshe hesitated. "The owners are in Israel to celebrate Rosh Hashanah with their relatives." Elaine took the phone, giving him her credit card. All the years we were together, people called me Mr. Lewis. It got to the point where it wasn't worth my time correcting them, explaining that Lewis was the name of her fourth husband, who was deceased.

The morning of Yom Kippur eve, we received a phone call that the moving van would arrive before noon. Calling West Elm, I explained the situation and agreed to pay a restocking fee, returning some of the merchandise that we purchased. We were both standing in front of the building awaiting the van to arrive. Opening the rear door, the mover lifted Elaine into the van to inspect the merchandise. Now we had fourteen mirrored floor-to-ceiling cabinets, three televisions, one old computer, and all our kitchen essentials. We were using paper plates, and paper cups, and buying coffee from McDonald's.

Feeling that we had completed our cycle of moving every two years, our two-year lease was due to be renewed at the end of Summer 2012. So secure was I about staying in New York that when I saw a sale on London Broil, I purchased ten steaks. Over the Labor Day weekend, a friend invited us to be his house guests in North Miami. Elaine always went to spas to decompress. Learning that Canyon Ranch, a spa in Tucson, Arizona, had renovated The Carillon, an old hotel on Collins Avenue and 68th Street, building two new towers to create a spa complex and condominium with direct access to the beach, a day before our flight back to New York, she suggested that we visit the onsite real estate office as prospective condo buyers. The broker offered a tour of the property, explaining that many owners purchased apartments, furnished them as investment properties, offered a two-year lease, and asked us if we wanted to see a vacant apartment. Exiting the lift on the 21st floor, we were shown a one-bedroom apartment with a balcony which gave us a view of the ocean and Intercoastal. The apartment looked like something she had a hand in furnishing. Squeezing my hand, she coyly asked what the monthly rent was on a two-year lease. Back at her office, she reviewed what the owner required for a two-year lease. Smiling, she announced it was two thousand dollars a month with free valet parking, use of all spa services and beach access. After signing the lease, which would start on 1st October, I kissed her, saying, "This is the smartest decision you have ever made. Now we have a permanent home."

Returning to New York, the owner agreed to allow us to terminate our lease. Now we had to give away our furniture. The only items we would ship were art, personal clothes, and Elaine's business records. Estimating the amount of money spent on boxes was close to fifteen hundred dollars, purchasing a dozen large storage bins at Home Depot. We were experts in hiring moving companies after getting three bids. Hiring a company called Flat Rate Movers, who guaranteed our belongings to arrive in 48 hours, we moved into our furnished apartment as promised. Our large storage containers were delivered. By the end of the week, I leased a Toyota Corolla. By the first week of living in Canyon Ranch, I was in search of a job. Elaine and I would drive north on Biscayne Boulevard, with strip malls on both the east and west sides of the highway, in search of a sales job in a decorative lighting store. Half a mile south of the 168th Street causeway, nestled on the corner of a strip mall with a kosher restaurant, was a lighting store called 4 U. Nothing like the stores on the Bowery, I asked to see the owner, who happened to be an Israeli named Ami. After a half-hour of conversation, he offered me a sales job at fifteen dollars an hour and a 5% commission. Thanking him, we both walked out of the store. Ami was behind us. "I gave you an offer, why did you walk out?" As I was opening the car door, I looked at him. "The fifteen dollars an hour is fine. I knew the markup; I expect a fifteen per cent commission on each sale." Ami thought for a moment. "Okay, I will give you ten per cent. When can you start?" Shaking his hand, I told him the next day.

Jamie and his family were in Vegas. He worked for two months at the Wynn, becoming one of the victims of course cutting where they fired five hundred people. Within days, he was hired by a casino off the Strip whose players were residents of Las Vegas. Every once in a while, I would ask him if he had heard from his sister. "I speak to her now and then. She's divorced, living in a place called Coral Springs with two kids, a girl named Skylar, and a boy named BJ." Always asking for her mobile number, Jamie refused to give it to me. His excuse was, "She doesn't want to talk to me."

On 12th February 2013, Jamie called me, saying that his sister had pancreatic cancer, giving me her telephone number. Calling the number, the voice on the other end sounded weak. I have not spoken to her since the meeting with my mother at the coffee shop in Manhattan fifteen years prior. After a minute's conversation, I asked if I could visit her. Her reply was, "Let me think about it." With that, the phone went dead. The next day, I called the same number; a nurse picked up the phone, telling me that she had just passed away, and recommending that I call her family for information on the burial. Having no information on how to contact her ex-husband, emotionally, I decided to remember happier times, from her birth to her twelfth birthday party at her favourite ice cream parlour, Serendipity. Calling Jamie to see if he was invited to the funeral, his answer was, "No."

In 2013, our lease at Canyon Ranch expired. The owner wanted to increase our rent by 50%. It took a day to find an apartment at One Lincoln Road, at the beginning of South Beach. Two weeks before our move-in date, two women walked into 4 U LIGHTING in search of art. While removing a painting, they created a domino effect, potentially destroying thousands of dollars' worth of inventory. Instinctively, I leaned in to stop the paintings from cascading. That one movement made my left foot feel like jelly; my ankle swelled to twice its size. That evening, I picked up Elaine and went straight to Mount Sinai ER for X-rays. The diagnosis was a ruptured Achilles tendon. After reading my x-rays, the young resident bandaged my foot and gave me the name of an orthopaedic surgeon. After signing the ER release form, I turned to Dr Cohen. "If I were your father, what would you recommend?" I asked. "See the surgeon as soon as possible," he replied. "From what I see, you may need to operate on your Achilles."

Elaine didn't have faith in the healthcare system in Miami. Realising that we couldn't afford Manhattan rents, we reached out to a friend who happened to be the director of orthopaedics at Scripps Medical Center in San Diego. I had Mount Sinai send my X-rays to Scripps. He recommended that I come within 72 hours; any further delay would be problematic. We arranged for VIP status with Flatrate movers to pick up our merchandise in Miami and deliver it to San Diego. All the containers I purchased at Home Depot, plus twenty boxes of her book *Less is More*, including her clothes, were in a storage locker two blocks away. Storing the containers reflected my insecurity that wherever we lived would not be our final home. As for our Toyota Corolla, an auto transport company would pick up the car at Canyon Ranch and deliver it to San Diego. Before leaving for San Diego, we contacted a friend, asking him to see if the building we had lived in had a one-bedroom apartment, which we would take sight unseen by the end of the week. Arriving in San Diego, I rented an Avis car and went to a motel about five miles from Scripps. The next morning, we arrived at the doctor's office, who viewed my X-rays and determined I did not need an operation. The plan was to put me in a cast for three months. We stayed in a motel for a week, returning to the same high-rise we had moved out of and signed a lease for the apartment. All we had was a mattress and a coffee table. Hobbling around Ikea with the help of a personal shopper, who, by chance, had Elaine's book on her desk, we furnished the entire apartment three days later. The mover came with all our merchandise. Contacting the driver who was transporting our Corolla, due to arrive in two days, we arranged where to drop off the car. The rental office of the building we lived in was very much aware of Elaine Lewis. This was our second time back in the same building, now back in La Jolla. Elaine reached out to her brother, who, during the interim, had a stroke and was unable to talk. After removing my cast, I visited my San Diego Home Depot, where again I was in the appliance department. After six months in San Diego, Elaine decided she wanted to go back to Miami and look for an apartment, arriving at the Fort Lauderdale airport. We were picked up by her gay bookkeeper, whom we had gotten a job at 4 U LIGHTING. After a week of looking for a place to live, she again made another decision to return to San Diego via Las Vegas. Luckily, I was able to stop the moving van from leaving Los Angeles, and also communicate with the driver who was bringing my car to Miami to turn around and meet us in Las Vegas. At this point, our credit was in the toilet. After spending a week in Vegas with my son, we drove back to San Diego, checking into a motel that had availability for three days. Every room in San Diego was sold out because of Comic-Con. The apartment we had moved out of was leased; the next available apartment wouldn't be ready for 30 days. Our only option was to find an extended-stay motel that included a kitchen. The only place we found was Extended Stay America in Temecula, about 58 miles outside of San Diego. I made my hangouts at Costco, sampling free food. Our life became like a travelling circus, going from motel to motel, changing credit cards to ten different addresses, and keeping up my payments on my credits. Finally, our apartment in La Jolla became available, moving back to the place where we started. As a couple, we proved our resilience, proving that a person who loves privacy to one who doesn't care. Moving from fifteen hundred square feet to three hundred square feet proved that our relationship was strong. A good majority of the time, we were living between apartments, hotels, and motels. In November 2014, Elaine and I truly evaluated our lives. All the wonderful places we lived in offered affordable housing, with one drawback: you needed a car. We were city people, growing up in apartment buildings. The bucolic setting of a suburban environment never worked for us. Elaine promised, "This is our last move." One of her Bangladeshi hairstylists invited us to be her house guests until we found a new apartment. Flatrate again picked up our belongings. We arrived by taxi at her home in Jackson Heights, Queens, at midnight on 3 January 2015. From the outside, the house looked great.

The entire house was freezing, and the heating system needed repair. The next morning, we took a taxi into Manhattan, remembering that a friend of mine, who owned a pizza store on Broadway, also owned The DaVinci, a boutique hotel across the street from the Symphony House, the building we had moved out of four years earlier. January to April are slow months in New York; hotel occupancy is low. The owner gave us a rate of fifty dollars per night. It was a unique experience, being back in my city as a tourist during January, wearing a ski jacket. Wanting to sell the car in San Diego, Elaine insisted that we should ship it to New York, saying that one of her best friends owned parking garages, giving her free parking. The car was en route, with instructions to offload it in front of the house we had left in Queens. The morning of the delivery, it was snowing. After a subway ride and a mile walk, the transportation rig was parked in front of the house. I called Elaine to ask if she had arranged a parking space. She answered that they had sold the company; parking in Manhattan was six hundred dollars a month. Elaine had a solution, offering her friend a hundred dollars a month to use her driveway. During our stay at the hotel, she suggested that we visit the building where she had grown up. Taking the subway to Brooklyn, we visited her old neighbourhood, Ocean Avenue, which she and I remembered as one of the upper-middle-class areas of Brooklyn. We were stunned by how the demographics had changed. Entering the lobby of the building where she had grown up was like transitioning from colour to black and white. Ringing the superintendent's apartment, a large person came to the door, introducing himself in a heavy Russian accent as Boris. Elaine told him the entire story of how her family had lived there for fifty years, wondering if there was a one-bedroom available. "You are lucky; we just have a one-bedroom and a two-bedroom vacant." Exiting the elevator on the sixth floor, he showed us a newly renovated, huge two-bedroom apartment for $3,000 a month. The one-bedroom was $2,500 a month. Thanking him, we walked over to Kings Highway, which we remembered as an upscale shopping area; the new stores reflected the changed demographic of the neighbourhood. Taking the subway back to Manhattan, we both agreed that Brooklyn was not an option.

We were ill-prepared for apartment hunting in January; our winter clothes had been given away when we left New York for Miami. Newly constructed luxury apartment buildings required forty times the monthly earnings to rent a one-bedroom apartment, upwards of $4,000 on a high floor, plus one month's rent and two months' security, plus a credit check. We checked none of the boxes. Our only chance of moving into an apartment was through Elaine's developer clients, who owned eighty per cent of the luxury residential buildings built before the turn of the century. Elaine started making phone calls. Her first call was to families who were the elite in New York real estate, owning large portfolios of residential buildings, who were engaged in a family dispute where both brothers were dividing the properties, therefore ending an impending legal battle. These calls resulted in lunch dates or meetings in their offices. Deciding that it would be best that she alone should handle the meetings, we now had to rehearse a story. When asked where she had been for seven years, she answered that she had sold her duplex a month before the 2008 financial crisis, moving to her apartment in Barcelona, just returning to New York in need of a one-bedroom apartment; she had decided to downsize. No one would dare to do a credit check on Elaine Lewis or ask for forty times her earnings. Throughout her career, she moved in a circle where all the people she knew were worth millions of dollars, all assuming that she was in their league. After three weeks at the DaVinci Hotel, multiple calls from Flat Rate, telling us if we did not take possession of our belongings by the end of the month, they would charge us a storage fee. One of her major clients owned a large luxury multi-family high-rise located in Midtown South and offered us a one-bedroom for $3,500 with one month's security. The building had an on-premises rental office; those who were told to forgo a credit check. After the move-in, we realised that we had too much stuff. The movers agreed to store it for free for six months. Being broke in New York, in every apartment we lived in, Elaine hung fifty framed pictures that were the story of her life, not ours. Everywhere we lived, we made the building handyman a member of our family.

The first thing I did was visit the Home Depot on West 23rd Street, Manhattan, and they immediately placed me in the appliance department. A good majority of the workers there were considered part-timers who didn't receive the benefits of full-time employees. During lunch breaks, I went down to the break room to discover that a good number of employees were homeless; on the money they made, they couldn't afford rent. These people were the result of a failed education system because none of them had marketable skills. I was the oldest person on the sales floor. Every two weeks, on my days off, I would take the Subway to Queens, either walking a mile or taking a bus, to visit my Toyota Corolla which was parked in the driveway of Elaine, a Bangladeshi hair stylist, to start the engine. This lasted until February. I decided to terminate the lease; the buyout was $5,000, which was split between three credit cards. On the days I worked at Home Depot, I began mentoring my fellow sales associates. Many of them had young families; all of them had dreams. Home Depot was their launching pad. My schedule varied from early opening to arriving mid-day until closing. We were constantly changing price tags. GE appliances were handling the logistics of all brands. Appliances were a commodity; smart consumers would search various online appliance websites, asking us to beat their prices. I usually offered them an extra ten per cent off the sales price with free shipping and installation. Essentially, Home Depot spent money on selling service contracts. Appliances had a slim profit margin, placing the department in the rear of the store so customers would have to pass various products that they might need. The item with the largest profit margin was household paint. The downside of the job was taking the abuse of customers, either in person or over the phone. According to the pyramid, the customer is always right. One night, I picked up the phone to a ten-minute tirade from a customer. After listening to her abuse, I explained that she didn't know what she was talking about. At the end of the conversation, she asked for my name. I said, "Fernando," and hung up.

The following morning, I was called into the Store Manager's office. He had come up the ranks of Home Depot to finally become a Store Manager. Thinking we were friends, he asked me if I had answered the phone last night, identifying myself as Fernando. I told him yes. After a few seconds, he told me that I was fired.

Elaine kept herself hidden; she rarely went uptown for fear of running into people she knew. The number one thing in her life was maintenance. Within a month, she duplicated the services that made her Elaine Lewis, recruiting hairstylists who would do her weaves, masseuses who came to the apartment, and manicurists a block away. Six months into the lease, she decided to move into a studio apartment, saving us $700 per month. Due to her talents in space planning, she was able to put everything from a one-bedroom apartment into the studio. There was no room to put the things that we placed in storage. After putting off several notifications that we were in arrears of payments, they notified us that they would auction off the contents of the storage bin in ten days. Neither of us remembered what was being stored; we approved the auction. A few weeks later, I landed a job at an appliance B2C business based in Bensonhurst, Brooklyn, dealing with new multi-family developers and Real Estate Management Companies. I was back taking subways, earning enough money to survive. Elaine used to wear six-inch heels. A decade earlier, she avoided taking care of it; now, at 83, she had bone-on-bone. We were seeking alternative treatments; someone recommended stem cells, which were not covered by insurance. The initial treatment was $5,000; we forgot to ask how much the follow-up treatment was, which ran between $1,500 and $2,000 per month. Next, she got a medical marijuana card to purchase CBD oil, which didn't work. In 2018, I was diagnosed with bladder and prostate cancer; neither of them metastasized. The bladder cancer resulted in two hospital stays, followed by two years of BCG* every three months. The prostate cancer was treated by an oncologist at Memorial Sloan Kettering who explained to me it was a choice of living without sex or possibly having sex with the cancer recurring. I always imagined being a stud in my senior year with a strong libido.

Now I was faced with a choice: nineteen straight days of radiation plus two years of female hormone shots to eliminate my testosterone. As a sex partner, I knew how to please my partner; as long as she was happy, I didn't care. Looking in the mirror, I realised I had great breasts. Elaine was in her mid-eighties; it seemed that a switch was turned off. The once most sexual woman no longer had any interest in sex. I had no complaints for twenty-five years. We went through hundreds of containers of Johnson & Johnson Baby Talcum powder and moisturising oils during sex play, which started on our trip to Japan. In mid-2019, I sensed something was wrong with her memory. I was seeing a neurologist who diagnosed that I had nerve damage, recommending that she visit my doctor for an evaluation. She returned, saying everything was fine. She never shared any medical information with me. On my next visit to the neurologist, he told me she had the early stages of Alzheimer's. My response was disbelief. She was a woman who did everything right; she didn't smoke, drink alcohol, or take drugs. Her diet consisted of steamed salmon at least four days a week, chicken on the other days, no dessert, and she was constantly working out. In early January 2020, the Real Estate Board of New York had their annual black-tie affair, with a cocktail reception before dinner, which was perfect for networking. This was an event we never missed. She suggested that I go alone. After many years of attending these events, I knew almost every important person in New York Real Estate. Our lease on the studio apartment was about to be renewed. My job at the appliance website was coming to an end. New York City offered tax abatement on new residential construction if the developer allocated twenty per cent of the apartments as affordable and eighty per cent at the market rate. Meaning they could charge anywhere from four to five figures a month, depending on the size and floor of the apartments. Twenty per cent became a lottery, with anywhere from fifteen to twenty thousand people on the list. This was not an option. As I networked, I hoped to meet one of Elaine's clients who had a vacant apartment that was constructed before 1980, who might offer us a deal. There were very few developers who could afford a rental building; most of them converted their properties to either co-ops or condominiums. Fifteen minutes before the dinner was to begin, I said hello to Gary, who introduced me to a colleague who was the COO of the largest portfolio of rental properties in New York City. After small talk, I asked if they could help us find an affordable apartment. After a few seconds, they told me to call them tomorrow; they might have something for us.

The following day, I called Gary's office. His secretary told me to contact the leasing department of a building that Elaine designed the models for fifty years ago. The people in the leasing office were waiting for us; they had two rent-stabilised apartments that were renovated to show us: apartment one on a lower floor, which was renovated, and one on the nineteenth floor facing west, being renovated, ready to move in on 29 February. Immediately, we signed the lease for the higher floor. Signing a fifty-page lease, we were finally set to live in what we considered our permanent home.

On 1 March 2020, we agreed to dispose of our IKEA furniture. With all of our moves, we weren't attached to any of our furniture, just our art. After our quarter of a century in the interior design business, we realised that both upholstered and case goods had zero appreciated value. The piece had to be either Art Nouveau, Art Deco, or antique with provenance. Elaine had a saying that good taste is not determined by the money you spend. All the movers transported were clothes, art, and sculptures. This apartment was the start of our new life without the pressure of going broke.

Fourteen days later, on 15 March 2020, the entire world stopped due to Covid. The experience we had was replicated by millions of people around the world. Again, we were one-on-one, but this time we had space. Elaine was acting erratically. She stopped eating and started repeating herself. We both belonged to the New York Center on Aging at New York-Presbyterian Hospital. Being referred to a specialist whose focus was on diagnosing AD*, she went through a battery of tests to determine cognitive impairment. The results came back that she was in the early stages of AD. She slept a good part of the day. The drugs prescribed were Memantine, to be given at night, including her sleep medication, 5mg Zolpidem. During the night, she would wake up, hallucinating, thinking that people were having a party in the house, accusing me of having conversations with girlfriends when I was in the toilet.

One evening, she walked out of the bedroom and sat on a chair, almost tipping over. I tried to steady her, but we both fell. I didn't have the strength to hold her limp body up. I called 999, and within fifteen minutes, the EMS arrived. I was able to pick myself up off the floor. The EMS team sat Elaine in a chair, but they couldn't wake her. They transported us to the NYP* Emergency Room, and I followed Elaine as she was wheeled from one test to another. Standing next to her on the gurney, I checked her pulse to see if she was alive. By 6:00 a.m., she woke up, asking where she was; she wanted to go home. The resident released her, and we took a taxi home. She acted as if nothing had happened.

The hospital arranged weekly visits from the Visiting Nurse Service. After evaluating her medication, I was advised to substitute Melatonin for Zolpidem. This simple change in medication stopped the hallucinations.

As senior citizens, New York City brought in hundreds of nurses from around the country to administer COVID-19 shots in the homes of housebound New Yorkers. By early January 2021, the out-of-state nurses visited us, giving us the first shot of the J&J vaccine. New York lifted its Covid restrictions on 15 June 2021. Everything was manageable. My most difficult task was getting her to eat three ounces of steamed salmon, trying to prevent her from losing weight. I ordered cases of Boost, a nutrient drink. I found myself taking short trips to purchase food, always afraid that when I came home, I would find her dead.

Her Alzheimer's Disease (AD) put me on the road to discovery. I began wondering why the scientific community could discover a vaccine for Covid, yet do so little to find a treatment for AD. Was it politics, or was the immediate death of thousands of people all at once what dictated finding a cure? AD ruined millions of families, but it didn't result in instant death. Alzheimer's was a bipartisan disease; a majority of both the Senate and House were over sixty years old, and anyone of them either had a loved one or a friend who had AD.

The darling of the Republican Party spent his final days on Earth with Alzheimer's. Finding a treatment or cure should be a bipartisan endeavour. I started a letter-writing campaign recommending that AD be included in the infrastructure bill. The goal was to rebuild the American family, which, as of this writing, consists of 6.7 million people aged 65 or older, increasing to 13% for people over 75 years old and their families. During my email campaign to either the elected official or their chief of staff, I didn't get a single response. My goal was ten billion dollars over five years to go to the NIH and WHO to fund research for treatment and a cure. Not one government official responded.

On the afternoon of 20 October 2021, we went to get our second Covid shot. We were told that the CDC had not given their final approval, recommending that we return in two days. Elaine could not walk back the ten blocks to her apartment. I usually try to coax her, but this time I hailed a taxi. Arriving in front of the lobby entrance, the doorman on duty opened the door. I told him to escort her into the building while I paid for our ride. Exiting the taxi, I asked the doorman where my wife was. Pointing to a body on the lobby floor, he said she had broken the bone in her leg, which was attached to her foot. This one incident was the beginning of her demise. During her hospital stay, I visited every day. There she was, wearing one of her wigs with makeup. After a week, the doctor recommended that she be placed in a rehab facility five long blocks from our home, sharing a room. Every day, I would visit for four or five hours and bring in food, which she refused to eat. During her stay, she had four surgeries. During her fifth and final surgery, we decided that she would rehab in a facility owned by the New York Archdiocese, Mary Manning, four blocks from our apartment. I was optimistic that with a couple of weeks of rehab, she could return home.

We Celebrated both our Birthdays in her private room with a cross facing the bed at the Rehab centre the odds of a Vampire attacking Elaine were nonexistent I asked them to remove the cross. I had difficulty accepting the Historical Jesus as white with blue eyes. From my understanding, he was born Jewish, and all he wanted to do was eliminate the corruption among Senior members of the Jewish Community. I doubt that he ever thought of creating a New Religious Movement.

Elaine was bed ridden with her foot placed in a sleeve called IPC (Intermittent Pneumatic Compression). An apparatus that is used to prevent blood clots. I began seeing a change she no longer asked for her makeup or blonde wig Every visit her tray of food was sitting there unneatened. Agreeing with her that the food was terrible, I began researching pre-cooked meals which I could warm up in the visitors' break room which had a mini-kitchen with a Refrigerator, sink, coffee machine, and Microwave. I had a problem all the meals came with sauces, She hated sauces, thinking that she would gain weight. Every week I would bring ten containers of a Nutrition drink called Boost, leaving notes for the staff to make sure she drinks it every morning. At the beginning of December, I Called her Orthopedic Surgeon, he told me that by Early January 2022, she might be able to put weight on her foot. Sitting next to her bed the doctor who worked at the Rehab Center suddenly shows up. I discussed my plans of bringing her home on the Fifteenth of December. Looking at me saying that he doubted she would make it, adding that he was going on a vacation to Florida. Friday the 10th of December, I discussed with the Rehab Social Worker what services I could get if I brought Elaine home. Reviewing her chart, she told me that they can arrange in-home Hospice Services. Looking at her I said she was not dying. Over the weekend I sat in her room watching football. She was alert when there was a touchdown. That Sunday I called our Hassidic Rabbi asking him to visit her to inspire her to eat. Rabbi Stone who we knew for ten years. We both emotionally adopted him even though we didn't follow his interpretation of JUDISM. Leaving the room hoping that the Rabbi would connect with her. After the nurses changed her diaper, I entered the room to kiss her, telling her that I planned for her to come home.

The next morning around 10 am my cell rang and the voice on the other end told me she had passed. Reviewing her chart, the voice on the other end told me she had a DNR and they couldn't intervene with life-saving measures. Was I in shock, not really, I was coming to terms with being alone during the two months she spent in Rehab Centers. Entering her room all I saw was a form wrapped in sheets. Looking at the body I was aware that she was fighting not to be an old Woman, using a Cane or Walker or being bed ridden. She always said that she wanted to be Cremated. I never had to arrange a funeral, my parents pre-planned it. So did her father every Jew had family burial plots as did various other religions, Jews didn't believe in the afterlife which is why they chose plain Pine Coffins which in time degraded with the Physical shell back into the earth. Jews as part of the laws of Moses have been Carbon Neutral since 5734. I wanted to donate her brain to do further studies on AD. Dogma dictated that the deceased of natural causes must be buried within 24 hours. Now I needed to find an affordable Jewish Funeral Home. Asking Google, recommended Plaza Jewish Community Chapel to pick up the body. Aware that the clock was ticking I had to decide whether to follow her request for Cremation or burial in the family plot. I needed a second opinion, reaching out to our friend the Rabbi who screamed into the phone JEWS DO NOT GET CREMATED. This was the first time I ever said NO to her. Remembering that her family had purchased a plot at Mount Ararat located in Farmingdale, the Capitol of cemeteries for the New York City Metro Area. There lies smart Jews who owned Real Estate and a

Burial plot and those whose only piece of Real Estate was the ground they were under.

From hundreds of friends, there were only four of us at the graveside: the Rabbi, Walter, and his boyfriend (they later married). The service was brief. We were reviewing invoices and writing cheques on the roof of the hearse. Our friend, the Rabbi, wanted $700, but settled for $500.

Returning home, I walked into an Elaine Lewis shrine. To this day, I have kept the remains of a floral arrangement that was sent by a friend. Like humans, they flourish, wither, and die. I consider them Elaine's ashes.

The question is: if you knew the date of your expiration, would you live your life differently? Excluding accidents and things beyond your control, in this limited time, would you strive to live a better life? Would you create things that would be a legacy, no matter how inconsequential they seem to the world around you, or would you just go along, waiting until you are pushed to the back of the shelf, like an expired shopping cart of groceries waiting to be disposed of?

All persons in this book, have their barcode expired. My son Jamie who decided to change his life now lives in las vegas with his wife, seventeen-year-old son, and nine-year-old daughter. Working as a senior casino host at Resort World Las Vegas

LESS IS MORE
A PRACTICAL GUIDE TO MAXIMIZING THE SPACE IN YOUR HOME
ELAINE LEWIS

Dear Congresswoman Cortez Your CNN PROFILE was amazing. Be aware that you are a Congresswoman for America and not hampered by the old ways of doing business in Washington. Working with me to sponsoring a bill to fund ALZHEIMER DISEASE RESEARCH AND TREATMENT WILL CREATE A LEGACY THAT WILL MILLIONS OF SUFFERS. I had sent an article which I hope the NY TIMES MAGAZINE SECTION PUBLISHES. Even though I do not reside in your district we are all NEW YORKERS. With the coming August Recess, we would appreciate it if you could visit us at our apartment at 500 East 77th Street to discuss your Sponsoring a bill attached to the infrastructure bill for ten billion dollars over five years to fund research and development of both a cure and treatment for Alzheimer's Disease. Doing this could be part of your legacy for neither the House nor Senate had the imagination or fortitude to create funding to help end the Plague of AD that affected 6,000,000 Americans. This should be a GLOBAL COLLABORATION.

THE 3 TRILLION DOLLAR INFRASTRUCTURE BILL MAY HOLD THE

KEY TO FINDING A CURE OR TREATMENT OF AD

ALZHEIMERS ROBBER OF THE NOW AND THE SOUL

My 34-year relationship with the most vibrant and brilliant woman I ever met was filled with adventure. She had a legacy in the New York Real Estate Community, renowned for her ability to make small, expensive apartments look huge. In the 1980s, she had model showcases in new developments across the Northeast.

Most of the new development was created by an architect, Phillip Birnbaum. Her office employed over fifty talented designers. Each showcase brought new business to her firm. We met in 1988 and became a team. She was eight years older than me. We would joke that when I was 14, she was 22. I never would have had a chance to start a relationship.

From 1992 until now, we moved 16 times across the country. I spent more money on moving supplies than it would cost to buy an Elsa Peretti piece of jewellery. She enjoyed the moves, as it was part of her DNA to set up apartments. As always, we always returned to New York.

In 2015, we returned to New York from San Diego, where we had lived for three years. She was always independent and in control of her schedule, keeping all appointments in a daily diary.

In 2016, I noticed that she was having memory problems. I thought it was the natural ageing process.

Concerned, I arranged for her to visit a neurologist for an evaluation. He gave her a prescription for Memantine 150mg. I never knew about the drug, as she was a private person. For personal reasons, I visited the same doctor who treated me for Carpal Tunnel and neck pains, giving me cortisone shots. Inquiring about my significant other's symptoms, the doctor told me she had the early onset of Alzheimer's Disease (AD), but "Don't worry, by the time it progresses, there will be a cure."

On 29 February 2020, we moved for the last time and committed to live our lives in New York. Relocation meant finding other health specialists, other than the doctors at NYU Langone. They were great, but at our age, we needed to find providers closer to where we lived on the Upper East Side of Manhattan. New York-Presbyterian was the most logical provider. Luckily, we were accepted by the Centre on Aging, which offered a team environment for the geriatric community. They became the gatekeepers for our medical needs.

New neighbourhood, new environment. The months of March and April 2020 were devoted to setting up our apartment. I noticed that something was amiss in her thought process and her ability to remember simple things and events that were part of our past life. I needed professional confirmation and set up a visit with Dr Michael Lin, a neurologist whose speciality was Alzheimer's. After tests, he confirmed that she had AD.

She was placed on Memantine, which is used to stem hallucinations and 5mg of Ambien to help her sleep. At 3 am, she would see people in our bed – a man and a child – and hear music. I slept with a flashlight to show her that what she was seeing was not there. Her eating habits changed. She ate slower and developed a cleanliness phobia, always cleaning the plates and drinking glasses. Her diet was salmon or chicken every night, yoghurt with fruit, egg salad, and vegetables. I did all the cooking, which I had done for thirty-two years. Before that, for the first two years of our relationship, she had a live-in housekeeper who did the cooking. Her eating habits changed; she went from 115 pounds to 100 pounds, from 4oz of salmon to 3oz, and wouldn't finish her dinner. Her dietician recommended that I put her on Boost Plus and that she drink three bottles a day. Feeding her became a constant battle. I feared that if she was hospitalised, she could lose a pound a day. That's why I wanted her to gain at least five pounds. It was impossible to stop her from watching her calorie intake.

Reading all the material on Alzheimer's, they say that a healthy lifestyle can prevent the disease. Her lifestyle ticked all the boxes. She didn't smoke, drink, or take drugs, and only ate salmon, chicken, or green salad. She had a personal trainer come in three times a week, and to top off the week, she had a masseuse come in three times. Her lifestyle was to be commended. Professionals might counter that she might have developed AD in her mid-seventies.

By the beginning of 2021, paranoia set in. She accused me of having a girlfriend and planning on leaving her. This mostly started at about 3 a.m., swearing that she read my thoughts and that I was packing my bags and leaving. At first, this would anger me, and I lashed back. At wit's end, I called the AD hotline, and they told me to apologise for something that I was not doing. No matter how much love and caring I gave her, she was fearful that I would desert her. At the counsel of her physician, we reduced the medication, eliminated the Ambien and Memantine bedtime combination, and put her on 5mg of Melatonin.

AD is all about caretaking, and in our case, we have no support. She never had children, and my son lives in Las Vegas. As a secretive person, she has kept her disease unknown to her friends. As a caretaker, you need someone to talk to. The Alzheimer's Association has a twenty-four-hour hotline where trained counsellors listen to your stories and give you tips. Currently, we are enrolled in a caretaker study sponsored by Weill Cornell. They give you a pre-programmed laptop, and you have Zoom conversations with a researcher who discusses healthy eating habits for thirty minutes. Then Elaine plays mind games, which are a click away on the laptop. The mentality of researchers is that the patient is too far gone in the disease, but they want to make sure that the caretaker is healthy. Unfortunately, that's the analysis of professionals. Once you get AD, there is no way to reverse the disease.

As the months progressed, she had trouble walking, for she was out of breath. Once independent, I had her go everywhere with me. My goal is to slow down the progression of the disease and have her doing things to make her think. Falling is a constant fear. When she fell, I tried to pick her up, and I could not handle the dead weight. I was too proud to call 999 for help. Finally, I realised that I could not do it on my own. Looking back on one incident that happened in the early morning of 9 April, I was working at my computer. She came from the bedroom and sat down, asking me what I was doing in her apartment, and that I should leave.

She was sitting on the chair next to me, looking like she was about to fall over. I tried to pick her up, and we both fell on the floor – me face down, and she on her back. It is rough to get off the floor when you are eighty. She was out. I called 999, and the FDNY

EMS came, followed by another ambulance service. They could not wake her. The decision was made to go to the New York-Presbyterian's emergency room. That was the last place I wanted to go because of Covid. We both went by separate ambulances – me to check out if I had a concussion, and her to be evaluated for any severe injury. During the entire six hours of probing, taking blood, scans, and other tests, she never woke up. I was concerned that she had a stroke.

At 6 a.m. on 9 April, she opened her eyes and asked me where she was. We were both discharged. To this day, she does not remember where she was.

Being aware that it was only a matter of time until her condition worsened, I enrolled her in clinical trials on an AD treatment by Eli Lilly.

As a caregiver, I asked my care professionals if they could give her either a CT (computed tomography) or MRI (magnetic resonance imaging) scan to learn how fast AD was progressing. Her doctor told me that her neurologist could track the disease progression by giving her tests called the Mini-Mental State Exam (MMSE) and the Mini-Cog test. These tests are designed specifically to pinpoint everyday mental skills, which use numerical scoring with a total of 30 points. A score of 20 to 24 suggests mild dementia, 13 to 20 suggests moderate dementia and less than 12 indicates severe dementia (aka Alzheimer's Disease). Every year, studies show AD patients' MMSE scores decline by two to four points a year.

Learning that the FDA has just approved Aducanumab, which goes by the brand name Aduhelm and is manufactured by Biogen (whose stock increased in value by 38%), I thought this was a ray of hope. Aduhelm would be administered by infusion once monthly for a price tag of $87,000 a year. Buried in this cost is Research and Development. With global sales, the Research and Development cost can be recouped within five years, and the rest is profit. If covered by Medicare, there would be a co-pay of $11,000, which may be lower when my supplemental insurance kicks in. Immediately, I contacted her physician, who told me that it was a waste of money and that the treatment should not have been approved. The approval was given to offer a ray of hope to 6,000,000 United States citizens who suffer from Alzheimer's Disease. What if the Federal Government and its team of scientists and researchers discovered the solution, both as a cure and treatment and licensed their findings to drug firms who guaranteed the cost of the drug would be affordable?

2021 proved that a treatment can be found in record time when 600,000 people died of COVID-19. Big Pharma was sitting on a solution that existed before the pandemic and only reacted when the Federal Government invested heavily to make it happen. What would happen if a million people died of Alzheimer's in 12 months? Would the government throw money at finding a cure? I bet they would.

In 1906, Alois Alzheimer discovered, during an autopsy of a patient who died naturally and a patient, Auguste Deter, a woman in her fifties, an unusual disease of the cerebral cortex. Alzheimer's became a recognisable disease between 1970 and 1979; science started research into the disease. By 1980–1989, Alzheimer's became known to the public with the death of movie star Rita Hayworth at the age of 68 in 1987. Her death put AD at the forefront of the American public's consciousness. Since then, many prominent Americans have succumbed to the disease, but quietly, rather than making the general public aware.

Alzheimer's was not a fashionable disease like breast cancer or any other cancer, which, by the nature of the disease, finds a home in parts of the human body. With advances in treatments, many cancers go into remission. Alzheimer's affects a single organ, the brain, and like Covid, G10, the World Health Organization should expand the Accelerator Partnership to discover either a cure or a treatment to slow the progress. The countries with the highest caseload—Finland, the United States, Canada, the United Kingdom, Iceland, Sweden, Switzerland, Norway, Denmark, The Netherlands, Belgium, Turkey, Saudi Arabia, and Kuwait—would be perfect partners in supporting the Group of Ten. Imagine if these twelve countries set aside 2% of GDP and collaborated on R&D, offering Big Pharma licensing on their developed treatments to slow down the progression or even a vaccine against contracting AD.

The above governments are spending billions of dollars on their citizens for healthcare treatment costs. The younger generation is filled with guilt because they do not have the time to care for their parents. Most AD patients are lucky to have a spouse who will take care of them until the late stage of the disease. They have no choice but to bring their loved ones to a special facility. Major public corporations that run nursing homes are now building special facilities to care for AD patients. The trend in age-restricted developments is to create communities that take their residents through the total life cycle. No longer does a senior have to search for a facility that offers special care for AD sufferers; it is already built into their community. Living in these communities is for seniors who have the financial means to buy a condo and pay monthly maintenance fees. What happens to seniors who were once rich but lost their savings in the 2008 financial crisis and are poor and alone? The answer is Medicaid, which picks up the total cost of living in an environment that is a warehouse of people who are ready to die. The cost of long-term care averages about $51,000 per patient per year. This cost is covered by the Federal Government. The projected number of AD sufferers is about 10,000,000 cases per year.

Seventy-two million Baby Boomers, people born between 1946 and 1964, and their children will suffer the indignity of Alzheimer's Disease (AD), which is not an immediate death and takes many years to progress. The toll, for both patients, caretakers, and government assistance, is in the billions of dollars. Political strategists dismissing a trillion-dollar cure for AD as not a national issue, or even a grassroots vote-getter, are mistaken. The average age of US Senators is 62 years old, and members of the House are 57 years old. As a group, they all get free health coverage. Even with the death of President Ronald Reagan, the GOP had control of the Senate, and they never took the lead in sponsoring a bill to fund Alzheimer's Research and create a coalition with Democrats who had control of the House. I am certain that somebody they know has a family member suffering from AD. Currently, both parties are negotiating a three-trillion-dollar package on INFRASTRUCTURE. I am certain there will be a lot of pork in it to appease the needs of state voters. During this negotiation, a real political leader should consider AD infrastructure as critical as roads and tunnels. For the American family, the infrastructure is crumbling. AD is a destroyer of generational wealth.

A government marketer who came up with the name "Warp Speed" for the COVID-19 vaccine will have to develop a catchy name for Alzheimer's Disease to entice global scientific collaboration. How about **HAL9000?**

alz.org®
800.272.3900

225 N. Michigan Ave., Fl. 17
Chicago, IL 60601

312.335.8700 **p**
866.699.1246 **f**

ALZHEIMER'S ASSOCIATION®

The Alzheimer's Association is a worldwide voluntary health organization dedicated to Alzheimer's care, support and research. Our mission is to lead the way to end Alzheimer's and all other dementia — by accelerating global research, driving risk reduction and early detection, and maximizing quality care and support. Our vision is a world without Alzheimer's and all other dementia®. Visit alz.org or call 800.272.3900.

Index: Billboard

2023

2022

2021

2020

2019

2018

Drake, “God’s Plan”

2017

Ed Sheeran, “Shape of You”

2016

Justin Bieber, “Love Yourself”

2015

Mark Ronson feat. Bruno Mars, “Uptown Funk!”

2014

Pharrell Williams, “Happy”

2013

Macklemore & Ryan Lewis feat. Wanz, "Thrift Shop"

2012

Gotye feat. Kimbra, "Somebody That I Used to Know"

2011

Adele, "Rolling in the Deep"

2010

Kesha, "Tik Tok"

2009

The Black Eyed Peas, "Boom Boom Pow"

2008

Flo Rida feat. T-Pain, "Low"

2007

Beyoncé, "Irreplaceable"

2006

Daniel Powter, "Bad Day"

2005

Mariah Carey, "We Belong Together"

2004

Usher feat. Lil Jon & Ludacris, "Yeah!"

2003

50 Cent, "In Da Club"

2002

Nickelback, “How You Remind Me”

2001

Lifehouse, “Hanging by a Moment”

2000

Faith Hill, “Breathe”

1999

Cher, “Believe”

1998

Next, “Too Close”

1997

Elton John, "Candle in the Wind 1997" / "Something About the Way You Look Tonight"

1996

Los Del Río, "Macarena (Bayside Boys Mix)"

1995

Coolio feat. L. V., "Gangsta's Paradise"
Hot 100 debut date: Aug. 19, 1995

1994

Ace of Base, "The Sign"
Hot 100 debut date: Jan. 1, 1994

1993

Whitney Houston, "I Will Always Love You"

1992

Boyz II Men, "End of the Road"

1991

Bryan Adams, "(Everything I Do) I Do It for You"

1990

Wilson Phillips, "Hold On"

1989

Chicago, "Look Away"

1988

George Michael, "Faith"

1987

The Bangles, "Walk Like an Egyptian"

1986

Dionne & Friends (Dionne Warwick, Gladys Knight, Elton John & Stevie Wonder), "That's What Friends Are For"

1985

Wham!, "Careless Whisper"

1984

Prince, "When Doves Cry"

1983

The Police, "Every Breath You Take"

1982

Olivia Newton-John, "Physical"

1981

Kim Carnes, "Bette Davis Eyes"

1980

Blondie, "Call Me"

1979

The Knack, "My Sharona"

1978

Andy Gibb, "Shadow Dancing"

1977

Rod Stewart, "Tonight's the Night (Gonna Be Alright)"

1976

Wings, "Silly Love Songs"

1975

Captain & Tennille, "Love Will Keep Us Together"

1974

Barbra Streisand, "The Way We Were"

1973

Dawn feat. Tony Orlando, "Tie a Yellow Ribbon Round the Ole Oak Tree"

1972

Roberta Flack, "The First Time Ever I Saw Your Face"

1971

Three Dog Night, "Joy to the World"

1970

Simon & Garfunkel, "Bridge Over Troubled Water"

1969

The Archies, "Sugar, Sugar"

1968

The Beatles, "Hey Jude"

1967

Lulu, "To Sir With Love"

1966

The Mamas & The Papas, "California Dreamin'"

1965

Sam the Sham and the Pharaohs, "Wooly Bully"

1964

The Beatles, "I Want to Hold Your Hand"

Notes: The group also finished with the No. 2 song of 1964, with "She Loves You. "

1963

The Beach Boys, "Surfin' U. S. A. "

1962

Mr. Acker Bilk, "Stranger on the Shore"

1961

Bobby Lewis, "Tossin' & Turnin'"

1960

Percy Faith And His Orchestra, "Theme From *A Summer Place*"

1959

Johnny Horton, "The Battle of New Orleans"

1958

Domenico Modugno, "Volare (Nel Blu Dipinto Di Blu)"

VARIETY

Motion Pictures that Changed Our Lives

1950s

1950: *Cinderella (1950)*
1951: *Quo Vadis (1951)*
1952: *This is Cinerama (1952)*
1953: *Peter Pan (1953)*
1954: *Rear Window (1954)*
1955: *Lady and the Tramp (1955)*
1956: *The Ten Commandments (1956)*
1957: *The Bridge on the River Kwai (1957)*
1958: *South Pacific (1958)*
1959: *Ben-Hur (1959)*

1960s

1960: *Spartacus (1960)*
1961: *West Side Story (1961)*
1962: *Lawrence of Arabia (1962)*
1963: Cleopatra (1963)
1964: *My Fair Lady (1964)*
1965: *The Sound of Music (1965)*
1966: *The Bible: In the Beginning (1966)* and *Hawaii (1966)* (virtual tie)
1967: *The Graduate (1967)*
1968: *2001: A Space Odyssey (1968)*
1969: *Butch Cassidy and the Sundance Kid (1969)*

1970s

1970: *Love Story (1970)*
1971: *Fiddler on the Roof (1971)*
1972: *The Godfather (1972)*
1973: *The Sting (1973)*
1974: *Blazing Saddles (1974)*
1975: *Jaws (1975)*
1976: *Rocky (1976)*
1977: *Star Wars: Episode IV - A New Hope (1977)*
1978: *Grease (1978)*
1979: *Kramer vs. Kramer (1979)*

1980s

1980: *Star Wars: Episode V - The Empire Strikes Back (1980)*
1981: *Raiders of the Lost Ark (1981)*
1982: *E. T.: The Extra-Terrestrial (1982)*
1983: *Star Wars: Episode VI - Return of the Jedi (1983)*
1984: *Ghostbusters (1984)*
1985: *Back to the Future (1985)*
1986: *Top Gun (1986)*
1987: *Three Men and a Baby (1987)*
1988: *Rain Man (1988)*
1989: *Batman (1989)*

1990s

1990: *Home Alone (1990)*
1991: *Beauty and the Beast (1991)*
1992: *Aladdin (1992)*
1993: *Jurassic Park (1993)*
1994: *The Lion King (1994)*
1995: *Toy Story (1995)*
1996: *Independence Day (1996)*
1997: *Titanic (1997)*
1998: *Saving Private Ryan (1998)*
1999: *Star Wars: Episode I - The Phantom Menace (1999)*

2000s

2000: *How the Grinch Stole Christmas (2000)*
2001: *Harry Potter and the Sorcerer's Stone (2001)*
2002: *Spider-Man (2002)*
2003: *The Lord of the Rings: The Return of the King (2003)*
2004: *Shrek 2 (2004)*
2005: *Star Wars: Episode III - Revenge of the Sith (2005)*
2006: *Pirates of the Caribbean: Dead Man's Chest (2006)*
2007: *Spider-Man 3 (2007)*
2008: *The Dark Knight (2008)*
2009: *Avatar (2009)*

OVERVIEW OF WOMENS FASHION 1956 TO 2000

GEMINI BY GOOGLE

Here's a breakdown of women's fashion trends by decade from 1950s to 2000s:

1950s:

- **Silhouette:** The ideal silhouette was hourglass-shaped, achieved with cinched waists, full skirts, and nipped bodices. Think poodle skirts, swing dresses, and fitted blouses.
- **Materials:** Popular fabrics included cotton, silk, and wool.
- **Icons:** Marilyn Monroe, Audrey Hepburn, Grace Kelly
- **1960s:**
- **Silhouette:** The silhouette became more youthful and mod. Think miniskirts, shift dresses, and pantsuits.
- **Materials:** New synthetic fabrics like nylon and polyester became prominent.
- **Icons:** Twiggy, Brigitte Bardot, Jackie Kennedy
- **1970s:**
- **Silhouette:** The 70s embraced a more relaxed and bohemian style. Think maxi dresses, jumpsuits, and wide-leg pants.
- **Materials:** Fabrics with textures like corduroy, denim, and crochet were popular.
- **Icons:** Farrah Fawcett, Bianca Jagger, Diane Keaton

- **1980s:**
- **Silhouette:** The 80s saw a return to power dressing with broader shoulders, bold colours, and geometric prints. Think padded shoulders, miniskirts, and leggings.
- **Materials:** A variety of fabrics were used, including synthetics like lycra and neon colours.
- **Icons:** Madonna, Princess Diana, Joan Collins
- **1990s:**
- **Silhouette:** Grunge and minimalism took centre stage. Think oversized flannels, slip dresses, and crop tops.
- **Materials:** Denim, flannel, and cotton were popular choices.
- **Icons:** Kate Moss, Winona Ryder, Courtney Love
- **2000s:**
- **Silhouette:** Fashion became more diverse in the 2000s. Low-rise jeans, cargo pants, and baby doll dresses were all popular trends.
- **Materials:** Denim remained a staple and new technologies brought in moisture-wicking fabrics for active wear.
- **Icons:** Jennifer Lopez, Britney Spears, Halle Berry

OTPS12735 NTM 1914OTEX1312
OTG319NTPH123OTPS1610

BABY

OLD TESTAMENT PSALM 127:3-5 CHILDREN ARE SEEN AS A GIFT OF GOD

NEW TESTAMENT MATTHEW 19:14 JESUS WELCOMES CHILDREN, COMPARES THEM TO THE IDEAL ENTERING THE KINGDOM OF HEAVEN

OLD TESTAMENT EXODUS 13:1- IMPORTANCE PLACES EMPHASIS ON THE FIRSTBORN, THEY WERE SEEN AS DEDICATED TO GOD AND WERE TO BE REDEEMED OR CONSECRATED

ADULT

OLD TESTAMENT GENESIS 3:19 DEATH IS SEEN AS A SEPARATION FROM GOD AND RETURN TO DUST.

NEW TESTAMENT PHILIPPIANS 1:23 DEATH IS THE SEPARATION FROM THE PHYSICAL BODY

OLD TESTAMENT PSALM 1610 GODS POWER OVER LIFE AND DEATH

www.ingramcontent.com/pod-product-compliance
Lightning Source LLC
LaVergne TN
LVHW041136150826
845673LV00001B/19

9798218554286